News under Fire

News under Fire

China's Propaganda against Japan in the English-Language Press, 1928–1941

Shuge Wei

This book is made possible by a publication subsidy from the Chiang Ching-kuo Foundation for International Scholarly Exchange in Taipei.

Hong Kong University Press
The University of Hong Kong
Pokfulam Road
Hong Kong
www.hkupress.org

© 2017 Hong Kong University Press

ISBN 978-988-8390-61-8 (*Hardback*)

All rights reserved. No portion of this publication may be reproduced or transmitted in any form or by any means, electronic or mechanical, including photocopy, recording, or any information storage or retrieval system, without prior permission in writing from the publisher.

British Library Cataloguing-in-Publication Data
A catalogue record for this book is available from the British Library.

Cover image: Sapajou, "The Lone Battalion," *North China Daily News*, October 30, 1977.

10 9 8 7 6 5 4 3 2 1

Printed and bound in Hong Kong, China

Contents

List of Illustrations	vi
Names of the Guomindang Government Organizations	viii
Abbreviation of Archives	ix
Notes on the Text	x
Acknowledgments	xi
Introduction	1

Part I: A Nation without a Voice

1. Bridge or Barrier: The Treaty-Port English-Language Press in China, 1920s — 21
2. Beyond the Front Line: The Jinan Incident — 46

Part II: Growing Pains

3. To Control the Uncontrollable: The Nanjing Government's International Propaganda Policy, 1928–1931 — 65
4. Shadowed by the Sun: The Mukden Incident and the Shanghai Incident — 96
5. Facing Dilemmas: China's International Propaganda Activities, 1932–1937 — 125
6. Friend or Foe: The Amō Doctrine — 162

Part III: Propaganda during the War

7. From Nanjing to Chongqing: International Propaganda in Wartime, 1937–1938 — 185
8. Confronting Encirclement: Chongqing, 1939–1941 — 219

Conclusion — 252

Glossary — 259
Bibliography — 263
Index — 278

Illustrations

Figures

Figure 1	The North China Daily News Building, 1925	25
Figure 2	The China Press Building, 1911–1929	28
Figure 3	Covers and front pages of *Millard's Review of the Far East* and the *New Republic*	31
Figure 4	"Time Will Tell Who Rules the Waves"	45
Figure 5	"The Road Hog"	62
Figure 6	"The Burdens of Office"	95
Figure 7	"Sayonara"	124
Figure 8	Tang Liangli	136
Figure 9	Hollington K. Tong	146
Figure 10	The *China Press* staff party	149
Figure 11	Yang Guangsheng	152
Figure 12	"A Damsel in Distress"	161
Figure 13	"A Little Boat May Leave a Big Wash Behind"	181
Figure 14	A weeping baby amid the ruins of the bombed Shanghai train station	195
Figure 15	China Campaign Committee	197
Figure 16	"Double Suicide?"	218
Figure 17	W. H. Donald and H. J. Timperley	235
Figure 18	H. H. Kung's financial support to rebuild the Press Hotel	238
Figure 19	Working in the dugouts	239
Figure 20	"The Lone Battalion"	251

Diagrams

Diagram 1	The structure of the Guomindang Ministry of Information, 1929	70
Diagram 2	The International Department members' military ranks	193

Illustrations

Diagram 3 The structure of the Guomindang international propaganda machinery, 1938 — 201
Diagram 4 Censorship data, International Department, December 1937–September 1938 — 205
Diagram 5 Selected payroll of the International Department — 223
Diagram 6 XGOY's broadcasting timetable to North America, 1940 — 232

Names of the Guomindang Government Organizations

Central Executive Committee 中央執行委員會
Central Party Headquarters 中央黨部
Executive Yuan 行政院
Investigation and Statistics Bureau of the Military Affairs Commission 軍事委員會調查統計局
Legislative Yuan 立法院
Military Affairs Commission 軍事委員會
Ministry of Communications 交通部
Ministry of Foreign Affairs 外交部
Ministry of Information 宣傳部
Ministry of the Interior 內政部

Abbreviation of Archives

AH: Academia Historica

CMA: Chongqing Municipal Archives

FOFC: Foreign Office Files for China, 1919–1980

GA: Guomindang Archives, Taipei

MSCGCEC: Minutes of the Standing Committee of Guomindang Central Executive Committee (Zhongguo Guomindang zhongyang zhixing weiyuanhui changwu weiyuanhui huiyi jilu)

PRFRUS: Papers Relating to the Foreign Relations of the United States

SCYDSL: Special Collections of the Yale Divinity School Library

SDCF: Confidential U.S. State Department Central Files, China, Internal Affairs 1930–1939

SHAC: The Second Historical Archives of China, Nanjing

SHSM: The State Historical Society of Missouri

SMC: Shanghai Municipal Council Archives

SMP: Shanghai Municipal Police Files

WGLP: Winston George Lewis Papers

Notes on the Text

I use pinyin to romanize Chinese names and titles of Chinese materials. But there are exceptions: names like Chiang Kai-shek, Hollington Tong, and T. V. Soong, which are established in English-language literature; geographical names that no longer exist, such as Mukden, and names quoted by contemporary authors in traditional form, like Nanking and Peking. To minimize confusion, I provide in the glossary a list of important personal names in pinyin, traditional spelling, and Chinese character. Chinese and Japanese personal names in this book are presented in traditional East Asian form—family name comes before the given name. Exceptions are made in the case of scholars who are well known.

The Guomindang and the Nationalist Party are interchangeable in this book.

The Nanjing government before 1938 refers to the Guomindang government led by Chiang Kai-shek. The Nanjing government after 1940 mentioned in this book refers to the puppet government established by Wang Jingwei.

Beijing is known as Peking in Western literature. The Guomindang government renamed the city Beiping (known as Peiping) in 1928. In 1949, the government of the People's Republic of China changed its name back to Beijing and continued to refer to the city as Peking until the 1970s. To avoid confusion, this book uses Beijing to refer to the city.

Acknowledgments

This work would have been impossible to produce without the generous assistance of a great number of people. I was fortunate to join a supportive intellectual community at the Australian National University (ANU). My deep gratitude goes to Tomoko Akami. Her extensive knowledge of propaganda history in East Asia and the great care with which she oversaw every aspect of my studies have been indispensable. I am very much indebted also to Brian Martin, who inspires me with his deep passion for Chinese history and his profound knowledge of international politics, as well as his eccentric jokes, which frequently escape his anarchistic mind beyond his desperate control. The guidance of Richard Rigby, whose views on the interaction between media and diplomacy are founded in part on a lifelong career as a diplomat, was invaluable. Benjamin Penny has always been kind to provide sharp comments on my chapters, sometimes even at short notice. Geremie Barmé's advice on book writing was illuminating and helpful. Thomas DuBois and Tessa Morris-Suzuki were, and continue to be, sources of inspiration. Each provided generous assistance and wise counsel on a range of intellectual and professional matters.

My friends and colleagues have supported me throughout the years of this project. I thank them for reading my chapters, bearing with my rambling thoughts, spoiling me with witty jokes, and kindling my desire to read more. Conversations with and comments from Nathan Woolley, Duncan Campbell, Zhu Yayun, Li Geng, Chen Liang, and Peter Cai have been extremely useful. Peter Van Ness offered valuable comments on the entire manuscript.

I have greatly benefited from my association with many other great scholars and research institutions. Rudolf Wagner of Heidelberg University, who initially inspired my interest in China's treaty-port press, has never been tired of sharing with me his profound understanding of Chinese media history. The Sinology Institute of the Heidelberg University generously helped me gain access to key databases at Berlin State Library. Parks Coble and Akira Iriye provided valuable suggestions on how to improve the manuscript. Colleagues at the Cheng She-wo Institute at Shih Hsin University—Eileen Chou, Frank Huang, Hsiao Hsu-chi, and Yang Hsiu-chin—created an inspirational and friendly environment for me to further develop my research.

Liao Min-shu, from National Cheng-chi University, helped me collect resources on several occasions. Discussions about perspectives on and approaches to Chinese history with her were even more delicious than the wonderful Taiwanese food and tea she introduced to me. Zhang Li and Hu Guotai from the Academia Sinica kindly offered a thorough introduction to the archives of the Institute of Modern History. Kawashima Shin of the University of Tokyo provided valuable advice on the political culture of the Guomindang government. I am grateful for the Virtual Shanghai Project which expanded my imagination of Shanghai in the 1930s with all kinds of images and maps. I thank Christian Henriot for kindly allowing me to include images from this wonderful project. I also thank Xiong Yuezhi for accepting my visit to the Shanghai Academy of Social Sciences.

Shu Sheng-chi was extraordinarily generous with his sources and deep knowledge of Chinese media history. Mareike Svea Ohlberg kindly shared her dissertation, which was unavailable at the ANU. Frank Bren put me in touch with Vicky Merchant, who shared with me a photo of W. H. Donald in her mother's personal collection. Sharon Strange, with her sharp eye for detail, provided excellent comments on style.

This project was mostly conducted before digital databases of treaty-port newspapers were available, so I relied much on the kindness of librarians and archivists at a variety of institutions. At the National Library of Australia, Dipin Ouyang has always been very helpful by purchasing microfilms of key newspapers and retrieving articles or images from original copies. Before his retirement from ANU's Menzies Library, Darrell Dorrington helped me obtain some crucial sources. Assistance from staff members at the Committee of the Guomindang Party History, Academia Historica, Shanghai Municipal Archives, Chongqing Municipal Archives and Nanjing Second Archives, State Library of New South Wales, the State Historical Society of Missouri, and the US National Archives and Records Administration were also essential for this project.

I wish to thank editors of Hong Kong University Press, Yuet Sang Leung, Sherlon Ip, and many others who saw the value of this project and worked diligently to bring it to fruition. Parts of Chapter 2 and Chapter 7 have appeared in *Modern Asian Studies* (January 2014) and *Twentieth-Century China* (May 2014). I thank the editors of the journals for allowing me to include revised version of them in this book.

I am deeply indebted to my parents and twin sister who have offered me unending encouragement over the years. None of them reads English well, so I can safely blame them here for all their unreserved support, which pushed me to swallow the many agonies of writing. I thank Poktori for his impatient proofreading with his paws. I thought he would poach some of my ideas in his own dissertation on whether to can or cane live mice. But he sadly did not live long enough to finish it. My ultimate thanks go to two boys, Roald and Lucas, big and small. I thank them for all the laughter and tears during the daily journey of life. And I thank them for making me a better person.

Introduction

It was one o'clock in the morning of December 8, 1941. Peng Leshan, the head of the radio office of the Ministry of Information's International Department in Chongqing, was waiting in front of the wireless receiver in his office to pick up news updates from contacts in Los Angeles. Suddenly a message came through his headphone—the Japanese army had attacked Pearl Harbor. The United States would wage war against the Japanese Empire. Alone in the office, he wondered whether the news was true or whether he had simply misheard it on account of his fatigue. Hesitating to report it to his superior Hollington Tong, vice minister of information, he decided to reflect on what he had heard before dialing Tong's number. Around four o'clock, the phone at Chiang Kai-shek's mansion rang—Tong reported the attack on Pearl Harbor to Chiang.[1] It was a fateful day for China, perhaps as much as it was for the United States. The attack drew America into a common war against Japan. It put an end to years of solitary and desperate resistance by the Chiang Kai-shek government and signaled a real possibility of victory in the prolonged Sino-Japanese War.

The Japanese attack on Pearl Harbor was not a bolt from the blue but an escalation of preexisting tensions between the United States and Japan. The public was keenly aware of mutual animosity well before the attack, a key dispute revolving around Japan's military action in China. A Gallup poll in 1939 suggested that 74 percent of the US public sympathized with China's cause. By September 7, 1941, 70 percent of the US public supported the idea of checking Japan's military expansion even at the risk of war.[2] On November 26, 1941, US Secretary of State Cordell Hull rejected Japan's demand for relaxing embargos and issued an ultimatum, requesting Japan to withdraw completely from China. The attack on Pearl Harbor constituted both a military measure against the economic sanctions and an effort to keep the US Pacific Fleet from interfering with Japan's further actions in Asia.

---

1. Hollington Tong, *Chiang Kai-shek's Teacher and Ambassador: An Inside View of the Republican China—General Stilwell and American Policy Change towards Free China* (Bloomington: Authorhouse, 2005), 119.
2. September 7, 1941, Japan, in George Horace Gallup, *The Gallup Poll: Public Opinion, 1935–1971* (New York: Random House, 1972), 69.

The US public's sympathy for China represented the general attitude in the Western world. Yet this sympathy was not won overnight; it was the result of long-term persuasion and conditioning. Only a decade earlier, in 1928, when the Nanjing government was first established, China was still commonly portrayed in the West as a country of antiforeign nationalists, which lacked the discipline of a modern nation such as Japan. What caused this sea change in opinion? Western opinion leaders' "obsession" with solving the Chinese riddle and their desire to share their knowledge about this exotic country were often cited as the cause. They combined China's pursuit of independence with their personal ambitions, prejudices, and fears.[3] Indeed, as T. Christopher Jespersen argued, the images of China often reflected Western public's assumption about itself.[4] Despite thorough investigation of the activities of Western journalists, businesspeople and diplomats, little has been said about China's endeavors to promote the change. Yet China has its own story to tell—a story about how a weak nation, given the context and constraints of its own times, utilized international propaganda to achieve national survival. This story also adds another dimension to the existing military and social history of the Sino-Japanese War, shedding light on how the conflict played out in the media.[5]

This book is a study of China's efforts to make its voice heard in the world press from the time of the establishment of the Nanjing government to the Japanese attack on Pearl Harbor. Challenging a perceived Chinese passivity in international propaganda, it demonstrates that advocating China's case was an important means for the Nationalist government to restore China's sovereignty in the absence of a strong military and economy. It argues that, in this propaganda war against imperialist encroachment, it was ironically the very product of imperialism—the treaty-port press—that

---

3. Warren I. Cohen, *The Chinese Connection: Roger S. Greene, Thomas W. Lamont, George E. Sokolsky and American–East Asian Relations* (New York: Columbia University Press, 1978); Paul French, *Through the Looking Glass: China's Foreign Journalists from Opium Wars to Mao* (Hong Kong: Hong Kong University Press, 2009); Mordechai Rozanski, "The Role of American Journalists in Chinese-American Relations, 1900–1925" (PhD dissertation, University of Pennsylvania, 1974); Stephen R. MacKinnon and Oris Friesen, *China Reporting: An Oral History of American Journalism in the 1930s and 1940s* (Berkeley: University of California Press, 1987); Jon Thares Davidann traced American statesman Henry Stimson's support for China's case from the Manchurian Crisis and discussed the role William Henry Chamberlin, the *Christian Science Monitor*'s expert on Japanese issues, and the role popular writers Pearl Buck and Nathaniel Peffer played in tarnishing Japan's image among the US public. See Jon Thares Davidann, *Cultural Diplomacy in US-Japanese Relations, 1919–1941* (New York: Palgrave Macmillan, 2007), 180–86; Karen J. Leong, *The China Mystique: Pearl S. Buck, Anna May Wong, Mayling Soong, and the Transformation of American Orientalism* (Berkeley: University of California Press, 2005).
4. T. Christopher Jespersen, *American Images of China, 1931–1949* (Stanford: Stanford University Press, 1996), xv.
5. Rana Mitter, *Forgotten Ally: China's World War II, 1937–1945* (Boston and New York: Houghton Mifflin Harcourt, 2013); Stephen R. MacKinnon, Diana Lary, and Ezra F. Vogel, ed. *China at War: Regions of China, 1937–1945* (Stanford: Stanford University Press, 2007); Hans J. Van de Ven, *War and Nationalism in China, 1925–1945* (London: Routledge, 2003).

constituted the best resource to connect China with the world press. It provided the basis for the establishment of an international propaganda institution. The absence of clear boundaries of nationalities, state and public actors greatly expanded China's opportunity to reach the world public. The ability of the government and the treaty-port press to adapt to each other's information system during national crisis fostered the development of China's international propaganda.

Propaganda by a Weak Country?

After the collapse of the Qing dynasty in 1911, China went through decades of chaos in a painful search for a new sociopolitical order. The lack of a legitimate central government gave rise to a period of "warlordism" during which regional militarists maneuvered for power and wealth. The Nationalist Party (Guomindang) nominally unified the country in 1928 under the leadership of Chiang Kai-shek. Despite Chiang's supremacy in military power, the government was in reality a coalition of regional warlords who had nominally pledged allegiance to the Nationalist Party but maintained substantial fiscal and administrative autonomy.[6] Chiang's authority was frequently challenged by political rivals within the party and by the Communists externally.[7] The economic situation of the young Nationalist government was equally bleak. Constant warfare with warlords and the Communists had depleted the government's coffers and caused considerable damage to the country's economy. While regional leaders blocked the collection of internal taxes in defiance of Chiang's authority, the country's low credit ratings and its volatile political conditions made it hard to attract foreign loans.

Japan's military aggression in China posed a grave threat to the fledgling government and the Chinese nation. From 1931, the Japanese army moved to seize Chinese territory, first in Manchuria, then in North China. Encouraged by private initiatives as well as Japanese government policies, Japanese trade expansion in China was more rapid than that of the other foreign powers.[8] Its constant demands on the Chinese government to suppress popular anti-Japanese activities provided a pretext for Japan's intervention in China's politics. Japan's determination to exercise direct colonial control in certain parts of China posed a sharp contrast to the indirect colonial penetration by Western powers, and this created a new type of foreign danger for China.

---

6. Parks Coble, *Facing Japan: Chinese Politics and Japanese Imperialism, 1931–1937* (Cambridge, MA: Harvard University Press, 1991), 27.
7. Hung-mao Tien, *Government and Politics in Kuomintang China* (Stanford: Stanford University Press, 1972), 45–72.
8. Mizoguchi Toshiyuki, "The Changing Pattern of Sino-Japanese Trade, 1884–1937," in *The Japanese Informal Empire in China, 1895–1937*, ed. Peter Duus, Ramon H. Myers, and Mark R. Peattie (Princeton: Princeton University Press, 1989), 4–5.

It not only undermined the Nationalist government's nation-building efforts but also gave rise to fear for the extinction of the Chinese nation among the Chinese public.[9]

Leaders of the Nationalist government were keenly aware of the reality that China was unable to stave off Japan's pressure single handedly. Having been trained at a Japanese military school, Chiang Kai-shek understood clearly that Chinese troops were incapable of standing up to the modern Japanese army. Moreover, a war with Japan would be political suicide for Chiang, destroying the delicate balance of forces that he had carefully constructed within the government and providing his rivals with an opportunity to overthrow his rule. For a weak nation with inadequate military and economic power to defend its territorial sovereignty, raising international pressure to curb Japan's ambition was essential. But how could China gain influence in the Western powers' foreign policy making?

Propaganda, "a concerted scheme for the promotion of a doctrine or practice,"[10] became an important means to gain and maintain power in international affairs from the time of World War I.[11] The rise in the use of propaganda was a result of greater mass participation in politics and the proliferation of communications technology, as well as increasing interaction among nations.[12] During the war, belligerents widely adopted propaganda as a way of strengthening the morale of their own forces and to sap that of their enemies.[13] The Soviet Union even set up long-term propaganda institutions, exploiting them to promote its political ideology worldwide.[14] In democratic countries, where the manipulation of political information was considered unethical, officials generally refrained from supporting propaganda activities after the war.[15] Acknowledging the power of public opinion, however, they wasted no time reverting to official propaganda when international crises intensified. By the end of the 1930s, propaganda had become an important instrument in international politics worldwide. As E. H. Carr observed in 1939, "New official or semi-official agencies for

---

9. Coble, *Facing Japan*, 6.
10. Edward Hallett Carr, *Propaganda in International Politics* (Oxford: Clarendon Press, 1939), 3.
11. Ibid.
12. Tomoko Akami, "The Emergence of International Public Opinion and the Origins of Public Diplomacy in Japan in the Inter-war Period," *The Hague Journal of Diplomacy* 3, no. 2 (2008): 101–2.
13. Harold Dwight Lasswell, *Propaganda Technique in World War I* (Cambridge, MA: MIT Press, 1971); George Creel, *How We Advertised America* (New York: Harper and Brothers Publishers, 1920); Philip M. Taylor, *The Projection of Britain: British Overseas Publicity and Propaganda, 1919–1939* (Cambridge: Cambridge University Press, 1981).
14. Edward Hallett Carr, *The Twenty Years' Crisis, 1919–1939: An Introduction to the Study of International Relations* (London: Macmillan, 1939), 137; Philip M. Taylor, *Munitions of the Mind: A History of Propaganda from the Ancient World to the Present Era* (Manchester and New York: Manchester University Press, 2003), 206.
15. See British officials' discussion of the function of propaganda in peacetime, in Taylor, *Projection of Britain*, 44–50.

the influencing of opinion at home and abroad were springing up in every country."[16] And propaganda "has never been so important a factor in politics as it is today."[17]

However, international propaganda was essentially a privilege of powerful nations that had the infrastructure and networks to transmit their views to an international audience. This echoed Carr's observation that "power over opinion cannot be dissociated from military and economic power."[18] During World War I, Britain's control over the transatlantic cables enabled it to monitor the output of telegraphic news sent from Germany to the United States and to continuously feed overseas representatives with news from the British perspective.[19] The United States spread its international propaganda networks in Europe, Latin America, and Asia by the Committee on Public Information. Benefiting from wireless technology, the committee widely explained American's aim in the war and advocated Wilson's gospel of democracy.[20] Since the late nineteenth century, Japan also developed a sophisticated submarine cable network to coastal cities in China, Korea, and Taiwan. Its state-sponsored news agencies had gained an essential foothold in the Chinese news market and become a presenter of Chinese issues in the international world.[21] Yet China by the late 1920s did not possess a single international news agency, nor did it have full sovereignty over cable transmissions within its own territory.[22] When a conflict between China and Japan occurred, China often found its voice drowned out by Japan's advanced propaganda machinery.

Existing literature on propaganda experiences of the strong powers, like Western countries and Japan, fails to shed light on China's case. While the Powers had military and economic strength to back up their propaganda efforts, China's propaganda did not have such support.[23] Like many other foreign-introduced strategies, ideas, and institutions, international propaganda had to go through a process of localization before it could function in the Chinese context.[24] Indeed, China's international

---

16. Carr, *Twenty Years' Crisis, 1919–1939*, 137.
17. Carr, *Propaganda in International Politics*, 3.
18. Carr, *Twenty Years' Crisis, 1919–1939*, 141.
19. Taylor, *Projection of Britain*, 58.
20. Erez Manela, *The Wilsonian Moment: Self-Determination and the International Origins of Anticolonial Nationalism* (New York: Oxford University Press, 2007), 48–70; Creel, *How We Advertised America*.
21. Daqing Yang, *Technology of Empire: Telecommunications and Japanese Expansion in Asia, 1883–1945* (Cambridge, MA: Harvard University Press, 2010); Tomoko Akami, *Japan's News Propaganda and Reuters' News Empire in Northeast Asia, 1870–1934* (Dordrecht: Republic of Letters, 2012).
22. Westel W. Willoughby, *Foreign Rights and Interests in China* (Baltimore: Johns Hopkins Press, 1920; Taipei: Ch'eng-Wen Publishing, 1966), 2:943–77. Citations refer to the Ch'eng-Wen edition.
23. The Powers in this book refers to Western and Asian empires that have substantial imperial interests in China.
24. Mittler argued that modern newspapers in China, instead of following the Western model, have gone through an indigenization process to cater for the Chinese market. See Barbara Mittler, "Domesticating an Alien Medium: Incorporating the Western-Style Newspaper into the Chinese Public Sphere," in *Joining the Global Public: Word, Image, and City in Early Chinese Newspapers, 1870–1910*, ed. Rudolf Wagner (Albany: State University of New York Press, 2007), 13–46.

propaganda experience had its own features. First, propaganda was not pursued by the state alone. Nonstate actors, particularly the treaty-port bilingual elites were crucial in making China's case known to the world. Second, transnational networks characterized China's propaganda experience. The resource it relied on to resist imperialist encroachment ironically was a product of imperialism—the English-language treaty-port press.

The English-Language Treaty-Port Press in China

The English-language treaty-port press in China has almost entirely escaped scholarly attention. Based on the static notion that the identity of a press derives from the language it uses, Chinese media historians have all but neglected the English-language treaty-port press as an integral part of the Chinese media.[25] Yearning to carve out an identity to fit into a neat nation-state framework, they have ignored the reality that identity itself is a fluid notion that takes shape through cultural encounters and exchange.[26] Others who believe that the English-language papers catered only to the expatriate community tend to regard this medium as unworthy of serious consideration. A scarcity of resources has also led to the neglect of the English-language press. Thomas Ming-heng Chao's *The Foreign Press in China* and Frank H. H. King and Prescott Clarke's *Research Guide to China-Coast Newspapers, 1822–1911* have mapped a diversified landscape of the treaty-port press in China from the late Qing to the early Republican era. Apart from a few papers available on microfilm or in digital form, most of the English-language papers were either lost or hidden, uncatalogued in Chinese provincial libraries. They appear only vaguely in scattered references in

---

25. Despite Lin Yutang's active engagement in English-language treaty-port journals in the 1930s, he failed to include them under the rubric "Chinese press" when discussing the history of the press in China; see Lin Yutang, *A History of the Press and Public Opinion in China* (Shanghai: Kelly and Walsh, 1937). Zeng Xubai only made passing reference to the English-language newspapers without any extended discussion of their political stances; see Zeng Xubai, *Zhongguo xinwen shi* [A history of China's journalism] (Taipei: Guoli zhengzhi daxue xinwen yanjiusuo, 1966). Discussion of the influence of the treaty-port press is also absent in a recent study of the Guomindang's news policy by Wang Lingxiao; see Wang Lingxiao, *Zhongguo Guomindang xinwen zhengce zhi yanjiu, 1928–1945* [News policy of the Guomindang government, 1928–1945] (Taipei: Jindai Zhongguo chubanshe, 1996). Literature on China's media history published in the People's Republic of China has operated largely within the ideological bounds of the "imperialism" model, in which the impact of the foreign empires have long been regarded as marred by exploitation. It often neglects the contribution of the treaty-port foreign press and narrowly considers it as merely an instrument of imperialist rule. Although Fang Hanqi briefly distinguishes the different attitudes toward China presented by British and American papers in the 1920s, he does not explore the significance of the press in China's domestic politics and foreign relations; see Fang Hanqi, *Zhongguo xinwen shiye tongshi* [General history of the press in China] (Beijing: Zhongguo renmin daxue chubanshe, 1992).
26. Rudolf Wagner, "Don't Mind the Gap! The Foreign Language-Press in Late-Qing and Republican China," *China Heritage Quarterly*, nos. 30/31 (June/September 2012), http://www.chinaheritagequarterly.org/features.php?searchterm=030_wagner.inc&issue=030.

studies on the activities of foreign journalists in China.[27] They have rarely been considered of historiographical interest, let alone worth investigating in terms of their editorial stances, financial backgrounds, connections with the state, or rivalries in the press market. An even larger problem, however, is that traditional historiography has tended to reduce Sino-foreign interactions to a simplified East-West dichotomy. The tensions between the foreign powers as the oppressors and China as the victim have been a popular theme that has strongly shaped public memory in China to date.

Scholars have recently begun to take notice of the significance of the English-language press in Chinese diplomatic history, but they have yet to investigate the treaty-port papers' interaction with indigenous elites.[28] Peter O'Connor's detailed study of English-language papers based in Japan demonstrated a transnational news networks in East Asia.[29] By examining the *China Critic* and *T'ien Hsia*, two English-language journals operating in Shanghai in the 1930s, Shuang Shen reveals a "cosmopolitan public" composed of Western-educated Chinese intellectuals who actively published in the English-language treaty-port press.[30] These seminal studies deepen our understanding of the dynamic media environment in the treaty ports, but they tend to emphasize the importance of the press for foreign readers, while neglecting its influence on Chinese politics. This book will look into this missing aspect and explore how the English-language press was used to restore China's sovereignty during the Sino-Japanese crisis and how the press influenced the formation of a centralized institution for international propaganda.

While the Chinese government lacked a channel to make its voice heard internationally, newspapers published in the foreign concessions and settlements integrated China into the world media system. Treaty-port journalists, editors, and foreign expatriates in general were highly regarded as credible sources by audiences in their home countries. Their writings about the exotic land and their observations of its people and political affairs continued to dominate the imagination of readers at home.[31] Sharing correspondents and news reports between the treaty-port press and metropolitan papers was also common practice. This further expanded the influence of the treaty-port journalists to the metropolitan audience. Savvy journalists who had connections with Chinese officials were favorite contacts for diplomats. They

---

27. Paul French, *Carl Crow: A Tough Old China Hand* (Hong Kong: Hong Kong University Press, 2006); French, *Through the Looking Glass*.
28. Feng Yue, *Riben zai Hua guanfang bao: Huabei zhengbao, 1919–1930* [Japan's official English-language paper in China: *North China Standard*] (Beijing: Xinhua chubanshe, 2008); Wu Yixiong, *Zai Hua Yingwen baokan yu jindai zaoqi de Zhongxi guanxi* [The English press in China and the Sino-Western relationship in the early modern times] (Beijing: Shehui kexue wenxian chubanshe, 2012).
29. Peter O'Connor, *The English-Language Press Networks of East Asia, 1918–1945* (Kent: Global Oriental, 2010).
30. Shuang Shen, *Cosmopolitan Publics: Anglophone Print Culture in Semi-colonial Shanghai* (New Brunswick, NJ: Rutgers University Press, 2009).
31. Robert A. Bickers, *Britain in China: Community Culture and Colonialism, 1900–1949* (Manchester: Manchester University Press, 1999), 22–59.

were frequently approached for opinion and inside information in case of diplomatic controversies.[32]

However, it would be wrong to consider the treaty-port press as homogeneous. The press was rife with tensions. Unlike regular colonies such as India where local economies and social life were dominated by a single empire, the Chinese treaty ports were operated by an assortment of foreign powers with different interests and ideologies. The presence of various imperial interests gave rise to fierce competition among papers for the power of discourse, information resources, and advertising markets. The emerging American press challenged the British news monopoly in China in the early twentieth century.[33] Yet temporary alliances were forged and dissolved between the two when Japanese and Chinese interests became involved in the press. Tensions did not end in the treaty ports but also existed between treaty-port expatriates and the metropolitan public. Instead of following the metropolitan view about Chinese issues, treaty-port communities tended to develop a relatively independent opinion that was sometimes at odds with the foreign policy maintained by their home countries.

The treaty-port press was characterized by transnational identities, partly due to the Chinese government's weak presence there. The treaty-port system was underpinned by extraterritoriality, which exempted foreign residents from the jurisdiction of Chinese laws. This protected foreign-registered newspapers from state intervention and gave rise to a complex and densely packed media environment, where conventional national boundaries did not apply and transnational registration, editorship, ownership, and subsidies became common practice.[34] As Bickers rightly points out, in practice the treaty-port system had effectively replaced the state as the defining organizational framework. It cultivated new identities among expatriates and attracted Chinese, regardless of whether they were professionals, gangsters, refugees, or traders.[35] Here, lines of identity of newspapers were complex, multilayered, and pragmatic.[36] It was common to find an English-language paper registered with one country, operated by nationals of another, with the funding provided by an interest group in a third country. Information was distributed by state-related actors,

---

32. See the consul general in Shanghai Edwin Cunningham's close connection with George E. Sokolsky, in Cohen, *Chinese Connection*, 86–87.
33. Yong Z. Volz and Chin-Chuan Lee, "Semi-colonialism and Journalistic Sphere of Influence: British-American Press Competition in Early Twentieth-Century China," *Journalism Studies* 12, no. 5 (2011): 563–65.
34. See the discussion of the transnational features of the Chinese press during the late Qing and Republican era by Bryna Goodman, "Networks of News: Power, Language and Transnational Dimensions of the Chinese Press, 1850–1949," *China Review* 4, no. 1 (Spring 2004): 1–10.
35. Robert Bickers and Christian Henriot, introduction to *New Frontiers: Imperialism's New Communities in East Asia, 1842–1953*, ed. Robert Bickers and Christian Henriot (Manchester and New York: Manchester University Press, 2000), 4–5.
36. Bryna Goodman and David Goodman, ed., *Twentieth-Century Colonialism and China: Localities, the Everyday and the World* (London and New York: Routledge, 2012), 10; Rudolf G. Wagner, "The Role of the Foreign Community in the Chinese Public Sphere," *China Quarterly* 142 (1995): 423–43.

independent groups, and individuals with an agenda that could not be simply categorized as imperialism, nationalism, or capitalism. Nor was the nationality of the editor a reliable indicator of a paper's editorial stance. Frequent changes of ownership between proprietors from different nations and hidden foreign subsidies further complicated the identity of the paper. There was deep interpenetration of news resources, funding, and personal networks among newspapers representing interest groups of different nations. The complex treaty-port media environment made it onerous for the Chinese government to exercise effective control of it. Ironically, it was exactly this lack of order that provided the Chinese intellectuals and officials, who had little prior engagement with this medium, the opportunity to penetrate it.

It is a common assumption that the English-language papers served the foreign community, whereas the Chinese press circulated among the Chinese. Yet the historical reality indicates that the two types of newspapers were more interdependent than is commonly recognized.[37] Editors of the treaty-port English-language papers, particularly those operated by Americans, had discovered a considerable numbers of bilingual Chinese readers. Most of them had educational experience abroad or in foreign-operated schools and universities in China.[38] Instead of being a passive audience, these bilingual elites actively engaged in the operation of the English-language papers, working as contributors, editors, or managers. Indeed, reading, writing, or even working in English had become fashionable among the bilingual elites. It partly reflected a dimension of their cosmopolitan identities and extensive life experience. When Sino-Japanese relations soured, those bilingual elites, who had been immersed in the treaty-port press, knew what sort of rhetoric appealed to Western audiences.[39] Their involvement in the press formed the initial basis for China's international propaganda, especially when an official framework was yet to be constructed.

The influence of the English treaty-port papers also extended to Chinese readers who did not have the language proficiency to read originals. The language barrier could easily be overcome by translation. Bryna Goodman's research has shown that a significant portion of the important news that appeared in Chinese papers was translated from foreign papers. Citation of a Western source, such as the *North China Daily News* or the *China Weekly Review*, enhanced the authority of the news. Those translations of the Western press frequently appeared in headlines, a privilege the Chinese sources did not enjoy.[40] Yet this was not a one-way flow of information. The Chinese bilingual elites constituted an important source of information

---

37. Bryna Goodman, "Semi-colonialism, Transnational Networks and News Flows in Early Republican Shanghai," *China Review* 4, no. 1 (Spring 2004): 64.
38. John B. Powell, *My Twenty-Five Years in China* (New York: Macmillan, 1945), 10.
39. The large number of bilingual intellectuals in the early Republic China was the result of the cultural policy of the United States and Japan. See Heng Teow, *Japan's Cultural Policy toward China, 1918–1931: A Comparative Perspective* (Cambridge, MA: Harvard University Press, 1999).
40. Goodman, "Semi-colonialism, Transnational Networks and News Flows in Early Republican Shanghai."

for foreign journalists through formal news exchange or informal conversations. As Stephen MacKinnon observed, few Western journalists spoke or read Chinese, but many had close ties with their Chinese counterparts through the English-language press.[41] Some journalists found it convenient to leak information to the foreign papers and then cite this material in Chinese translation to avoid censorship and social awkwardness in the Chinese community.[42] These invisible and personal information networks expanded the power of English treaty-port press and enabled its tentacles to reach the deepest corners of Chinese politics and society. This also explains why so many interest groups were eager to gain influence in this seemingly unimportant medium and why the competition over the control of the key papers was fierce.

The translingual flow of information nevertheless could not erase national and racial boundaries. Although many Chinese popular newspapers sought to benefit from the conditions of extraterritoriality by registering abroad as foreign assets, the level of protection they received from foreign administrations was much more limited than that extended to the English-language papers run by foreigners. When controversies arose with the Chinese government, foreign legations usually refused to protect journalists with Chinese backgrounds yet could not ignore similar situations with their own nationals.[43] It was still the foreign-operated English-language papers that enjoyed the highest level of independence from state intervention in China.

Such independence was unattainable for commercial Chinese newspapers either. It is true that the rise of commercial newspapers, as well as the rapid professionalization of journalistic training in the 1920s, led to a more independent and less politically partisan press. Yet commercialization did not foster political freedom to the level intellectuals wished to achieve. The quest for profit pushed the Chinese press owners to provide more social and entertainment news while avoiding sensitive political debates so as to avoid trouble with the government.[44] Although the English-language papers were also commercial, they targeted a small number of foreign and Chinese elite readers who paid more attention to politics and culture than social entertainment. This required the papers to engage in deep political debates and in information digging.

The treaty-port press provided a broader platform than Chinese-operated papers to discuss Chinese domestic and international politics. The high level of political independence constituted the source of credibility and power of the English-language press in both international and Chinese domestic news markets. Such an information

---

41. Stephen R. MacKinnon, "Toward a History of the Chinese Press in the Republican Period," *Modern China* 23, no. 1 (January 1997): 11–15.
42. Goodman, "Semi-colonialism, Transnational Networks and News Flows in Early Republican Shanghai," 77.
43. See Eugene Chen's case in Goodman, "Semi-colonialism, Transnational Networks and News Flows in Early Republican Shanghai," 78.
44. Timothy Weston, "Mining the Newspaper Business: The Theory and Practice of Journalism in 1920s China," *Twentieth-Century China* 31, no. 2 (April 2006): 4–31.

enclave attracted people from all over the country who were open to diversified ideas and looking for a space to pursue an alternative form of information order. Indeed, preserving a locale where messages were considered more credible in the news market was never the Nationalist government's intention. Its existence simply reflected the government's inability to extend control over treaty ports. It also challenged the state's traditional propaganda strategies and the top-down information order that the party tried to establish. Yet it was undeniable that the press constituted a valuable channel that China desperately needed to reach an international audience. Such an ambiguous situation required the Guomindang government to deal with the treaty-port press with great caution.

Treaty-Port Press and International Propaganda Institution

The information order in the treaty-port press was distinctive from that pursued by the Nationalist government elsewhere in China. In 1924, Sun Yat-sen reorganized the Nationalist Party along Leninist lines. A Ministry of Propaganda was established following the organizational structure of its counterpart in the Soviet Communist Party. The propaganda system placed great emphasis on thought control and ideological indoctrination. Various schemes, including censorship, political training, distribution of propaganda outlines and publications, were exercised through party organizations on a central and local level.[45] The party propaganda system implemented a top-down form of information control. Based on the belief that the party represented public interests and that it was equipped with the knowledge to solve China's problems, propaganda officials considered it imperative to educate the public with Sun Yat-sen's Three People's Principles. Although national leaders acknowledged that European and American ideals of liberty and equality had initially inspired the revolution in China, they regarded the pursuit of personal freedom not useful to further guide China's revolution. It was the party that had the freedom of expression, not the individual.[46] This logic ran contrary to the values held in the treaty-port press, where independence and credibility, as mentioned above, were the key factors determining how far a message could travel. The clash of values developed into tensions between the treaty-port journalists and the conservative Guomindang members when the former joined the government's propaganda system after the war.

The development of international propaganda policy needs to be understood in light of the dimensions of China's international environment as well as its domestic political culture. Just like William Kirby observed, during the Republican period

---

45. John Fitzgerald, *Awakening China: Politics, Culture, and Class in the Nationalist Revolution* (Stanford: Stanford University Press, 1996), chapters 6 and 7.
46. Fitzgerald, *Awakening China*, 215.

(1912–1949) "everything important had an international dimension."[47] From 1931 to 1941, Chiang Kai-shek's foreign policy experienced a paradigm change, from taking a position against foreign coercion, particularly that of Britain, to an anti-Japanese policy. Yet the transition did not follow a linear path, and the line between friend and foe was unclear, particularly during the mid-1930s.[48] While the Guomindang government was alert to Japan's desires for Chinese territory, it was also concerned about the Western powers' encroachment on China's sovereignty. Officials of different political groups often debated about who China should ally with to fight against whom. The lack of consensus and a definite diplomatic line led to the government's ambiguous attitude toward the treaty-port press: while it pursued an alliance with the Western-operated papers to denounce Japan, it was relentless in its efforts to challenge the Powers' extraterritorial privileges in the press.

Factional politics among Chiang Kai-shek, Wang Jingwei, and Hu Hanmin, which involved rivalries for control of the government, impaired the formation of a unified and coherent system of international propaganda. Conservative party members who were reluctant to abandon the party's anti-imperialist tradition continued to raise hurdles for the implementation of propaganda policies aimed at forming an alliance with Western powers. Attempts at building a strong international propaganda system by civilian leaders were contradicted by the continuing militarization of politics and administration in the 1930s. The concentration of propaganda resources became possible only after Chiang Kai-shek's ascendance to the leadership following the outbreak of the Sino-Japanese War.

The relations between the English-language treaty-port press cohorts and the Nationalist government should be analyzed in two phases, divided by the outbreak of the full-scale Sino-Japanese War in 1937. During the prewar period before a centralized propaganda institution had been established, the most vibrant force to advocate China's case was the English-language treaty-port papers operated by bilingual Chinese and foreign nationals. Despite several institutions' involvement in international propaganda, their efforts were conducted in an ad hoc manner without consistent policy guidelines. The government made considerable adjustments to the transnational treaty-port press at this stage. Facing a complex media environment in the treaty ports, where the boundaries of national identity were not always clear cut, the government sought to infiltrate the press by camouflaging its connections with some of the distinguished papers and journalists. Scholars have tended to perceive the Guomindang government and the press as dichotomous opposites whose

---

47. William C. Kirby, "The Internationalization of China: Foreign Relations at Home and Abroad in the Republican Era," in *Reappraising Republican China*, ed. Frederic Wakeman Jr. and Richard Louis Edmonds (Oxford: Oxford University Press, 2000), 179.
48. Youli Sun, *China and the Origins of the Pacific War* (New York: St. Martin's Press, 1993).

relationship was characterized by the former's suppression and the latter's resistance.⁴⁹ This study demonstrates that the relation between the two was far more complex. Apart from challenging the independence of the press, the government also sought to adapt to the transnational media environment. Communication between the Western press and Chinese communities was not only increased by the pressure to maximize profit in the news market and journalists' innate desire to dig out news, but also by the government's efforts to incorporate the treaty-port press into its propaganda system.

After the war, the treaty-port press cohorts were under great pressure to adapt to the government's propaganda system. Having to abandon the news infrastructure and resources in the treaty ports, they sought institutional accommodation in the party-state. Despite their desire to uphold the liberal journalism learned in US-influenced institutions, they had to make compromises to the party's surveillance of information transmission during wartime. A special structure was thus established to accommodate this group of outsiders who had no roots in the party to help them fit in with the existing propaganda bureaucracy. Chiang's effort to insulate them from external pressure was essential to guarantee their office's efficiency. Julia Strauss's seminal study on the Nationalist government's institution building argued that the institutions' ability to insulate themselves from external intervention was essential to maintaining their daily operations and therefore to achieving mid- and long-term goals.⁵⁰ Her analysis is germane to understanding the development of the international propaganda institution. Yet the international propaganda office benefited from insulation only temporarily. The strategy soon proved to be the poison to quench the thirst, since it further isolated the institution from other political factions with which collaboration was imperative. It also made the propaganda office vulnerable, since its independence, and the credibility derived from it, became increasingly hinged upon Chiang's support. Yet Chiang, who was by no means committed to liberal values, was ready to exploit the intelligence role of the office at the cost of its efficacy of publicity.

Compared to the Guomindang's domestic propaganda system, the international propaganda office established in 1937 placed greater emphasis on professionalism and qualifications than on seniority and commitment to the party's ideologies. Indeed, the officials who used to serve the treaty-port press had tried to eke out a space in the government where they could maintain a certain level of independence. Yet compromise was inevitable. The institution was not strictly a modern, Weberian bureaucracy operating on the basis of impersonal recruitment procedures and a clearly defined distribution of power based on administrative protocols. Instead, it was strongly patriarchal. Philip Kuhn argued that the Qing Chinese state was a

---

49. Lee-hsia Hsu Ting, *Government Control of the Press in Modern China, 1900–1949* (Cambridge, MA: Harvard University Press, 1974).
50. Julia C. Strauss, *Strong Institutions in Weak Polities: State Building in Republican China, 1927–1940* (Oxford: Clarendon Press, 1998).

"bureaucratic monarchy," characterized by the simultaneous coexistence of an autocratic monarchy with a routinized bureaucracy.[51] This model could also be used to understand the international propaganda department. Apart from the codes and ethics used to regulate staff members of the department, Chiang could always find a channel to monitor its daily operations, influence its censorship policy, and ensure its output to fit his larger political plans. A sense of community was nurtured through informal networks based on people's native place, alumni connections, experiences as colleagues, and chains of friendship.

The person Chiang Kai-shek put in charge of establishing the propaganda system was Hollington Tong (Dong Xianguang), a US-trained bilingual journalist. While his name rarely appears in books on the involvement of foreign journalists in China's war and revolution, Tong played a key role in linking the Nationalist government with the treaty-port press and in founding an international propaganda department in the party. Yet the process was not always pleasant. He constantly found himself sandwiched between his commitment to liberal ideals and the necessity to adapt to the conservatism of the party. And his experience mirrored many intellectuals of the time who struggled to gain more independence when nationalism became the dominant ideology that pushed people to make decisions based on national interests during wartime.

Structure and Outline

Scholarship dedicated to the history of the Chinese media has tended to examine propaganda policies and media texts separately and has often obscured their interaction. In each media battle, trial and error was an integral part of the formative process of building an effective international propaganda system. This book combines discourse analysis with studies on policy making and institution building. It traces how China's fractured government carried out a propaganda scheme in spite of Japan's advanced international news network.

This book adopts a two-tiered structure: each chapter on the historical development of Guomindang propaganda policy is followed by a section that analyzes how the Sino-Japanese conflict was discussed in the treaty-port press during the given period. The purpose is to integrate the analysis of media policies with that of actual reporting in newspapers. Given the transnational feature of the treaty-port media environment, the national identity of a newspaper in this book is based on its source of funding, which significantly affected its editorial line. "Propaganda" in this study mainly refers to news propaganda—the use of news in the English-language press as

---

51. Philip A. Kuhn, *Soulstealers: The Chinese Sorcery Scare of 1786* (Cambridge, MA: Harvard University Press, 1990).

a tool of diplomacy.⁵² "News," on the contrary, carries a broader meaning, applying to both the reporting of facts and political commentary on recent events.

In my case studies, I pay particular attention to the interactions between the texts that appeared in the press and their social and political context. Media texts are not generated in a social vacuum. They are often a response to a context, which may be an opponent's propaganda or a particular opinion popular among the public. Although it is impossible to discern precisely to whom an article was initially directed, juxtaposing texts from several rival sources usually provides a good indication in this regard. The juxtaposition is also important to track the flow of information between treaty-port papers and from treaty-port press to the metropolitan papers in Britain and the United States. For each case, I will examine how Japan and China presented their sides of the story in the treaty-port press. The opinions of the British- and American-controlled treaty-port papers will be discussed to reveal their engagement in this media battle. This will be followed by a review of press opinion in London and New York in order to trace whether and to what extent Chinese and Japanese views were accepted by the metropolitan press.

The case studies are meant to demonstrate two points. First, they seek to reflect the nuanced and multilayered treaty-port press environment and the various political tensions behind it, especially through examination of a particular paper's choice of words and cross-referencing with other papers representing different interest groups. Second, the competition for news reporting between China and Japan was more about establishing the context of the news than reporting the news itself. As Edward L. Bernays put it, "there has to be fertile ground for an idea to fall on and grow."⁵³ Unable to retrieve historical reality most of the time, newspapers of both sides had paid great attention to cultivating favorable contexts for their reports, so as to make their versions of the story appear more authentic and thus acceptable among the readers.

There are obvious limits to what this study can accomplish, one of them being the assessment of the efficacy of propaganda. For decades, the question of whether propaganda can effectively change people's minds has been the topic of much debate. Scholars approaching the question with different analytical models come to different conclusions, and I do not intend to join the debate. Rather, I follow Warren Cohen's injunction to "chart lines of access to decision-makers and to the public"⁵⁴ and present the neglected factors that might lead to certain changes. The ability to transmit one's views, as he suggests, does not guarantee influence, but no influence is possible without the ability to convey opinions to audiences. This study traces China's

---

52. See the explanation of the term "news propaganda" in Akami, "The Emergence of International Public Opinion and the Origins of Public Diplomacy in Japan in the Inter-war Period," 102.
53. Edward L. Bernays, *Propaganda* (New York: Liveright Publishing, 1928), 109.
54. Cohen, *Chinese Connection*, 2.

endeavors to gain access to the world press. Second, various forms of media and publications contribute to national image building, such as movies, radio, travelogues, and popular novels.[55] While there is considerable scholarship on this, the treaty-port English-language press remains underresearched. This book examines how news was employed as an intangible power to shape the minds of the foreign public. Third, discourse analysis does not examine what actually happened in the past but what was reflected in the press. The press may not necessarily be able to discern truth during or immediately after an event, but it reflects certain parts of it and records what people perceive the truth to be, based on the prevailing attitudes.

This book comprises three sections. Part I describes the Chiang Kai-shek government's weak position in international propaganda during the early years of the regime, when connections with the treaty-port press had not yet been established. Chapter 1 sketches out the backgrounds of the key British- and American-owned English-language papers in the treaty ports in the late 1920s and China's efforts to compete with Japan in international news reporting before 1928. Chapter 2 examines China and Japan's confrontation in the English-language press during the Jinan Incident in May 1928—the first military conflict between the Nationalist government and Japan after Chiang Kai-shek established the Nanjing government.

Chapters 3–6 form the second part of the book. They address the formative period of China's propaganda system before the full-scale Sino-Japanese War. Chapter 3 deals with the Nationalist government's attempts to build an international propaganda system from 1928 to 1932. It explores the government's efforts to regulate treaty-port papers protected by extraterritoriality and to window dress its own papers with foreign capital and editors. The Mukden Incident (1931) and the Shanghai Incident (1932), which instigated another battle of words between China and Japan in the English-language press, tested the Nationalist government's international propaganda system. Chapter 4 analyzes the position and strategy that the major newspapers adopted during the two incidents. In Chapter 5, I trace the development of China's international propaganda from 1933 to June 1937, a period characterized by the government's appeasement of Japan and Chiang taking two positions simultaneously. While suppressing anti-Japanese voices in the domestic press, he secretly subsidized the prominent anti-Japanese English-language papers. Chapter 6 uses the press's reaction to the statement of the Amō Doctrine (1934) to reveal how China and Japan both failed to form a unified line in the press, due to complex political circumstances.

Part III explores the Nationalist government's propaganda policy after the outbreak of the Sino-Japanese War. Chapter 7 traces the establishment of a centralized international propaganda system led by Hollington Tong. Analyzing the Nanjing Incident of

---

55. Chang-tai Hung, *War and Popular Culture: Resistance in Modern China, 1937–1945* (Berkeley: University of California Press, 1994); Michael A. Krysko, *American Radio in China: International Encounters with Technology and Communications, 1919–1941* (Houndmills: Palgrave Macmillan, 2011).

1938, this chapter reveals how the system organized international propaganda against Japan through its extensive network. The final chapter examines how Tong operated the propaganda institution after Chiang Kai-shek moved the capital to Chongqing. Troubled by the lack of resources and constant bombing by the Japanese, Tong's office also had to compete with the Communist Party for the attention of foreign correspondents and to undermine the propaganda efforts of the Wang Jingwei regime through a clandestine branch office in Shanghai.

During my years of reading the *North China Daily News*, the foremost treaty-port newspaper of the time, I have collected many cartoons drawn by the paper's talented White Russian artist Georgii Avksent'ievich Sapojnikoff, known by his pen name Sapajou.[56] To recapture the historical events and political circumstances, I end each chapter with one of his cartoons published between 1928 and 1940—when the paper ceased publication under Japanese pressure.

---

56. Richard Rigby, "Sapajou," *East Asian History*, nos. 17/18 (June/December 1999): 131–68.

Part I

A Nation without a Voice

1
Bridge or Barrier

The Treaty-Port English-Language Press in China, 1920s

The English-language press has a fairly long history in China. The first English-language newspaper, the *Canton Register*, appeared in Canton's local foreign community in 1827.[1] By then, foreigners had already been resident on China's coast for more than two hundred years.[2] Because of the small number of people in these communities, the running of periodicals had long been unviable. The foreigners shared similar values nurtured by Christianity, and their economic interests were closely connected with the operation of the East India Company.[3] When trade with China began to thrive, the foreign community expanded, and the monopoly of the East India Company gradually impeded the growth of local independent businesses. As the call for free trade grew stronger, foreign residents in China felt the need to make their appeal heard in their home countries, where colonial policies were crafted.

The *Canton Register* was established to challenge the monopoly of the East India Company. Realizing that their criticism could draw attacks from the company, editors of the *Register* led by A. S. Keating softened their stance after the first issue. To avoid further confrontation, Keating turned the paper into a news carrier, focusing on factual reports. In 1831, William W. Wood, who lost his position as editor of the *Register* because of his intransigent attitude, started a weekly of his own. The journal, named the *Chinese Courier and Canton Gazette*, focused on editorials. It claimed to have a sense of justice and overtly urged ending the monopoly of the East India Company.[4] Wood considered the *Register* as its rival and frequently vented his anger at the *Register*'s betrayal of its original stance. His editorial line was partly encouraged by his American citizenship and the financial assistance of an American company.

---

1. Frank H. H. King and Prescott Clarke, *A Research Guide to China-Coast Newspapers, 1822–1911* (Cambridge, MA: Harvard University Press, 1965), 16; P. L. Simmonds, "Statistics of Newspapers in Various Countries," *Journal of the Statistical Society of London* 4, no. 2 (July 1841): 136.
2. Macao and Canton were the only ports that allowed Westerners to conduct trade and set up a residence before the Opium War; King and Clarke, *Research Guide to China-Coast Newspapers*, 15; Hosea Ballou Morse, *The Chronicles of the East India Company Trading to China, 1635–1834* (Cambridge, MA: Harvard University Press, 1926).
3. King and Clarke, *Research Guide to China-Coast Newspapers*, 15.
4. *Chinese Courier and Canton Gazette*, no. 1, July 28, 1831.

The dispute of the two papers over trade issues translated into mutual personal attacks of the chief editors, which eventually culminated in the announcement of a duel between Keating and Wood.[5] The duel did not take place. Yet the dramatic beginning of the treaty-port press industry in China foreshadowed some key features in its later development: the focus on treaty-port interests and the tensions among papers representing different interest groups.

Over the next hundred years, English-language periodicals in China thrived with the development of the treaty-port system. Backed by gunfire, the Powers, then led by the British Empire, opened a series of coastal ports for trade and laid down regulations that would facilitate their commercial profits. They obtained the rights to lease land, build premises, and start their own businesses and administrative bodies. All their activities were protected by extraterritoriality, a legal regime that subjected foreign sojourners to the jurisdiction of their own consuls. Underpinned by this legal privilege, the treaty-port system created a new grey area of contested sovereignty and control, where foreign residents together with their premises and agencies extended the tentacles of empires within China.[6] Indeed, the system challenged the Chinese government's already-limited authority over its territory, but it also provided the world with a window to peer into this otherwise mysterious land.

The treaty-port newspapers were an effective bridge to tighten communications not only among foreign communities in China but also between treaty ports and the metropolitan centers. Their reports about China were highly valued by audiences in their home countries as a primary introduction to Chinese politics and society. As Robert Bickers points out, accounts of China's treaty-port papers became the "persuasive knowledge" about the country and shaped British understandings and imaginations of the land.[7] Meanwhile, discussion of affairs in their home countries in the treaty-port press also kept expatriates abreast of the developments at home and thus reinforced their connections and loyalty to their country of origin. Apart from serving treaty-port papers, many prestigious journalists also worked as correspondents for other international newspapers. J. B. Powell, for example, was both chief editor of the Shanghai-based *China Weekly Review* and a correspondent for the *Chicago Tribune* during the 1920s. While serving the *China Press*, Larry Lohrbas and J. Butts covered Chinese issues for the *Manila Bulletin* and the *Chicago Daily News*.[8] Diplomats also tended to regard the treaty-port papers as a reliable source of

---

5. King and Clarke, *Research Guide to China-Coast Newspapers*, 17.
6. Nicholas Rowland Clifford, *Spoilt Children of Empire: Westerners in Shanghai and the Chinese Revolution of the 1920s* (Hanover: Middlebury College Press, 1991), 17; Wesley R. Fishel, *The End of Extraterritoriality in China* (Berkeley: University of California Press, 1952), 5–6.
7. Robert Bickers, *Britain in China: Community Culture and Colonialism, 1900–1949* (Manchester: Manchester University Press, 1999), 22–59.
8. "Principal newspaper correspondents in Shanghai who send news abroad to supplement what is given out by the regular agencies," no. I-O-9121, Shanghai Municipal Files.

information, quoting them frequently in their discussion of China-related issues and consulting distinguished treaty-port journalists for information and advice concerning their investigation of local conflicts. The treaty-port papers' strong influence of public opinion in their home countries as well as the correspondents' close ties with diplomats made them an important channel for China to have its voice heard abroad.

The close connection between expatriates and the metropolitan centers has all too easily created two myths: first, that opinions of foreign papers in China represented the interests of their home empires, with their allegiance tightly attached to their metropolis.[9] Second, that treaty-port newspapers were operated by foreign residents as one entity, pursuing similar goals to deepen imperial expansion in China. After years of working and living in treaty ports, foreign residents tended to develop an independent view about international affairs based on their local interests. Such a view often became pronounced in the papers they published. Meanwhile, the treaty ports were collectively administered by various Powers, each having its own vision about the region and which interests to pursue. The coexistence of diverse foreign communities caused tensions and sometimes helped forge strategic alliances between communities. Indeed, the treaty-port press could also create barriers imbued with hostilities that deterred the flow of information. Yet it was exactly these conflicts and ambiguities that provided opportunities for Chinese editors and politicians to penetrate into this medium in which they had little presence.

Before examining the Guomindang government's involvement with the English-language press during the Sino-Japanese conflicts in the 1930s, it is necessary to conduct a brief review of the key English newspapers in China during the 1920s and explore how China and Japan sought to extend their influence through this medium. By introducing three important English-language periodicals controlled by British and American interests and the rivalry between Japan and China in extending influence in the treaty-port English-language press, this chapter will reveal a contentious and transnational media environment in China's treaty ports.

The *North China Daily News*

The *North China Daily News* was the most important English-language paper in China during late nineteenth and the first half of the twentieth century. It was founded in Shanghai in 1864 by the amalgamation of two enterprises: the weekly *North China Herald* (established in 1850) and the *Daily Shipping and Commercial News* (established in 1860). The paper boasted a daily circulation of 8,000 in the early 1930s, an impressive figure if one considers that the *Central Daily News* (*Zhongyang*

---

9. Wang Boheng, "Zhongguo zhi xizibao" [Western newspapers in China], in *Minguo congshu* [A series of books on Republican China], vol. 2, no. 48, ed. Huang Tianpeng (Shanghai: Shanghai shudian, 1930), 139.

ribao), the official organ of the Guomindang government published in Chinese in the capital city Nanjing, sold no more than 10,000 copies.[10] Its circulation continued to grow throughout the 1930s. In 1935, the paper sold around 10,000 copies per day.[11] Up to 1937, the daily circulation rose to more than 10,400 copies, accounting for 35 percent of the circulation of the English-language dailies in Shanghai and more than 16 percent of the total for all of China.[12] As Zhao Minheng, a contemporary journalist, observed, the education standard of the average reader of the paper was "higher than that of any other popular daily newspapers either in China or abroad."[13]

Another contemporary journalist, Wang Boheng, who was conversant with the English-language press because of his own employment with the *Peking Daily News*, commented:

> The *North China Daily News* is as prestigious as the *Shen bao* and *Xinwen bao* [two of the most popular Chinese newspapers]. . . . It is capable of shaping the public opinion of foreign communities in Shanghai. Whenever an important event occurs, the *Daily News* would be highly relied upon as a source of information, frequently quoted even by Chinese newspapers.[14]

"Impartial not neutral" was the *Daily News*' editorial policy set by the *Herald*'s chief editor Samuel Mossman in 1861. However, the paper was not as "impartial" as advertised, in the eyes of the Chinese and American readers. They perceived the paper as an organ of the Shanghai Municipal Council, the British-led administrative body of the International Settlement of Shanghai, and thus an instrument to promote British imperial interests and reflect British metropolitan opinions. Their perception was true. The municipal council was the open patron of the *Daily News*, frequently providing the paper with subsidies and exclusive news.[15] When an accident occurred in the International Settlement, the municipal council often gave the *North China Daily News* the opportunity by to inspect the scene first while keeping journalists of other papers outside.[16]

The sophisticated news network of the *Daily News* was another reason for its stranglehold on the press market. It had contracts with nearly all important news agencies

---

10. Thomas Ming-heng Chao (Zhao Minheng), *The Foreign Press in China* (Shanghai: Institute of Pacific Relations, 1931), 76.
11. Rudolf Loewenthal, "The Present Status of the Press in China," *A Reprint from the Collectanea Commissionis Synodalis* 8, no. 11 (November 1935): 934.
12. See a pamphlet edited under the auspices of the Department of Journalism, Yenching University, Ch'en Tzu-Hsiang, *The English-Language Daily Press in China* (Beijing: Collectanea Commissionis Synodal, 1937).
13. Chao, *Foreign Press in China*, 53.
14. Wang Boheng, "Zhongguo zhi xizibao," 140.
15. Hu Daojing, "Shanghai de ribao" [Shanghai dailies], in *Shanghai xinwen shiye shiliao jiyao* [Selection of materials on history of journalism in Shanghai] (Taipei: Tianyi chubanshe, 1977), 293.
16. "The Departure of Editor Green of the N. C. D. N.," *China Weekly Review*, July 5, 1930, 168.

Figure 1
The North China Daily News Building, 1925. From Virtual Shanghai Project (Institut d'Asie Orientale).

around the world, including Reuters of Britain, the Associated Press of America, Havas of France, Wolff of Germany, and Stefani of Italy.[17]

Such a wide range of news sources surpassed that of any other papers in China. In spite of their international scale, these news agencies lacked coverage on Chinese affairs, and no Chinese news agency at the time was able to provide a credible service to fill the information gap. As a result, these news agencies looked to the *Daily News* to supply reports on Chinese issues. The *Daily News* created its news network in China by mobilizing the British missionaries for news collection. The missionaries reported local events regularly to the paper's headquarters in Shanghai on a voluntary basis, their recompense being a free copy of the *Daily News*. A vast social network of missionaries, which reached the most interior parts of China, including Gansu, Xinjiang, and Yunnan, became a unique news network for the paper and enabled it to become the key provider of Chinese information in the news market.[18]

17. Chao, *Foreign Press in China*, 53; Hu Daojing, "Shanghai de ribao," 293–94.
18. Hu Daojing, "Shanghai de ribao," 293.

As a prominent British treaty-port paper and an "official organ of the Municipal Council," the paper kept strong connections with the *Times* in London. The *Times* constantly endorsed the *North China Daily News* by purchasing its news and subsidizing correspondence.[19] Despite the support, the *Daily News* did not follow the *Times*' editorial line uncritically. The stance of the *Times* in international affairs was influenced by the British Foreign Office, which reflected Britain's national interests rather than merely those of the treaty ports. It actively sought a compromise with China in the 1920s when China's anti-British sentiments were running high. Representing the interests of treaty-port-based British citizens, who bore the brunt of Chinese nationalist movements, the *Daily News* was neither willing to bow to China's popular protests nor to concede Britain's extraterritorial rights. Such an attitude, notoriously known as "diehardism," characterized the paper when Rodney Gilbert and Owen Mortimer Green (O. M. Green) were in charge during the 1910s and the 1920s.

The independent attitude of the *Daily News* was nevertheless commonly shared among the treaty-port communities. In an article published in the *Manchester Guardian* in May 1927, Arthur Ransome cogently termed it "the Shanghai mind":

> The Shanghailanders hold that their loyalty begins at home and their primary allegiance is to Shanghai. They proclaim that property is in danger when they need British troops to defend them, but have shown . . . that the acceptance of this assistance does not in any way prevent them from doing what they can do to make impossible the realization of a British policy which they do not like.[20]

Despite the different stances between the metropolitan British government and the treaty-port papers—the center and the periphery of the British Empire—it was still too easy for the ordinary treaty-port audience to mistake the opinion of the *Daily News* for that of the British government.[21] This misunderstanding often gave rise to confusion over British policies and thus created barriers for amity between China and Britain.

Meanwhile, the *Times* was not blind to the recalcitrant stance held by the treaty-port papers. Although the *Times* relied on the latter for information about Chinese affairs, it was ready to block items inconsistent with its own position. This filtering of information drew strong protests from Rodney Gilbert. He blamed the *Times* for "stubbornly persist[ing] in misrepresenting conditions [in China]" in the hope of pleasing the "timid and weak diplomats."[22] Officials of the British Foreign Office also sought opportunities to change the treaty-port papers' die-hard attitude and to

---

19. Haward to Lints Smith, February 24, 1932, MLMSS 7594/3, Winston George Lewis Papers (hereafter WGLP), concerning W. H. Donald, together with papers of the Donald family. Library of New South Wales, Sydney.
20. Arthur Ransome, "The Shanghai Mind: An Obstacle to British Policy," *Manchester Guardian*, May 2, 1927.
21. Richard W. Rigby, "Sapajou," *East Asian History*, nos. 17/18 (June/December 1999): 135.
22. Gilbert Rodney to J. O. P. Bland, August 22, 1926, MLMSS 7594/5, WGLP.

ameliorate Britain's imperialistic image in China that had been created by the paper. O. M. Green was frequently asked to soften his editorial line. After the Guomindang government withdrew postal services from the paper in 1929, Green was advised by the consul general to tone things down.[23] Vexed by Green's editorial style, Miles Lampson, the British minister to China from 1926 to 1933, used all of his influence to replace Green in 1930.[24] As a result, Green resigned at the end of July 1930. Edwin Howard, who was appointed as his successor, adopted a more sympathetic attitude toward the Guomindang government. The change in the editorship did not, however, completely relieve the tension between the metropolitan paper and the treaty-port press. Howard continued to complain about the *Times*' distortion of reports supplied by the *Daily News*. He believed that the *Times* owed his paper a "deep debt of gratitude" for its coverage of the Chinese issues and urged the paper to raise payment for the service of the *North China Daily News*.[25]

The *China Press*

The *China Press* was one of the most distinguished English-language dailies in Shanghai from the 1910s to the 1940s. The paper was cofounded by Thomas F. Millard, a prominent American journalist, and the British-trained Chinese diplomat Wu Tingfang in 1911.[26] Registered in Delaware, United States, the China Press Company was a Sino-American enterprise, with Wu Tingfang as its trustee.[27] Investors in the paper included Charles R. Crane, the Chicago manufacturer who became US minister to China in 1920–1921; Benjamin Fleischer, the owner of the Yokohama-based *Japan Advertiser*; Tang Shaoyi, a (US) Columbia University–trained diplomat who became Republican China's first prime minister in 1912; and two of the largest American concerns in China, namely the Standard Oil Company and the British-American Tobacco Company.[28]

Despite its semi-Chinese ownership, the paper was fully staffed by Americans in its early years. Millard secured a strong managing and editing team for the paper: Fleischer, who had successfully saved the *Japan Advertiser* from financial loss and guided it into profit in two years, became the paper's business manager; C. Herbert Webb, former editor of the *Chicago Examiner*, served as the paper's assistant editor;

---

23. Bickers, *Britain in China*, 151.
24. Ibid.
25. Edwin Howard to Lints Smith, February 24, 1932, MLMSS 7594/3, WGLP.
26. Millard came to China originally as a correspondent for the *New York Herald* to cover the Boxer Rebellion in 1900. Before *Millard's Review*, Millard had founded the first Sino-American joint newspaper in China, the *China Press*, in Shanghai.
27. Bryna Goodman, "Networks of News: Power, Language and Transnational Dimensions of the Chinese Press, 1850–1949," *China Review* 4, no. 1 (2004): 1–2.
28. Mordechai Rozanski, "The Role of American Journalists in Chinese-American Relations, 1900–1925" (PhD dissertation, University of Pennsylvania, 1974), 91.

Figure 2
The China Press Building, 1911–1929. From Virtual Shanghai Project (Institut d'Asie Orientale).

and Carl Crow, Millard's fellow alumnus of the University of Missouri, was appointed as the chief writer.

Together, they determined to create a channel to present America's interests and point of view in East Asia while transmitting a Chinese voice abroad.[29] The establishment of the paper was also motivated by their desire to break what they saw as an Anglo-Japanese monopoly of news in China:

> China and the Chinese at present have no adequate means through the columns of the daily press, of promptly and continuously presenting their point of view, and of refuting misrepresentations designed to injure China, and which impair her national prestige and credit. It is said "China has no voice." The *China Press* is designed to correct this condition.[30]

Millard's team initially held an ambitious vision for its press business in China. Under the same general management, it planned to establish three daily newspapers, in Beijing, Tokyo, and Shanghai, respectively; two weekly papers (one in English and

---

29. Thomas F. Millard, "*China Press* Reverts to Original Design," *China Press*, August 29, 1931, k3.
30. Millard's prospectus, February 25, 1911, quoted in Rozanski, "Role of American Journalists in Chinese-American Relations," 95.

one in Chinese); two monthly magazines (one in English and one in Chinese); and an annual yearbook. The only enterprise that succeeded, however, was the *China Press*.³¹

The *China Press* created a sensation in the Shanghai newspaper market after the release of its first issue. The paper not only challenged the traditional British format but also took a unique journalistic style. "Our worst crime," in Carl Crow's words, was to carry news on the front page instead of following the traditional British style to "conceal it in the back of the paper among shipping or auction advertisement." For a community accustomed to the traditional British layout, the design was initially considered as done in "bad taste." Another major innovation was to give prominent position to Chinese news instead of news of the United States and Europe.³² This again challenged the convention of the foreign community, who took primary interest in developments in their home countries and cared little about Chinese affairs beyond treaty ports. Some readers, for example, were "shocked" to see that the paper reported on Hankou floods in great detail. Stories about the drowning of thousands of Chinese and the destruction of millions of dollars' worth of crops were particularly criticized as the paper's evidence of "poor journalism."³³ Yet editors of the paper insisted in printing Chinese stories on a national scale, which eventually became an example followed by others.

Both Japanese and British interest groups watched the establishment of an American paper with suspicion. While the idea of starting the *Press* was being formulated, the Japanese minister and his staff questioned American minister Calhoun about the paper and expressed their concern about its purpose. On June 22, 1911, the Yokohama Specie Bank in Shanghai bought the *Shanghai Times* "for Japanese interests" from J. C. Ferguson,³⁴ which was considered by the American legation in Beijing as Japan's answer to the founding of the *Press*.³⁵ The British-owned paper, the *North China Daily News*, also saw the *China Press* as an unwelcome rival and sought to thwart its publication. The *Daily News* not only undermined the establishment of the *Press* by dissuading its potential Chinese shareholders from investing in the paper,³⁶ but it also urged British advertisers and subscribers to boycott the paper in the ensuing years.³⁷ In the early 1910s, American investments in Shanghai were small, and about 80 percent of the press advertising in Shanghai was controlled by

---

31. Rozanski, "Role of American Journalists in Chinese-American Relations," 94.
32. Carl Crow, "Former China Press Men Recall Paper's Early Struggles, Triumphs," *China Press*, August 29, 1931, k3.
33. "Twenty-Five Years of the China Press," *China Press*, October 10, 1936, c75.
34. Ibid.; for detailed information about the establishment of the *Shanghai Times*, see Rozanski, "Role of American Journalists in Chinese-American Relations," 110.
35. Rozanski, "Role of American Journalists in Chinese-American Relations," 94.
36. John B. Powell, *My Twenty-Five Years in China* (New York: Macmillan, 1945), 10.
37. "The Departure of Editor Green of the *North China Daily News*," *China Weekly Review*, July 5, 1930, 168; John Maxwell Hamilton, "The Missouri News Monopoly and American Altruism in China: Thomas F. F. Millard, J. B. Powell, and Edgar Snow," *Pacific Historical Review* 55, no. 1 (February 1986): 34.

British firms or agencies.³⁸ The boycott caused serious financial troubles for the paper. To maintain operation of the *Press*, Millard had to go back to the United States to raise funds.³⁹ His refusal to take the British side in World War I further drained the popularity of the *Press* among British advertisers.⁴⁰ These financial difficulties finally forced Millard to relinquish his editorship in 1917.

In 1918, the *China Press* was sold to Edward I. Ezra, a British opium merchant. Ezra bought the paper in an attempt to build up a newspaper chain, together with his previous acquisition, the *Shanghai Evening Star*. After his death in 1921, Sun Yat-sen controlled the paper for less than a year before Ezra's heirs reclaimed the paper and operated it until 1929.⁴¹ In December 1930, a Chinese syndicate led by Zhang Zhuping acquired the paper. The constant change of ownership revealed a fierce competition among various interest groups to expand their influence in the treaty-port English-language press. Yet the Chinese-operated paper did achieve a commercial success. In the mid-1930s, the *Press* sold around 5,000 copies on weekdays and 8,000 copies on Sundays. This amounted to 8 percent of the total domestic circulation of the English-language dailies in China or more than 16 percent locally.⁴²

The *China Weekly Review*

Before the 1930s, the American newspaper enterprises in China were unable to compete with their British counterparts. In the shadow of Reuters and the *North China Daily News*, American publishers found it hard to maintain a competitive daily in Shanghai. The first profitable US daily, the *Shanghai Evening Post and Mercury*, came only after 1930. Falling behind in daily news reporting, nevertheless, American editors focused on the publication of magazines. The *China Weekly Review* was one of the most important weeklies in the treaty ports. The journal had a strong connection with the "Missouri mafia"—graduates of the University of Missouri who were actively engaged in journalistic work in China between the 1910s and the 1940s. It became a platform for this group to wield influence on the development of China's modern journalism.

The *China Weekly Review* (originally named *Millard's Review of the Far East*) was established in 1917 by Thomas F. Millard with the assistance of John B. Powell, an alumnus of the University of Missouri. Referring to Herbert Croly and Walter Lippman's the *New Republic* and Oswald Garrison Villard's the *Nation* as

---

38. Millard to Lansing, October 12, 1915, quoted in Rozanski, "Role of American Journalists in Chinese-American Relations," 267.
39. Ibid.
40. Hamilton, "Missouri News Monopoly and American Altruism in China," 34; Powell, *My Twenty-Five Years in China*, 10.
41. Ch'en, *English-Language Daily Press in China*, 11.
42. Ibid.,12.

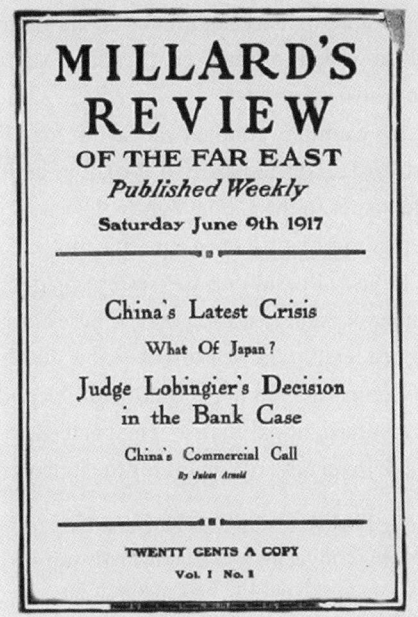
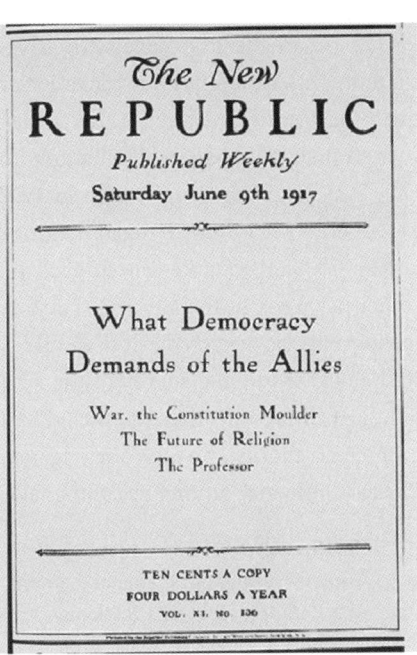

Figure 3
Covers and front pages of the *Millard's Review of the Far East* and *New Republic*.

models for their publication, Millard and Powell not only followed those journals' liberal editorial style but also precisely copied the layout of the *New Republic*. The *Review* began the first page with editorial comments and highlights of the main content. This straightforward manner greatly appealed to treaty-port readers. Many treaty-port editors influenced by American journalism later introduced the same style to their own papers. Hollington Tong, for example, adopted the layout for his *Yong bao*, established in Tianjin in 1925. Millard sold the paper to Powell in early 1919, and Powell soon changed the title of the paper to the *China Weekly Review*.

The *China Weekly Review* enjoyed an average circulation of four to five thousand copies per week in the late 1920s and early 1930s.[43] In addition to Western readers, the journal also attracted a considerable number of readers among the Chinese bilingual elites. Through a survey of the *Review*'s readership, Powell discovered a sizable bilingual Chinese readership, including intellectuals and students of missionary and municipal schools who took a strong interest in international affairs.[44] He specified the *Review*'s influence among the bilingual Chinese in an advertisement for the journal:

> Its [the *Review*'s] circulation is chiefly among English-reading Chinese and foreigners throughout China and among Chinese residing overseas, particularly in the Philippines, Straits Settlements, etc. [It is] considered the best medium for reaching Chinese officials, professional and businessmen interested in foreign trade or Sino-foreign relations.[45]

Clearly, he considered the bilingual readership a great attraction to win more subsidies and contracts from international companies.

Unlike the *North China Daily News*, the *Review* was enthusiastic about China's Nationalist movement. Both Millard and Powell were staunch supporters of Sun Yat-sen. They advocated a "hands-off" policy by foreign powers toward Chinese affairs. Powell commented:

> In regard to policy, the *Review* has consistently supported the program of an independent China that would be able to look after her own affairs and not become a colonial appendage of other European or Asiatic nation. . . . It has supported the Open-Door Policy, Chinese autonomy in respect to tariff, as well as the abolition of extraterritoriality; in reference to China, it has continuously advocated a policy of political, economic and industrial reconstruction that would place the nation on an equal footing with other nations of the world. Only in this way will the so-called Far Eastern questions be solved, because a weak China constantly excites the covetous ambitions of other nations, while a strong China will have a stabilizing effect on world affairs.[46]

---

43. Chao, *Foreign Press in China*, 76; Carl Crow, *Newspaper Directory of China* (Shanghai: Carl Crow, 1935), 118.
44. Powell, *My Twenty-Five Years in China*, 12–13.
45. An advertisement of the *China Weekly Review* collected by Carl Crow, in *Newspaper Directory of China*, 143.
46. Quote of Powell's statement of the *Review*'s editorial policy in Chao, *Foreign Press in China*, 76.

It was hard to determine whether the journal advocated China's independence because of its editors' sympathy for the nation or because of their desire to promote US national interests—an integrated China was conducive to the implementation of the Open Door doctrine. The stance, nevertheless, appealed to many Chinese bilingual intellectuals, especially American-returned scholars and professionals, such as Hu Shi and Hollington K. Tong. These Chinese intellectuals regularly contributed articles to the journal, and many became important sources of information for the *Review*.[47] Editorials of the journal also flowed into Chinese native–language papers through translation. Based on his extended experience in journalism, Carl Crow confirmed that "practically everything" that appeared in *Millard's Review* was translated and "widely published" in the Chinese press.[48] Indeed, the actual influence of this journal went far beyond what its circulation figures suggested.

Despite the *Review*'s sympathy with the Nationalist cause, it was not a propaganda organ of the Nationalist Party. The *Review* was an independent journal, known for its progressive, leftist position upheld by its chief editor, John B. Powell. Its criticism of the Guomindang government's weak military capacity and the nonresistance policy was bitter during the Mukden Incident (Chapter 4). The journal's relationship with the US government also varied on different occasions. Toward the end of World War I, the US government established a branch of the Committee on Public Information in Shanghai to advocate Wilson's idea of self-determination for weak nations to a Chinese audience. The *Review*, whose office was in the same building and on the same floor as the committee, served as its information channel.[49] During the 1920s, Powell himself was frequently approached by the US Department of State for exclusive information or assessment of Chinese attitudes about foreign affairs, such as extraterritorial issues.[50] However, the journal did not always share the same line with the US government. In 1935, for example, the *Review*'s protest against Japan's aggression in China ran contrary to the US government's isolationist policy. Facing the Japanese consul general's complaint about the *Review*'s anti-Japanese tone, Edwin Cunningham, the US consul general in Shanghai, had to emphasize the difference between the US official view and the *Review*'s position.[51]

The *Review*'s relationship with the British press in Shanghai was also complex. The US periodicals shared many common features with British papers. Apart from publishing in the same language, newspapers and journals of the two nations also shared

---

47. Neil L. O'Brien, *An American Editor in Early Revolutionary China, John William Powell and the "China Weekly/Monthly Review"* (New York: Routledge, 2003), 19.
48. Quoted from Bryna Goodman, "Semi-colonialism, Transnational Networks and New Flows in Early Republican Shanghai," *China Review* 4, no. 1 (Spring 2004): 64.
49. Hans Schmidt, "Democracy for China: American Propaganda and the May Fourth Movement," *Diplomatic History* 22, no. 1 (January 1998): 4–5.
50. US Department of State, Papers Relating to the Foreign Relations of the United States, 1929, vol. 2, 642.
51. Ibid., 2:375.

correspondents and contributors. George E. Sokolsky, who frequently wrote for the *North China Daily News*, for example, published regularly in the *Review*. In 1919 the *Review* allied with the British-owned *North China Daily News* and *Peking and Tientsin Times* to expose Japanese smuggling of morphine in China. Their joint reports stirred a huge anti-Japanese sentiment among the Chinese public in early 1919.[52] However, the coalition was temporary. It dissolved in the late 1920s when the papers' different approaches toward Japan emerged. In 1928, while the American papers still carried an anti-Japanese tone, their British counterparts came to believe that Japan's resistance to the abolition of extraterritorial rights corresponded to Britain's similar pursuit, and Japan's actions in Manchuria helped to bolster the general imperial interests in China. The political differences between the US and British papers degenerated into an open dispute in 1929 when the *North China Daily News* was banned from using the postal service by the Guomindang government.

The rivalry between British and American papers had long caused tension in the treaty ports. With the burgeoning American community in China, the American expatriates were no longer satisfied to be represented by British papers. They were eager to break the Britons' domination of the press and nurture their own sense of community. Unlike the British papers, which championed imperialist rule in China, American editors saw the US interest primarily as "cultural and moral." They tended to expand American's democratic model in China and supported the country's national independence. Apart from Americans' mission-like passion to make their values accepted worldwide, the altruistic rhetoric served America's economic interests: while British trade in China was based on special rights and the sphere of influence it secured, American interests would be best protected by keeping the Chinese market open.[53] This rhetoric simply sugarcoated the otherwise exploitative imperialist intention, making America's imperial expansion much more hidden and thus acceptable to the Chinese. Many Chinese treaty-port elites supported the American-operated periodicals through regular contributions and registration. Yet British editors chastised America's rhetoric as hypocritical and irresponsible. H. G. W. Woodhead, editor of the British-owned *Peking and Tientsin Times*, openly denounced the American community as a "semi-parasite" who took advantage of the treaty rights garnered by other Powers:

> Americans—business and professional men, missionaries, etc.—owe the fact that they have been able to reside and pursue their lawful avocations in China entirely to the so-called "unequal Treaties." But, unlike Great Britain and France, they did not secure these Treaties by force, but by semi-parasitism.... American envoys

---

52. *Millard's Review of the Far East*, January 4, 154–55; *Millard's Review of the Far East*, January 18, 1919, 195; *Millard's Review of the Far East*, January 18, 229.
53. Yong Z. Volz and Chin-Chuan Lee, "Semi-colonialism and Journalistic Sphere of Influence: British-American Press Competition in Early Twentieth-Century China," *Journalism Studies* 12, no. 5 (2011): 563–65.

followed in the wake of the victorious armies and fleets of other Powers, and without sharing in the risks and hazards of war secured from the Chinese the same (or similar) privileges as those which had been won by other Governments.[54]

He believed that Americans, who genuinely perceived that China's nationalist movements were free from Bolshevik influence, had misunderstood the situation in China.[55]

Japan's English-Language News Network in China

Japan and China both began to construct their news networks in China in the 1910s. Yet by 1928, Japan's international news agencies were much more advanced than those of China. Japan's news service in China began with the Tōhō news agency, established in 1914 in Shanghai. It signaled Japan's strong objective to build its own news empire. While Reuters had branch offices only in Beijing, Shanghai, and Tianjin, by 1919 Tōhō had expanded its service to Hangzhou, Nanjing, Mukden, Jinan, and Canton.[56] Apart from conducting news propaganda, the agency was also responsible for collecting intelligence.[57] In 1920 the ministry moved Tōhō's headquarters from Shanghai to Tokyo and turned it into a state apparatus supervised by the Ministry of Foreign Affairs of Japan. The support from the ministry rose from initial amount of ¥19,000 per year to ¥500,000 in 1920.[58]

The reorganized Tōhō agency achieved quick success after arriving in China's news market. To break Reuters' monopoly, Tōhō sold its news in China at aggressive discounts. It offered news services to foreign newspapers at the very low rate of 10 Mexican dollars per month—the currency used in the treaty ports—which stood in stark contrast to the Mex$200–500 charged by Reuters.[59] While Reuters charged Chinese newspapers Mex$25 per month, Tōhō asked only Mex$10 from Chinese newspapers and supplied news to Japanese papers for free.[60] Reuters' Far East manager, W. Turner, was aware of the huge subsidy provided by the Japanese government to Tōhō and feared that Japan's low-price service would squeeze Reuters out of

---

54. H. G. W. (Henry George Wandesforde) Woodhead and *Shanghai Evening Post and Mercury, Adventures in Far Eastern Journalism: A Record of Thirty-Three Years' Experience* (Tokyo: Hokuseido Press, 1935), 204–5.
55. Ibid., 204.
56. FO371/6668/100, Foreign Office Files for China, 1919–1980 (hereafter FOFC).
57. Tomoko Akami, *Japan's News Propaganda and Reuters' News Empire in Northeast Asia, 1870–1934* (Dordrecht: Republic of Letters, 2012), 95.
58. Tsūshinshashi kankōkai, ed., *Tsūshinshashi* [A history of news agency] (Tokyo: Editor, 1958), 158; Akami, *Japan's News Propaganda and Reuters' News Empire in Northeast Asia*, 96.
59. According to Andrew James Nathan's estimation of the exchange rate in the 1920s in Shanghai, Mex$1 was equivalent to approximately US$0.78. See Andrew James Nathan, *Peking Politics, 1918–1923: Factionalism and the Failure of Constitutionalism* (Berkeley: University of California Press, 1976), xiii.
60. FO371/6668 [F3934/3934/10], a confidential letter dated July 18, 1921 to Acting Secretary of Chinese Affairs by a reliable press representative from Tokyo, FOFC.

the Chinese market.⁶¹ His concern was fully justified. The generous subsidies from Japan's Ministry of Foreign Affairs, estimated to range from ¥450,000 to ¥500,000 per year, with an optional extra of ¥100,000 for telegram fees, greatly empowered the agency to challenge Reuters' stranglehold on China.⁶² By 1928, Tōhō had won contracts with most of the newspapers in China, English language and Chinese language alike. Its news reports were even utilized by metropolitan papers and were frequently quoted in key metropolitan papers, such as the *Times* and the *New York Times*. Tōhō continued its operations in China until 1929 when Rengō news agency, revised its agreement with Reuters and took over Tōhō's business in China.⁶³

Japan also controlled several English-language papers in China, the first being the *Manchuria Daily News*, established in Dalian in 1908 by the South Manchuria Railway Company.⁶⁴ The initial purpose of the paper was to propagate the Japanese cause in Manchuria to the outside world. In its early years, the *Daily News* was a news carrier rather than a political forum. Local news about Japanese construction activities in Manchuria dominated its pages. Elaborate political editorials were rare. As Sino-Japanese relations intensified in the late 1920s, the paper was gradually transformed into a staunch supporter of the Japanese occupation of Manchuria and was commonly perceived by both Chinese and Westerners as an organ of Japanese propaganda, despite its claim to be an "independent daily."⁶⁵

Another important English-language newspaper run by the Japanese was the *North China Standard* based in Beijing. The paper was founded in 1919 by Japan's Ministry of Foreign Affairs with an annual financial support of Mex$60,000.⁶⁶ In addition to explaining Japanese views and activities in China, the paper also had the goal of competing with a Chinese-operated English-language daily, the *Peking Leader*, to offset the anti-Japanese influence that the *Leader* exerted on foreign and Chinese readers. The *Standard* tried hard to squeeze the *Leader* out of the Chinese market. As a contemporary journalist wrote, the two fought "like cats and dogs."⁶⁷ Although the *Leader* passed into American control in 1925, the change of ownership

---

61. FO 371/8028 [F647/647/10], W. Turner memorandum and private letter to "Ross" RN, December 5, 1921, quoted in Peter O'Connor, "Endgame: the English-Language Press Networks of East Asia in the Run-up to War, 1936–41," *Japan Forum* 13, no. 1 (2001): 69.
62. Akami, *Japan's News Propaganda and Reuters' News Empire in Northeast Asia*, 136. The value of the yen against British pound was approximately ¥10.1 to £1 in 1920. See Takatoshi Ito, *Japanese Economy* (Cambridge, MA: MIT Press, 1992), 21–22.
63. Akami, *Japan's News Propaganda and Reuters' News Empire in Northeast Asia*, 139.
64. See Feng's discussion on the establishment of the *Manchurian Daily News*, Feng Yue, "Zaoqi Riben zai Hua baoyeshi chutan" [Discussion on Japan's newspaper in China in the early period], *Riben yanjiu* [Japanese studies] 4 (2006): 72–73.
65. Ibid.
66. O'Connor, "Endgame," 69.
67. Chao, *Foreign Press in China*, 28.

did not shift its editorial direction, and the *Standard* continued to see the *Leader* as its primary rival. Although the *Standard* was not welcomed by the American press in the north, its anti-Guomindang stance achieved immense popularity in the Beijing Legation Quarter and among die-hard foreign merchants in Shanghai. Its ties with the most powerful warlord faction, the Fengtian Clique, also allowed it to be directly involved in China's political struggles.[68]

In addition to establishing English-language papers in North China, Japan also tried to control newspapers operated by British and Americans in Shanghai. The *Far Eastern Review: Engineering, Finance, Commerce* was one of the examples. This monthly journal was originally founded in Manila in 1904 by an American national, George Bronson Rea, and moved to Shanghai in 1912. The journal maintained offices in New York, London, Paris, Berlin, and Tokyo. Its large network enabled the journal to reach audiences worldwide. Apart from providing engineering and financial information, the journal carried long editorials on political issues in East Asia. Its wide scope attracted readers in various fields. By the late 1920s, the *Far Eastern Review* had an estimated monthly circulation of six thousand copies, making it a highly competitive player in the English-language press market in Shanghai.[69]

Rea was initially sympathetic to China's desire for autonomy and opposed Japan's growing power in the Pacific. He endorsed the Open Door policy in China and saw Japan as a potential enemy of the United States. In his pamphlet *Japan's Place in the Sun*, he warned that Japan was secretly and heavily arming itself for a possible war with the United States.[70] The *Far Eastern Review* was the prime platform for the dissemination of his political ideas. While the Chinese government did not yet have its own English-language paper to present its case, the *Far Eastern Review* had in effect become one of its most effective propaganda channels. Apart from editing the journal in the 1910s, Rea was also involved in Chinese politics. An expert on railways, he was technical secretary to the Ministry of Communications of the Beijing government, working for several senior Guomindang officials, including Sun Yat-sen and Sun Ke (also known as Sun Fo). He later became technical secretary to China's Industrial Commission under Minister Ye Gongchuo (known as Yeh Kung-cho) at the Paris Conference.[71] With a pro-Chinese journal and active engagement in Chinese politics, Rea appeared to be a firm advocate of China's interests.

However, in 1920 Rea suddenly shifted sides, becoming a supporter of Japanese interests. He changed the editorial policy of the *Far Eastern Review* and published

---

68. Feng Yue, "Jindai Jingjin diqu yingwenbao de yulun yu waijiao pingxi" [Review of the opinions and diplomatic functions of the English-language newspapers in Beijing and Tianjin in modern times], *Beijing hangkong hangtian daxue xuebao* 23, no. 3 (2010): 93.
69. Chao, *Foreign Press in China*, 78.
70. George Bronson Rea, *Japan's Place in the Sun* (Shanghai: Far Eastern Review, 1915).
71. Noel H. Pugach, *Paul S. Reinsch: Open Door Diplomat in Action* (Millwood: KTO Press, 1979), 113.

several books and pamphlets justifying Japanese interests in China.[72] Rea's reversal was so abrupt that even his associate, the coeditor of the *Far Eastern Review*, William. H. Donald was caught by surprise. Donald resigned from his editorship and openly declared his disapproval of Rea's new policy.[73] Rea's shift was investigated by the Office of Naval Intelligence of the United States and the American legation in Beijing. The cause of his change of heart remains something of an enigma. Some scholars argue that the shift was driven by his intention to temper the American-Japanese conflict and thus protect American interests in China—realizing that the aggressive rhetoric of the Open Door policy would lead to an actual war with Japan. They believe that Rea decided to withdraw rhetorical support for the territorial and administrative integrity of China and to promote cooperation with Japan, which could preserve order in East Asia.[74] This view overemphasizes Rea's commitment to US national interests while neglecting the economic benefits behind his choices. Although Rea explained that he "had become tired of fighting China's battles when their own statesmen were selling their country to Japan,"[75] the American investigators believed that the problem lay elsewhere, namely that Chinese officials had failed to pay the bill presented to them by Rea for his pro-Chinese publicity in the *Far Eastern Review* at the time of the Paris Peace Conference.[76] John B. Powell, editor of the *China Weekly Review*, confirmed in his letter to the US military attaché that Rea had complained about being "unfairly treated" by Chinese leaders "in view of the great amount of service he had done for them."[77] When Rea was on the verge of breaking ties with the Chinese government, Japan promptly invested in the magazine and transformed it into one of its key propaganda organs in Shanghai.[78] It was estimated that the Japanese government paid US$100,000 a year to the journal.[79] Indeed, obtaining Rea's support was a significant coup for Japan: it both strengthened its own foreign propaganda network and weakened that of China.

Another important paper that fell into Japanese hands was the *Shanghai Times*. The paper was officially registered as a British daily and operated by a British subject, E. A. Nottingham. Yet beneath the veneer of British ownership lay Japanese interests. The police office in the French Concession in Shanghai discovered that the paper not only received a grant from the Yokohama Specie Bank but also accepted

---

72. George Bronson Rea, *The Greatest Civilizing Force in Eastern Asia* (Shanghai, 1924); George Bronson Rea, *Japan's Right to Exist* (Shanghai, 1920).
73. Editorial notice by William. H. Donald, *Far Eastern Review*, March 1920, 153.
74. Frederick B. Hoyt, "George Bronson Rea: From Old China Hand to Apologist for Japan," *Pacific Northwest Quarterly* 69 (April 1978): 61–70.
75. "George Bronson Rea," MLMSS 7594/5, WGLP.
76. Ibid.; "George Bronson Rea: Character of and Activities in Far Eastern Affairs," February 16, 1920, MLMSS 7594/5, WGLP.
77. "John B. Powell to Military Attaché," June 1920, MLMSS 7594/5, WGLP.
78. "George Bronson Rea," MLMSS 7594/5, WGLP.
79. See Peter O'Connor's quotes from FO 371/445 [P1870/260/150] in O'Connor, "Endgame," 68.

subsidies from the Japanese government starting in 1924.⁸⁰ A Japanese source, however, dated Japanese government's control of the *Shanghai Times* back to 1915 and revealed that Tōhō had purchased the paper with the support of the Japanese consul general in Shanghai, Ariyoshi Akira.⁸¹ Although the *Shanghai Times* never openly acknowledged its ties to Japanese interests, its pro-Japanese editorial line raised suspicion among Western journalists in China. The American Carl Crow believed the paper was controlled by Japan although it was owned and edited by the British.⁸² John B. Powell also regarded Nottingham's editorship as nominal.⁸³ The Shanghai Municipal Police made an investigation of the paper in 1924 and confirmed that the presumed property of a British subject "appeared to be controlled by Japanese."⁸⁴

Japanese interest groups were also keen to obtain control of the *Shanghai Mercury*, a paper traditionally considered to be representing British views. A large number of *Mercury* shares had passed into Japanese hands in 1917. By 1921, the Japanese controlled more than half of the paper's shares, with another third held by an American, Carl Crow. Although the paper was registered as a British concern, the British held only one-sixth of the total share. The Japanese dominance of the paper created hostility among the British directors of the board. Tensions escalated to the point that Japanese representatives tried to squeeze the two unfriendly British directors, A. K. Craddock and J. D. Clark, out of the board. The move caught the attention of the British Foreign Office. By quoting a report from the *North China Daily News*, officials indicated their worry that the Japanese would make the paper a propaganda organ for Japanese interests by inserting paragraphs of strong Japanese support in the *Mercury*'s columns. "Here in Shanghai everybody whose views are of importance would understand such paragraphs and discount them; but abroad their effect might be, if not actually injurious at least very much the reverse of British ideas."⁸⁵

China's English-Language News Network

Compared with the Japanese news network in China, China's foreign propaganda network was underdeveloped. By 1928, China still had no efficient national or international news agency of its own. Most of China's domestic and international news was transmitted by foreign news agencies, particularly Reuters, which had begun operating in China in 1872. Reuters stationed special correspondents in practically all the principal telegraphic centers in China and controlled the channel of news

---

80. U38-2-715, Compte-rendu de renseignements no. 104/2, July 9, 1932, Concession Française de Shanghai, Services de Police, Shanghai Municipal Council Archives.
81. Akami, *Japan's News Propaganda and Reuters' News Empire in Northeast Asia*, 96.
82. Paul French, *Carl Crow: A Tough Old China Hand* (Hong Kong: Hong Kong University Press, 2006), 28.
83. Powell, *My Twenty-Five Years in China*, 359.
84. No. I.O.-9212, Shanghai Municipal Police Archives.
85. FO 371/6668 [F 3934/3934/10] Major R. B. Denny to Mr. Lampson, October 24, 1921, FOFC.

distribution.[86] Indeed, it had become the narrator of Chinese affairs whenever events took place. Not only did the press in other countries rely heavily on Reuters for Chinese news, native papers also looked to it for information on Chinese domestic affairs.[87] Yet Reuters' domination was not impregnable. In the late 1920s, its position faced a significant challenge from Japan's Tōhō, Havas of France, the Tass agency of Russia, and the United Press of the United States.[88] Amid the fierce competition among foreign news agencies, none of China's own news agencies was strong enough to compete. The privilege of interpreting Chinese issues was still held tightly in the hands of foreign agencies.

The lack of a strong Chinese-owned news agency did not go unrecognized. Since the beginning of the twentieth century, Chinese journalists had tried to organize news agencies in various forms.[89] Efforts came primarily from individuals who registered news agencies of their own and sold their services to their warlord patrons. Such private news agencies mushroomed during the late Qing and early Republican periods. It has been estimated that by 1926 the number of news agencies in China had reached 155.[90] However, despite the large number, the quality of their services was far from satisfactory. Since most agencies relied on local warlords for funding, their services were focused on promoting the interests of their patrons.[91] They ended up becoming a source of rumors rather than reliable information. The warlords' patronage also prevented these private agencies from expanding their business beyond their patrons' borders. The majority of these private agencies, therefore, remained local organizations.

Realizing that news agencies run by individual journalists were prone to factional manipulation, newspapers sought to form large-scale news agencies by grouping themselves into news cooperatives. In 1910, sixty-seven Chinese papers organized the National Press Development Committee (Quanguo baoye jujin hui) in Nanjing and devised a plan to build a national news agency. The plan was ambitious: they aimed to combine media sources in Beijing, Shanghai, Manchuria, Mongolia, and Xinjiang in the hope of establishing a nationwide news network. Once the national supply was in place, the network would seek to extend its service worldwide.[92] However, after the fall of the Qing dynasty, many of the small newspapers, vulnerable to political and social changes, ceased publication, and the plan for a national news agency was

---

86. Chao, *Foreign Press in China*, 48.
87. Zeng Xubai, *Zhongguo xinwen shi* [A history of China's journalism] (Taipei: Guoli zhengzhi daxue xinwen yanjiusuo, 1966): 571.
88. Graham Storey, *Reuters' Century, 1851–1951* (London: Parrish, 1951), 204–6.
89. The first Chinese-owned news agency, the Zhong Xing news agency, was established in 1904. See Zeng, *Zhongguo xinwen shi*, 571.
90. Ibid.
91. Ibid., 573.
92. Ibid., 571.

abandoned. After the Paris Peace Conference, Chinese concerns over the monopoly of news by foreign news agencies intensified. In May 1920, two leading newspapers in Guangzhou, the *72 Hang shang bao* and *Xinminguo bao*, rallied 120 newspapers and news agencies across the country and established the National Press Cooperating Committee (Quanguo baojie lianhe hui). Inspired by the model of the Associated Press, the committee intended to create a news agency by combining the sources of its member newspapers. The committee also envisaged expanding the national network abroad by sending correspondents to key European cities and securing contacts with Chinese students abroad.[93] Grand as their plan was, the committee's operation was constantly hindered by struggles among warlords. Unable to survive in the unstable political environment, the committee soon broke up.

Owners of big newspapers also sought to set up news agencies, making them a suborganization of the paper.[94] The relatively influential ones were the Guowen news agency established by Hu Zhengzhi, managing director and editor of *Dagong bao* in Tianjin, and the Shenshi News Agency initiated by two of the most prominent Chinese dailies in Shanghai, *Shen bao* and *Shishi xin bao*. Yet by 1928 these agencies offered services only in Chinese for vernacular papers. They had failed to forge direct links with the foreign press.

Aside from such private efforts, the Guomindang government in Guangzhou also made attempts to build a national news agency. It established the Central News Agency (Zhongyang tongxunshe) within the Ministry of Information in 1924, hoping to develop it into a national agency. Without a long-term plan or a streamlined structure, the agency remained a loose organization, unable to compete with the Guowen and Shenshi news agencies, let alone Tōhō and Reuters.[95] In 1927, immediately after Chiang Kai-shek established his regime in Nanjing, the government's Ministry of Foreign Affairs set up the Guomin (also known as Kuomin) news agency, with the goal of making the Chinese case to the outside world. It became the only Chinese news agency to offer an English-language service. Based in Shanghai, the agency boasted a strong management team led by Zhang Sixu (known as Samuel H. Chang) and Li Cai (also Lee Choy). Both had received university degrees in the West and possessed extensive experience in operating English-language papers in China. Despite this, the agency did not have sufficient funding to hire its own correspondents. It had to rely on translating and rewriting news from Chinese papers to maintain its news supply. Its close ties with the government, which ensured it had priority in gaining

---

93. Ge Gongzhen, *Zhongguo baoxueshi* [The history of China's newspapers] (Hong Kong: Taiping shuju, 1964), 255.
94. Shenshi dianxunshe, *Shi nian: Shenshi dianxunshe chuangli shi zhounian jinian* [Ten years: The tenth anniversary of the Shenshi News Agency] (Shanghai: Shenshi dianxunshe, 1934).
95. Feng Zhixiang, *Xiao Tongzi zhuan* [A biography of Xiao Tongzi] (Taipei: Zhuanji wenxue chubanshe, 1975), 3.

exclusives from both the Ministry of Foreign Affairs and Ministry of Finance, was the main reason the agency was quoted by the foreign press.[96]

In parallel with the failure to build a strong news agency were Chinese officials' repeated attempts to control an influential English-language paper. The need for an English-language paper had been felt since the late Qing. The Chinese government's first attempt to establish an English-language press of its own was made in 1909 by Yan Huiqing (W. W. Yen), then an official in the news department of the Ministry of Foreign Affairs. Yan established the *Peking Daily News* with funding from the ministry and edited the paper himself.[97] The paper aimed to explain China's diplomatic policy abroad so as to influence the opinions of foreign diplomats as well as Western-returned Chinese intellectuals. Fearing his official position might harm the paper's credibility, Yan soon passed the editorship to W. C. Chen, who eventually sold the paper to Zhu Qi in Guangdong because of financial difficulties after the fall of the Qing.[98] Although the paper remained under Chinese ownership, it was edited by a Scottish journalist, Alexander Ramsay, whose loyalty was firmly attached to British interests.[99] Meanwhile, Yuan Shikai also subsidized the *National Review* to represent his voice.[100] The paper was established by Tang Yuanzhan (known as Tong Yuen-cham), and edited by a Briton, Walter Kirton.[101]

After the fall of Qing rule, the warlords and members of the elites in Beijing also invested in English-language papers. The *Peking Leader* was an attempt by Beijing officials to expand their influence among English-language readers. The paper was founded in 1920 by the Research Clique (Yanjiuxi), a powerful political group headed by Liang Qichao. The group invited Diao Minqian (known as M. Tukzung Tyau),[102] an expert on Chinese foreign relations, to edit the paper. After Diao left Beijing, the paper became a rumor monger for warlords. Wang Boheng, who was then a reporter at the paper, recalled that he often found his coverage of the war between Zhili and Fengtian cliques censored to suit the paper's political bias and his articles completely

---

96. Chao, *Foreign Press in China*, 6.
97. Shi Zhaoji, *Shi Zhaoji zaonian huiyilu* [Memoir of Alfred Sze about his early years] (Taipei: Zhuanji wenxue chubanshe, 1967), 77.
98. Shen Jianhong, *Bansheng youhuan: Shen Jianhong huiyilu* [The memoir of Shen Jianhong] (Taipei: Lianjing Publishing, 1989), 57–58; Hollington K. Tong (Dong Xianguang), *Yi ge nongfu de zishu* [Hollington Tong's autobiography: A self-introduction of a farmer], trans. Zeng Xubai (Taipei: Taihai xinsheng baoshe, 1973), 30–34.
99. George Ernest Morrison, *The Correspondence of G. E. Morrison* (Cambridge: Cambridge University Press, 1976), 376.
100. Rudolf Wagner, "Don't Mind the Gap! The Foreign Language-Press in Late-Qing and Republican China," *China Heritage Quarterly*, nos. 30/31 (June/September 2012), http://www.chinaheritagequarterly.org/features.php?searchterm=030_wagner.inc&issue=030.
101. "China Looks Up to the Future," *New York Times*, October 4, 1910, 4.
102. Diao later became director of the Intelligence and Publicity Department of the Ministry of Foreign Affairs, Nanjing.

rewritten by editors who felt no shame in distorting facts and contributors' ideas.[103] In 1925, an American, Grover Clark, gained control of the paper, becoming both editor and president.[104] Yet American patronage did not save the paper from frequent financial difficulties due to the small number of subscriptions in North China and a business downturn caused by endless military disturbances. Moreover, the paper's American identity together with financial hardship made it ideal prey for local warlords. In 1927, Hallett Abend, coeditor of the paper, found that the *Leader* was receiving regular allowances from Feng Yuxiang, a northern warlord sympathetic to Bolshevism.[105]

Members of the Guomindang also attempted to gain a position in the English-language press. After the 1911 revolution, the Guomindang, under the instruction of Sun Yat-sen, founded the *China Republican* (also known as *China Gazette*) in the French Concession of Shanghai. The paper was edited by Ma Su, Sun Yat-sen's English secretary; Hollington K. Tong, a graduate from the Journalism School of the University of Missouri; and R. I. Hope, a Briton of Indian extraction. Chesney Duncan, editor of the *Hong Kong Telegraph*, also frequently contributed to the paper. Its anti-Yuan policy soon caught the attention of the Chinese elite and government.[106] In 1913, the paper was closed down by the consul general of France in Shanghai upon the request of the Yuan government. Ma Su, who was of Chinese and French parentage, was deported from China and Chesney Duncan threatened with prosecution.[107]

After the Guomindang established its authority in Guangzhou, the party started a semiofficial English paper, the *Canton Gazette*, operated by Li Cai. The paper supported the left wing of the party and gained popularity in the mid-1920s when Guangzhou was the revolutionary political center of China. It attracted prominent foreign journalists like Hallett Abend, who later became the *New York Times*' key correspondent in China, and gained editorial assistance from Chen Youren (known as Eugene Chen), the foreign minister of the Guangzhou government.[108] However, after the Guomindang moved its capital from Guangzhou to Wuhan in November 1926, its influence quickly waned.

In Wuhan, the Guomindang started a political journal called the *People's Tribune*. The paper was set up by Chen Youren and Mikhail Borodin, a Comintern agent in China, with the help of two American journalists, William and Rayna Prohme, who were sympathetic to Bolshevism. The *Tribune* aimed to inform a foreign audience about the Wuhan government's ideology and achievements. The paper was mailed

---

103. For Wang Boheng's observation of the role Western newspapers played in China, see "Zhongguo zhi xizibao," 148.
104. Chao, *Foreign Press in China*, 74.
105. Hallett Abend, *My Life in China, 1926–1941* (New York: Harcourt, Brace and Company, 1943), 52.
106. G. E. Morrison to Yen Ho-ling, November 4, 1913, in Morrison, *Correspondence*, 238–39.
107. Morrison, *Correspondence*, 112.
108. Abend, *My Life in China*, 15–19.

daily to a list of more than five thousand individuals and radical organizations across the world provided by Borodin.[109] However, the *Tribune* did not operate for long because of the Guomindang's internal struggles. The paper was suppressed by Wang Jingwei after it carried an article by Soong Qing-ling (Madam Sun Yat-sen) criticizing the Guomindang for having betrayed Sun's doctrines.[110]

The fierce competition for control of the English-language papers and news resources indicated that Chinese intellectuals and officials were fully aware of the importance of the English-language press in connecting China with the outside world. Yet their efforts to penetrate the press industry were often disrupted by the turbulent political environment. The constant change of the division of power in the local and central government rendered it difficult for governments to formulate a long-term news policy or offer stable funds for news organizations. Without an effective news agency or an English-language paper to gain a foreign audience, the reach of Chinese propaganda was restricted: China's side of the story could be heard only when the foreign-controlled agencies or papers chose to quote its version. Such a disadvantage manifested itself fully in the Jinan Incident in 1928.

---

109. Milly Bennett, edited and annotated by A. Tom Grunfeld, *On Her Own: Journalistic Adventures from San Francisco to the Chinese Revolution* (Armonk, NY: M. E. Sharpe, 1993), 176.
110. Emily Hahn, *The Soong Sisters* (New York: Doran and Company, 1941), 115; Peter Rand, *China Hands: The Adventures and Ordeals of the American Journalists Who Joined Forces with the Great Chinese Revolution* (New York: Simon & Schuster, 1995), 61.

TIME WILL TELL WHO RULES THE WAVES

Figure 4
Sapajou, "Time Will Tell Who Rules the Waves," *North China Daily News*, November 23, 1934.

2
Beyond the Front Line

The Jinan Incident

The Jinan Incident was the most serious military clash between China and Japan in the 1920s. It put an end to the brief period of Sino-Japanese amity and foreshadowed the more drastic collisions between the two in 1931 and beyond. In April 1928, Chiang Kai-shek launched the second Northern Expedition against the warlord-backed Beijing government led by Zhang Zuolin. As Chiang's troops marched toward Jinan, the provincial capital of Shandong, the Japanese government dispatched troops to the city, claiming that it was responsible for protecting the two thousand Japanese nationals there and their property. On the morning of May 3, fighting broke out in Jinan between Chiang's army and the Japanese troops. Intensely nationalistic soldiers of both sides committed atrocities that further inflamed the conflict. On May 7, without conferring with his superiors in Tokyo, the Japanese commander General Fukuda Hikosuke presented Chiang with a twelve-hour ultimatum that Chiang was unable to accept. This led to the Japanese army's large-scale attack and bombing of Jinan city on the second day. By May 11, the Japanese had driven Chiang's troops out of the city and governed the area through a puppet organization composed of Chinese citizens. Instead of continuing the fight with Japanese forces, Chiang bypassed Jinan to resume the expedition northward. It was not until March 1929 that Japan, under pressure from Western powers, returned Jinan to the Guomindang government.[1]

The incident immediately came under the spotlight of the press and became widely discussed in the following months. Both China and Japan engaged in a bitter dispute about the basic facts surrounding the event. Beyond the front line, there was a battle of words in the media, which was equally fierce and intensive. A detailed review of the battle shed light on the intricate relationships among newspapers controlled by different interest groups in China. It vividly reflected how China was plagued by its lack of media resources, political consensus, and media strategy compared to Japan's

---

1. Akira Iriye, *After Imperialism: The Search for a New Order in the Far East, 1921–1931* (Cambridge, MA: Harvard University Press, 1965), 193–205; C. Martin Wilbur, "The Nationalist Revolution: From Canton to Nanking, 1923–28," in *The Cambridge History of China*, ed. John King Fairbank (Cambridge: Cambridge University Press, 1983), 12:703–5; William Fitch Morton, *Tanaka Giichi and Japan's China Policy* (Folkestone: Dawson, 1980), 118; Donald A. Jordan, *The Northern Expedition: China's National Revolution of 1926–1928* (Honolulu: University Press of Hawai'i, 1976), 158–61.

powerful news machinery. Difficulty lay not only in the lack of media resources but also in the lack of favorable public opinion. For the first time, the Guomindang officials felt the urgency of building an international news propaganda network. Yet the lesson was learned through a painful defeat.

Responses to the Jinan Incident

Benefiting from a powerful news network, the Japanese media's response to the Jinan Incident was swift, consistent, and intensive. The first dispatch about the military conflict came shortly after fighting broke out. Before any investigation of responsibility had been made, the Tōhō news agency had dispatched accounts from Beijing to the world, asserting that the trouble was caused by looting carried out by Chinese soldiers.[2] In the hours following the outbreak of fighting, dispatches concerning the incident continued to be distributed from Tōhō's branch offices in China. Despite their different sources, all messages consistently stuck to the explanation of "looting," with each report bringing new details of crimes. Japanese soldiers were thus portrayed as innocent defenders who were "compelled" to return fire at the disobedient Chinese looters. By the end of the first day, at least seven dispatches were sent from Tōhō, all blaming Chinese soldiers for the fighting.[3] The misconduct of Chinese soldiers was presented in the press as the only reason for the conflict, reinforced by consistent statements and repetition. It should be noted that the first few reports on the incident were likely to be decisive in forming public opinion, since they gave readers their first basic information on events and were thus likely to influence any future judgements.

Tōhō's reports went unchallenged in the English-language press for days. China's lack of an effective news network was to some degree responsible, but this alone could not explain a complete absence of its views on the conflict. The situation was exacerbated by the state of communications with forces on the battlefield. To isolate the armies of the northern warlords, the Nationalist troops had cut rail lines linking Jinan with Nanjing, Beijing, and Qingdao prior to the battle.[4] The telegraph lines along the rail lines were also destroyed. Communication with Jinan, therefore, relied solely on two wireless stations in the city, one controlled by the Japanese and the other by the Chinese. Soon after the clash began on May 3, Japanese soldiers destroyed the Chinese wireless station, which left the Japanese station the only channel for communications.[5] Destruction of the Chinese station not only impeded the transmission

---

2. See quotes of Reuters' reports on the Jinan Incident, in "How the Japanese Reported the Tsinan Incident," *China Weekly Review*, May 12, 1928, 311–13.
3. Ibid.
4. "Chinese Defy Tokyo, Cut Tsinan Railway," *New York Times*, May 1, 1928, 12; "Communications Cut," *China Press*, May 1, 1928, 1.
5. See the memoir of Shen Yiyun, the wife of China's then Foreign Minister Huang Fu, Shen, *Yiyun huiyi* [Shen Yiyun's memoir] (Taipei: Zhuanji wenxue chubanshe, 1968), 2:371.

of news but also affected general communications between Jinan and Nanjing. It was reported that the Guomindang government could reach Chiang only by first telegraphing to Yanzhou, about sixty miles south of Jinan, and then sending messages by courier.[6] The lack of efficient communications on the Nationalist side left Japan in control of all messages from Jinan to the outside world.

Had alternative explanations been offered by other foreign media sources, Japan's version may not have so easily prevailed. Despite Tōhō's heavy stake in China's news market, it was still Reuters that occupied the primary position globally. Reuters also enjoyed greater credibility than Tōhō in reporting events in Jinan because of its third-party position. Yet an alternative view from Reuters did not appear. Rivalry between Tōhō and Reuters in China was primarily a matter of business, not politics. Instead of giving balance to non-Japanese sources or remaining skeptical of the Japanese version, Reuters completely followed the Japanese line, reporting that the trouble had arisen from looting by Chinese soldiers.[7] The two agencies together monopolized outgoing reports of the incident and established the cause of "looting" as a fact in the press.

Compared with Japan, China's response was slow and inconsistent. The official Guomin news agency's report first appeared in the *North China Daily News* on May 5. It maintained that the shooting occurred when Japanese troops arrested several members of the Nationalist propaganda corps and threatened to shoot anyone attempting to pass through a Japanese-controlled barricade.[8] Yet Guomin's version was unable to challenge the account of the event established by British and Japanese news agencies. Reports from the *China Press*, one of the few papers that recorded the source of its information, clearly indicated the marginal position of Guomin in the news market. Among the 168 reports concerning the first ten days of the incident, only 14 were quoted from Guomin, while 107 came from Reuters and 47 from Tōhō.

China also suffered from the inconsistency of its own versions. Multiple explanations concerning the origin of the fighting were distributed. The various accounts not only confused foreign audiences but also severely damaged China's credibility. Shortly after Guomin's interpretation found its way into the press, Chiang Kai-shek and Huang Fu, minister of foreign affairs, issued another account on May 5, stating that the incident was caused by Japanese troops shooting Chinese soldiers when the latter passed through Japanese-controlled streets.[9] Chiang's version dropped the reference to Chinese propagandists yet asserted that the conflict had begun with a clash between the two groups of troops. Another account circulating in the press

---

6. "How the Japanese Reported the Tsinan Incident," *China Weekly Review*, May 12, 1928, 311.
7. "Japanese and Southerners Clash at Jinan," *North China Daily News*, May 4, 1928, 13.
8. "The Chinese Version," *North China Daily News*, May 5, 1928, 18.
9. "End Tsinan-fu Fight Both Sides Accused," *New York Times*, May 6, 1928, 1.

claimed that Japanese soldiers had prevented Nationalist forces from crossing the railway line in order to protect fleeing northern troops.[10] Although all versions blamed Japan for the fighting, the disagreement on the basic reason was liable to give the impression that the Chinese were fabricating their accounts, unsure of how to effectively justify their aggression. The existence of multiple accounts was a result of the Guomindang government's lack of institutions for systematic foreign propaganda. There seemed to be no coordination between the official agency, Guomin, and the Guomindang's top leaders regarding explanations of the cause of the incident. Meanwhile, Chiang and Huang's protest about the Japanese soldiers' ruthless killing of Commissioner of Foreign Affairs for Shandong Cai Gongshi and the other staff members present in the bureau had been frequently cited by Chinese papers since May 6.[11] Yet it failed to appear in the foreign press.

This inconsistency reflected the Guomindang officials' distrust of the power of propaganda and hesitation to involve it in military planning. After the fighting broke out, Chiang Kai-shek was not keen to publicize the affair internationally, fearing that extended exposure of the incident would complicate the issue and undermine attempts to reach an immediate agreement with Japan. After all, the completion of the Northern Expedition was more important than confrontation with Japan in Shandong at the time.[12] A quick solution could perhaps be found by negotiating with Japanese forces locally. Accordingly, Chiang's reaction was twofold: while seeking a cease-fire with Japanese military officers on the front line, he also appealed for mediation to foreign consulates in China, especially those of Britain and the United States.[13] Yet both approaches failed: demands of Japanese generals were too high; meanwhile, the foreign consulates refused to mediate unless a request to do so was received from Japan as well.[14] This was tantamount to a denial, since Japan had clearly expressed its objection to any third-party mediation.

The Guomindang government changed its foreign propaganda strategy on May 8 when Japanese forces began to bomb Jinan. Believing that the absence of China's voice was due not to a lack of moral ground but the lack of a channel, the Nanjing leaders began to seek a new way to distribute China's views.[15] Instead of publicizing news inside China and passively waiting for the foreign media to transmit it abroad,

10. "Nationalist Statement," *Times*, May 5, 1928, 12.
11. "Dui Ri baoju zhi fenkai" [Rage against Japanese atrocities], *Shen bao*, May 6, 1928, 13–14; "Cai Gongshi xunnan shimo ji" [The death of Cai Gongshi], *Shen bao*, May 9, 1928, 10.
12. *Shi lüe gao ben* [Chiang Kai-shek's manuscripts], May 17, 1928 (Taipei: Academia Historica, 2003), 3:316.
13. Chiang Kai-shek's telegraph about the Jinan Incident, May 4, 1928, in *Zhonghua Minguo zhongyao shiliao chubian: Dui Ri kangzhan shiqi; xubian* [Collection of important historical materials: The anti-Japanese war; Sequel] (Taipei: Zhongguo Guomindang zhongyang weiyuanhui dangshi weiyuanhui, 1981), vol. 1, 126.
14. Consul General at Shanghai (Cunningham) to the Secretary of the State, Papers Relating to the Foreign Relations of the United States (hereafter PRFRUS), vol. 2 (1928), 137–38.
15. Chen Gongbo, "Women duiyu Tianzhong baoxing de zhuzhang" [Our opinion on the outrages by the Tanaka government], *Geming pinglun* 3 (1928): 5.

Nanjing sought direct access to foreign audiences. The first step was to report the Jinan Incident to the League of Nations, calling upon it to intervene.[16] On May 11, Tan Yankai, chair of the Nationalist Government Council, issued an official appeal to the secretary-general of the League of Nations, in which Tan gave a thorough account of the Chinese interpretation of the incident and appealed to the League to arrange an international inquiry into the incident.[17] By doing so, Nanjing officials indicated to the world that they had faith in their version of the events. Yet the League rejected China's appeal on May 13, on the grounds that the League still recognized the Beijing government as the official government of China, not that of Nanjing. Fully aware of their lack of legitimacy prior to their appeal, Guomindang leaders still saw it as an opportunity to publicize their case before the court of international opinion, since any move by the League of Nations would be monitored by the world press.[18] Hu Hanmin, one of the top leaders of the Guomindang, indicated such a plan in his correspondence with Huang Fu:

> [T]he Nanjing Government has not gained recognition from the League of Nations, yet issuing the appeal with the support of the Beijing government will boost the prestige of the northern warlords. The League was controlled by the big powers, with a British national being the president and Japan strongly influencing its political decisions. China has no chance to win. Even if the League intervened, it would only conduct investigations of the incident, offering no immediate solutions. That is why the United States refrains from stepping in. Nevertheless, we should appeal to the League for propaganda purposes. . . . The chance of winning is always slim when it comes to the rivalry with the Powers. But publicizing our causes is better than remaining silent.[19]

To further reinforce China's position, the Guomindang government openly appealed to US president Calvin Coolidge, inquiring about "the attitude of the American government and the people towards this grave situation created by Japan."[20] The appeal, which appeared in the *New York Times*, reviewed the incident at length from China's perspective. The government sent high officials as "special envoys" to key capitals. Among them, Wu Chaoshu (C. C. Wu) was sent to Washington, Wang Chonghui to London, Wang Jingwei to Geneva, Hu Hanmin and Li Shizeng to Paris, and Sun Ke (Sun Fo) to the Hague and Berlin. Their job was to form a liaison between key foreign newspapers and Chinese sources, to give public talks on the Jinan Incident, and to elicit support from government officials in the target countries.[21] Prior to his trip,

---

16. "China to Ask League for Tsinan Inquiry," *New York Times*, May 8, 1928, 1.
17. "China Presents Her Case to the World," *China Weekly Review*, May 19, 1928, 356.
18. Hu Hanmin, "Shandong shijian tichu Guojilianmeng de jingguo" [How the Jinan incident was presented to the League of Nations], *Geming wenxian*, vols. 19–21, 1396.
19. Hu Hanmin's telegram to Huang Fu, May 12, 1928, quoted in Shen, *Yiyun huiyi*, 383.
20. "China Asks Coolidge Our Stand on War by Japan in Jinan," *New York Times*, May 14, 1928, 1.
21. "Hu Hanmin, Sun Ke, Wu Chaoshu zi Bali zhi Tan Yankai zhuxi deng chenshu dui Jinan yijian dian"

Beyond the Front Line

Wu intimated to US journalists that the object of his mission to Washington was "to make the Nationalist case clear to the United States" and "to make sure America will not be led astray by propaganda."[22] These emissaries hoped to draw Western countries into a mediation of the situation, but Chinese officials knew that these countries would not intercede until they had a clearer understanding of the situation. With the Japanese interpretation dominant in the foreign press, making the Chinese version acceptable to foreign audiences was a prerequisite for securing foreign support.

Japan: Making the Jinan Incident the Second Nanjing Incident, 1927

In addition to its advanced news networks, Japan also enjoyed a favorable public opinion. Japan shared with Western powers their "foreign" identity and experience of colonization in China. For them, China's antiforeign sentiment was a commonly shared difficulty. Resentment against China could easily be stirred up if Japan was able to convince Western readers that the Jinan Incident was simply a further example of an outrage committed by the Chinese against foreigners.

To invoke anti-Chinese feelings among Westerners, Japanese journalists attempted to portray the Jinan Incident as a second Nanjing Incident that had occurred during the first Northern Expedition. On May 24, 1927, Guomindang troops defeated northern warlords in Nanjing. Upon arrival, they looted and killed foreigners throughout the city. American and British warships on nearby rivers responded by shelling Chinese forces, causing heavy Chinese casualties and damaging properties. Chiang Kai-shek later blamed the acts on communist elements within the army, an explanation that Westerners were ready to accept. Negotiations on the settlement of the Nanjing affair dragged on for more than a year. It was not until April 1928, less than a month before the Jinan Incident took place, that the Guomindang government was able to reach an agreement with the United States regarding an apology and the amount of compensation.[23] Settlement with Britain was still pending because of a deadlock on issues related to the revision of treaties.[24]

The Nanjing Incident offered a favorable precedent for Japan to justify its own actions in Jinan. The two incidents shared many common features: both cases occurred during the nationalistic Northern Expeditions, and both involved clashes between Guomindang troops and foreigners. Furthermore, the Nanjing Incident was the most recent example of Sino-foreign conflict. The foreign community's memory of

---

[Telegraph about opinions on the Jinan Incident, sent by Hu Hanmin, Sun Ke, Wu Chaoshu from Paris to Tan Yankai], May 12, 1928, *Zhonghua Minguo zhongyao shiliao chubian: Dui Ri kangzhan shiqi; xubian,* vol. 1, 147; Shen, *Yiyun huiyi,* 382.

22. "Nanking Sends Wu Here on Shandong," *New York Times,* May 11, 1928, 4.
23. "The Secretary of State to the Minister in China (MacMurray)," April 4, 1928, PRFRUS, vol. 2 (1928), 337.
24. "Mr. MacMurray's Brilliant Diplomatic Victory," *Far Eastern Review,* April 1928, 154.

the Guomindang's lawless actions was still fresh in people's minds, and resentment against Nationalist troops had not been allayed because of the incomplete settlement of the case.

Japanese journalists deliberately reported details of the Jinan case following the Nanjing model. Tōhō's repetition of the scenes of looting mentioned above is an example. It should be noted that the Japanese account of the looting may not have been accurate. Reports from neutral sources, such as the *Manchester Guardian* and the *New York Times*, failed to confirm the looting. Contemporary scholars have also been unable to verify whether the looting had actually taken place or whether the scale was as intensive as in Tōhō's version of events.[25] Japan's reporting nevertheless repeatedly referred to the communist element and the internal chaos of the Northern Expedition Army—the same way that the Nanjing Incident was covered—despite the fact that Chiang had excluded the Communists from the army in 1927.[26]

Nonetheless, Japan's strategy of linking the two incidents had its drawbacks. It invited readers to question Japan's expedition to Shandong in the first place. While the Nanjing Incident was initially a clash between Chinese soldiers and Western civilians, the Jinan Incident was a battle between Chinese and Japanese troops. Indeed, the presence of Japanese troops in Jinan had increased the possibility of a military clash. Without good justification for reinforcing troops in Jinan, Japan's claim to be a victim remained weak, since the incident could easily be perceived as trouble that Japan had brought on itself.

Justifying the Japanese expedition to Shandong was difficult. The expedition was a result of the inability of the Tanaka Giichi government to rein in military ambitions. Since the autumn of 1927, Chiang Kai-shek had made several attempts to persuade Japan not to intervene in Shandong. He had repeatedly promised that he would not tolerate antiforeign activities by his troops and had given assurances that he would work to protect the lives and property of foreigners in China.[27] To seek further amity with Japan, Chiang replaced the Western-educated Minister of Foreign Affairs Wu Chaoshu with the Japanese-educated Huang Fu in February 1928, even though some top leaders in Nanjing strongly opposed Huang's appointment.[28] Meanwhile, the Tanaka cabinet also hesitated before dispatching more troops to Jinan. Neither the prime minister nor the general staff was fully convinced that the expedition was

---

25. Iriye, *After Imperialism*, 199–200; C. Martin Wilbur, "The Nationalist Revolution: From Canton to Nanking, 1923–28," in *The Cambridge History of China*, ed. John King Fairbank (Cambridge: Cambridge University Press, 1983), 12:703–5.
26. Tōhō's reports on the Jinan Incident, quoted in "How the Japanese reported the Tsinan Incident," *China Weekly Review*, May 12, 1928, 311.
27. MacMurray to the Secretary of the State, April 13, 1928, PRFRUS, vol. 2 (1928), 130–31; Zhonghua Minguo shishi jiyao bianzuan weiyuanhui, *Zhonghua Minguo shishi jiyao* [Historical records of the Republican China], January–June 1928 (Taipei: Zhongzheng shuju, 1978), 503.
28. MacMurray to the Secretary of the State, February 29, 1928, PRFRUS, vol. 2 (1928), 323–24.

necessary.²⁹ Yet the military had its own views. Pressure from the War Ministry finally forced Tanaka to accept the expedition in mid-April 1928.

Japan's propaganda also faced challenges from its domestic audience. On May 5, Tokyo newspapers, with the exception of *Nichi nichi shimbun*, blamed the Japanese government's hostile policy for the conflict in Jinan.³⁰ They believed that Japan's dispatch of forces to Shandong not only failed to protect Japanese property but also severely harmed trade with China. Japanese commercial interests in Shandong, which "amounted to no less than $440,000,000 for the current fiscal year," "were too large to incur the ill-will of the Chinese, who were their best customers."³¹ Furthermore, some argued that the troops, which were intended to protect the inhabitants, only gave other forces a pretext to attack. They maintained that troubles could have been avoided if no Japanese troops were present.³² Were the intention to protect Japanese nationals genuine, the government could have temporarily relocated Japanese civilians to the nearby city of Qingdao instead of leaving them in Jinan to face possible military conflict, challenged the domestic papers.³³ Japanese propaganda thus was caught in a dilemma: the more Japanese nationals suffered in the Jinan Incident, the more Japan could blame China for its "barbarism" and thus justify its use of force, but at the same time, casualties among Japanese nationals would enrage the domestic public. The War Ministry was believed to have tried to withhold reports on Japanese casualties for fear that "publication of exceptionally heavy Japanese civilian losses would have a detrimental effect politically throughout the country."³⁴

Meanwhile, Zhang Zuolin also sought to reap political gains from the Jinan Incident. Soon after the incident began, Zhang distributed a message to the press, offering to assist Japan with arms and ammunition.³⁵ Zhang's offer immediately raised people's suspicions concerning Japan's connections with the Beijing government. Rumors began to circulate in the press accusing Japan of using the Jinan Incident to assist the northern army. While Japan insisted that its action in Jinan was to protect its nationals, Zhang's rhetoric in the press embroiled Japan in China's internal struggles. Yet, only two days later, Zhang did an about-face and issued a protest to the Japanese diplomats in Beijing, demanding that Japanese troops withdraw from Chinese territory.³⁶ On May 9, he circulated another message announcing a temporary cessation of the civil war because of the Sino-Japanese conflict.³⁷

29. Iriye, *After Imperialism*, 196.
30. "Tokyo Papers Blame Cabinet," *New York Times*, May 6, 1928; "Situation of the Utmost Gravity: Comment of Press," *China Press*, May 6, 1928, 1.
31. "Correspondence," *China Press*, May 17, 1928, 4.
32. "Press Criticism of Tanaka," *New York Times*, May 7, 1928, 1.
33. Ibid.
34. "End Tsinan-fu Fight; Both Sides Accused," *New York Times*, May 6, 1928, 18.
35. "Chang Tso-lin's Offer," *Times*, May 5, 1928, 12.
36. "Chang Protest to Japan," *New York Times*, May 6, 1928, 1.
37. "Chang Tso-lin Favors Truce between North and South before Tsinan," *North China Daily News*, May 10, 1928.

China's Dilemma

In 1928 China was unfavorably positioned in the court of public opinion. Two features characterized its image in the Western press: disorder and antiforeignism. China's anti-imperialist feelings reached a peak in the 1920s. In 1924, Sun Yat-sen wrote nationalism into the Three People's Principles, which specified the importance of overthrowing imperialism and achieving racial and national equality with other nations of the world.[38] In 1925, the May Thirtieth Movement elevated anti-imperial sentiment to a new level, particularly against the British.[39] The Northern Expedition launched in 1926 led to further aggravation. The National Revolutionary Army with Bolshevik support had reclaimed the British settlements of Hankou and Jiujiang, and had also threatened foreign lives and property after taking Nanjing. These events provided Western audiences with the context to believe that Nationalist armies were likely to create another antiforeign incident in Jinan.

Nevertheless, leaders in Nanjing clearly understood that China, as a weak country, could not afford to confront all other Powers at the same time. Chiang was concerned about Britain's attitude and worried that if diplomatic measures failed, China would have to confront Japan militarily.[40] The Jinan case required the Nanjing government to shift its diplomatic strategy: from anti-imperialism, particularly against Britain, to a focus on Japan.

This shift was not easy. With antiforeign sentiment running high among the Chinese public, any political group, whether they were Nationalists, Communists or warlord faction, understood the need to address public anger toward imperialism and mobilize it for its own use. Although Chiang severed relations with the Soviets after eliminating the communist element in the Nationalist Revolutionary Army and adopting a moderate attitude toward foreign countries, he could not afford to totally abandon anti-imperialist rhetoric. Campaigns against extraterritoriality continued, and negotiations on the control of tariff rates dominated China's diplomacy.

Not all Guomindang leaders supported Chiang's overtures to the West. For example, Li Shizeng, one of the top leaders of the party, tried to dissuade Chiang from reporting the Jinan Incident to the League of Nations, regarding such an effort as futile.[41] Other left-wing members of the Nationalist Party, in their continuous opposition to Chiang, condemned his resort to the League as "begging for mercy" (*qi lian*), which betrayed the party's anti-imperialist tradition. An editorial in the *Geming pinglun*, an official paper of Guomindang leftists, exemplifies this attitude:

---

38. Sun Yat-sen, *San Min Chu-I* [Three People's Principles], trans. Frank Price (Shanghai: Commercial Press, 1928).
39. Richard W. Rigby, *The May 30 Movement: Events and Themes* (Canberra: Australian National University Press, 1980), 112–13.
40. *Shi lue gao ben*, 3:300.
41. Li Shizeng to Zhang Jingjiang and Huang Fu, May 13, 1928, quoted in Shen, *Yiyun huiyi*, 384.

> How stupid and humiliating it is to beg other imperialist powers to help China out of Japan's threat! . . . There is no fundamental difference between Japan and other imperialist countries. The only difference is that Japan acted more directly while other Powers coerced China in a concealed manner. Whichever way they pursue, their goal is the same, that is, to obtain special rights in China.[42]

The Opinion of the Treaty-Port Press

Members of the foreign diaspora in China were not merely a passive audience in the Jinan case; they also had their own interests to serve. Fearing that China's nationalism would push foreign powers to further relinquish their special rights, many Britons in the treaty ports supported Japan's defense of its own interests in Shandong, believing such a pursuit would strengthen the general imperial interests in China. Despite the end of the Anglo-Japanese alliance in 1923, the two countries still saw each other as allies rather than enemies in the 1920s when competition between the two was not as intense as it would become later. Many people on both sides quietly hoped for the return of the alliance when their interests were threatened by Chinese nationalism or the growing influence of the United States.[43] Yet for American progressives who saw an independent and open China as the best market for American exports as well as a means to check Japan's rise in the Pacific,[44] events in Jinan provided them with a chance to attack foreign intervention in China's affairs. These divergent goals translated into a split view in the British and American press in the treaty ports: the British press strongly upheld the Japanese argument, whereas US papers displayed sympathy for China's cause.

The support of British papers for Japan was explicit. They accepted both Japan's version of the facts and its rationale. In early May, the two largest English-language papers in China, the *North China Daily News* and the *China Press*, both endorsed the Japanese version. A cursory glance at the headlines indicates that the papers firmly followed the Japanese interpretation: "Chiang Kai-shek Reported to Be Powerless to Control Undisciplined Soldiers Who Have Got Out of Hand in City,"[45] "Outburst of Looting by Southern Troops,"[46] "Japan Losing Patience under Calumnies of

---

42. Xing Cun, "Jinan shijian zhi waibao yulun" [Foreign newspapers' opinions on the Jinan Incident], *Geming pinglun* 3 (1928): 53.
43. Hosoya Chihiro, "Britain and the United States in Japan's View of the International System, 1919–1937," and Ian Hill Nish, "Japan in Britain's View of the International System, 1919–1937," both in *Anglo-Japanese Alienation, 1919–1952*, ed. Ian Nish (Cambridge: Cambridge University Press, 1982), 57–76 and 3–57; Ian Hill Nish, *Alliance in Decline: A Study in Anglo-Japanese Relations, 1908–1923* (London: Athlone Press, 1972).
44. George Ephraim Sokolsky, *The Tinder Box of Asia* (New York: Doubleday, Doran & Co., 1932); Carl Crow, *Four Hundred Million Customers* (New York: Harper Brothers, 1937).
45. *China Press*, May 4, 1928, 1.
46. *North China Daily News*, May 5, 1928.

Nanjing."⁴⁷ While it was generally professional practice for a journal to report a controversial issue with phrases such as "alleged by," this caution was absent when the papers quoted Japanese sources. In contrast, Chinese sources were usually labelled as "unfounded." The editor of the *North China Daily News* once stated that "we are inundated with correspondence, manifestoes, student resolutions, copies of telegrams sent abroad, all putting the Chinese view of the Tsinanfu affair. . . . [But] we regret to say that we cannot open our columns to propaganda of this kind."⁴⁸

British editors readily accepted the link between the Jinan Incident and the looting of Nanjing that was widely presented by Japanese sources. The *North China Daily News* endorsed the view that the Jinan affair was the Guomindang's "attempt to reproduce the Nanking outrage as the result of the recent diplomatic indulgence in negotiations for a settlement of that affair."⁴⁹ With the Nanjing Incident unresolved and anti-British sentiments running high in the preceding five years, the British were sympathetic to the Japanese explanation. They trusted Japanese sources not because they found the account of looting more persuasive but because those reports cogently reminded them of their own experiences. "It would be idle to deny," confessed the editor of the *North China Daily News*, "that some of the Southern troops have a bad reputation for looting and arrogance. At a crisis like the present, this cannot be ignored."⁵⁰ The *China Press* also supported this view, saying:

> Undisciplined [Nationalist] soldiers on nearly every occasion seem to get beyond the control of their commanders. At Hankow, at Nanking, in Nantao and Chapei, to mention only the instances of the past year, scenes of carnage, chaos and indiscriminate brigandage have characterized every change of government. Innocent citizens have been shot down, valuable property burned, and in other ways the terrible toll of warfare has been made needlessly more horrible. Now Tsinan is suffering from the same degrading lawlessness.⁵¹

The British papers also upheld Japan's justification for its expedition to Shandong. They intimated that "after the experiences of the British in China, it is difficult to be very censorious over the decision of the Japanese government to defend the lives and property of their nationals by the dispatch of troops."⁵² They believed that Japan "in her vast interests in Shandong, has every reason for acting in defense of her own."⁵³ And it "would have gravely neglected her duty if she had not."⁵⁴

---

47. *North China Daily News*, May 15, 1928.
48. "The Chinese View of Tsinan," *North China Daily News*, May 10, 1928, 6.
49. "From Rodney Gilbert," *North China Daily News*, May 5, 1928.
50. "Notes and Comments: The Responsibility at Tsinan," *North China Daily News*, May 9, 1928, 6.
51. "Tsinan—a Repetition of Nanking?" *China Press*, May 5, 1928, 12.
52. "North and South May Sink Differences and Unite in Present Situation," *China Press*, May 8, 1928, 1.
53. "Chinese View of Tsinan," 6.
54. "The Judgement on Tsinan," *North China Daily News*, May 16, 1928, 6.

Although the Jinan Incident was basically a Sino-Japanese affair, the British communities used it as an opportunity to vent their anti-Chinese views. Criticism went well beyond the incident itself, expanding to a condemnation of the Chinese nation. The British press believed that the Jinan Incident only reaffirmed China's underdeveloped status and its uncivilized nature. "Now and again," stated the *China Press*, "the foreign residents of China are jerked back a few centuries to be reminded that, however modern living conditions in Shanghai may have been made, they are still living on the fringe of a civilization which is back in the Middle Ages."[55] Thus, the trouble in Jinan, instead of being caused by Japan, was invited by China itself. The editor of the *North China Daily News* sarcastically commented:

> The Chinese have only themselves to thank that many of their nationals are dead and the prospects of the northern campaign gravely imperilled. And the question arises, will the Chinese never learn sense? What good did they do themselves by the raid on Hankow? The Concession was left to them. But the moral ascendancy, the honor due to those who could have hit back and did not, passed to Great Britain. What good did the Nanjing outrages do? What could it have profited even if the Southern army in Tsinan had wiped out every Japanese in the place? By every one of these Incidents the Chinese leaders put themselves a stage lower in the eyes of the civilized world and remove their country yet further from that position of acknowledged equality in the family of nations which they so ardently desire.[56]

When Japan bombed Jinan on May 8 and decided to dispatch more troops to Shandong, the British papers slightly shifted their pro-Japanese stance, suggesting that Japan's actions were unwarranted. Even though the British communities were ready to accept the Japanese version and blame China for starting the clash, they still viewed any escalation unfavorably, fearing that the Sino-Japanese fighting could extend to a new round of antiforeign activities in China. In an editorial of May 11, the editor of the *North China Daily News* called for a joint investigation into the incident in order to make an immediate settlement possible. The paper also approved of Nanjing's reaction to the incident for the first time, commending Nanjing for localizing the dispute and successfully preventing popular outbursts in the region.[57] Editorial columns, where pro-Chinese comments were previously rejected as propaganda,[58] now began to carry Chinese voices and to quote protests against British expatriates' slant toward Japan.[59] Meanwhile, the paper became cautious about further Japanese

---

55. "Tsinan—a Repetition of Nanking?," 12.
56. "The Tsinanfu Explosion," *North China Daily News*, May 7, 1928, 6.
57. "An Atmosphere of Reasonableness," *North China Daily News*, May 11, 1928, 6.
58. See editors' explanations of their rejection of Chinese sources: "The Chinese View of Jinan," *North China Daily News*, May 10, 1928, 6.
59. "Correspondence: A Chinese Voice," *China Press*, May 12, 1928, 4.

moves. It advised Japan to minimize its military operations,[60] and cited rumors from the treaty ports that Japan's action in Jinan was aimed at intervening in China's civil war, in the hope of gaining a favorable position to secure its Manchurian interests.[61]

The *China Weekly Review* and the *Peking Leader*, two of the most popular American-owned papers, had taken a decisively anti-Japanese attitude from the outset, disagreeing with the account provided by the Japanese authorities. Rather than relying on Japanese reports, the *Review* relayed the information provided by H. J. Timperley, Beijing correspondent for the *Manchester Guardian*, regarding his reports as "the first impartial accounts by a neutral witness."[62] Timperley's reports differed from Japanese versions. Before the incident, he characterized the initial southern troops' occupation of Jinan as "peaceful" and "exemplary." He also confirmed that Chiang's soldiers were "friendly disposed toward foreigners."[63] Regarding the origin of the clash on May 3, Timperley claimed that the fighting began when Japanese soldiers fired on Nationalist troops passing by in the street. Instead of regarding the fighting as the result of looting, he saw the confrontation as a continuation of a series of Sino-Japanese clashes, including the shooting of a Nationalist officer on the previous day and the detention of Nationalist street lecturers by the Japanese.[64]

Apart from quoting non-Japanese sources, the *China Weekly Review* also condemned the British papers' support for Japan, believing that they had assisted in the distribution of Japanese propaganda. In a front-page editorial on May 12, the *Review* singled out the three British dailies—the *North China Daily News*, the *China Press*, and the *Shanghai Times*—for having allied with Japan "without awaiting reports from American and British or other neutral sources in Tsinan."[65] The readiness displayed by the three British newspapers for blaming China for the trouble, stated the *Review*, "indicated that 'die-hard' stock in Shanghai [wa]s again on the up-turn."[66] In the next issue, on May 19, the journal continued to criticize the British papers, arguing that the Jinan Incident was "unfairly reported in the *China Press*."[67] The *Peking Leader*, while not accusing the British papers of sympathy for Japan, warned them to treat Japanese sources with caution. Whatever the causes, commented the *Leader*, the case itself had inevitably stirred furious feelings between China and Japan. Their passion may have resulted in grossly exaggerated reports of what happened on the ground. In such circumstances, warned the *Leader*, it was "particularly

---

60. "Japanese Press for Early Withdrawal," *North China Daily News*, May 13, 1928.
61. "The Chinese War: Japanese Hint to Chang," *Times*, May 21, 1928, 16; "The Situation in North China," *North China Daily News*, May 23, 1928, 6.
62. "The Clash between the Nationalist and the Japanese in Tsinan," *China Weekly Review*, May 12, 1928, 306–7.
63. Ibid.
64. Ibid.
65. "Foreign Diehard Press Blames Chinese," *China Weekly Review*, May 12, 1928, 305.
66. Ibid.
67. "Correspondence," *China Weekly Review*, May 19, 1928, 354.

necessary to exercise caution both in accepting as valid reports which may be circulated and in voicing condemnation of one side or the other."⁶⁸

Disagreement over the facts and justifications as put forward by Japanese sources aroused suspicion of Japan's motives. Editors of the *Review* saw the incident as an effort by Japan to block the advance of Nationalist troops and assist the warlords in Beijing. They also explained that the incident was created to "shift the Japanese people's attention to the foreign complication" so as to turn attention away from Japan's troubled domestic politics.⁶⁹ By clashing with the Guomindang government, the editors believed that Japan hoped to extract some concession from the Nationalists and win a favorable position in negotiations over its special interests in Shandong and Manchuria as well as over the tariff problem.⁷⁰

While China lacked its own English-language network to present its case, the American treaty-port papers provided a channel for a pro-Chinese voice to the outside world. But the effect was limited. The American treaty-port journals were less popular than the British-operated dailies. Compared to the *North China Daily News*, which sold about eight thousand copies daily in the early 1930s,⁷¹ the *China Weekly Review* had a circulation of only four to five thousand per week.⁷² It was still the Japanese version endorsed by British papers that dominated the public opinion in the treaty ports.

Metropolitan Opinion from London and New York

The views presented in the British treaty-port press were largely echoed by the largest newspaper in London, the *Times*, although the paper was less pronounced in venting anti-Chinese sentiment. As a paper representing British business interests, it supported Japan's justification of its actions in Jinan. It saw the incident as arising from looting by Chinese soldiers.⁷³ The editorial on May 5 gave a detailed account on the start of the clash: "Looting of Japanese property by individuals followed, and when the Japanese battalion stationed in the quarter interfered, 2,000 Nationalist soldiers quartered close at hand came to the rescue of the criminals and opened fire on the Japanese troops."⁷⁴ The editorial continued to commend the Japanese government for treating the incident "with sobriety and sound judgement" and blamed the escalation

---

68. Quote from the *Peking Leader* in the *China Weekly Review*, May 19, 1928, 364.
69. "Japan's Intervention a Blessing in Disguise," *China Weekly Review*, May 19, 1928, 351.
70. Ibid.; "The Japanese Version," *China Weekly Review*, May 12, 1928, 309.
71. Thomas Ming-heng Chao, *The Foreign Press in China* (Shanghai: Institute of Pacific Relations, 1931), 53.
72. Ibid., 76.
73. "Fighting in Shantung," *Times*, May 4, 1928, 16; "Looting at Tsinanfu," *Times*, May 4, 1928, 16; "The Tsinanfu Outrage," *Times*, May 7, 1928, 16.
74. "The Chinese Puzzle," *Times*, May 5, 1928, 13.

of fighting on the Guomindang whose passion had gone "beyond bounds."⁷⁵ The correspondent of the paper also saw the conflict as a repeat of the Nanjing Incident by undisciplined Nationalist soldiers and rejected the explanation offered by Nanjing:

> The Nanking Foreign Minister's version of the origin of the outbreak and his statement of the Japanese troops are not regarded by foreigners here as credible. Barbarous conduct is incompatible with the strict discipline of the Japanese Army. . . . It is a matter of universal comment here that the career of the Nationalist Army has been marked by outrageous conduct in many places, and that it is easy to believe that it has been guilty of further atrocities. In fact, the Nationalist Government, instead of making frank amends for the Nanking outrages, has endeavored to evade responsibility by making unfounded countercharges against foreigners and to instil the bitterest anti-foreign feeling into the Army. It will need a great deal of evidence to the contrary to shake the conviction that the Tsinanfu outbreak is the work of the powerful extremist element which pervades the whole Nationalist movement, and is as active today as it was when Borodin was present in person to lead it.⁷⁶

However, most of the paper's discussion of the incident focused on the event itself, rarely venturing to criticize China's underdevelopment and lawlessness, as did the press in the treaty ports. The paper did not seek to interpret the incident as an outburst of China's antiforeign sentiment by ordinary Chinese soldiers at the front but believed that it was staged by extremist leaders in the Guomindang government who intended to use the Jinan outrage, together with the Nanjing Incident, to exert pressure on foreign powers to make concessions in the revision of the treaties.⁷⁷

Although the American treaty-port papers challenged the Japanese interpretation, their views do not appear to have found their way into newspapers back home. The prominent US newspaper the *New York Times* largely maintained a neutral stance on the Jinan Incident, with slight indications of sympathy for the Japanese cause. Unlike most of the foreign press, which gained its information on the Jinan event from Reuters and Tōhō, the *New York Times* derived its information from the Associated Press news agency and from its own Chinese correspondents, namely Henry F. Misselwitz and Hallett Abend. All these sources cautiously took a balanced view, giving space to accounts from both sides. Yet this newspaper still turned to news from Japanese sources when it was the only news available. After fighting broke out on May 3, for example, the Japanese side of the story dominated coverage of the fighting. Japanese casualties were reported frequently while details of Chinese losses were seldom mentioned.⁷⁸ Chinese soldiers were portrayed as ruthless

---

75. Ibid.
76. "Tsinanfu Outrage," 16.
77. "Japan and China: Severe Fighting in Shandong," *Times*, May 9, 1928, 16.
78. "Many Japanese Killed," *New York Times*, May 4, 1928, 1; "Japanese Charge Atrocities," *New York Times*, May 6, 1928, 1; "Tokyo Plans to Send New Force to China," *New York Times*, May 7, 1928, 4.

killers who slaughtered Japanese civilians[79] and burned and buried Japanese soldiers alive,[80] whereas similar charges against Japan that were popular in China's domestic papers were absent from the foreign press.

The *New York Times* was critical of both Japan and China. Editors of the paper were not convinced by the Japanese explanation that the fighting was started by prearranged looting. They saw Japanese reports on the looting and the subsequent Chinese atrocities simply as an effort to "make a second Nanking Incident out of the affair."[81] Neither did they agree that Japan had staged the fight to block the advance of Nationalist troops, since "Japan has quite enough problems on her hands at the moment to avoid new ones and no war could be as useful to her for some years as a period of peace."[82] The paper saw the incident more as "spontaneous quarrels" arising in times of acute tension[83] and urged a settlement of the conflict as soon as possible. The anger toward Japan expressed in the American treaty-port papers was absent here. Instead, the paper maintained a neutral yet detached attitude, waiting for events to take their own natural course.

Indeed, China was defeated in the foreign propaganda battle over the Jinan Incident. Despite its various attempts to present its case in the press, China's voice was drowned out by Japanese propaganda both in the treaty-port press and metropolitan papers abroad. This failure can be attributed to China's disadvantages in text and context: China's inefficient dissemination of news and its indecisive propaganda policy greatly limited the quantity and quality of its discourse. The negative image of China of being an anti-imperialist and disordered country also diminished the credibility of its news. Yet behind these disadvantages lay the root of the problem—the unsettled political situation. The constant changes of government thwarted China's official and unofficial efforts to establish a national news network. The threat from the northern warlords and China's intricate relations with the imperialist powers deterred the Nanjing regime from formulating decisive foreign propaganda policies. The lack of coordination within the Guomindang government gave rise to inconsistent accounts in the press. Furthermore, its disputes with the Powers over national sovereignty impacted on public opinion in treaty ports and abroad, estranging the very audience to which it sought to appeal. The failure to effectively employ the domestic and foreign media prompted the Guomindang government and unofficial experts to invest in improving China's foreign propaganda institutions. Through trial and error, a national international propaganda institution was in the making.

---

79. "Many Japanese Killed," 1.
80. "Reported Burned to Death," *New York Times*, May 7, 1928, 4.
81. "Japanese Charge Atrocities," 1.
82. "British Warships on Way to China," *New York Times*, May 10, 1928, 3.
83. "New Chinese Troubles," *New York Times*, May 12, 1928, 16.

Figure 5
Sapajou, "The Road Hog," *North China Daily News*, May 7, 1928.

Part II

Growing Pains

3
To Control the Uncontrollable

The Nanjing Government's International Propaganda Policies, 1928–1931

By the end of 1928, the officials in Nanjing keenly felt the importance of constructing an international propaganda apparatus. At the Guomindang's Third National Congress, China's deficient international propaganda network had become the target of general censure. Proposals for the construction of a powerful international propaganda institution were repeatedly raised.[1] The incentive for Nanjing to improve its foreign publicity derived not only from China's painful lessons from the Jinan Incident but also from the dire need of the newly inaugurated government to establish its international prestige. While the underdevelopment of China was excessively exploited as the main pretext for foreign powers to continue their treaty privileges, redressing the negative portrayal of the country became a necessary diplomatic strategy to fend off foreign powers' encroachment on China's national sovereignty.

Despite the sheer necessity of establishing an international propaganda institution, the weakness of the Guomindang government to build such an apparatus was obvious: news transmission was controlled by foreign cable companies and foreign news agencies; Nanjing had no jurisdiction over foreign-operated media organizations within China. Conservative government officials were not ready to forgo the anti-imperialist sentiment and to seek amity with Western powers. This partly led to a lack of coordination and consensus among ministries to deal with unfriendly newspapers and foreign journalists. Indeed, international propaganda was still a novel strategy for the young government. There was no clear vision how it should be institutionalized and who should lead the propaganda work. The fact that international propaganda was incorporated as a subdivision attached to the party propaganda system was an indication of the officials' lack of understanding of the fundamental difference between domestic propaganda and propaganda targeting international audiences. Yet the lack of consensus in the government nevertheless provided opportunities for some officials experienced with treaty and foreign press to seek alternative solutions outside of the party system.

---

1. Guomindang disanci daibiao dahui ti'an, Huiyi jilu, 3.1/3.12; 3.1/14.17, Guomindang Archives (hereafter GA).

The Origin of International Propaganda Policy

On June 1928, the Nationalist forces conquered Beijing. The warlord-based government was dissolved, and Chiang Kai-shek declared his unification of China. By then, the Nanjing government had officially ended the phase of military rule and entered into a political tutelage period. The basic rationale for the tutelage period was to allow the enlightened group (*xian zhi xian jue*), particularly the members of the Guomindang, to educate the unenlightened (*hou zhi hou jue*) and prepare them for constitutionalism.[2] Underneath the principle lay the barely hidden condescension of the Nationalist elites toward the Chinese people, whom they regarded as ignorant of democracy and the modern way of governance. Supervision and training by the political elites were required before democratic rules could be adopted, and the principle of tutelage was therefore introduced to justify the dominance of the Nationalist party ideology in shaping the government's propaganda policies. After World War I, many of the officials in Britain and the United States began to perceive the maintenance of government-endorsed propaganda institutions as a legacy of totalitarian dictatorship.[3] Yet, in China, the very exercise of thought control was accepted as an educational process among the Guomindang officialdom, allowing the people to learn about democratic rules under the party's guidance.

Propaganda became an important part of Guomindang party affairs particularly after the May Forth Movement in 1919, when Sun Yat-sen came to realize the potential power of organized mass publicity.[4] Sun did not see Marxist-Leninist ideology as useful to solve China's problems, yet he still admired the efficiency of the party organization of the Soviet system.[5] As soon as Sun reorganized the Nationalist Party and established his regime in Guangzhou in 1924, a Ministry of Information, modeled on its Soviet counterpart, was installed to supervise the government's propaganda. The ministry emulated not only the architectural design of the Soviet system but also its great ambition for indoctrination and passionate desire for thought control.[6] While in the West propaganda practices focused on persuasion techniques, propaganda systems following the Soviet model intended to penetrate every corner of one's life

---

2. Edmund S. K. Fung, *In Search of Chinese Democracy* (Cambridge: Cambridge University Press, 2000), 30.
3. Philip M. Taylor, *The Projection of Britain: British Overseas Publicity and Propaganda, 1919–1939* (Cambridge: Cambridge University Press, 1981); Andrew Defty, *Britain, America, and Anti-Communist Propaganda, 1945–53: The Information Research Department* (London: Routledge, 2004), 27.
4. John Fitzgerald, *Awakening China: Politics, Culture, and Class in the Nationalist Revolution* (Stanford: Stanford University Press, 1996), 216–17.
5. Wang Qisheng, *Dangyuan, dangquan yu dangzheng, 1924–1949 nian Zhongguo Guomindang de zuzhi xingtai* [Party membership, power and struggle: The organization of Guomindang, 1924–1949] (Shanghai: Shanghai shudian chubanshe, 2003), 13.
6. Peter Kenez, *The Birth of the Propaganda State: Soviet Methods of Mass Mobilization, 1917–1929* (Cambridge: Cambridge University Press, 1985), 4.

with one ideological message.⁷ Guomindang propaganda officials considered the promotion of Sun's Three People's Principles as their priority and were eager to censor information unfriendly to the party. Their primary goal was to attain unity in opinion so as to strengthen the one-party rule.⁸ Unlike most of the other ministries, such as the Ministry of Foreign Affairs and the Ministry of Communications, which were supervised by the Executive Yuan belonging to the state, the propaganda ministry (translated as Ministry of Information by Guomindang officials) was a party organ, directly subject to the control of the Central Executive Committee. This arrangement was indicative of the government's strong emphasis on thought control. An international office was established in this party-dominated propaganda ministry to supervise propaganda targeting foreign audiences.

This party-led international propaganda institution was a distinctive structural design. It should be noted that institutions with similar functions in other countries were mostly affiliated with the state, such as the Ministry of Information in Britain, the Committee on Public Information in the United States and the Center for Foreign Service (Zentralstelle für Auslandsdienst) in Germany. Even the foreign propaganda organ in the Soviet Union, the All-Union Society for Cultural Relations with Foreign Countries, was a state-initiated agency.⁹ In China, international propaganda was previously conducted by people close to diplomatic circles. Although propaganda was mostly organized in an ad hoc manner, without an institutional structure or any form of systematic planning, the practice was usually initiated by the state rather than the party.

It is hard to find documents explaining how the decision was made. Yet the structural design at least reflected an ideological fervor that captured the Guomindang officialdom in the late 1920s and the party members' desire to export revolution the way Soviet propaganda machinery had done. Many Nanjing officials regarded Sun Yat-sen's thought as an all-encompassing theory to guide revolutions around the world. Following Sun's advocacy of the universal commonwealth (*datong*), they believed that the world had been divided into two camps: the imperialist powers and the suppressed colonies. The best way to restore China's national sovereignty was to cooperate with other weak nations and collectively strive for equal rights against the imperialist powers.¹⁰ After Sun's death, commitment to his ideology became a strategy for different political factions to claim authority in the party. The line between genuine belief in Sun's thought and exploiting the political legitimacy it represented

---

7. Mareike Svea Ohlberg, "Creating a Favorable International Public Environment: External Propaganda as a Global Concept with Chinese Characteristics" (PhD dissertation, Heidelberg University, 2013), 53.
8. Fitzgerald, *Awakening China*, 216–17.
9. Katerina Clark, *Moscow, the Fourth Rome: Stalinism, Cosmopolitanism, and the Evolution of Soviet Culture, 1931–1941* (Cambridge, MA, and London: Harvard University Press, 2011), 38.
10. Kuoda guoji xuanchuan de biyao yiji fang'an, Guomindang disanci daibiao dahui ti'an, Huiyi jilu, 3.1/3.12 GA.

was increasingly obscured. The surge of this ideological enthusiasm was the result of a power struggle in domestic politics.

This ideological passion, with a strong anti-imperialist undertone, ran especially high during the early years of the Nanjing decade, when the revolutionary leaders were encouraged by their triumph over the warlords and the reclamation of Hankou and Jiujiang concessions from the British Empire in 1927. After Chiang Kai-shek militarily unified China, anti-imperialism continued to be the dominant discourse. Chiang strongly pushed for the revision of unequal treaties, hoping the proactive response to these international disputes would both cater to anti-imperial public sentiments domestically and make the presence of the new government felt across the world.[11] This strong claim to the Guomindang's ideological line at this particular moment reflected the top leaders' sense of insecurity, despite their military edge over other warlord factions.

The desire for ideology dissemination also revealed the frustration of the Chinese elite in adapting to the new world order. Despite China's military and economic weakness, many of the elites believed that the power of China derived from its enduring culture. They were reluctant to give up the traditional Chinese world view, which positioned China as the center of civilization, and to accept the new order based on nation-states and structured by racial hierarchies and military strength. They were particularly disturbed to be described as "uncivilized," "savage," or "barbaric," words the Chinese had long used to define other ethnical groups or non-Chinese neighbors.[12] The sheer imbalance between China's self-esteem and disrespect from foreigners strongly propelled Nationalist leaders to spread Sun's thought globally, so as to make China's culture and political stance understood by the world. A proposal from a Nanjing official cogently reflected the national pride generally held among the Nationalists:

> China is a country with thousands of years of civilization and history, a huge population, a vast territory and rich natural resources. All of them are incomparable heritage for this brilliant nation and for the world. Yet the country is now unfairly treated and being exploited by the imperialist powers.... China needs to make its cause known to the world. It is the only way for this nation to complete its revolution and thus contribute to the development of the world.[13]

---

11. Chiang's speech delivered on December 10, 1928, "Beifa chenggong hou zui jinyao de gongzuo" [The most important tasks after the Northern Expedition], in Chiang Kai-shek, *Zongtong Jianggong sixiang yanlun zongji* [Chiang Kai-shek's thought and speeches] (Taipei: Zhongguo Guomindang zhongyang weiyuanhui dangshi weiyuanhui, 1985), 332.
12. Wang Ermin, *Wan Qing zhengzhi sixiang shi lun* [The political thought of the late Qing period] (Taipei: Xuesheng shuju, 1969), 183.
13. Kuoda guoji xuanchuan, Guomindang disanci daibiao dahui mishuchu, Huiyi jilu, March 21, 1929, 3.1/14.17, GA.

Attaching the international propaganda office to the party was also likely the result of a power struggle at the center. After all, most of the existing propaganda sources were controlled by Guomindang leftists rather than Chiang Kai-shek's clique. Given the leftists' entrenched influence in the party, it was not surprising to see an international propaganda office established within their domain. However, such a design, which might have fit the political situation of the late 1920s, severely constrained Guomindang's propaganda practices in the following decades. And its long-lasting impact on later propaganda structures in the People's Republic of China was certainly beyond what the initial planners were able to envision.[14]

The International Propaganda Institution and Legal Regulations on the Press

In 1928, officials of the Ministry of Information established the International Division (Guoji ke) to supervise China's international propaganda. The division thus became an extension of the domestic propaganda system. It consisted of an editing and a translation office. The former was responsible for devising international propaganda plans and compiling propaganda materials. The latter served as a conduit to connect the party with the outside world, using a two-pronged approach: it collected and translated foreign discussions on the Guomindang governance for the reference of party members, and it translated the party's ideology and important policies into foreign languages for distribution abroad.[15]

This design failed to acknowledge the different natures of domestic and foreign propaganda. While the former for the Guomindang was about forming consensus and exercising a top-down manner of thought control, the latter concerned persuasion of audiences of foreign countries, most of whom were committed to liberal values. Authority of information constituted the power of the domestic propaganda system, yet, for its international counterpart, credibility of sources was the key for attracting attention and support.

Confined by structural design, the international propaganda office was operated mostly by domestic propagandists whose vision and strategy did not allow them to break the shackles of traditional party propaganda: promoting ideology through sermonizing and repetition. They probably had no idea that the more Sun's thought was repeated, the less emotional power they contained. Through repeated, mundane

---

14. See Mareike Ohlberg's analysis of the party-dominated foreign propaganda system in China, in "Creating a Favorable International Public Environment."
15. "Zhongyang xuanchuanbu zuzhi tiaoli" [Organization of the Ministry of Information], in *Zhongguo di'er lishi dang'anguan, Zhongguo Guomindang zhongyang zhixing weiyuanhui changwu weiyuanhui huiyilu* [Minutes of the Standing Committee of the Guomindang Central Executive Committee] (hereafter MSCGCEC) (Guilin: Guangxi shifan taxue chubanshe, 2000), 10:201–2.

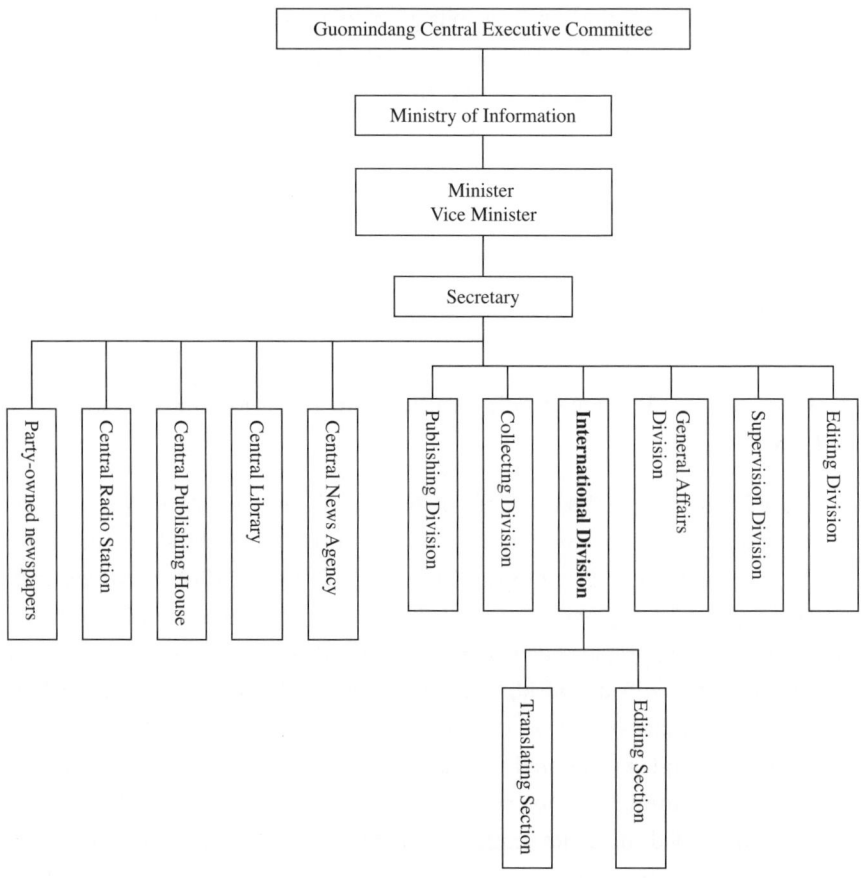

Diagram 1
The structure of the Guomindang Ministry of Information, 1929.
Source: MSCGCEC, 10:204.

reference to ideological discourses, sometimes out of the necessity to follow political formality, the passion initially carried by this rhetoric was drained dry. The first years of the Nanjing decade had seen a steady growth of the translation and publication of the doctrines of the Guomindang, such as Sun Yat-sen's Three People's Principles and articles on Sun's thought.[16] Establishing the Nanjing government's authority was another important task of the international propaganda office. Two dominant themes ran through the propaganda materials: unification and construction. Publications endorsed by the government kept assuring the foreign public that China was a unified nation under the rule of the Nationalist Party, that regional warlords had been eliminated, and that the government led by Chiang Kai-shek enjoyed

---

16. Zhongguo di'er lishi dang'an guan, *Zhongyang dangwu yuekan* [Monthly of the Guomindang affairs] (Nanjing: Nanjing chubanshe, 1994), vol. 20 (February 1930), 81; Sun Yat-sen, *San Min Chu-I*; "San Min Chu I and the Age of Great Harmony," *China Critic*, May 23, 1929, 408.

absolute control over the country.¹⁷ Propagandists were anxious to affirm faith in the Nanjing government, promoting the idea that the government was not only able to dismantle the deeply flawed warlordism but also capable of building a new modern nation.¹⁸

However, neither the party's ideology nor the claims of the new government appealed to the foreign public. Impediments came both from suspicion of the propaganda motives and the contrast between propaganda materials and reality. Foreigners were highly sensitive to government- or party-related publications. The abuse of propaganda during World War I had tainted the term with a sinister flavor. Propaganda as a concept began to be linked with partial information, manipulation of thoughts, and political deception. It implied a calculated intent on the part of the propagandists.¹⁹ Publications related to propaganda were firmly resisted by the Anglo-American public. The dissemination of the Guomindang's ideology directly fell into the category of "official" propaganda and thus enjoyed little credibility among foreign audiences. Foreign journals rarely discussed Sun's thought or republished articles on such a topic from Chinese sources. Among the few articles commenting on Sun's thesis, an air of disdain could easily be detected. The *Times* in London, for example, described the Three People's Principles as Sun's "curious vade-mecum of government" and perceived it as nothing more than an "amalgam of miscellaneous Western ideas with Chinese preconceptions."²⁰

The most damaging blow to the Nanjing government's propaganda system was that reality did not live up to the claims of the party. Despite the party's high-sounding resolution to achieve democracy, the newly inaugurated Nanjing government failed to follow democratic principles. The government was characterized by a one-party dictatorship. The Organic Law, which set out the government's structure, stipulated that the Nationalist Party was the highest organ of power and that the government served to implement policies made by party institutions. In practice, as a result of the tradition of interlocking personnel, party institutions greatly overlapped with those of the government sectors. The party was essentially the state.²¹ The division of the five powers within the government, which was originally designed to avert dictatorship, not only failed to bring about a more democratic leadership but also made the already clumsy bureaucracies even more cumbersome, creating a high potential for despotism and corruption.

Furthermore, the unification of China was only nominal. The Nanjing government was challenged by a serious rebellion in 1930. Threats primarily came from

---

17. Tsung-hsi Ch'en, *General Chiang Kai-shek: The Builder of New China* (Shanghai: Commercial Press, 1929).
18. Min-ch'ien T. Z. Tyau, *Two Years of Nationalist China* (Shanghai: Kelly and Walsh, 1930).
19. Taylor, *Projection of Britain*, 2–5.
20. "Dawn in China?" *Times*, October 12, 1928, 17.
21. James Claude Thomson, *While China Faced West: American Reformers in Nationalist China, 1928–1937* (Cambridge, MA: Harvard University Press, 1969), 9.

Feng Yuxiang, Yan Xishan, and Li Zongren, who belonged to different factions but drew together in their common opposition to Chiang Kai-shek. Although Chiang crushed the rebellion with the help of Zhang Xueliang in October 1930, the underlying threat to Chiang's rule and the actual revival of the civil war severely tarnished the image of stability and unification that Nanjing had strived to present to the world.[22] Politicians who lost power in their struggle with Chiang or disagreed with Chiang's governance allied to protest his rule. These malcontents, led by Wang Jingwei, ranged from the former Wuhan leftists to the rightist Western Hills faction.[23] Threats also came from local insurgents in perpetual revolt against authority and from the Communists.[24]

Fully aware of the possible negative impact of the status quo on their propaganda efforts, Nanjing officials were intent to suppress information or opinions that were unfavorable to the government. Its first order, the Rules for Censorship on Publications, was issued as early as January 10, 1929. The rules specified that any publication should respect Sun Yat-sen's thought and follow the doctrines, policies, and decisions of the Guomindang. Publications that propagated communism, distributed rumors, fomented dissension, or opposed the Guomindang would be considered "reactionary" and punished by the government.[25]

After laying out what should be censored, the party began to work on how to conduct the actual censorship. In August 1929, the Central Executive Committee of the party passed the Methods of Postal Censorship in Key Cities, requiring the regional municipal governments to install censorship offices and withhold public or personal mail with content that harmed the cause of the party.[26] A month later, on September 23, the party furthered its control through another order, the Methods of Newspaper Registration, which demanded that all newspapers and news agencies register with regional propaganda agencies. Certificates for publication could be denied to any newspaper that "contained reactionary information" or was "liable to undermine social security."[27] Newspapers that failed to respond to the registration order would be banned from postal delivery by the Ministry of Information. Having

---

22. Ironically, Zhang's intervention on behalf of the Nanjing government in 1930 increased Chiang's mistrust of him. See Rana Mitter, *The Manchurian Myth: Nationalism, Resistance, and Collaboration in Modern China* (Berkeley: University of California Press, 2000), 56–57.
23. The West Hills faction (1925–1927) led by Lin Sen favored expulsion of Communists from the Guomindang. See C. Martin Wilbur, *The Nationalist Revolution in China, 1923–1928* (Cambridge: Cambridge University Press, 1983): 31–33.
24. Akira Iriye, *After Imperialism: The Search for a New Order in the Far East, 1921–1931* (Cambridge, MA: Harvard University Press, 1965), 269.
25. Zhongguo di'er lishi dang'anguan, *Zhonghua Minguo shi dang'an ziliao huibian* [Collections of historical records of the Republic of China], vol. 5, no. 1 Culture (1) (Nanjing: Jiangsu guji chubanshe, 1994), 74–75.
26. "Quanguo zhongyao dushi youjian jiancha banfa," in MSCGCEC, 9:207–8.
27. "Chuban tiaoli yuanze," in Zhongguo di'er lishi dang'anguan, *Zhonghua Minguo shi dang'an ziliao huibian*, vol. 5, no. 1, Culture (1), 76–77.

granted the certificate for publication to a periodical, the ministry still retained the authority to withdraw its rights to publish, should it engage in antiparty propaganda.[28]

The Publication Law, enacted in 1930, was the legal backbone of the Nanjing government's control of the press. The law primarily inherited principles of the previous orders on censorship and registration. It introduced a registration system, requiring popular newspapers to register with the Ministry of the Interior and party-related papers to register with the Ministry of Information. Advised by Dai Jitao and Chen Lifu, the law extended the scope of "harmful speech" by forbidding any information that *intended* to undermine the Three People's Principles, the Guomindang, the government, or the interests of the nation.[29] It thereby transformed the previous content-based censorship into a restriction of subversive intentions. Since evaluation of intention was a highly subjective matter and the discretion to assess the intention of a journal was solely held by the party, the new law, in fact, expanded the party's authority to control the flow of information.

Battling with Extraterritoriality

Foreign-operated news agencies and newspapers in the treaty ports were one of the main obstacles for the Nanjing government to effectively control outgoing information. These sources, which tended to view Chinese issues from a parochial perspective, fell beyond Nanjing's jurisdiction. The underdevelopment, disorder, and instability of China were ongoing themes for their reports. Knowing that foreign papers were the most trusted sources of information on Chinese issues among overseas audiences, Nanjing leaders saw the foreign-operated news organizations as the very producers of negative portrayals of China and instigations of anti-Chinese sentiments.[30] Regulating the foreign-operated media in China, therefore, became a pressing task.

In February 1930, the Guomindang government passed a Registration Order for the Foreign Press, attempting to place foreign papers under Chinese control.[31] Yet the attempt was not successful, because of the existence of extraterritoriality, which stipulated that foreigners were exempted from the jurisdiction of China but were bound by the laws of their home countries. The system nullified any Chinese efforts to control foreign-registered or foreign-owned papers. To avoid Nanjing's censorship, many Chinese editors tried to obtain extraterritorial protection by registering their papers abroad and operating them in foreign concessions. As a result, the dissent that the government was eager to suppress was commonly found in the treaty-port

---

28. "Ribao dengji banfa," in Zhongguo di'er lishi dang'anguan, *Zhonghua Minguo shi dang'an ziliao huibian*, vol. 5, no. 1, Culture (1), 77.
29. "Chuban fa," in Zhongguo di'er lishi dang'anguan, *Zhonghua Minguo shi dang'an ziliao huibian*, vol. 5, no. 1, Culture (1), 78–84.
30. "Waibao dengji banfa," *Zhongyang dangwu yuekan*, vol. 19, February 1930.
31. Ibid.

press and was transmitted widely through the circulation of those papers beyond China's regional and national borders. Nanjing understood that its censorship efforts would be doomed to failure if papers with extraterritorial protection were left unregulated. To tighten the control, its primary yet challenging task was to abolish extraterritorial rights.

Extraterritoriality was imposed upon China from the mid-nineteenth century. Initially, through the General Regulation of Trade, which was incorporated into the Treaty of the Bogue in 1843, the British managed to secure the provisions that British subjects involved in criminal cases in China were to be tried according to British law. In 1844, the United States quickly took advantage of these inroads into the Manchu polity and signed the Treaty of Wanghia with the Qing government, in their case enlarging the provision to include civil cases. They also secured a "most favored nation" clause, which guaranteed that US nationals would automatically become recipients of any corresponding rights or privileges thenceforward granted to other foreigners by the Chinese. Over the years, other Powers obtained the same extraterritorial rights via various treaties and extended the scope of extraterritoriality. These extraterritorial terms underpinned the whole structure of foreign privilege in China.[32]

Chinese perception of extraterritoriality underwent a marked change over the years. When Chinese negotiators first granted extraterritorial rights to foreigners, they considered extraterritoriality as a temporary expedient to ease the legal difference between China and the Powers. They saw the treaty system as a way of fitting Westerners into the Chinese Empire by managing their own affairs, troubling the Qing government as little as possible.[33] As Pär Cassel pointed out, the origin of extraterritoriality was compatible with the legal pluralism tradition of the Qing dynasty.[34] Yet with the growing expansion of treaty rights of the foreign powers as well as the awareness of national sovereignty among the Chinese people, some Chinese elites began to view treaty rights as a foreign encroachment. Anti-Qing parties also constantly used the granting of extraterritoriality to attack the Qing's inability to deal with foreigners. Such rhetoric found a large audience among the general public who were eager to see the end of the Qing's rule. After the fall of the Qing empire, the Nationalist Party continued to oppose the unequal treaty system and blame foreign invasion for the decline of China in modern times. Thus, by the end of 1928, extraterritoriality had become the most acute issue for the Nanjing government. Socially,

---

32. Wesley R. Fishel, *The End of Extraterritoriality in China* (Berkeley: University of California Press, 1952), 2–7.
33. Nicholas Rowland Clifford, *Spoilt Children of Empire: Westerners in Shanghai and the Chinese Revolution of the 1920s* (Hanover: Middlebury College Press, 1991), 18; John K. Fairbank, "System in the Chinese World Order," in *The Chinese World Order: Traditional China's Foreign Relations*, ed. John K. Fairbank (Cambridge, MA: Harvard University Press, 1968), 257–75.
34. Pär Cassel, *Grounds of Judgment: Extraterritoriality and Imperial Power in Nineteenth-Century China and Japan* (New York: Oxford University Press, 2012).

the existence of extraterritoriality challenged the national pride of the Chinese people, reminding them of the downfall of their nation and the loss of national sovereignty. Politically, extraterritoriality not only damaged the prestige of the Nanjing government but also undermined its authority: foreign concessions often became the hiding place for refugees and rebels, making it difficult for the government to deal with political dissidents.

The Nanjing government began negotiating a revision of the treaties immediately after it conquered Beijing. Abolition of extraterritoriality was the focal part of the negotiations. Nanjing believed that extraterritoriality in China was an outdated system that severely violated Chinese sovereignty.[35] Instead of facilitating justice, it only complicated the existing jurisdiction standard and incurred antiforeign sentiments that could fuel extreme acts threatening foreign life and properties. Furthermore, China's improved legal system after the establishment of the Nanjing government rendered the so-called foreign tutelage on China's jurisdiction construction unnecessary.[36]

The disputes between foreign powers and Nanjing, however, did not revolve so much around whether to abolish extraterritoriality—foreign powers had unanimously agreed to relinquish their extraterritoriality over time. Disputes were more concerned with how to abolish it. In 1929, while China was eager to terminate it immediately, foreign powers led by Britain preferred a "gradual and progressive" approach, believing a prolonged process was most practical, given China's incompetent legal system and domestic chaos.[37] They expressed doubts about the independence of China's judicial system, considering the system as being controlled by the Nationalist Party rather than a civil government.[38] They also argued that it was not proper to withdraw protection of foreign nationals before Nanjing could achieve political stability across the country.[39]

China's international propaganda, which was devoted to boosting Nanjing's reputation and authority, was an important diplomatic strategy to refute the Powers' justification of their exterritorial privileges. Instead of passively waiting for the progress of treaty revisions, Nanjing officials proactively pushed the boundary of press control. They used sovereign rights already in their hands to make inroads into the extraterritorial privileges of the foreign papers. Their primary weapons were postal control and the rights of deportation.

35. "China's Note on Extraterritoriality," *China Critic*, May 9, 1929; "Chinese Opinion on the Abolition of Extrality," *China Critic*, July 25, 1929.
36. Fishel, *End of Extraterritoriality in China*, 152; also see the summary of the negotiation on extraterritoriality in "Abolition of Extraterritoriality," *China Critic*, May 2, 1929; "Chinese Opinion on the Abolition of Extrality."
37. Iriye, *After Imperialism*, 256; Fishel, *End of Extraterritoriality in China*, 150.
38. See Dr. Ho Shih-tsung's summary of the Powers' position on treaty negotiations, first published in the *Shanghai Times*, April 7, 1929, quoted in "Foreign Opinions in the Abolition of Extrality," *China Critic*, July 18, 1929.
39. Fishel, *End of Extraterritoriality in China*, 169–70.

Postal Ban

Nanjing's censorship system was not completely powerless in regulating the foreign-operated press. Although it had no legal rights to conduct prior censorship or penalize disobedient papers the way it did the domestic press, it was still able to limit the distribution of the treaty-port papers with the sovereign power it did possess—postal control. Despite political disturbances, governments of different levels since 1896 had spent relentless efforts building a nationwide postal network. The postal system, which reached every town and village of the country, as Lane J. Harris argued, was essential to the protection of China's territory integrity and administrative independence.[40] The Chinese government partially restored postal rights during the Washington Conference, when the Powers agreed to withdraw control over postal offices by the end of 1922, under the condition that they maintain operation of post offices in treaty ports and the position of codirector general of the postal system continued to be held by a foreigner.[41] After the fall of the Beijing government following the Northern Expedition, the Nationalist government moved the headquarters of the postal system and reduced the authority of Henri Picard-Destelan, the then–codirector general. With the resignation of Destelan in February 1929, the Nanjing government reclaimed its postal control outside of the treaty ports.[42]

The Nanjing government's first postal ban on the English-language press was imposed on an American-owned newspaper in Tianjin, the *North China Star*. On February 5, 1929, the Ministry of Communications withdrew postal services from the paper because of an article written by C. D. Bess of the United Press in which he predicted that serious political trouble was inevitable between the Northern generals and Nanjing in the spring of 1929.[43] The *Star* was registered at the American consulate general, with three-fifths of its capital stock belonging to Charles J. Fox, a well-known lawyer. Ironically, the *Star* was regarded by the British press as "notoriously pro-Guomindang."[44] The ban by the very government it sympathized with not only left the editors of the paper in shock but also took C. T. Wang, the then Chinese minister of foreign affairs, by surprise.

---

40. Lane Jeremy Harris, "The Post Office and State Formation in Modern China, 1896–1949" (PhD dissertation, University of Illinois, 2012).
41. See quote from *Shen bao*, December 1, 1921, in Huang Jianhui, "*Shen bao* jiuwen jiedu 47: Huashengdun huiyi yu chefei geguo zai Hua youju" [News in *Shen bao*: Washington Conference and the abolition of foreign post offices in China], *Shanghai jiyou* [Shanghai philately] 11 (2011): 42.
42. Jia Xiutang, "Nanjing guomin zhengfu wei shouhui youzheng guanli quan suozuo de nuli" [The Nanjing government's efforts to restore postal control], *Lanzhou xuekan* [Journal of Lanzhou], no. 10 (2009): 203–5.
43. MacMurray to the Secretary of State, February 13, 1929, Papers Relating to the Foreign Relations of the United States (hereafter PRFRUS), 1929, vol. 2, 754; *China Weekly Review*, February 16, 1929, 476; March 16, 1929, 85.
44. See a pamphlet edited by the *North China Daily News and Herald*, *China's Attempt to Muzzle the Foreign Press*, May 20, 1929, 9.

Apparently, the postal ban was not a coordinated decision within the government. The Central Executive Committee issued the order without prior consultation with the Ministry of Foreign Affairs or any other appropriate authorities.[45] After learning about the ban, C. T. Wang worried that it would discourage C. J. Fox, a long-term Nationalist sympathizer, from supporting China's cause and that C. J. Fox's brother Albert W. Fox, a well-known journalist in Washington, might publicize the case to the US public. Despite Wang's desire to lift the ban, the leaders in the Central Executive Committee were unwilling to cooperate. Only after Fox officially expressed regret for publishing the article, as the committee had demanded, was the ban finally lifted.[46]

If the ban on the *Star* only caused minor friction between the Nanjing government and a foreign-operated paper, the withdrawal of the postal service of the *North China Daily News* instigated an intense battle. The case not only reflected the long-harbored animosity between the Chinese government and the British treaty-port paper but also illuminated the underlying tensions among papers of different nationalities in Shanghai and the disagreement between British diplomats and British treaty-port journalists.

As mentioned in Chapter 1, the British-operated *Daily News* was commonly regarded as the official organ of the Shanghai Municipal Council. The paper was known for its imperialist tone, treating China the way a mother country would treat a rebellious colony.[47] It was this condescending manner that drained the Guomindang government's patience. On April 18, the Standing Committee of the Central Executive Yuan, the highest administrative body of the Nanjing government, resolved to suspend the mail privilege to the *North China Daily News* and ordered the deportation of George E. Sokolsky, a distinguished contributor to the paper. The resolution was introduced by Ye Chucang, head of the Ministry of Information. Ye severely criticized the *North China Daily News*' anti-Chinese tone and blamed the paper for having "repeatedly and maliciously attacked the Guomindang government and the Guomindang, hoping to create dissension within ranks of the Guomindang and to discredit China in the eyes of the world."[48] Ye further explained that the postal ban was the last resort in response to the inaction of the British consulate general to the repeated protests of China's Ministry of Foreign Affairs against the paper's misreporting of facts.[49] To enforce the ban, the government ordered Customs to cooperate in

---

45. MacMurray to the Secretary of State, March 12, 1929, PRFRUS, 1929, vol. 2, 757–58.
46. Thomas Ming-heng Chao, *The Foreign Press in China* (Shanghai: Institute of Pacific Relations, 1931), 73.
47. "Overlooking the Point in the NCDN Case," *China Monthly Review* 48 (1929): 527.
48. "Threat against NCDN," *North China Daily News*, April 19, 1929, 14; "Nanjing Threatens British Paper Ban," *New York Times*, April 21, 1929, 5.
49. *China Weekly Review*, April 27, 1929, 352. "Nanking Threatens British Paper Ban," *New York Times*, April 21, 1929, 5.

stopping the circulation of the paper overseas and forbade government organizations and officials to advertise in, subscribe to, or read the paper.⁵⁰

The postal ban on the *Daily News* was a double-edged sword for Nanjing. While the underdevelopment of China was the common pretext for Western powers to strengthen extraterritorial protection for their nationals, the case was exploited by the British papers as evidence of the Nanjing government's maladministration. Not being informed of the reason for the ban, the paper openly interpreted it as the government's response to its editorial article "Freedom of the Press," in which the paper displayed contempt for the Nanjing government's warning to foreign newspapers.⁵¹ By explaining the ban with a single and insignificant editorial article, the paper tended to downplay its traditional anti-Guomindang stance while accentuating the government's suppression of expression.⁵² The paper also sought to amplify the implication of the case by warning all foreign firms that their fate was "wholly dependent on the whims and vagaries of the gentlemen at present in power in Nanjing"⁵³ and that the Nanjing government, "which knows little of law," could adopt the same ban on their mail, deny their rights to pass anything through customs, and hence ruin their business ultimately.⁵⁴ In response to Nanjing's request for the change of editorial policy, O. M. Green, the chief editor of the *Daily News*, replied with an outright denial, saying that the "policy for over three-quarters of a century, where it touched Chinese questions, has always been framed with a view to the best interests of the Chinese people."⁵⁵

Apart from protesting Nanjing's ban in its own editorials, the *Daily News* allied with other die-hard British papers in a joint criticism of Nanjing's action. Its closest ally was the *Peking and Tientsin Times*, edited by Henry George Wandesforde Woodhead, a trenchant defender of British treaty rights in China. The *Tientsin Times* commented that the *Daily News*' case was a "flagrant violation of treaty rights" by the Nanjing government and complained that the "inexperienced and intolerant politicians" in Nanjing only revealed their despotism and corruption by suppressing the press.⁵⁶

Although the *North China Daily News* presented itself as a defender of the freedom of speech for all treaty-port papers, its stance hardly received sympathy from the American-run *China Weekly Review*, its long-term competitor. The *Review* applauded

---

50. "Zhongguo Guomindang zhongyang zhixing weiyuanhui disanci changwu huiyi jilu," [Minutes of the third conference of the Standing Committee of the Guomindang Central Executive Committee], April 18, 1929, in MSCGCEC, 8:29–30; "Threat against NCDN," 14; "Ban on North China Daily News," *China Critic*, May 9, 1929, 366.
51. *China's Attempt to Muzzle the Foreign Press*, 9, 15–16.
52. "Nanking and the N.-C. Daily News," *North China Daily News*, May 6, 1929, 6.
53. *China's Attempt to Muzzle the Foreign Press*, 12.
54. Ibid.
55. Editorial by O. M. Green in the *North China Daily News*, June 7, 1929, quoted in "Has the NCDN Promised to be Good?," *China Weekly Review*, June 15, 1929, 98.
56. "Freedom of the Press," *Peking and Tientsin Times*, April 20, 1929.

Nanjing's action, believing that the editorial line of the *Daily News* would be "labelled seditious in any sovereign country"[57] and that no country would put up for a minute with the constant attacks and pin-pricking attitude of this foreign newspaper.[58] It also criticized the *Daily News*' conceited attitude in reporting Chinese issues, warning that foreign journalists would invite punishment if they continued to dictate to the Chinese how they should manage their country.[59]

The *China Weekly Review* saw the postal ban as the government's effort to break up a secret international propaganda organization known as the "Shanghai Committee." According to the *Review*, the committee had been distributing confidential pamphlets all over the world, "paint[ing] conditions in China in the blackest light possible" so as to hamper China's treaty revision process.[60] For many years, the *Daily News* had been nominally in charge of the committee. Yet the *Review*'s observation remained open to debate. The so-called secret propaganda organization was an unofficial publicity organization established by the Constitutional Defence League in 1925. It later transformed into the Shanghai Publicity Bureau, with a goal to disseminate propaganda that could strengthen the rule of the Shanghai Municipal Council and counter the efforts of the Comintern. Its aim was never fixed on being "anti-Guomindang," although its pro-SMC publication on treaty revision and the abolition of extraterritoriality created such an impression. With the decline of the Comintern in late 1927, the organization shifted its target from countering communist propaganda to altering the "die-hard" image of the British communities in China.[61] Instead of collaborating with the "die-hard" *North China Daily News*, the organization aimed to remedy the negative image created by the British paper.

The *China Critic*, an English-language paper operated by independent Chinese intellectuals, also lent its support to the Nanjing government's postal ban. Indeed, the *Critic*'s liberal tradition had its limit: while appealing for free expression in the domestic press, it believed that the government was entitled to suppress any foreign paper that was prejudiced in its coverage of Chinese issues. Here, nationalism transcended liberalism and became the primary criterion to assess the position of the foreign press. The *Critic* not only criticized the *Daily News*' inveterate misinterpretation of China to audiences abroad but also took the opportunity to criticize the "Shanghai mind" syndrome popular among British journalists.[62]

---

57. "Overlooking the Point in the NCDN case," *China Weekly Review*, May 25, 1929, 527.
58. "The Kuomintang Action against Mr. Sokolsky and the North-China Daily News," *China Weekly Review*, April 27, 1929, 352–53.
59. "Has the NCDN Promised to be Good?" 98.
60. "Overlooking the Point in the NCDN Case," 527–28.
61. Robert Bickers, "Changing Shanghai's 'Mind': Publicity, Reform and British in Shanghai, 1928–1931," a lecture given at a meeting of the China Society on March 20, 1991, 16–18.
62. "What Ails the Press of Shanghai?" *China Critic*, March 6, 1929, 121–22.

The "Shanghai mind" was a term coined by Arthur Ransome in his article published in the *Manchester Guardian* in May 1927. It referred to the British rigid adherence to their imperialistic privilege in treaty ports, even though the privilege was no longer valid. The harm of the Shanghai mind manifested itself fully in issues related to the treaty revision process. The British government's attempts to compromise were constantly undermined by the treaty-port papers' intransigency. Editors of the *Critic*, who observed the disunity, questioned "whether the Labor Government represents the British people or the British press [in Shanghai] is really representative of them,"[63] indicating that "the government of Shanghai does not hold itself responsible to the diplomats or the Powers they represent."[64] The paper warned that British trade with China, which was based on mutual goodwill, could be affected by Shanghai-minded propaganda if the die-hard papers continued to pursue their hostile stance.[65] By exposing the difference between the die-hard views and the British diplomatic attitude, the *Critic* aimed to isolate the *Daily News* and urge the British Foreign Office to check the paper's anti-Nanjing stance.

The *Daily News*' independent line was a constant problem for the British Foreign Office. Miles Lampson, British minister to China between 1926 and 1933, had repeatedly instructed the treaty-port community to act with "patience and self-sacrifice" and let the Chinese determine their own fate. Yet O. M. Green and Rodney Gilbert, who edited the paper in the late 1920s, continued to act in their own way.[66] Proud of their independence, they considered themselves as the only people who dared to "tell the unflattering truth about China to a world hypnotized by the flummery of diplomats and politicians in Peking, Whitehall, and Washington and by the deceptive dreams of missionaries and uplifters who saw a bright future amidst the chaos of China's unending civil wars."[67] Such an attitude raised awareness both in London and Shanghai. While the American press in China aided Washington's policy, complained Colonel L'Estrange Malone, a visiting Labor Member of Parliament, the British press hindered London's.[68] Many of the social workers in Shanghai also admitted that O. M. Green was "quite frankly a serious menace to British interest in this country."[69] "If anyone would murder Green," wrote Warren Swire, a distinguished British merchant in Shanghai, "I would gladly pay for his defense and the education of his orphans."[70] After Nanjing banned the *Daily News* from postal delivery, Green

---

63. "British Friendship and Propaganda," *China Critic*, December 11, 1930, 1181–82.
64. "Shanghai Mind Reveals Itself," *China Critic*, April 24, 1929, 394.
65. "British Friendship and Propaganda," *China Critic*, December 11, 1930, 1181–82.
66. F4425/10/10 contained the statement, quoted in Clifford, *Spoilt Children of Empire*, 175.
67. Ibid., 66.
68. "The British and the American Press in China," *China Weekly Review*, November 20, 1926, 317.
69. F2942/194/10 (1925) undated letter from a Miss Arnold, quoted in Clifford, *Spoilt Children of Empire*, 66.
70. Quoted in Robert Bickers, *Britain in China: Community Culture and Colonialism, 1900–1949* (Manchester: Manchester University Press, 1999), 151.

was advised by the consul general to tone things down. Yet he refused to yield to the British metropolitan authority and believed that his criticism of the Chinese government was serving the interest of the Chinese public "whose own opinions were stifled by the rigorous control of the press."[71] This intransigence eventually led to the end of his editorship with the paper. In 1930, Lampson used all his influence to replace Green with Edwin Howard, *Times* correspondent in India.[72] The editorial standpoint of the paper changed noticeably from this point on. Fault-finding criticism of Nanjing ceased, and a generally more objective approach became the norm of the paper in the 1930s.[73]

Deporting Foreign Journalists

Another strategy of the Nanjing government to control the English-language press was to deport unfriendly foreign journalists. Again, hindered by extraterritoriality, the government did not possess the legal power to expel a foreigner. Any successful deportation would require cooperation from foreign legations. Yet the journalists who were considered threats by Nanjing officials were valuable sources of information for foreign diplomats. This occasionally resulted in a lack of cooperation or even protest from foreign legations as a response to Nanjing's deportation orders. Deportation therefore frequently ended in empty demands or embarrassing compromises from China.

The deportation of Hallett Abend is a vivid example. On June 17, 1929, C. T. Wang sent a note to John Van Antwerp MacMurray, US minister to China, demanding Abend be deported from China. Wang complained that Abend's news dispatches had consistently been biased and unfair to the Guomindang government and that his libelous publications were likely to harm Sino-American relations or mislead overseas US citizens. Wang particularly complained about two of Abend's dispatches: one concerning an attack on Chiang Kai-shek's wife Soong May-ling (a.k.a. Madam Chiang), the other revealing Feng Yuxiang and Zhang Xueliang's denunciation of the Nanjing leaders.[74] Meanwhile, the Nanjing government tried to cut his connection with the US press by denying to offer him telegraph and cable services and warning other correspondents from forwarding his dispatches. To isolate Abend socially, the Nanjing Ministry of Foreign Affairs forbade officials to receive or visit him.[75]

71. FO 371/13950 [F2545/2016/10], decode dispatch from Sir. M. Lampson, April 24, 1929, FOFC.
72. Bickers, *Britain in China*, 151.
73. Richard W. Rigby, "Sapajou," *East Asian History*, nos. 17/18 (June/December 1999): 136; Robert Bickers, "Shanghailanders: The Formation and Identity of the British Settler Community in Shanghai," *Past and Present* (1998): 159.
74. C. T. Wang to MacMurray, June 17, 1929, *PRFRUS*, 1929, vol. 2, 763–64.
75. "Nanking in Drive on Correspondents," *New York Times*, July 9, 1929, 6.

Abend arrived in China in 1926. Under George E. Sokolsky's advice and introduction, he went to Guangzhou, then the headquarters of the Guomindang, and worked for the local Chinese-owned English-language newspaper, the *Canton Gazette*. Years of frequent communication with the Guomindang's top leaders, including T. V. Soong and Eugene Chen, led Abend to develop a critical view of Chinese domestic politics. His Guangzhou days also left him with a deep impression of the lawlessness and rule of force in China. Abend later joined the American-operated paper, the *Peking Leader* and concurrently served as a foreign correspondent for the *New York Times* in Beijing. Discovery of the warlord's subsidy for the *Leader* reinforced his understanding of backdoor politics in China. His observation of China's deeper flaws in society and politics was fully evident in his dispatches to the *New York Times*. These reports stood in sharp contrast to Chiang's claim that China had restored order after 1928.

The *New York Times* had undergone a major reorganization of its correspondents in China in the mid-1920s, which resulted in a different political stance. Abend was appointed in this context. For a considerable period prior to the occupation of the Yangtze valley by the Nationalists, the *New York Times* employed Thomas F. Millard, former editor of the *Millard's Review / China Weekly Review*, as its China correspondent. Millard had adopted a sympathetic attitude toward the Chinese revolution and attempted to contextualize Chinese revolts in terms of China's long-term struggle for nationalism and independence. Yet a few weeks before Shanghai was captured by Guomindang forces in 1927, the *New York Times* suddenly replaced Millard with Frederick Moore, an East Asian specialist with a different view. Moore perceived the Chinese nationalist movement as a threat manipulated by the Soviets. Diverging from Millard's "hands-off" policy toward China, Moore urged armed intervention on the part of the United States with cooperation from Great Britain and Japan. However, Moore's policy drew so much protest from readers that the publisher, Adolph S. Ochs, had to recall him and replace him with a new correspondent, Hallett Abend.[76] Although Abend did not advocate foreign intervention in Chinese issues, he shared Moore's distrust of the Guomindang government, believing it was incapable of bringing an end to the years of chaos. It was this attitude that eventually saw his name appear on the government's blacklist.

Neither the US legation in China nor the *New York Times* surrendered in the Abend case. MacMurray, who was personally on good terms with Abend, refused to deport him on the grounds that deportation was a mode of punishment not recognized in the United States and that he had no authority to deport a US citizen.[77]

---

76. It was reported that Adolph S. Ochs had received more than four thousand letters of protest against Moore's articles. "The *New York Times* and Its China Correspondents," *China Weekly Review*, July 13, 1929, 283–84.
77. Memorandum by the Assistant Secretary of State (Johnson), *PRFRUS, 1929*, vol. 2, 766–67. MacMurray to the Secretary of State, July 10, 1929, *PRFRUS, 1929*, vol. 2, 767.

The *New York Times* also acted defiantly against pressure from China's Ministry of Foreign Affairs. It neither recalled Abend nor transferred him to another country as the ministry required. Instead, the *New York Times* immediately moved him from Beijing to Shanghai, where he could have better access to foreign-controlled cables.[78] During the days when Abend was trapped in Beijing, the *New York Times* dispatched Herbert L. Matthews to approach him in a semiofficial capacity, working as his correspondent and filing his dispatches out of China. While the Chinese government shunned Abend, the Japanese proactively courted him. They offered to send Abend's dispatches via the Japanese-owned telegraph system and provided him with news from their perspective.[79]

The tension between Hallett Abend and the Guomindang government remained unchanged until April 1931. Following mediation by the new American minister, Nelson T. Johnson, C. T. Wang finally agreed to resolve the dispute after receiving Abend's letter, which Wang saw as an attempt to express "regrets for his unfair and false reports."[80] Abend, however, insisted he had never apologized for his reporting. What he regretted was the controversy itself and the government's objection to his manner of handling the news.[81] The whole deportation drama nevertheless exposed the Nanjing government's inability to deal with unfavorable foreign journalists.

Such a deportation failure was not a rare occurrence. It also happened to Sokolsky, then a correspondent for the *North China Daily News*. Sokolsky had a long and diversified experience working in China. At one point, he was close to Sun Yat-sen and had worked as a key person linking student leaders of the May Fourth Movement with Sun's followers.[82] He was involved in English-language papers of various backgrounds and political stances, including the *North China Star*, *Shanghai Gazette*, the *China Weekly Review*, the *North China Daily News*, the *Japan Advertiser*, and the *Far Eastern Review*. His marriage to Rosalind Peng, a close friend of Soong May-ling and the Soong family, brought him into the center of Chinese politics.[83] His insight into Chinese politics became the most important reference for some American diplomats and journalists.[84] However, his independent editorial style made it hard for others to discern his political loyalties. In 1921, he associated closely with ardent defenders of China like W. H. Donald, Thomas F. Millard, and John B. Powell, advocating China's independence and America's involvement in China's market. Yet, only two years later,

---

78. Abend, *My Life in China*, 105.
79. Ibid., 108.
80. Ibid., 126.
81. Ibid.
82. Warren I. Cohen, *The Chinese Connection, Roger S. Greene, Thomas W. Lamont, George E. Sokolsky and American–East Asian Relations* (New York: Columbia University Press, 1978), 73.
83. Bryna Goodman, "Semi-colonialism, Transnational Networks and News Flows in Early Republican Shanghai," *China Review* 4, no. 1 (Spring 2004): 71.
84. Cohen, *Chinese Connection*, 86.

he shifted sides and began to write for his prior enemy, George B. Rea, publicizing Japan's perspective in the *Far Eastern Review*. While seeking good terms with the Guomindang leaders, such as T. V. Soong and C. T. Wang, he continued to write articles criticizing the Nationalist Party's undemocratic rule and untalented leadership. Unable to harness his wild pen, the Nanjing government decided to drive him out of the country. His attack on the C. C. Clique, a political faction run by the Chen brothers—Chen Guofu and Chen Lifu, eventually brought him a deportation notice in April 1929. The deportation nevertheless ended in silence. Mediated by the American minister and T. V. Soong, the case against Sokolsky was diluted by the attacks on other related journalists and eventually subsided without any expulsion.[85]

The Review of Cable Contracts

Foreign ownership of the cables, protected by extraterritoriality, had prevented China from conducting censorship on outgoing dispatches. Despite Nanjing's continuous efforts to stifle dissention via various regulations and the censorship apparatus, information considered seditious by the government could still be transmitted freely via foreign cables. The lack of cable rights also diminished the Nanjing government's ability to reduce the price of outgoing dispatches. To save time, most press messages had to be sent at urgent rates, which cost around $0.4 (gold) per word to Europe.[86] This high rate far exceeded the budget of most of the Chinese newspapers and news agencies, which led to a lack of a Chinese voice abroad.[87] According to a Chinese telegraph administration report in 1926, about 1.5 million messages were dispatched from China to other countries. Yet the total amount of messages sent abroad through the Japanese Telegraph Administration was nearly double that of China.[88]

China's cable communications with other countries were mainly monopolized by three foreign companies: the Great Northern Telegraph, a Danish corporation but largely British owned and controlled; the Eastern Extension, a British company; and the Commercial Pacific Cable, an American enterprise with three-fourths of its stock owned by foreign cable interests. The Great Northern Company controlled cables connecting Vladivostok, Nagasaki, Shanghai, Amoy, and Hong Kong. It also operated cables in north European waters and owned land telegraphs across Russia and Siberia, which connected its eastern and western cable systems. The Eastern Extension operated a cable system from Hong Kong to Singapore, where further connection with Europe was established. It also owned the cable from Hong Kong to

---

85. Ibid., 168.
86. "Cable Contracts and the Press," *China Critic*, January 23, 1930, 77–78.
87. "News Facilities for China," *China Critic*, April 4, 1929, 267.
88. "Today's Cable Conference at Nanjing," *China Critic*, March 20, 1930, 275.

Fuzhou and Shanghai. The Commercial Pacific had a cable that linked Shanghai to San Francisco via Manila, Midway, and Honolulu.[89]

Japan controlled cables connecting Shanghai with Nagasaki and Fujian with Taiwan (Formosa). It also claimed Germany's cable rights in China after World War I and the privilege was tacitly approved by the United States after Japan offered the United States equal cable landing rights on Yap, an island strategically located between the US cable ports in Hawaii and the Philippines.[90]

The year 1929 provided an opportune moment for the Nanjing government to review its cable contracts, since most of the foreign companies' contracts with China were to expire at the end of 1930 and new rules were to be settled before the deadline. Nanjing placed great emphasis on the treaty revision and organized an International Communications Committee to prepare for it. The committee, led by Zhuang Zhihuan, was composed of representatives from the Ministry of Communications, Ministry of Foreign Affairs, Ministry of Finance, and the Ministry of War.[91] The committee determined to withdraw the foreign companies' right to build cables and land submarine cables within Chinese territory; to reduce the period of cable lease from twenty years to two years; to reclaim control of the cable infrastructure, including the landing of cables and cable poles; and to increase China's share of the revenue generated by cable transmissions.[92]

However, China's resolute plans were thwarted by its lack of funds to repay a £535,000 debt to the Western cable companies and to purchase their cable facilities.[93] The foreign cable companies constantly used these debts as leverage to deny the Nanjing government's demands. Knowing that cable was China's only channel of communication to the outside world and that China could not afford any disconnection in case negotiations broke down, the companies refused to make concessions.[94] They made a concerted demand to extend the current contract for another twenty years and refused to relinquish their ownership of the landing stations in port

---

89. Westel Woodbury Willoughby, *Foreign Rights and Interests in China*, vol. 2 (Taipei: Ch'eng-wen Publishing, 1966), 946–47; Jorma Ahvenainen, *The Far Eastern Telegraphs: The History of Telegraphic Communications between the Far East, Europe, and America before the First World War* (Helsinki: Suomalainen Tiedeakatemia, 1981), 207–12; Xia Jinlin, *Studies in Chinese Diplomatic History* (Shanghai: Commercial Press, 1933), 191–92.
90. Japan and the United States signed a treaty that settled the Yap Island dispute on February 11, 1922. See Lester H. Brune and Richard Dean Burns, *Chronological History of U.S. Foreign Relations: 1607–1932* (New York: Routledge, 2003), 442.
91. "Today's Cable Conference at Nanking," *China Critic*, March 20, 1930, 275.
92. Jiaotong bu ni ju jiejue Dadong, bei quan'an banfa qing jian he chenggao [Opinions of the Ministry of Communications in regard to the issue of Great Northern Company and East Extension Company], April 30, 1929, Nanjing Second Historical Archives, *Minguo dang'an shiliao huibian* [Collection of historical records of the Republic of China] (Nanjing: Jiangsu guji chubanshe, 1994), vol. 5, no. 1, Economy (9), 659.
93. Ibid.
94. Xingzhengyuan cheng shuixian dianxin jiaoshe jingguo [Executive Yuan's reports on the negotiation of submarine cables], March 21, 1931, *Minguo dang'an shiliao huibian*, 5, no. 1, Economy (9), 683.

cities. The first round of negotiations in 1930 was concluded with disappointment for China. Instead of reducing the period of cable leases to two years as the Nanjing government had planned, Zhuang conceded to a fourteen-year lease term and failed to reclaim the companies' rights to operate cable services in China.[95]

The concessions made by the committee subjected Zhuang to severe public censure. Regional telegraph worker unions repeatedly sent representatives to Nanjing to demand Zhuang be punished. The petition was directed both against foreign coercion and the weakness of the central government. Without a response from the government, telegraph staff in Fuzhou and Xiamen cut foreign cable lines as soon as the current contract had expired.[96] Although undiplomatic, the sabotage created practical difficulties for the foreign companies to continue operating cables in China. It also assisted Chinese officials at the negotiation table, who could cite the popular pressure to push for the reclamation of cable rights.

The cable rights negotiations dragged on much longer than the Nanjing government had expected. In new rounds of negotiations, the foreign companies focused on delaying the revision process, hoping that procrastination would transform the status quo into an acquiesced agreement the way many of the foreign privileges were initially acquired. In 1931, the Mukden Incident interrupted the negotiations. Afterward, Japan's cable privileges from Shanghai to Nagasaki became the major excuse for the Danish, British, and American companies to maintain their cable rights.[97]

Penetration of the Treaty-Port Press

Suppressive policies such as postal ban and deportation did not characterize the Guomindang government's daily propaganda operations. These policies usually instigated debates and protests in the press, and particularly during this surge of dispute, hidden alliances among newspaper would surface. This visible suppression helped the Guomindang government to develop a deeper understanding of the intricate power dimension of the treaty-port press. With such knowledge, invisible penetration into the daily operation of the press became possible.

To compensate for the lack of news agencies and effective cable control, some Nanjing officials, as well as treaty-port elites, continued to purchase, subsidize, or establish English-language papers in the treaty-port cities. The majority of such efforts were conducted in a clandestine manner. Faced with the complex and sometimes chaotic

---

95. "Woguo yu Dadong Dabei gongsi shuixian jiaoshe guoqu yu xianzai" [The past and present of China's negotiations with the Great Northern and East Extension companies], *Guowen zhoubao* 10, no. 20 (1933).
96. Zhongguo renmin zhengzhi xieshang huiyi quanguo weiyuanhui wenshi ziliao yanjiu weiyuanhui, *Wenshi ziliao xuanji* [Selection of historical materials] 23, nos. 66/68 (Beijing: Zhongguo wenshi chubanshe, 2000), 142–43.
97. Jiaotongbu guanyu Dadong Dabei Taipingyang san shuixian gongsi dianxin jiaoshe jingguo qingxing zhi xingzheng huiyi ti'an gao, April 18, 1933, *Minguo dang'an shiliao huibian*, 5, no. 1, Economy (9), 688.

treaty-port media environment, members of the elite did not seek to challenge the existing structure but skillfully adapted to it by blurring the national identity of their papers. When the water was deep and muddy and the order undefined, the best chance for China to eke out some space in the English treaty-port press was to penetrate the system and act according to established norms. Complex as the media environment was, it was exactly this lack of a clear order that provided Chinese elites with an access to the medium. Indeed, there were two types of international propaganda forces that coexisted in China. One was the centralized party-led institution mentioned in the beginning of the chapter; the other was these separate and independent propaganda resources camouflaged with transnational identities. The two forces were not mutually exclusive. Many of the papers apparently operated by bilingual elites secretly received official subsidies. Yet there were clear attempts by the elite to distinguish themselves from the government, so as to establish credibility with their sources. While the existence of the latter revealed the former's weakness in centralizing propaganda resources, it also complemented it and accomplished what it desired but could not achieve.

The *Peking Leader* had been in financial difficulty since 1928. Its popularity waned rapidly with the move of the Chinese capital from Beijing to Nanjing. The Nanjing government purchased the *Peking Leader* from the American editor Grover Clark, who, by the latter half of 1929, was unable to maintain operation of the paper. The government reorganized the paper, renamed it the *Leader* and appointed Diao Minqian, a member of the Ministry of Foreign Affairs, as its managing director. Li Bingrui (Edward Bing-shuey Lee), who was educated in Canada, was appointed one of the editors.[98] Operated by the Ministry of Foreign Affairs, the paper received a monthly subsidy of 3,000 yuan from the Ministry of Information.[99] After nearly a decade of American ownership, the *Leader*, which was originally founded by Beijing officials (Chapter 1), had eventually returned to Chinese hands.

Before passing to Chinese control, the *Peking Leader* was considered a liberal paper, independent of both the Guomindang government and the American legation. Clark was a disobedient nuisance in the eyes of many American diplomats in Beijing. In 1927, the paper firmly opposed the proposed American loan to the South Manchuria Railway for the development of south Manchuria. When the Nationalist troops approached Beijing at the end of the Northern Expedition, rumors were rampant in the Legation Quarter that the "Southern Communists" would repeat the Boxer atrocities of 1900. Upon the legation's offer to provide "adequate protection" of American properties, Clark rejected the overture, saying that he was quite content under the protection of Chinese law. Whenever legal disputes with Chinese firms occurred, the paper preferred to fight the case out in Chinese courts than to claim

---

98. Chao, *Foreign Press in China*, 74.
99. "Zhongyang caiwu weiyuanhui dishiwuci huiyi jilu," MSCGCEC, 9:480.

extraterritoriality. This further embarrassed members of the American legation who were keen to maintain the extraterritorial system. The paper's attack on Japanese atrocities during the Jinan Incident also enraged Japanese companies. When Clark refused to change his stance, many Japanese firms cancelled their advertising contracts in protest.[100] However, the *Leader*'s anti-extraterritoriality and anti-Japanese tone did not suggest that it was a Nationalist propaganda asset. During the Northern Expedition, it was found to be subsidized by the Northern warlord Feng Yuxiang with Russian money.[101]

The *Leader* was the only Chinese-controlled English-language paper in North China. The purchase of the paper was of strategic importance to Nanjing. It not only enabled the Guomindang's view to be heard in North China but helped counter the anti-Nanjing views held by the die-hard British paper, the *Peking and Tientsin Times*, published in the same area. However, distant from the Yangtze area—Chiang Kai-shek's political center—the paper was vulnerable to political and military struggles in the North. During the Central Plains War, insurgent warlords led by Feng Yuxiang, Yan Xishan, and Li Zongren, took control of Beijing. The paper was seized by warlords, and all of its Chinese employees were expelled. Having no interest in serving the insurgent government, the paper's American editor E. H. Hunter resigned, and the vacuum was filled by Lenox Simpson (known as Putman Weale), a China-born British national. Simpson followed in his father's footsteps and joined the Imperial Maritime Customs in 1896 at the age of nineteen, a job he quit after the Boxer Rebellion in 1900. He served the *Daily Telegraph* as a Beijing correspondent from 1911 to 1914, and later worked as an adviser to military warlords in Beijing. Simpson was an active treaty-port writer. During his editorship at the *Leader*, he was critical of both the policies of the Guomindang government and the imperialist stance of the Shanghai Municipal Council.[102] Yet Simpson's association with the *Leader* was brief. The Guomindang reclaimed Beijing in October 1930, and Simpson was assassinated a month later after being appointed as Tientsin customs commissioner.[103]

Apart from the purchase of the *Leader* in Beijing, Nanjing officials also sought to penetrate the stronghold of the English-language press in Shanghai. The *Shanghai Mercury* was briefly subsidized by the government after the Jinan Incident. The *Mercury* was a well-known British paper established by J. D. Clark in 1879. The paper reached its height at the turn of the twentieth century when it broke the *North China Daily News*' monopoly on Reuters' service in China. Since 1904, Japanese interests had kept influencing the paper. By 1917, nearly half its shares were bought by the

---

100. Chao, *Foreign Press in China*, 74–75.
101. Abend, *My Life in China*, 52–54.
102. Bickers, *Britain in China*, 33–35. "Putman Weale and His 'New Order' in Peiping," *China Weekly Review*, May 17, 1930, 436.
103. "The Death of Mr. Lenox Simpson," *China Critic*, November 20, 1930.

Japanese. British nationals controlled no more than 20 percent of the shares, with the remaining 30 percent held by Americans. The paper naturally turned into a promoter of Japanese interests. The overt pro-Japan stance ruined the popularity of the paper. Circulation dropped sharply in the 1920s, and by 1929 the paper was on the verge of bankruptcy. The editor of the *Mercury* approached the Guomindang Ministry of Information for financial support. Realizing that a British-operated English-language paper was better received by foreign audiences, the ministry provided 2,000 yuan per month with the condition that the Guomindang would coedit the paper.[104] The party's limited assistance nevertheless failed to pull the paper out of its financial quagmire, but a merger eventually did. The paper was purchased by the American merchant, C. V. Starr, who combined the *Mercury* with the *Shanghai Evening Post* to form the new *Shanghai Evening Post and Mercury*. Under new management, the *Post* soon developed into a successful Shanghai evening paper in the 1930s.

With the support of the government, Li Bingrui established a political weekly, the *Chinese Nation*, in Shanghai in June 1930.[105] The journal received a monthly 3,000-yuan allowance from the party and became one of its major outlets.[106] Yet Li was reluctant to reveal the journal's connection with the government, fearing that government backing might undermine the journal's credibility. The government invited Lin Wenqing (also Lim Boom Keng), a British-trained doctor who was then the president of the University of Amoy, to lead the paper.[107] Lin's editorship was a guise to cover the party's involvement. When the *China Weekly Review* introduced the journal as a magazine edited by "prominent members of the Kuomintang Party,"[108] Li asked the *Review* to make a correction immediately, emphasizing that the *Chinese Nation* was owned by a "private company."[109] Yet the journal was far from as "private" as it claimed. The International Division of the Ministry of Information continued to supply articles to the journal. Some were published as excerpts integrated in the "editorial comments." Some were published entirely as front-page editorials. "Yen Hsi-shan's Motive for Establishing a Government," which appeared on July 30, 1930, as a front-page editorial, for example, was supplied by the party.[110]

Apparently, Nanjing did not have a clear plan of how foreign propaganda should fit into the existing party system. While the focus on ideological dissemination worked against the objective to promote China's national image, most of the practical

---

104. "Xuanchuan," August 1929, MSCGCEC, 9:167; *Zhongyang xuanchuanbu yizhou gongzuo gaikuang*, August 12–18, 1929, 3.3/50 Huiyi jilu, GA.
105. MSCGCEC, 11:453.
106. MSCGCEC, 12:126, 391, 13:21–22.
107. *Xiada zhoukan* [University of Amoy weekly] 10, no. 4 (1930): 15; Liu Guoming et al., eds., *Zhongguo Guomindang bainian renwu quanshu* [Complete collection of biographies of key members of the Guomindang] (Beijing: Tuanjie chubanshe, 2005), 2:1488.
108. "The *Chinese Nation*, Weekly Paper Makes First Appearance," *China Weekly Review*, June 28, 1930, 152.
109. "The *Chinese Nation*," *China Weekly Review*, July 12, 1930, 235.
110. *Zhongyang dangwu yuekan*, 28:225–27.

operations were conducted by staff members in the Ministry of Foreign Affairs who at least had experience in dealing with a foreign audience. Official involvement in the treaty-port press was nevertheless clumsy and limited. The most vibrant resources of international propaganda lay in the treaty-port bilingual intellectuals who were familiar with a Western mind-set and shared the urge to promote China's international reputation.

Disturbed by foreign newspapers' interpretations of the Jinan Incident, China's bilingual elites in Shanghai founded an English-language weekly, the *China Critic*. The long-term editors of the journal included Gui Zhongshu, Lin Yutang, Ma Yinchu, Liu Dajun, Zhao Minheng, and many other distinguished scholars who had received university degrees in the West. The editors stated that their initiative was to "prevent the repetition of events that have made the month of May so unhappily memorable [due to the May Thirtieth Movement and the Jinan Incident]."[111] Liu Dajun also confirmed in his letter to Hu Shi that the journal was published to "counter Japan's harmful propaganda."[112] The publication of the journal, as Hu Shi recollected, was not merely an impulse driven by the acute situation during the Jinan Incident. The need for a "representative publication," "independent of governmental control and popular prejudices (anti-imperialist sentiment)," had long been felt, and the *China Critic* intended to "strengthen the friendly relations between China and the outside world" and to promote "better understanding between China and the other Powers."[113]

The relationship between the *China Critic* group and the Nanjing government was delicate. The publishers claimed themselves to be a "voluntary" and "independent" group of Chinese, "who were interested in a fair presentation of all issues arising between China and the other Powers."[114] However, their self-proclaimed independence was frequently under suspicion. The editorial board of the *Critic* was close to Sun Yat-sen's son, Sun Ke, the then-head of the Legislative Yuan. Sun contributed frequently to the journal, especially in the first few issues. Some key founders of the *Critic* also held important positions in the Nanjing government. Zhang Xinhai (H. H. Chang), for example, joined the Ministry of Foreign Affairs in June 1928. Liu Dajun, a graduate of University of Missouri, majoring in economics and statistics, became the head of the statistics department in the Legislative Yuan, supervised by Sun. Despite all the personal connections with the government, there was no concrete evidence showing that the paper was receiving any government subsidy. The paper's harsh criticism of some of the party's domestic policies also indicated its distance from the Nanjing regime. Yet the difference between the group and the government

---

111. "Foreword," *China Critic*, May 31, 1928, 1.
112. Hu Shi, *Hu Shi riji quanji* [Complete collection of Hu Shi's diary], *1928–1930* (Hefei: Anhui jiaoyu chubanshe, 2001), 417.
113. Ibid.
114. Ibid.

was much less distinctive when dealing with foreign affairs. Before 1933, the journal largely endorsed the government's position regarding Sino-Japanese conflicts. It also became one of China's effective propaganda outlets during the Manchurian Crisis in the early 1930s.

Another important Chinese-controlled English-language paper was the *China Press*. In 1930, a Chinese syndicate led by Zhang Zhuping acquired the paper from Edward I. Ezra's family for 260,000 taels. John B. Powell learned from his private yet "authoritative" sources that Wellington Koo was the principal shareholder in the new organization, having advanced 100,000 in local currency for the purchase of the paper.[115] Constant changes of ownership blurred the paper's editorial line, as Hollington K. Tong observed: "the founder's objective, namely to remove international misunderstanding and place before the world Chinese views and thoughts" had remained dormant as the paper was "tossed alternatively from the Chinese to the Americans, from Americans to the British, and from the British back to Chinese."[116]

Zhang soon organized a board of directors made up of four foreigners and four Chinese. This arrangement was intended to create the impression that the paper was a jointly operated enterprise. The four Western board members were Chauncey P. Holcomb, an American attorney in Shanghai; William T. Findley, an American optician; E. L. Marsh, a medical practitioner; and William H. Donald, adviser to Zhang Xueliang and formerly the *New York Herald*'s correspondent in China.[117] Apart from Donald, none of them had experience in journalism. They lent their fame and credibility to the paper yet were seldom involved in editing and managing the *Press*. Donald was indeed active in the reorganization, yet his service to the *Press* was brief. It was believed that Donald came to assist the reorganization on Wellington Koo's request.[118] Soon after he finished his task in 1932, he withdrew from the board, and Xu Xinliu, Chinese representative to the Shanghai Municipal Council, took over the position.[119] The active control of the paper was in the hands of the Chinese members led by Hollington K. Tong as the managing director.[120]

Tong's career spanned both journalism and politics. He was the first Chinese graduate from the School of Journalism at the University of Missouri in the United States. In Missouri, he was taught by John B. Powell, who later joined Thomas Millard in

---

115. Douglas Jenkins, Consul General, to Nelson T. Johnson, American Minister to Peiping, February 24, 1931. 893.911/266, Confidential US State Department Central Files (hereafter SDCF), China, Internal Affairs 1930–1939.
116. "China Press Celebrates Twentieth Anniversary," *China Weekly Review*, September 19, 1931, 119.
117. "*China Press* Changes Hands: New Board of Four Foreign, Four Chinese Directors Named," *Shanghai Evening Post and Mercury*, February 20, 1931.
118. Douglas Jenkins, Consul General, to Nelson T. Johnson, American Minister to Peiping, February 24, 1931. 893.911/266, SDCF.
119. "Shanghai zhi xinwen shiye" [A history of Shanghai press], *Shanghai xinwen shiye shiliao jiyao* [Materials on the history of newspapers in Shanghai] (Taipei: Tianyi chubanshe, 1977), 1:57.
120. *Zhonghua Minguo shi dang'an ziliao huibian*, Culture, 1:133.

China and cofounded the *Millard's Review of the Far East*. His acquaintance with Powell paved the way for his later role with *Millard's Review*, and his experience at the University of Missouri facilitated his connections with the "Missouri mafia," a group of graduates from the University of Missouri who practiced journalism in China in the 1930s and the 1940s. After graduation, Tong became a member of the first class of the Pulitzer School of Journalism at Columbia University. The Columbia experience put Tong in touch with many energetic classmates who later became key figures in the journalistic field. They remained friends with Tong in the following years. Carl W. Ackerman was one of them. In 1942, thirty years after their graduation, Tong was the vice minister of the Ministry of Information of the Guomindang government, and Ackerman was dean of the Pulitzer School. At this time, they collaborated to set up a wartime journalism school in China, staffed by Columbia and underwritten secretly by the Office of Strategic Services.[121]

Upon Tong's return to China in 1913, Sun Yat-sen recruited him to the *Republican China*, an English-language paper Sun had set up in Beijing to undermine Yuan Shikai's authority.[122] When *Republican China* closed down at the end of 1913, Tong moved to the *Peking Daily News*, a newspaper owned by the Communications Clique, a pro–Yuan Shikai group led by Zhou Ziqi and Ye Gongchuo. The paper was subsidized by several governmental ministries including the Ministry of Communications and the Ministry of Foreign Affairs.[123] Its main rival was the *Peking Gazette*, edited first by Henry G. W. Woodhead and then Eugene Chen.[124] Tong pursued an anti-Japanese stance during his service to the *Peking Daily News*. Such an attitude offended the Anhui Clique, a powerful warlord faction supported by Japan. As a result, he was forced to resign in the mid-1910s. The experience with the two papers, nevertheless, offered Tong a real taste of China's sophisticated politics and the complex relations between the political factions and the press.

Despite Tong's short-lived service to the *Peking Daily News*, his relationship with Xiong Xiling, then in charge of China's oil and mining affairs, and the Missouri mafia was long-lasting. Tong had been Xiong's secretary for many years. In a trip to Washington to prevent the United States from loaning money to Japan for the development of Manchuria, Tong worked closely with Wellington Koo, then China's minister to the United States. As Tong acknowledged, such close connections with the top political leaders in North China enabled him to directly observe the activities

---

121. James R. Boylan, *Pulitzer's School: Columbia University's School of Journalism, 1903–2003* (New York: Columbia University Press, 2003), 182.
122. Zhuang Zheng, "Sun Zhongshan chuangban yingwen *Minguo xi bao*" [Establishment of the *Republican China* by Sun Yat-sen], *Dang'an yu shixue* [Archives and history] 1 (1998): 63.
123. See Andrew James Nathan, *Peking Politics, 1918–1923: Factionalism and the Failure of Constitutionalism* (Berkeley: University of California Press, 1976), 63.
124. Hollington Kong Tong, *Dong Xianguang zizhuan: Yi ge nongfu de zishu* [Hollington Tong's autobiography: A self-introduction of a peasant] (Taipei: Taiwan xinsheng baoshe, 1973), 39.

of China's top officials and "gain deep insight into China's politics."[125] Meanwhile, he resumed close ties with fellow Missouri alumni, particularly Millard and Powell. He joined the *Millard's Review / China Weekly Review* and worked as its associate editor and Beijing correspondent for ten years.[126]

Tong also nurtured a good relationship with China's largest press syndicate, the Shen bao company. In 1925, he established his own Chinese-language paper, *Yong bao*, in Tianjin. The paper's anti-Japanese stance and its independent attitude received support from Shi Liangcai and Zhang Zhuping, the owners and operators of China's largest newspaper, *Shen bao*. Tong later assisted Shi in negotiating with C. J. Ferguson for the purchase of *Xinwen bao*. The experience strengthened their relationship and paved the way for their later cooperation during Tong's editorship with the *China Press*.[127] Tong's professional ability and his extensive social networks in the press and politics made him a leading figure in China's treaty-port press.

Tong tried hard to maintain the American element of the *China Press* after he took over the editorship. He continued to register the paper in Delaware, United States, so as to enhance the paper's credibility as well as to gain extraterritorial protection. He preserved the paper's American-style layout and hired many American journalists as its reporters and editors. Malcolm Rocholt, for example, served the *China Press* as a reporter in 1931. Earle Selle, who later worked for the *Advertiser* in Honolulu and became famous for his biography of W. H. Donald, joined the *Press* as an editor around the same time.[128]

Despite all these American elements, the reorganized *China Press* represented Chinese interests. The new managing team was "doing its utmost" to feature Chinese news in its papers in order to compete with the British-owned *North China Daily News*,[129] which paid handsomely for exclusive services supplied by Reuters and the United Press. In addition to the regular Reuters, Guomin, and Transocean news services, the *Press* also obtained exclusive services from the Shenshi News Agency, a private news agency organized by the largest Shanghai native papers *Shen bao* and *Shishi xin bao*. The goal of the paper was to break the monopoly on Chinese news by Reuters and other large foreign news agencies.

Tong considered the paper to be a platform to neutralize China's antiforeign image and to promote friendship between China and the Western powers. He perceived cooperation and mutual understanding with foreign powers to be "most desirable for the early realization of China's national aspirations."[130] With regard to various foreign interest groups in Shanghai, Tong claimed that the paper would "promote the welfare

---

125. Ibid.
126. Ibid.
127. Ibid., 44–47.
128. Malcolm Leviatt Rosholt, *The Press Corps of Old Shanghai* (Rosholt, WI: *Rosholt House*, 1994), 11.
129. Chao, *Foreign Press in China*, 72.
130. Ibid.

and prosperity of Shanghai as a whole," indicating its contention with the Shanghai mind, a mentality that focused primarily on British imperial legacies. Concerning Chinese domestic politics, Tong claimed that the paper would "take no sides." Yet he did not rule out the possibility of making "constructive criticisms of measures and policies" when necessary.[131]

Much as the Chinese board members wanted to accentuate the paper's American ownership, the Shanghai Municipal Council and the American legation tried to downplay the American influence in the paper. Stirling Fessenden, the chairman of the Shanghai Municipal Council, once denounced the US influence in the paper, stating that "the only American interest in the *China Press* of any consequence was a small number of shares" held by those "who never took the slightest interest in the paper."[132] Edwin S. Cunningham, American consul general, even questioned the existence of American stakes in the paper. He believed that none of the foreign board members "had any financial interests in the concern but acted in that capacity for the purpose of emphasizing the fact that the *China Press* has an American charter."[133] The paper's American registration also raised concerns among the China-based American diplomats. Knowing that Zhang Zhuping was occasionally critical of the Nanjing government, the American consuls feared that the paper's registration would entangle the US legation in a tussle between the paper and the Nanjing government. The legation, therefore, tried to revoke the paper's American registration through the Division of Far Eastern Affairs in the Department of State. The attempt was unsuccessful since there was no legal basis in Delaware, where the paper was registered, to revoke the registration.

Despite all the efforts from the government and the elites, China did not have the luxury of time to wait for its own news network to become mature. The Japanese invasion soon dragged the country into another round of propaganda battles before its fledgling propaganda system was ready to fight.

---

131. Ibid.
132. Stirling Fessenden to Hollington Tong, May 19, 1931, Q3–6–88, Shanghai Municipal Council Archives.
133. Edwin S. Cunningham to the Secretary of State, Washington, June 10, 1935, 893.911/310, SDCF.

Figure 6
Sapajou, "The Burdens of Office," *North China Daily News*, September 26, 1929.

4
Shadowed by the Sun

The Mukden Incident and the Shanghai Incident

On September 18, 1931, a section of the railroad owned by Japan's South Manchuria Railway was dynamited. The Japanese Kwantung Army, accusing Chinese soldiers of the bombing, responded by invading Manchuria. Within hours, the army controlled the major cities of southern Manchuria—Mukden (Shenyang), Yingkou, Andong, and Changchun. Within days, the Japanese occupied most of Liaoning and Jilin (Kirin) Provinces. Within a year, Japan established the puppet Manchukuo government and exercised control over the majority of northeast China. The victory in Manchuria whetted the appetite of the Japanese military for more success in China. On January 28, 1932, the Japanese navy bombed Chinese residential areas in Shanghai, marking the beginning of another serious Sino-Japanese conflict, known as the Shanghai Incident. Historians tend to link the two events together as part of the Manchurian crisis.

By 1931, the Chinese government and the elites had secured several English papers to counter Japan's propaganda. Yet the increase of news outlets did not guarantee a favorable image of China. When basic historical facts could not be verified immediately after the conflict, competition of news reporting became a competition of skills to create favorable contexts for the news. Reports that prevailed in the media may not have been the most accurate ones, but rather those that corroborated existing stories took precedence. The interaction between media text and opinion context is delicate: the context constitutes a framework that determines the credibility of texts. Yet the framework is not static. Over time, it will also be shaped by texts. While Japanese papers' skillful reference to China's antiforeign tradition continued to undermine China's discourse, the power of its versions were wearing thin when facts, accumulated during the two incidents, continued to relate Japanese troops' ruthless behavior in China. The Shanghai Incident was the tipping point when international public opinion started to shift from sympathy to skepticism of Japan's war intentions. Yet the change could not be taken for granted. This chapter explores this battle of words in detail.

Response to the Mukden Incident

After the Mukden Incident, one of the issues that remained at the heart of the media discussion was who started the fight. Although contemporary historians in hindsight commonly believe that the Japanese soldiers staged the explosion to provide a pretext for war, back in 1931 the cause of the fight was unclear. Within twenty-four hours after the outbreak of the incident, the Japanese War Ministry had issued a communiqué blaming the Chinese troops for both bombing the South Manchuria Railway and attacking Japanese railway guards.[1] This version was distributed through the London *Times* via Reuters in Tokyo.[2] The statement remained unchallenged for a day, until China's official response was seen in the treaty-port paper the *North China Daily News* on September 20, mildly responding that the action by Japanese troops was "entirely unprovoked."[3]

The slow reaction from the Chinese side was a result of its lack of communication infrastructure. At the time of the Mukden Incident, Nanjing had no substantial control over outgoing cables. China still relied heavily on foreign news agencies for information transmission. After the Japanese army occupied Mukden, it required dispatches from the city to be relayed to Tokyo before being passed on to Shanghai.[4] The army also seized wireless stations in Mukden and installed its own censors to intercept information favorable to China.[5]

Japan: Beyond the Incident

Japan's explanation as to why the Mukden Incident started was not entirely coherent in the beginning. Disagreement occurred between the War Ministry and Ministry of Foreign Affairs. While the former blamed China for the fighting, the latter was inclined to view the incident as "bravado on the part of a number of hot-headed senior officers"[6] and demanded the military officers on the front line to withdraw their troops immediately.[7] The inconsistency offset the advantage that Japan gained by presenting its case in the press before China was able to respond. Yet the split did not last long. After the outbreak of the incident, newspapers in Japan vied to report on the daily progress of the Kwantung Army to meet the market demands for news. The ubiquitous coverage of the incident enflamed the general public's war fever,

---

1. "Collision at Mukden Conflicting Reports, City Occupied," *Times*, September 19, 1931.
2. Ibid.
3. "The Chinese Version," *North China Daily News*, September 20, 1931, 11.
4. "Japanese Censorship in Manchuria," *China Critic*, November 12, 1931, 1095.
5. Daqing Yang, *Technology of Empire: Telecommunications and Japanese Expansion in Asia, 1883–1945* (Cambridge, MA: Harvard University Press, 2010), 77.
6. "Japanese Views Changing," *North China Daily News*, September 21, 1931, 18.
7. "Regret over Mukden Expressed at Tokyo," *New York Times*, September 20, 1931, 1.

and the enthusiasm toward Japan's empire building obliged the Ministry of Foreign Affairs to drop its criticism of the army and to adopt the latter's explanation of how the incident started.[8]

As the Kwantung Army continued to advance in Manchuria, the cause of the incident initially alleged by Japan—protection of the railway—became increasingly inadequate to justify its extensive military actions. Many foreign correspondents traveled to Mukden to investigate the incident and returned with a story blaming Japanese troops for staging the conflict.[9] Realizing that continuous elaboration of the railway explosion was of no avail, the Japanese-controlled English paper, the *Far Eastern Review*, gradually downplayed the episode and contextualized the incident in the larger Sino-foreign conflict.

The *Far Eastern Review* put forward the murder of Nakamura Shintaro as the cause for Japan's military actions. Nakamura was a military spy who traveled as a civilian to the Manchurian interior with his interpreter and assistants in June 1931 to make survey maps.[10] In August 1931, newspapers reported that he had been apprehended and shot by Chinese soldiers after they discovered his identity.[11] The case instigated strong domestic protest in Japan against China's contempt for Japanese rights in Manchuria. The Nanjing government initially denied that the incident had ever taken place.[12] It eventually opened an investigation into the case but failed to agree with Japan about the basic facts. The case remained unsolved when the Mukden Incident broke out.

The *Far Eastern Review* perceived the Nakamura case as the catalyst for the Mukden Incident. This largely followed the same argument proposed by Japanese domestic papers. An article in the *Asahi shimbun*, quoted by the *North China Daily News*, best reflected how the Japanese press explained the origin of the Mukden Incident:

> The murder of Captain Nakamura was like pouring petrol on a pile of wood, while the destruction of a section of the South Manchuria Railway line was equivalent to applying a match, thereby cutting the rope with which the Japanese bag of patience was tied.[13]

Nakamura was portrayed as an innocent soldier, with his identity as a spy unknown to the public. By frequently referring to his death, the *Review* sought to remind the

---

8. Louise Young, *Japan's Total Empire: Manchuria and the Culture of Wartime Imperialism* (Berkeley: University of California Press, 1998), 60–88.
9. "How the Japanese Troops Captured Mukden," *China Weekly Review*, October 10, 1931, 203.
10. Sandra Wilson, *The Manchurian Crisis and Japanese Society, 1931–33* (London: Routledge, 2002), 19.
11. "Japan-China: Mukden & Markets," *Time* magazine, September 28, 1931; Marius B. Jansen, *Japan and China: From War to Peace, 1894–1972* (Chicago: Rand McNally College, 1975), 377; Daniel B. Ramsdell, "The Nakamura Incident and the Japanese Foreign Office," *Journal of Asian Studies* 25 (1965): 51–67.
12. "Japanese Occupation of Manchuria," *China Weekly Review*, October 3, 1931, 180; Ramsdell, "Nakamura Incident and the Japanese Foreign Office," 51–67.
13. "Press Comment in Japan," *North China Daily News*, September 21, 1931, 18.

readers of China's ill treatment of foreigners, which provided a context for Japan's reaction to the railway explosion.

The *Review* also linked the Nakamura case with the death of John Thorburn to raise the foreign community's fear for the Guomindang's abolition of extraterritoriality. Thorburn was a nineteen-year-old Briton. He secretly left home on July 1, 1931, to join Guomindang forces engaged in the first encirclement campaign against the Communist Party in Jiangxi Province. In a nighttime melee on the Shanghai-Nanjing railway line, he fatally wounded two Chinese gendarmes. He was subsequently seized and secretly executed.[14] The case remained unsolved when the Mukden Incident happened. While negotiations on the abolition of extraterritoriality had reached a critical stage, the case reinforced Shanghailanders' concern for their safety in a post-extraterritorial age. George Bronson Rea, editor of the *Far Eastern Review*, took advantage of this fear, arguing that both the Nakamura and Thorburn cases sent a warning to foreigners that "the Chinese military officials have taken the law into their own hands,"[15] irrespective of the extraterritoriality enjoyed by foreign nationals. Nakamura, according to Rea, was shot because "the military may have accepted literally the government's proclamation that extraterritoriality [was] abolished; secret orders may have been issued in regard to the treatment of suspicious foreigners arrested outside the concession areas."[16] By invoking the extraterritoriality issue, the journal implied that Japan was not only to protect its own rights but to defend the rights of all foreign communities in China. Support for the Japanese case thus amounted to defending the foreign nationals' own interests.

The Nakamura case, nevertheless, was not always effective in strengthening Japan's argument. Criticism was vociferous. Many complained that the case had been given excessive attention, which obfuscated the true origin of the Mukden Incident. In the minutes of the Council of the League of Nations, the Nakamura case was frequently mentioned as if it was the cause of the Sino-Japanese situation in Manchuria of that time.[17] Even the Japanese press complained that the delegates of the Powers in Geneva did not understand the genuine facts of the Manchurian Incident since they referred to the Nakamura case only, completely ignoring the destruction of the South Manchuria Railway.[18]

The 1915 Sino-Japanese Treaty, known as the Twenty-One Demands, was also cited by the paper as the cause of the incident. All subsequent incidents that embittered relations between the two countries could find their roots in China's refusal to

---

14. For more on the Thorburn case, see Robert A. Bickers, *Britain in China: Community Culture and Colonialism, 1900–1949* (Manchester: Manchester University Press, 1999), 148–49.
15. "Approaching the Showdown," *Far Eastern Review*, September 1931, 532.
16. Ibid.
17. "Japanese Press and League: Delegates Do Not Understand Essential Facts," *North China Daily News*, September 26, 1931, 18.
18. Ibid.

recognize the binding nature of this treaty.[19] Indeed, condemnation of the misrule of the Chinese government had quietly replaced the self-defense rhetoric, thus justifying the Japanese occupation of Manchuria as a way to discipline China on behalf of all foreign powers.

The journal constantly attacked the Chinese government as "weak," "inefficient," "corrupted," and "powerless."[20] Although China claimed sovereignty over Manchuria, argued the journal, its control over the region was nominal. China was neither able to defend its territory against the menace of Russia nor cease domestic hostilities.[21] The underlying message was, if the Chinese government is unable to govern the region wisely, why not give power to Japan, which has accumulated vast interests in the area? Another Japanese-controlled English newspaper, the *Manchuria Daily News*, echoed the view by quoting a line from the Bible: "One who does not know how to improve one's possessions shall be deprived of what one has."[22] However, no matter how these papers defended Japan's vested interests in Manchuria, they were sensible not to touch on the sensitive subject of claiming territorial rights. The *Far Eastern Review* kept repeating that Japan had no territorial desires in Manchuria and its troops were stationed there only to maintain stability.[23]

Anti-Communism was another important theme repeated by the *Review* to justify Japan's military occupation of Manchuria. It explained that Japan's military action was not only to maintain order but also to guard against Russia's potential aggression. "When the time was propitious," claimed the paper, "the great Red Army would move and take over China's land."[24] It was clear even at the height of the Manchurian crisis that the Soviet Union was not an imminent danger to Japan. Introducing the Soviet factor into the Mukden Incident was an apparent effort to serve Japan's propaganda rhetoric. This line of argument was well received by some. William Riddell Birdwood, master of Peterhouse, commented on the Mukden Incident in his letter to his friend John Simon, the new foreign secretary, that "I know [it] sounds all wrong, perhaps immoral, when she [Japan] is flouting the League of Nations, but . . . her [Japan's] presence fully established in Manchuria means a real block against Bolshevik aggression."[25]

Western powers' colonial precedents were also used by Japanese editors to justify the occupation of Manchuria. "What is just and good for Great Britain in India,

---

19. "The Validity of a Treaty," *Far Eastern Review*, September 1931, 534.
20. "Has Japan the Right to Defend Herself?" *Far Eastern Review*, October 1931; "Militarism Must Go!" *Far Eastern Review*, December 1931.
21. "The Validity of a Treaty"; "Has Japan the Right to Defend Herself?"
22. "The Daren Devil Who Quotes Scripture," *China Weekly Review*, October 24, 1931, 286–90.
23. "Statement by Japan," *North China Daily News*, September 26, 1931, 18.
24. "Has Japan the Right to Defend Herself?"
25. Birdwood to Simon, November 6, 1931, Simon Papers, Foreign Affairs, 1931, quoted in Christopher G. Thorne, *The Limits of Foreign Policy: The West, the League, and the Far Eastern Crisis of 1931–1933* (New York: Capricorn Books, 1973), 177.

in Egypt and in Mesopotamia; for France in Algeria and Morocco; for Italy in the Mediterranean and for the United States in the Caribbean, must also be just and good for Japan in Manchuria," read one of the front-page editorials of the *Far Eastern Review*.[26] The style of language that the Japanese editors adopted contained a strong imperial flavor. An argument from the Japanese domestic press quoted by the *North China Daily News* read, "Japan . . . should act like a parent who spanks a naughty, spoilt child sternly yet sympathetically."[27] The condescending view based on the premise that the Chinese were inferior people in need of paternal guidance had long been popular among Japanese officials. As early as the mid-1920s, Japanese diplomat Shidehara Kijūrō had been vocal about such an attitude. As the British ambassador to Japan, Charles Eliot, observed, Shidehara believed that:

> The Chinese . . . were like young children, naughty children no doubt, and fond of playing most dangerous tricks, but still mere children, and not to be taken too seriously, as he thought we and the Americans did, each in our own way.[28]

Meanwhile, loyal readers of the *North China Daily News* would find such a tone familiar. Articles of a similar vein could be found daily in the paper under Rodney Gilbert and O. M. Green's editorship in the 1920s.[29]

China: Facts, Facts, Facts

China was no longer defenseless in the English-language press. The *Leader* in Beijing and the *China Critic* in Shanghai were the main positions to counter Japan's version. However, the negative spin of international opinion continued to plague China's propaganda. While the Chinese anti-imperialist manner still remained fresh in the memory of many foreign expatriates, the tension over treaty revision kept reinforcing China's anti-foreign image. How to separate the anti-Japanese rhetoric from the broader anti-imperialist movements became a pressing task for China's propaganda.

Chinese-operated English-language periodicals pursued a narrow interpretation of the cause of the incident. Instead of citing previous Sino-Japanese frictions to justify China's position, the editors tended to focus on the incident itself, believing that the "undisputable facts" about Japan's military activities and atrocities was the best way to counter Japan's "misstatements."[30] Chinese editors paid considerable attention to reviewing the explosion on the South Manchuria Railway. Their goal was

---

26. "Has Japan the Right to Defend Herself?"
27. "Press Comment in Japan," *North China Daily News*, September 21, 1931, 18.
28. Quote from Richard Rigby, *The May 30 Movement: Events and Themes* (Canberra: Australian National University Press, 1980), 139.
29. Bickers, *Britain in China*, 28.
30. "Newspaper Appeal to World," *Leader*, October 7, 1931, 6; "Special Notice," *China Critic*, September 24, 1931, 911.

twofold: first, to prove that Chinese troops were entirely unprovoked; and second, to reveal that Japan had planned the whole scheme to exploit the bombing as a pretext for the occupation of Manchuria. But both tasks were difficult. There were no Chinese eyewitness accounts of what had happened when the incident broke out. No one saw the explosion and the resulting damage. The only eyewitnesses were the Japanese soldiers who had killed the alleged Chinese bombers. Even if there were Chinese survivors, chances of them being able to tell their side of the story were slim, since Japan had seized all wireless stations in Mukden after the incident and was strictly scrutinizing all outgoing messages via cables.[31]

Instead of confronting Japanese accounts directly, Chinese-operated journals and Nanjing officials, who were keen to publicize China's case worldwide, tended to challenge Japan's version in a subtle manner by inviting foreign journalists to investigate the explosion. Two days after the incident, Zhang Xueliang arranged a special train for foreign journalists who desired to visit the scene of the Japanese occupation in Manchuria.[32] The visit inevitably forced Japan to prove its version of events. Yet the more details Japan provided, the more flaws were noticed. Foreign journalists returned with a growing suspicion about the Japanese version. One journalist reported to the *China Weekly Review* that after the investigation trip he found the whole Japanese explanation "weak in a hundred different places . . . and every time some correspondent or military observer has called attention to a weak point, the Japanese have always come back with a new and more involved explanation."[33] He confessed that he finally gave up "patching the various Japanese explanations in disgust" and totally understood why "foreign correspondents in Mukden have not been able to find a single foreigner in the city who believes the Japanese explanation of the so-called 'Pei-ta-ying Incident' [Mukden Incident]."[34]

Editors of the *Leader* also directed readers' attention to the swift and organized reaction by the Japanese army immediately after the "accident," implying that the incident was carefully planned.[35] Ironically, the editors, when arguing this point, relied heavily on factual materials provided by Japan's news agency Rengō, whose reports recorded every major Japanese military movement. Yet behind this smart move was the painful reality that China's own information supply was insufficient and that editors had to gather any materials available to them.

Indeed, Chinese editors made conscious attempts to "localize" the discussion of the incident, trying hard to divert the readers' attention away from the larger Sino-foreign

---

31. "Japanese Censorship in Manchuria," 1095.
32. "Journalists Visit Mukden," *Leader*, September 20, 1931, 1.
33. "How the Japanese Troops Captured Mukden," *China Weekly Review*, October 10, 1931, 203.
34. Ibid.
35. "Real Facts Known from Interviews," *Leader*, September 22, 1931, 10; "Doubts Cast on Japanese Statement," *Leader*, September 24, 1931, 1.

conflicts, particularly the extraterritoriality issue. During the three months following the outbreak of the Mukden Incident, neither the *Leader* nor the *China Critic* ever mentioned the extraterritoriality debate. The omission was not a truthful reflection of the shift of public interest. For the foreign communities in Shanghai, the Mukden Incident was a remote case, but the extraterritoriality debate was their priority. In November 1931, British residents in Shanghai had organized a mass meeting to oppose negotiation on extraterritoriality, which indicated that extraterritoriality issues still dominated public opinion in the treaty ports despite the lack of coverage by Chinese-controlled papers. Clearly, the silence surrounding the extraterritoriality debate was an attempt by the Chinese-operated papers to downplay the current Sino-foreign disputes and to separate the Sino-Japanese conflict from them.

The *China Critic* and the Tanaka Memorial

To persuade the other Powers that they shared a common interest with China against Japan's aggression was not an easy task. Japan's invasion of Manchuria posed no immediate danger to their interests. Neither Britain nor the United States had any substantial investment in Manchuria. In hindsight, the Mukden Incident marked the beginning of a series of military adventures by the Japanese in the 1930s and 1940s. Yet this reality could not have been predicted in the early 1930s. The incident could have just been an insignificant confrontation that might have easily escaped the attention of the world media. Rana Mitter cogently reminded us of the remote location of Manchuria as a factor in the difficulties of evoking popular nationalism elsewhere in the country.[36] If nationalizing the event was already challenging, internationalizing the incident was even worse. It was therefore imperative for Chinese propagandists to lead the public imagination by creating a context to give the case a broad and long-lasting significance. The Tanaka Memorial accordingly entered the debate in the treaty-port press.

The *China Critic* pioneered the invoking of the Tanaka Memorial as evidence of Japan's aggressive intentions. The memorial was first published in the December 1929 edition of the journal.[37] Although current historians believe that the document was a Soviet forgery, the memorial was widely accepted as authentic in the 1930s and 1940s because of the close correspondence between the plans presented in the memorial and Japan's military actions.[38]

---

36. Rana Mitter, *The Manchurian Myth: Nationalism, Resistance, and Collaboration in Modern China* (Berkeley: University of California Press, 2000), 189.
37. Meirion Harries and Susie Harries, *Soldiers of the Sun: the Rise and Fall of the Imperial Japanese Army* (New York: Random House, 1991), 162.
38. Martin J. Manning and Herbert Romerstein, *Historical Dictionary of American Propaganda* (Westport, CT: Greenwood Publishing, 2004), 272–73.

The Tanaka Memorial was claimed to be a confidential document provided by Prime Minister Tanaka Giichi to the emperor in mid-1927, in which he presented Japan's plan for world conquest:

> In order to conquer China we must first conquer Manchuria and Mongolia. In order to conquer the world, we must first conquer China. . . . Having China's entire resources at our disposal we shall proceed to conquer India, the Archipelago Asia Minor, Central Asia, and even Europe.[39]

The memorial advocated that a "blood and iron" policy be applied to establish Japan's authority in East Asia and saw the United States as an obstacle to Japan's imperial expansion.

The *Critic* used the memorial with great caution. In its issue of September 24, the journal primarily focused on Tanaka's plan for Manchuria, seeking to establish a connection between the Mukden Incident and the document.[40] Tanaka's suggestion that Manchuria and Mongolia should be conquered to facilitate Japan's larger expansion was quoted to refute Japan's claim that it had no territorial desire in China.[41] His view that Korean immigration should be mobilized to assist Japan's conquest of Manchuria was also cited to explain Japan's intention in the Wanbaoshan Incident, when a local irrigation dispute between Korean immigrants near Changchun developed into large anti-Chinese riots in Korea two months before the Mukden Incident.[42] All quotes from the memorial closely revolved around the Manchuria incident itself.

Editors continued to cite the memorial in subsequent issues. On October 15, they published another two excerpts: one concerning the significance of the conquest of China and the other stating that the United States was a potential impediment for Japan's leadership in the world. Clearly, by selecting these parts of the memorial, the editors intended to draw the United States into the Sino-Japanese dispute. However, they were careful not to push this line too hard. They specified that their publication of the memorial was only to remind the Chinese of the existence of this secret document.[43] Apart from a direct quotation of the memorial, they refrained from adding any comments on the excerpts, fearing that an explicit attack on Japan would only reveal China's propaganda purpose and accordingly damage the authenticity of the document.

The *Critic* referred to the memorial again on November 12, with the purpose of reinforcing the authenticity of the document and to "convince the reader of the

---

39. See quotation of the memorial in Carl Crow, *Japan's Dream of World Empire: The Tanaka Memorial* (New York: Harner and Brothers, 1942), 28–29; "Tantrums of Tanaka," *China Critic*, October 15, 1931, 1008–9.
40. "Official Document, Tanaka Memorial," *China Critic*, September 24, 1931, 923.
41. Ibid.
42. Akira Iriye, *After Imperialism: The Search for a New Order in the Far East, 1921–1931* (Cambridge, MA: Harvard University Press, 1965), 291.
43. "Tantrums of Tanaka," 1008–9.

accuracy of the Memorial in the prediction of Japanese aggressive acts."[44] Instead of citing the memorial alone, the author placed the extracts side by side with the Japanese military actions over the last few months, to create the impression that Japan had "signed [its] signature to the document by [its] own deeds."[45] At the end of the article, the author abandoned his implicit style, warning Western readers directly that the memorial not only concerned China but also threatened Russia and the United States, two countries Japan regarded as major obstacles on its way to world conquest.[46]

Altogether, it took the *Critic* three articles, stretching over ten weeks, to present its full interpretation of the memorial, from primarily seeking to connect it with the Mukden Incident to warning the world of Japan's menace. This achieved at least some impact in the United States. The memorial was reproduced in the United States in the *Communist International* magazine in late 1931. The document drew wider attention in February 1934 when it was quoted at length in the front-page article of the first edition of the *Plain Truth* magazine, published by Herbert W. Armstrong.

Opinions of the Treaty-Port Papers and the Metropolitan Press

The *North China Daily News*, led by its new editor, Edwin Howard, took a mixed attitude in the Mukden Incident with a slight leaning toward the Japanese account of events. It expressed deep sympathy for Japan's vital interests in Manchuria and praised the Japanese for "endur[ing] with remarkable patience a series of affronts [from China]."[47] By quoting statistics about "bandit raids within the Japanese railway zone since 1906," "the number of Japanese victims between 1926 and 1929," and "the loss of Japanese army and police in resisting bandit attacks," the editor lamented that Chinese military forces seldom "effectively and sincerely" endeavoring to suppress these bandits who threatened the life, property, and enterprises of the Japanese people.[48] British nationals, complained the *Daily News*, suffered from a similar disorder and lack of protection. Such a line resonated with the *Far Eastern Review*'s discussion of the Thorburn case. The paper claimed that "the failure of Nanjing to give satisfaction in the Thorburn case merely illustrated the impossibility of its winning foreign confidence."[49]

The *Daily News*' stance on the Manchurian crisis reflected the general view held by Anglo-American communities in Shanghai. Randall Gould, who was then

---

44. "Tanaka the Prophet," *China Critic*, November 12, 1931, 1098–101.
45. Ibid.
46. Ibid.
47. "The *Times* on Manchuria," *North China Daily News*, September 22, 1931, 20.
48. "Bandit Menace in Manchuria: What Japan Has Suffered in Recent Years," *North China Daily News*, September 24, 1931, 15.
49. "Foreign Press Opinion," *North China Daily News*, September 21, 1931, 18.

correspondent of the *Shanghai Evening Post and Mercury*, the largest American-controlled evening paper, observed that opinion concerning the Mukden Incident among foreigners in Shanghai was divided and that a large number of Americans and most Britons were willing to accept the Japanese argument.[50] The foreign expatriates in China, without the pressure to remain neutral as newspapers did, could be much more pronounced in their pro-Japanese view. In fact, British nationals believed that Japan was trying only to follow the steps of other empires and extend its own influence. Being stalwart supporters of imperial interests themselves, they saw no reason to challenge these Japanese acts. As Gould recalled, Colonel Amery's statement in London was welcomed in Shanghai:

> I confess that I see no reason why, whether in act, or in word, or in sympathy, we should go individually or internationally against Japan in this matter. . . . Who is there among us to cast the first stone and to say that Japan ought not to have acted with the object of creating peace and order in Manchuria and defending herself against the continuous aggression of a vigorous Chinese nationalism? Our whole policy in India, our whole policy in Egypt, stands condemned if we condemn Japan.[51]

However, it would be irresponsible to argue that the *Daily News* carried a pro-Japanese tone. The paper strongly opposed Japan's military action, believing "there [was] no excuse for the Japanese officers to strike the blow without consulting their government."[52] It frequently addressed the Japanese army as "invaders"[53] and quoted Chinese sources at length about Japan's militant aggression in Manchuria. The paper gave space to voice China's case in its Letters to the Editor section, where harsh condemnation like "Japan is fooling the world" or "Japan's intention towards China is an open secret to all" could commonly be found.[54] It carried eyewitness accounts by foreign residents in Manchuria who denounced the Japanese for starting the incident by bombing the railway and described how Japanese troops bullied and robbed civilians.[55] Indeed, the paper was cautious not to provoke the Chinese public any further, as this might lead to another large-scale antiforeign popular movement. No matter how the paper's allegiances swung between the two sides, one message had clearly been sent: keep off Shanghai and restore peace soon.

The advance of the Japanese military as well as the lack of resistance by the Chinese government soon ignited public anger among the Chinese in Shanghai. Following the pattern of the May Fourth and May Thirtieth Movements, students gathered in

---

50. Randall Gould, *China in the Sun* (Garden City, NY: Doubleday, 1946), 310.
51. Ibid.
52. "The *Times* on Manchuria."
53. "Japanese Position Strengthened," *North China Herald*, September 22, 1931, 398.
54. Letters to the Editor, *North China Daily News*, October 7, 1931, 5.
55. "Another View of Mukden," *North China Daily News*, September 30, 1931, 5.

the street and demonstrated against both the Japanese invasion and the nonresistance policy pursued by the Nanjing government. In response, Japan sent more warships to the Huangpu River.⁵⁶ The *Daily News* revealed deep concerns over the stability of the city and advocated that peace and order be maintained "at any cost" by the local authorities "if they wish Shanghai to continue its prosperity at all."⁵⁷ The paper severely condemned the widespread boycott activities in Shanghai, fearing that they would exacerbate the crisis:

> The measure of boycott adopted by China is as much inhuman and cold-blooded in the eyes of humanity and as much infringement on international law as an aggressive war itself. This [the boycott] is a living death, much crueller than war in view of the fact that the former kills a man inch by inch while the latter does at once.⁵⁸

For the *Daily News*, returning justice to the Far East was much less important than bringing the conflict to a swift conclusion. Although editors of the paper agreed that Japan bore some responsibility in instigating the boycotts, and forcing the Chinese to purchase Japanese goods was inappropriate, they still suggested that China and Japan should "try to forget" their personal and international grievances "like a true man" and mediate "calmly" for an "immediate solution."⁵⁹ The paper became impatient with the League of Nations' inability to solve the problem, warning that indecision would lead to calamity.⁶⁰ As the chief editor explicitly commented in an editorial, "There is no need to weigh up the grievances of either side."⁶¹ The top priority for both countries, he believed, was the speedy restoration of peace.

Compared with its stance during the Jinan Incident, the *North China Daily News* had apparently toned down its die-hard perspective when it came to the Manchuria Incident. Ironically, while the treaty-port paper began to accept China's point of view, the British metropolitan papers, the London *Times* in particular, ignored it. The *Times*' sympathy lay with Japan. It appreciated Japan's development in Manchuria and believed that Japan's military action was the result of China's long-term disrespect for Japanese vital interests in Manchuria.⁶² British correspondents claimed Japan had created "a flourishing oasis in a howling desert of Chinese misrule" and "established order where order was not known before."⁶³ Yet Japan's contribution received only

---

56. "Order in Shanghai," *North China Daily News*, October 13, 1931, 4.
57. Ibid.
58. "Japan's Protests," *North China Daily News*, October 13, 1931, 4.
59. "Selling Goods by Force," *North China Herald*, October 13, 1931, 54.
60. "Before the League," *North China Daily News*, September 30, 1931, 6.
61. Ibid.
62. "Fighting in Manchuria," *Times*, September 21, 1931, 13.
63. "Japan in Manchuria," *Times*, November 2, 1931, 13.

China's hostile reactions.[64] "Under such provocation," claimed the paper, "it is no wonder that Japan should have asserted herself."[65]

The paper drew on the British imperial experience to justify Japan's military action. It endorsed J. O. P. Bland's view that "Japan's position with regard to Manchuria today is almost similar to ours vis-à-vis Egypt."[66] It also acknowledged that "the work of Japan is indeed of a sort that makes particular appeal to the people of the British Empire," since "nowhere is it better understood how vital are the material interests of Japan in Manchuria, which supplies her with foodstuffs and primary products, and provides her with a market for her manufactured goods."[67]

The *Times* resumed a die-hard tone to blame the British government's concession to Chinese nationalism. It argued that Japan shouldered the consequences of an antagonized Sino-British relationship in the 1920s: "If British rights had been safeguarded by the British government, this particular and most provocative part of the Chinese plan to injure the position of Japan in Manchuria could not have been carried out."[68]

Indeed, Britain was caught between "the maintenance of a traditional friendship" with Japan and the "defence of principles" as a signatory of the Covenant of the League of Nations.[69] Considering the common imperial interests it shared with Japan, Britain was reluctant to criticize its old ally. Yet as a key member of the League, considerable hope was placed upon Britain to restore peace in East Asia. This hesitation translated to inaction, which not only drew China's complaint against its partiality toward Japan but also harmed the League's reputation. To save Britain from this quagmire, the *Times* repeatedly blamed China for the escalation of the crisis, accusing it of intransigence toward Japan's request and efforts to internationalize the regional crisis. "In the present dispute," expressed the paper, "the Council's [Council of the League of Nation] championship of peace does not in the least mean that it has any sympathy with the 'pinpricking' policy in which Chinese Governments have indulged only too often in present years."[70]

The key American paper in Shanghai, the *Shanghai Evening Post and Mercury*, firmly pursued an anti-Japanese line after the incident. Despite his personal liking for Japan and its people, the owner of the paper, Cornelius Vander Starr, believed that Japan had gone too far during the Mukden Incident. "Up to now," he said to his chief editor Theodore Olin Thackrey, "I've never tried to lay down specific policy for

---

64. "Japan and China," *Times*, September 9, 1931, 13.
65. "Japan in Manchuria," 13.
66. "Points from Letter, Japan and Manchuria," *Times*, October 23, 1931, 17.
67. "Japan in Manchuria," 13.
68. "British Investments in China," *Times*, November 10, 1931, 10.
69. "Japan in Manchuria," 13.
70. "Manchuria and the League," *Times*, September 26, 1931, 11.

the *Post*, but on this Manchuria thing—I must. We are against it!"[71] Yet to uphold the anti-Japanese view was not easy. The paper's reports from Manchuria needed to survive Japan's censorship. Numerous telegrams from the *Post* filed from Mukden to Shanghai were held up, rewritten, or edited by Japanese censors.[72] The *Post* also faced strong challenges from its Japanese-controlled competitors, the *Far Eastern Review* and the *Shanghai Times*.

However, the biggest obstacle came from the paper's own editorial writer H. G. W. Woodhead's staunch advocacy of Japan's interests. Woodhead was a prominent British die-hard journalist. Starr invited him to join the *Post* in 1930 and granted him full independence in writing, hoping his prestige in Shanghai would bring more British readers. Yet, after the outbreak of the Mukden Incident, Woodhead's strong defense of Japanese interests gravely offset the *Post*'s anti-Japanese stance. Although he did not believe that Japan had the intention to fight on behalf of other Powers in Manchuria, he maintained that its winning would inevitably strengthen the other Powers' interests in China.[73]

Among the foreign-operated English-language papers, the *China Weekly Review* maintained the most hostile stance against Japan's action in Manchuria. The paper challenged Japan's "self-defense" explanation from the beginning, criticizing Japan for its military presence, atrocities to civilians, and dishonesty before the League.[74] The editors believed that Japan's occupation of Manchuria aimed to "break up the nation" and nullify the open-door policy in China.[75]

Articles from the *Review* served as ideal propaganda materials for Chinese interest groups because of its third-person perspective. In 1932, the Shanghai Bar Association, for example, published an English pamphlet opposing Japanese aggression in Manchuria and Shanghai. Out of its twenty-five articles dealing with the Manchurian case, twenty-two were *Review* editorials originally published between late September 1931 and early April 1932.[76]

Nevertheless, the *Review*'s criticism of Chinese domestic disorder was as bitter as was its condemnation of Japan. It ridiculed China's weak military: "Look at China! In what respect could she compete with Japan? Will her four hundred million brothers

---

71. Gould, *China in the Sun*, 310.
72. "Japanese Censorship in Manchuria," 1095.
73. H. G. W. Woodhead and *Shanghai Evening Post and Mercury*, *The Sino-Japanese Crisis: Being a Reprint of a Selection of Articles Appearing in "The Shanghai Evening Post and Mercury" October 1931–June 1932* (Shanghai: Printed by the Mercury Press for the South Manchuria Railway Co., 1932), 3.
74. "Japanese Military Occupation of South Manchuria," *China Weekly Review*, September 26, 1931, 127; "The Japanese Militarists," *China Weekly Review*, September 26, 1931, 136; "An Outrageous Act of War," *China Weekly Review*, October 24, 1931, 284; "Japan Defies the League of Nations—League Leaves China in the Lurch," *China Weekly Review*, October 3, 1931, 167.
75. "Evidence of Japan's Real Objective in Manchuria," *China Weekly Review*, October 31, 1931, 321.
76. K. N. Lei and Shanghai Bar Association, *Information and Opinion Concerning the Japanese Invasion of Manchuria and Shanghai from Sources Other Than Chinese* (Shanghai: Shanghai Bar Association, 1932).

come together to the same front, or are those brothers all useful in fighting against Japan?"[77] It blamed Chinese leaders' miscalculation of the nonresistance policy, arguing that nonresistance not only disgraced the nation but also confused world opinion.[78] By invoking the Kellogg Pact, a state of war should exist. Yet China's failure to return fire created no warlike situation, which provided the State Department of the United States with the justification for not intervening.[79] The nonresistance policy, stated the journal, made it difficult for other countries to offer China any practical help while China itself had chosen not to fight.[80]

The *Review*'s anti-Japanese line contrasted with the neutral stance adopted by the American metropolitan paper the *New York Times*. The paper carried more than two hundred articles about Manchuria in the month following the outbreak of the incident.[81] Despite the close follow-up, it refrained from taking sides. Fully aware of the League of Nations' weakness in solving the Sino-Japanese conflict, the paper still advocated that the United States should follow the League's decision while avoiding any commitment of joint action with the League in solving the conflict.[82] Only after Japan's air assault on Jinzhou, which shook the United States' faith in a withdrawal of Japanese troops, did the US government agree to send representatives to the Council of the League to collectively curb Japan's aggression. However, the move, as interpreted by the paper, was only for the "convenience" of the procedure. The paper stressed that "we are merely sitting in on the conference.... There is no implication that we are pro-Chinese or pro-Japan. We are pro-world and pro-peace."[83] Like the *North China Daily News*, the *New York Times* was more eager to restore peace than to achieve moral justice. As Akira Iriye cogently pointed out, there was a mixture of moral globalism and fear of military involvement in Asia that characterized American press opinion.[84]

The Mukden Incident once again highlighted the necessity for international propaganda by the Nanjing government. In October 1931, the government urgently allocated 100,000 yuan to subsidize international cable transmissions. Welcoming

---

77. "How Can China Find Her Way Out?" *China Weekly Review*, November 7, 1931, 369.
78. "The Failure of Policy of Non-resistance," *China Weekly Review*, December 5, 1931, 20–21.
79. "To What Extent Has Japan Violated International Agreements?" *China Weekly Review*, October 10, 1931, 222.
80. "Some Significant Elements in the Sino-Japanese Situation in Manchuria," *China Weekly Review*, October 17, 1931, 246.
81. Based on a keyword search of "Manchuria" in the historical database of the *New York Times* for articles between September 18 and October 18, 1931.
82. "Stimson Appeals to China and Japan," *New York Times*, September 24, 1931, 1; "Doubt Foreign Step Is Needed in China," *New York Times*, September 20, 1931, 28.
83. "Press Comment on Our Cooperation with League," *New York Times*, October 17, 1931, 3.
84. Akira Iriye, *Across the Pacific: An Inner History of American–East Asian Relations* (New York: Harcourt, Brace & World, 1967), 180.

the policy, Nanjing leaders nonetheless were critical of the ad hoc manner in which foreign propaganda work was organized.

> Our foreign propaganda lacks long-term planning and effort. Everyone realizes the importance of foreign propaganda and promotes it when the nation is threatened by external forces, yet few care about it when peace returns. Propaganda only produces an effect with ongoing efforts. Without a daily continuous preparation, foreign propaganda would not yield promising results when conflicts occur.[85]

In November 1931, Fang Zhi and Zhang Junqi repeatedly appealed to the Nanjing government to organize a centralized foreign propaganda agency to counter Japan's foreign propaganda.[86] Yet a few months later, before the government was able to make any concrete improvements, another Sino-Japanese conflict broke out in Shanghai.

The Shanghai Incident

Anti-Japanese boycotts and popular movements were widespread in Shanghai after the Mukden Incident. Tensions between Chinese and Japanese communities escalated at the turn of 1932. On January 18, Japanese monks were attacked by a party of fifty to sixty Chinese in Shanghai, leaving one dead and several injured. Rear Admiral Shiozawa Kōichi, Japanese naval commander at Shanghai, used this disturbance as a pretext to present demands to Wu Tiecheng, the mayor of Chinese Shanghai. Although Wu unconditionally accepted all the demands, around midnight on January 28, the Japanese navy still bombed Zhabei, a densely populated Chinese suburb adjoining the International Settlement. This marked the beginning of the Shanghai Incident.

The incident was commonly considered an extension of the unresolved Manchurian dispute. Unable to withstand Japan's advance in Manchuria, Chinese elites perceived boycott and noncooperation as the "only way that a weak country can even her score with a militaristic country like Japan."[87] These approaches not only aimed to "make the Japanese living in this country uncomfortable and their business unprofitable"[88] but also were a way to vent Chinese public anger toward the Japanese military as well as the Nanjing government's nonresistance policy.[89] The Japanese community in Shanghai was equally inflamed. It lodged complaints against Chinese violence to the

---

85. Guoji xuanchuan jinxing banfa, Zhang Junqi's proposal, November 16, 1931, conference papers, 4.3/27.42, Guomindang Archives.
86. Ibid.
87. "Cowardice of the Japanese Militarists," *China Critic*, September 24, 1931, 912.
88. Ibid.
89. Parks Coble, *Facing Japan: Chinese Politics and Japanese Imperialism, 1931–1937* (Cambridge, MA: Harvard University Press, 1991), 36–37; Donald A. Jordan, *Chinese Boycotts versus Japanese Bombs: The Failure of China's "Revolutionary Diplomacy" 1931–32* (Ann Arbor: University of Michigan Press, 1991), 3.

Japanese consulates and repeatedly pressed military authorities to take action against Chinese hostilities.[90]

There were also various hidden connections between the Shanghai and Mukden incidents. The Shanghai Incident was partly driven by the Japanese navy's jealousy over the Kwantung Army's success in Manchuria.[91] As the Japanese army occupied the whole of Manchuria without meaningful resistance from the Chinese, the navy also anticipated an easy victory in Shanghai. Furthermore, the incident was a conspiracy of the Kwantung Army and the Japanese navy to divert Western powers' attention away from the establishment of Manchukuo.[92] Tanaka Ryūkichi, then the military attaché to Shanghai, testified in 1956 that from October 1931 Itagaki Seishirō of the Kwantung Army had secretly asked him to organize a series of incidents in Shanghai to distract the world's attention from Manchuria. Following the request, Tanaka, with the help of Kawashima Yoshiko, bribed some Chinese and staged the attack on Japanese monks on January 18.[93] The assault fit so well into the tense situation in Shanghai that neither the Chinese nor the Japanese ever suspected the true reasons for the attacks.

Shanghai was an international city with three authorities supervising its territories: the Shanghai Municipal Council, mostly representing the Anglo-American interests, ruled the International Settlement; the Conseil d'Administration Municipale, backed by the French government, controlled the French Concession; and the Chinese government was in charge of the remainder. The three parts were so closely connected, geographically and socially, that any attack in one part would cause significant disturbance to the others. The city held the largest foreign economic interests in China. While Great Britain and the United States together had no more than US$40 million invested in Manchuria, Britain alone had direct business investments in Shanghai worth US$737.4 million, while the US business interests valued at US$97.5 million.[94] Indeed, no fighting in Shanghai could be regarded as "local." While Chinese

---

90. Donald A. Jordan, *China's Trial by Fire: The Shanghai War of 1932* (Ann Arbor: University of Michigan Press, 2001), 6–8.
91. Coble, *Facing Japan*, 44; Akira Iriye, *The Origins of the Second World War in Asia and the Pacific* (London and New York: Longman, 1987), 17.
92. Coble, *Facing Japan*, 47; Harumi Goto-Shibata, *Japan and Britain in Shanghai, 1925–31* (New York: St. Martin's Press, 1995), 136–37; Wen Jize, *Jiuyiba he yi'erba shiqi kang-Ri yundong shi* [A history of the anti-Japanese movement during the Mukden and Shanghai Incidents] (Beijing: Zhongguo gongren chubanshe, 1991), 204–7; Peter Duus and John Whitney Hall, *The Cambridge History of Japan: The Twentieth Century* (Cambridge University Press, 1988), 297.
93. Goto-Shibata, *Japan and Britain in Shanghai*, 135–36, 204–5.
94. Charles Frederick Remer, *Foreign Investments in China* (New York: Macmillan, 1933), 97–98. Based on press reports, V. Wellesley estimated British investment to be £250 million in early 1932, which included shipping and insurance interests, investments in railways and in government bonds, banking, and trade of all kinds. See memorandum by Sir V. Wellesley, February 1, 1932, in *Documents on British Foreign Policy*, series IX (London: Her Majesty's Stationery Office, 1946), 288.

propagandists were trying hard to internationalize the Sino-Japanese dispute, the Japanese bombs in Zhabei effectively did the job for them.

As the media center of East Asia, Shanghai housed correspondents from key international newspapers and news agencies. Foreign journalists were not merely passive observers but active participants, providing intelligence information to the politicians with whom they associated. The *New York Times*' correspondent Hallett Abend, after learning of Admiral Shiozawa's intention to bomb Zhabei regardless of Mayor Wu's compliance, warned US consul Cunningham and T. V. Soong about the crisis. It may have been at that point that Soong mobilized his hundreds of antismuggling police to fend off Japan's attack.[95] Thousands of foreign residents in Shanghai also became the best third-party witnesses to this Sino-Japanese fighting. Unlike the Mukden case, when Zhang Xueliang needed to organize Western journalists to travel to Mukden to investigate the conflict, the Shanghai Incident took place right in front of the foreign journalists. Equipped with the best news facilities in China, the correspondents were able to expose the Shanghai Incident to the world public immediately. This minimized China's disadvantage in international communication infrastructure and reduced the chance for Japan to dominate the flow of information.

China also had a good story to tell. It enjoyed the moral high ground in the face of Japan's ruthless bombings and killings in Chinese territory. Many of the civilian areas, including refugee camps, the Commercial Press, and its libraries, were engulfed in flames. These facts, which were witnessed by foreign residents, were strong propaganda material for China to strengthen its position as a victim. Confident of their own righteousness, Chinese officials temporarily lifted all censorship from local newspapers, wireless, and cable offices, so as to publicize Japan's violence to the outside world as widely as possible.[96]

Japan nevertheless did not entirely lose its competitive edge. The legacy of its positive image remained strong, and the peace and order it promised to bring after the incident was attractive to many foreign residents. A large number of Shanghai expatriates considered Japan, whose triumph boosted the reputation of foreigners in general, as "one of them." As Archibald Trojan Steele, a contemporary US journalist, described, applause from Europeans and Americans for Japanese action in Shanghai could commonly be heard in bars, at street corners, and in offices: "Well, it's about time somebody was knocking sense into the Chinese and bringing a little order into this country. Perhaps the Japanese are the ones to do it."[97] In the face of a Sino-Japanese conflict, foreigners sometimes supported Japan not necessarily because they were impressed by the Japanese cause but because they deplored Chinese rule. Japan

---

95. Jordan, *China's Trial by Fire*, 41.
96. "Japanese Attempt to 'Buy Up' Shanghai Newspapers," *China Weekly Review*, March 19, 1932, 68.
97. Archibald Trojan Steele, *Shanghai and Manchuria, 1932: Recollections of a War Correspondent* (Tempe: Arizona State University, 1977), 1.

could still score points by exposing China's weakness and accentuating Japan's affinity with Western powers. Knowing their advantages and limits, China and Japan refined their strategies and engaged in a new round of propaganda battles.

China's Strategies

During the Shanghai Incident, China's propaganda focused increasingly on allying with the Anglo-American powers while isolating Japan. Both government officials and intellectuals were eager to drop the anti-imperialist tone and redefine the criteria by which "friends" or "enemies" were identified. At the government level, Yan Huiqing, Chinese delegate in Geneva, had reported the incident to the League of Nations immediately after Japan's bombing of Shanghai and invoked the Covenant of the League to solve the Shanghai crisis.[98] On January 30, Luo Wengan, the Oxford-trained foreign minister, circulated a statement in the English-language press in Shanghai, confirming that China would firmly "adhere to the Covenant of the League of Nations, the Brian-Kellogg Pact and the Nine Power Treaty—by all of which military aggression and war as an instrument of national policy are renounced and condemned."[99] To be sure, the declaration was more a propaganda strategy than a reflection of China's trust in the League and the international treaties. T. V. Soong, vice president of the Executive Yuan, openly expressed his concern over the limits of the international agreements, believing that they were "of use only when backed by force."[100] Yet, by expressing China's firm adherence to the international treaties, the government sought to create the image that China was the Western powers' closest follower, willing to observe and defend the world order. As the *North China Daily News* rightly pointed out, the Chinese delegation thought that it had nothing to lose by taking its case before the League. The more publicity it obtained, the more it would be to their advantage.[101]

To further ameliorate relations with foreign powers, the Chinese-controlled treaty-port journals completely avoided printing articles about the revision of extraterritoriality or any issues that might remind the Westerners of China's anti-imperialist past. For the first time, they frequently addressed the Western countries as "friendly powers," a title that they would not have even conceived of using in the years leading up to the Shanghai Incident when Sino-foreign relations were tense.[102] The *China Critic* even began to criticize Chinese nationalist activities, stating that "blind passion and prejudice" against the West were unhelpful to China's development and that

---

98. Yan Huiqing, *Yan Huiqing zizhuan* [Autobiography of W. W. Yen] (Taipei: Zhuanji wenxue chubanshe, 1973), 173.
99. "50,000 Cheer Troop Trains for Shanghai," *China Press*, January 31, 1932, 1.
100. "The Significance of the Warfare around Shanghai," *People's Tribune*, March 1932, 82–83.
101. "China and the League," *North China Daily News*, February 13, 1932, 9.
102. T. V. Soong et al., "Japan's Challenge to the Civilized World," *People's Tribune*, February–March 1932, 13.

"discriminating hostility to the foreigner and all his works can lead people astray."[103] The *China Press* argued that both the Chinese and Western public were the victims of Japanese aggression. It attributed the depression in the London stock market to the instability in the East Asia and warned that the capture of Shanghai and other ports of China by Japan would lead to widespread bankruptcy among Chinese commercial and industrial establishments.[104] In addition, the paper provided graphic descriptions of Japanese atrocities in the International Settlement and eyewitness stories about attacks on foreign residents by Japanese soldiers.[105]

The Chinese public in Shanghai also dropped its anti-imperial sentiments and singled out Japan as China's sole enemy. Posters urging all Chinese to befriend Westerners while antagonizing the Japanese were put up on the doors and windows of Chinese shops along Nanjing Road and elsewhere in the International Settlement. The posters, written in red, bold Chinese characters, read:

> All my countrymen, see exactly who is your enemy. Distinguish your friends from your enemies. All foreigners (other than Japanese) are friendly to us, and we should not do anything to hurt their feelings.[106]

Some of the Chinese shops and institutions put up posters welcoming the arrival of the US Asiatic Fleet, which was sent to Shanghai to protect American interests and restore the neutrality of the International Settlement.[107] It was unclear who initiated these activities or whether there were any government support behind it. But they sent a clear message to foreign residents that the Chinese had changed their antiforeign attitude and considered Japan to be their only foe.

Chinese treaty-port paper editors deliberately connected the Shanghai case with the Mukden Incident, arguing that the origin of the Shanghai situation could "only be traced to the situation created by Japan's aggression in Manchuria."[108] Linking the two incidents was a way to keep the Manchurian case in the international forum so as to restrain Japan's activities in Manchuria. It also provided the audience an opportunity to revisit the Manchurian case based on its renewed understanding of the Japanese militancy shown in Shanghai. While Chinese reports on Japan's war crimes in Manchuria were overshadowed by Japanese propaganda and were commonly held as untrustworthy, the Shanghai Incident helped to redeem credibility in China's sources and to prove that Japan was capable of severe brutality in warfare. Moreover,

---

103. "Anti-Foreignism Is Not Enough," *China Critic*, January 21, 1932, 67–68.
104. "Shanghai and the Manchurian Question," *China Press*, February 9, 1932, 12.
105. "Japanese Detain British Woman in Chapei for 5 Terrible Days," *China Press*, February 4, 1932, 1; "Chapei Becomes Far-off 'No-Man's Land' to Writer, Marooned between Firing Lines," *China Press*, February 4, 1932, 9; "Nipponese War on Women Takes Horrible Toll," *China Press*, February 5, 1932, 9.
106. "Only Japanese Called Enemies in Red Posters," *China Press*, February 6, 1932, 9.
107. Ibid.
108. "Shanghai and the Manchurian Question," *China Press*, February 9, 1932, 12.

Japan's occupation of Manchuria and its subsequent attack on Shanghai corroborated the Tanaka Memorial. Combining the two cases simply made Japan's world-conquest plan more real. In an article in the *People's Tribune*, T. V. Soong reminded the readers of the Tanaka Memorial by drawing on the Manchurian and Shanghai incidents:

> Having occupied Manchuria, which is as big as France and Germany combined, without serious opposition from Europe or America, and seeing that the rest of the world is still preoccupied with domestic and foreign problems of its own, Japan is determined to put forward her programme of conquest of China by planting her power in Shanghai which is the greatest metropolis of trade and finance in the Far East.[109]

In contrast to the lack of resistance in the Mukden Incident, the Chinese army put up a meaningful defense in Shanghai. The resistance by the Nineteenth Route Army together with the snipers sent by Du Yuesheng, leader of the underground Green Gang, dealt a heavy blow to Japanese naval forces. The defense at the front line greatly benefited China's propaganda. Although neither Japan nor China declared war, the severe military confrontation created a de facto war status, tense enough to invoke the Covenant of the League, the Nine-Power Treaties, and the Kellogg Pact, all of which were designed to prevent warfare. The signatory powers, therefore, were pushed to intervene. The high morale displayed by Chinese soldiers and civilians during the resistance also greatly boosted China's prestige. Henry L. Stimson, US secretary of state, for example, praised the Chinese infantry as "heroic" and believed that the country deserved "more moral sympathy" because of the spirit displayed among its people.[110]

Having sensed the power of military resistance in the battle of propaganda, Chinese officials repeatedly proclaimed their commitment to defend Shanghai. On January 29, Chiang Kai-shek openly expressed that if China should be pushed beyond what could be accepted, it would "go to war even if it would die in defeat."[111] He also published a lengthy front-page article in the *People's Tribune*, glorifying the Nineteenth Route Army's heroism, referring to the troops as a "chivalrous army" that would "fight to the last man and the last bullet" against the Japanese soldiers. He concluded that the "Chinese warriors have the noble cause of humanity and international justice to give up their lives for."[112] T. V. Soong, in the same issue, echoed Chiang's view:

> The manhood of China, armed only with rifles, machine guns and gas pipe mortars, as opposed to the most modern fighting equipment the world had seen,

---

109. T. V. Soong et al. "Japan's Challenge to the Civilized World," 12–13.
110. Henry Lewis Stimson, *The Far Eastern Crisis: Recollections and Observations* (New York: Harper, for the Council on Foreign Relations, 1936), 135–36.
111. Chiang Kai-shek's telegram to Foreign Ministry, January 29, 1932, quoted in Jordan, *China's Trial by Fire*, 50.
112. Chiang Kai-shek, "The 19th Route Army Resists—to the Last!" *People's Tribune*, February–March, 1932, 1–7.

is battling along for the independence of the country so solemnly guaranteed by international agreements to which all the Powers are party.[113]

These statements, nevertheless, were aimed at appealing to emotions rather than reflecting reality. Chiang was far from ready for a war at that point and would try by all means to avoid it. In contrast to the verbal support for military resistance, the government's actual support for the Nineteenth Route Army was minimal. The Nineteenth Route Army belonged to Chiang's rival, the Guangzhou Clique. During the Shanghai Incident, Nanjing sent only nominal reinforcements to the army. Some troops Chiang promised, such as the Third and Fourteenth Divisions, did not arrive until March 7, after the fighting had ceased.[114]

Japan's Strategies

Japanese officials took various measures to suppress unfriendly reports. On January 23, Yano Makoto, chargé d'affaires of the Japanese legation, called Zhang Xueliang, ordering the closure of the *Leader* because it reported a Korean manifesto. Yano also demanded an apology from the paper and the arrest of its editor, Li Bingrui. Zhang rejected the request but had to close the paper to avoid trouble with Japan. It was unclear whether closing the *Leader* right before the attack on Shanghai was part of Japan's scheme to suppress discussion of the forthcoming crisis. It nevertheless displayed definite attempts by Japan's Ministry of Foreign Affairs to muffle anti-Japanese voices in North China when Sino-Japanese conflicts in Shanghai grew more intense. In Shanghai, Japanese officials tried to win foreign journalists support by bribery. On January 27, Takahashi Sankichi, then assistant to the military attaché, approached the *New York Times* correspondent Hallett Abend with a monetary gift, asking him to be conciliatory toward Japan and its actions.[115]

Japan maintained its traditional "self-defense" argument in the press, insisting that its action aimed to protect Japanese nationals in Shanghai who were severely threatened by China's anti-Japanese movements. Rear Admiral Kouichi Shiozawa, commander of the First Japanese Fleet in Chinese waters, blamed Chinese "lawlessness" and "disorder" for the start of warfare, saying it was China's chaos as well as the presence of a large number of "undisciplined troops" that necessitated the navy's shelling of Zhabei.[116] The Japanese government's statement on February 7 strengthened Shiozawa's view, confirming that Japan's action was stimulated by Chinese

113. T. V. Soong et al., "Japan's Challenge to the Civilized World," 11.
114. See Stimson's note in *Far Eastern Crisis*, 110.
115. Hallett Abend, *My Life in China, 1926–1941* (New York: Harcourt, Brace and Company, 1943), 176–77.
116. See quote of Shiozawa's proclamation, in "Swift Action Follows Admiral's Warning: Chinese Withdrawal Urged," *North China Daily News*, January 29, 1932, 13.

soldiers' continuous harassment of the Japanese despite Mayor Wu's acceptance of Shiozawa Kōichi's demands.[117]

While China tried to isolate Japan from the Powers, Japan sought to strengthen its connections with them by citing Western precedents as models of its military action. Shiozawa argued that Japan's shelling of Zhabei was a necessary response to an acute situation: the Shanghai Municipal Council had proclaimed a "state of emergency," and the military and naval forces of other countries had respectively taken various actions to protect their nationals in Shanghai. Japan was acting in accordance with the foreign powers' general defense plan and was fighting for all foreigners. Shiozawa hinted that Japan's response only intensified an already acute situation. Japanese foreign minister Yoshizawa Kenkichi drew a parallel between Japan's current actions and Britain's reaction in 1927 when its nationals in Shanghai were threatened by the Guomindang's Northern Expedition troops. He argued that what Japan did now was "exactly the same" as the British reaction back then.[118] If the British attack was justified, so was that of Japan.

Knowing that to deny Japan's brutal actions in Shanghai was of no avail, editors of the *Far Eastern Review* deliberately avoided details of the fighting and took a realistic view by warning Western audiences about the consequences of antagonizing Japan. The journal argued that foreign powers, particularly the United States, would wreak havoc on its economy if it got involved in the Sino-Japanese conflict. By listing Western powers' investment in Japan, it indicated that any conflict with Japan would put these investments at stake.[119] The journal also claimed that the United States, in order to confront Japan's navy, would have to abandon all its Pacific policies, build a fleet at least three times as powerful as that of Japan, and convert Manila into a military base. Even with such an enormous initial expenditure, it would be of little benefit to the United States if Japan had fortified its submarine defenses.[120] Clearly, editors of the journal tried to urge readers to go against their moral obligations and to consider the case from a pragmatic perspective.

The journal also warned its audience that China did not deserve the Western powers' favor. Quoting an American historian's comments on the Sino-Japanese War of 1895, Rea indicated that China would remain chaotic and repay foreign assistance with hatred:

> Her [China's] armies never once scored a victory. . . . Her fleet on which many hopes had been based, was driven ignominiously to the shelter of fortified ports. Her commanders showed themselves all incompetent, and many, cowards. Her

---

117. See full quotation of Japan's official explanation of its intervention in Shanghai, February 7, in Kiyoshi Karl Kawakami, *Japan Speaks on the Sino-Japanese Crisis* (London: Macmillan, 1932), 122–23.
118. "Japan Considering Expeditionary Army," *New York Times*, January 30, 1932, 1.
119. "Foreign Investments in Japan," *Far Eastern Review*, January 1932, 13.
120. "America Cannot Fight Japan," *Far Eastern Review*, March 1932, 111.

administration was as inefficient and corrupt in the hour of the nation's peril as it notoriously was in time of peace; and her people, while they had acquired some sense of nationality, were still an inchoate mass, in which self-interest was the only motive power and blind fury replaced patriotic endeavour. . . . [I]t was the duty of foreign powers, and not any part of the duty of China to save China from aggression and dismemberment.[121]

The journal drew on China's domestic chaos to attack its "peace-loving" argument. "In the past decade," it maintained, "[China's] pitiless armies have massacred more of their own defenceless people than were killed in the world war."[122] If China was indeed committed to a love of peace and an abhorrence of militarism, questioned the journal, why was this great peace-loving nation unable to settle its own political differences except by an appeal to the sword? The *Review* warned its US readers in Shanghai that they would fall into the trap set by China's propagandists if they kept pursuing an anti-Japanese line:

> Chinese would have America fight Japan while they sit on the sidelines watching both combatants go down to defeat and disaster. They would then garner their fruits of victory. . . . If we win, we lose, and the Chinese would be the only gainers.[123]

Ironically, Rea ruthlessly denied the statement of the *People's Tribune* that the *Far Eastern Review* was "a violent pro-Japanese organ," claiming that the journal was "a better Chinese Nationalist and more loyal friend of Sun Yat-sen than ninety per cent of his Janus-faced disciples who ignobly departed him to accept lucrative positions under every military tyrant from Yuan to Chiang."[124] While elaborating on the journal's support for Sun Yat-sen against his warlord enemies during the 1910s, Rea was tight lipped about Sun's pursuit of national independence. Nor did he mention the journal's change of political patron and stance in the 1920s. He insisted that his observation of Chinese affairs was grounded in "facts" and "events," and his judgement was based on concerns for the "inarticulate millions" of Chinese who were "enslaved" by the Chinese militarists.[125]

Treaty-Port Opinions

The British- and American-operated press formed a united anti-Japanese line during the Shanghai Incident. The *North China Daily News*, which used to sympathize with Japan, adopted an anti-Japanese stance during the Shanghai crisis. The *Shanghai*

---

121. "Again, Stay out of It," *Far Eastern Review*, January 1932, 1.
122. "Basic Problems," *Far Eastern Review*, January 1932, 15.
123. Ibid., 3.
124. "Our Friendship for China," *Far Eastern Review*, January 1932, 6.
125. Ibid., 7.

Evening Post and Mercury and the *China Weekly Review* denounced Japan's aggression and repeatedly urged the Japanese soldiers in the International Settlement to "get out!"[126] Editor of the *Post* Randall Gould believed that "no other Shanghai newspaper hit the Japanese so hard" in its reporting of the Shanghai attack and the subsequent incident in Manchuria than did the *Post*.[127]

The treaty-port papers were most critical of the atrocities committed by Japanese soldiers in Shanghai. Graphic descriptions of Japanese bayoneting civilians, killing women and children, or organized bombing of civilian districts could be found daily in various newspapers. Japanese civilians also came under criticism. Journalists regarded those civilians who coalesced into vigilante units and named themselves *rōnin* in memory of the rugged lordless samurai as "extremely cruel" mobs, beating, stabbing, and shooting the Chinese at random.[128] Such a portrayal severely challenged the traditional impression that Japanese civilians were a gentle, patient people who held decorum in high regard. A. T. Steele confessed that he found himself caught between the fine impression of the Japanese people and the brutal behavior of the Japanese marines and civilians in Shanghai, not knowing which represented the true Japanese.

> I found it difficult to comprehend that these cold-blooded killers could have had any connection with the island of soft hills, pretty temples, kindly people and colorful kimonos I had visited only a few weeks before.[129]

The "facts" of Japan's brutal activities challenged the popular belief that Japan would bring order to the settlement. The *Post* indicated that if China's rule in the settlement was bad, Japan's could only be worse, since during the past several decades foreigners had never had such trouble with the Chinese.[130] The *North China Herald* also questioned whether Japan was authorized to "teach China a lesson" and whether in doing so Japan maintained the proper dispassion of an instructor.[131]

Indeed, the Japanese propaganda machine started to lose steam in front of the naked facts exposed by foreign witnesses. Despite Japanese diplomats repeatedly promising to respect China's national sovereignty, the nonstop bombardment of Chinese cities proved the contrary.[132] In remote Manchuria, the Japanese were still able to suppress reports and challenge the credibility of information unfavorable to Japan. They were unable to do so in Shanghai, where every move of the Japanese

---

126. "To Those Who Have Abused a Trust—Get Out!" *Shanghai Evening Post and Mercury*, February 1, 1932. "Again—Get Out!" *Shanghai Evening Post and Mercury*, February 4, 1932.
127. Gould, *China in the Sun*, 149.
128. "Thousands of Priceless Books Destroyed in Library Flames," *Shanghai Evening Post and Mercury*, February 2, 1932.
129. Steele, *Shanghai and Manchuria*, 7.
130. "Thousands of Priceless Books Destroyed in Library Flames."
131. "A Bad Breach," *North China Herald*, February 9, 1932, 204.
132. "Dangerous Misrepresentations," *Shanghai Evening Post and Mercury*, February 2, 1932.

soldiers was scrutinized by interested and inquisitive foreigners. As Henry L. Stimson observed, when it came to the criticism of Japanese atrocities, "Japan had no defenders. None of the explanations put forth by her (Japan) carried for a minute with our press or our people."[133] The *China Weekly Review* overtly warned foreigners "Don't pay any attention to what the Japanese *say*. Just watch what they are *doing*."[134] A. T. Steele admitted that his distrust of Japan started from witnessing the Japanese killings in 1932, and the experience had left a deep scar in his memory.[135]

The foreign community's anger also came from Japan's use of the International Settlement as a military base to attack the Chinese soldiers. It not only "jeopardized" the neutrality of the settlement and threatened the lives and property of the foreign nationals,[136] but also created the impression that foreign powers endorsed the Japanese attack.[137] Yet the biggest concern was the fiscal stability of the settlement. Chinese taxpayers based in the settlement had collectively notified their intention not to pay any taxes if the Shanghai Municipal Council failed to observe neutrality and return peace soon.[138] Since the greater part of the revenue of the council came from the Chinese, the council leaders could not afford to ignore such a notice.

In response, Japan proposed establishing demilitarized zones, fifteen to twenty miles in width, around the principal trading ports in China, notably Shanghai, Hankou, Tianjin, Guangzhou, and Qingdao.[139] The proposal equated to an extension of the foreign settlement. While the Chinese were doing their utmost in abolishing extraterritoriality and subsequently closing the foreign settlements, Japan's proposal catered to the foreigners who wished to preserve their treaty privileges. The British press claimed little interest in the proposal. A Reuters report showed that the United States had secretly favored demilitarized zones.[140]

Metropolitan Opinions

In contrast to the unified anti-Japanese line adopted by the British- and American-controlled treaty-port papers, the gap between metropolitan papers of the two countries was large. Although both deplored the atrocities Japan had committed, their

---

133. Stimson, *Far Eastern Crisis*, 146.
134. "Be Careful, Gentlemen, or the Japanese Will Have You Holding the Bag Again!" *China Weekly Review*, February 13, 1932, 344.
135. Steele, *Shanghai and Manchuria*, 7.
136. Ibid.
137. "Dangerous Misrepresentations," *Shanghai Evening Post and Mercury*, February 2, 1932; "Neutrality of the Settlement," *North Herald*, February 2, 1932, 159; "Confusion in Hongkew: Col. Stimson's Statement," *North China Herald*, February 2, 1932, 131; "Shells Fall in Settlement," *North China Daily News*, January 31, 1932, 17.
138. "Some of the Dangers That Threaten Shanghai," *China Weekly Review*, February 20, 1932, 358.
139. "The Latest Proposal from Tokyo—Demilitarized Zones," *China Weekly Review*, February 13, 1932, 327.
140. "Demilitarization Proposal," *North China Daily News*, February 16, 1932, 6.

interpretations of the cause and the implications of the incident varied. The London *Times*, for example, displayed an overt slant toward the Japanese case. Drawing a parallel between the British navy's protection of Shanghai in 1927 and the current action by the Japanese, it argued that Japan, considering the "close proximity of a large and notoriously ill-disciplined force of Chinese troops," had a sound reason to defend its nationals in Shanghai.[141] The paper also showed sympathy with Japan's loss in the anti-Japanese boycotts and its difficulties with dealing with the Chinese government. It blamed China's lack of an authoritative government and its officials' "habitual procrastination and evasions." It argued that "in such circumstances some display of force by Japan was not condemned by reasonably minded persons."[142]

The London *Times* believed Japan's action was only to punish China without any interest in China's territory or sovereignty. Although Lord Cecil and many other diplomats had urgently warned the British to change their attitude and open their eyes to Japan's military ambitions in the whole of China and its menace to other British colonies in the Pacific, particularly India, Canada, and Australia,[143] the paper lent no support to Cecil's view. It quoted many opponents who believed Cecil was exaggerating the situation and referred to Japan as Britain's "old ally" whose friendship and military strength was vital to British interests.[144] It believed that a "generous but ignorant sympathy with an imaginary 'China' is the greatest danger today to universal peace."[145]

The *New York Times*, on the contrary, resonated with the anti-Japanese line pursued by the US treaty-port's press in Shanghai. The paper saw Japan's action as an "invasion."[146] It referred to Japan's bombing of Chinese civilians as living testimony to Japanese "savagery."[147] The Mukden Incident, argued the paper, had previously been considered as a "good case" for Japan in terms of its entitlement to "stand upon her treaty rights" and her suffering from "provocation from irresponsible Chinese officials."[148] Yet Japan's use of force in Shanghai had "alienated many neutral supporters and sympathizers" and raised people's suspicion toward its intentions in Manchuria.[149] The paper saw Japan's militancy in Shanghai as a menace to the balance of power. Since the incident took place right before the Geneva Conference of Disarmament, editors of the paper worried that the tension created by Japan would alter the naval

---

141. "Anxious Hours in Shanghai," *Times*, January 29, 1932, 13; "The Shanghai Crisis, Japanese Action in China," *Times*, February 27, 1932, 11.
142. "Critical Hours in Shanghai," *Times*, February 2, 1932, 13; a similar view was also voiced in "The Shanghai Crisis," *Times*, February 27, 1932, 11.
143. "The Shanghai Crisis, British Policy in Far East, Respect for Collective Treaties," *Times*, February 18, 1932, 13.
144. "The Shanghai Crisis, U.S. Policy in the Far East," *Times*, February 29, 1932, 13.
145. "The Shanghai Crisis, Japanese Action in China," *Times*, February 27, 1932, 11.
146. "Japan's Intentions Asked by Stimson," *New York Times*, January 29, 1932, 3.
147. "Pity of It," *New York Times*, January 30, 1932, 16.
148. "Both in the Wrong," *New York Times*, January 31, 1932, E1.
149. Ibid.

plans set by Herbert Hoover[150] and undermine America's two basic policies in China: the Open Door policy and respect for China's integrity.[151]

The Mukden and Shanghai incidents offered the Chinese state and intellectuals a deeper understanding of this new political strategy. Propaganda was not only about the text but also about the interaction with certain contexts that enabled the argument to prevail. Benefiting from a unified anti-Japanese line, Chinese editors strove to shift from an anti-foreign stance to an anti-Japan focus. Yet the shift was premature and unstable. The Nanjing government's propaganda plans were further complicated by the dilemma that it faced between appeasing Japan and confronting it in the mid-1930s.

---

150. "Tension May Alter Hoover Navy Plans," *New York Times*, January 29, 1932, 1.
151. "China: The Vast Arena of World Rivalries," *New York Times*, February 7, 1932, XX1.

Figure 7
Sapajou, "Sayonara," *North China Daily News*, May 13, 1932.

5
Facing Dilemmas
China's International Propaganda Activities, 1932–1937

The Nanjing government survived the Mukden and the Shanghai Incidents at a bitter cost. Apart from significant numbers of military and civilian casualties, enormous damage to buildings and infrastructure, and the huge impact on local businesses and industries, the Guomindang government effectively lost its sovereignty over all of Manchuria and the right to deploy troops within the Shanghai area. The Shanghai Truce (May 1932) and the mediation of the League of Nations failed to rein in Japanese militancy. The Japanese army had established the puppet state Manchukuo in Manchuria during the fighting in Shanghai and succeeded in getting it recognized by the Japanese government in September 1932.[1] In January 1933, the Japanese army crossed the Great Wall and advanced farther south to Jehol (Rehe) Province, attempting to expand its invasion to North China.

Keenly aware of China's military weakness and domestic disunity, Chiang Kai-shek had tried hard to avoid a full-scale war with Japan. He busied himself with anti-Communist campaigns in southwestern China and adopted the policy of "first internal pacification, then external resistance" (*rangwai bixian annei*), arguing that China would not be able to resist Japan until the internal menace of the Communists was eliminated. To avoid conflagration with Japan, Chiang had to contain popular anti-Japanese sentiments, which reached a peak after the Manchurian crisis.

Chiang's policy was unpopular among both the public and officials. A leftist periodical, *Chun qiu*, argued that Nanjing's timidity, instead of halting Japan's advance, had whetted the appetite of the Japanese army for further attacks. Even *Shidai gonglun*, a journal usually identified with the C. C. Clique, a political faction close to Chiang, complained that nonresistance would damage public morale.[2] The policy of internal pacification not only drew protests from Chiang's own brother-in-law, Finance Minister T. V. Soong, but was also exploited by his rivals as ammunition

---

1. Louise Young, *Japan's Total Empire: Manchuria and the Culture of Wartime Imperialism* (Berkeley: University of California Press, 1998), 40; Yoshihisa Tak Matsusaka, *The Making of Japanese Manchuria, 1904–1932* (Cambridge, MA: Harvard University Press, 2001).
2. Parks Coble, *Facing Japan: Chinese Politics and Japanese Imperialism, 1931–1937* (Cambridge, MA: Harvard University Press, 1991), 76–77.

to weaken his control. Instead of targeting Chiang directly, Wang Jingwei held Zhang Xueliang, one of Chiang's key military supporters, responsible for the loss of Manchuria and Jehol and demanded Zhang's resignation. Indeed, in the mid-1930s Chiang was caught between Japanese military pressure and domestic anti-Japanese sentiments.

This dilemma also plagued China's diplomacy. Internationally, China had to juggle the policy of appealing to Western powers for a common resistance against Japan with attempts to appease Japan's militancy. The weakness of China's military revealed during the Shanghai Incident reaffirmed the reality that China was unable to defend itself single-handedly, and forming an alliance with Western powers was essential. The early 1930s had seen China's continuous efforts to abandon its antiforeign tradition to seek an alliance with Western powers. Yet Japan's renewed aggression in North China indicated to the Nanjing government that this diplomatic approach was incapable of blocking Japan's military advance immediately. Japan's withdrawal from the League of Nations in March 1933 further diminished China's hope of relying on international authorities to solve Sino-Japanese disputes. What the Nanjing government direly needed was a solution to counter Japan's military threat. From 1933 the Nanjing government began acceding to Japanese demands in the hope of gaining time to continue national construction. It toned down its anti-Japanese stance and reached a series of cease-fire agreements to maintain temporary "peace." However, the political cost of this new approach was heavy. It forced the government to move even further from the Party's anti-imperialist tradition. It also nullified the government's previous international approach and redefined the Sino-Japanese conflict as a regional issue. The change left Western powers unclear about China's real intentions.

While military confrontation was not an option, more attention was paid to the development of nonmilitary strategies to resist Japan's aggression. Propaganda was one of them. Beneath the appeasement to Japan were the government's continuous efforts to strengthen its news network. For a regime fraught with political dilemmas, factional struggles, and international threats, however, the process was plagued by conflicts.

Lytton Commission

After the Shanghai Truce, the Shanghai Incident gradually receded to the background in the international media. The Manchurian issue, where the deeper Sino-Japanese dispute lay, recaptured public attention. The main focus of the media was on the investigation by the Lytton Commission. In response to repeated appeals by the Chinese government, the League of Nations decided to send out a commission of inquiry to investigate the Manchurian and Shanghai incidents. The commission, headed by V. A. G. R. Bulwer-Lytton, the second Earl of Lytton of the United Kingdom, included

Major General Frank Ross McCoy from the United States, Heinrich Schnee from Germany, Count Aldrovandi-Marescotti from Italy, and General Henri Claudel from France. As a third-party investigator, the commission was commonly considered as a referee in the Sino-Japanese conflict. Its account would not only exert moral pressure on the "aggressor" in the court of international public opinion but also influence the League's later decisions on East Asian affairs.[3] The investigation began on March 14, 1932, and in the three months that followed the commission travelled to Shanghai, Nanjing, Beijing, and Manchuria to collect primary information on the development of the Manchurian crisis. It then stayed in Tokyo for two weeks in July before moving to Beijing to draft the final report of the inquiry, which took until the September of that year.

During the commission's six months' stay in China, the Nanjing government organized a series of propaganda activities targeting the commission and the League. Apart from the government's urge to present its case to the world, its efforts were also motivated by the necessity to counter Japan's propaganda activities. From 1932, the Ministry of Foreign Affairs of Japan had launched a series of worldwide propaganda campaigns to promote Japan's view. It sent diplomats and prominent Japanese intellectuals to the United States and Europe to advocate Japan's vested interests in Manchuria and distributed pamphlets around the world claiming that Japan's action in Manchuria was based solely on self-defense.[4] In China, the ministry funded the Press Union to translate Rengō agency reports into English and send them to the foreign press in Shanghai.[5] The South Manchuria Railway Company supported H. G. Woodhead, special writer for the American paper the *Shanghai Evening Post and Mercury*, to voice Japan's position.[6] According to the *China Weekly Review*, Henry W. Kinney, head of the propaganda department of the South Manchuria Railway Company, frequently contributed articles to newspapers in Shanghai about Japan's contribution to the development of Manchuria. After the Shanghai Incident, he was sent to the United States to investigate the status of public opinion so as to keep Japanese officials and leaders of the South Manchuria Railway Company better advised on propaganda policies.[7]

The Manchukuo government hired the editor of the *Far Eastern Review*, George Bronson Rea, as its representative at the General Assembly of the League of Nations. Before setting off to Geneva, Rea called on US consul general in Shanghai

---

3. Ian Hill Nish, *Japanese Foreign Policy in the Interwar Period* (Westport, CT: Greenwood Publishing, 2002), 86–87.
4. Sandra Wilson, "Containing the Crisis: Japan's Diplomatic Offensive in the West, 1931–33," *Modern Asian Studies* 29 (1955): 337–72.
5. "The Japanese Squabble over Propaganda Money," *China Weekly Review*, June 11, 1932, 42; also see Press Union, *The Shanghai Incident Misrepresented* (Shanghai: Press Union, 1932).
6. "Preparing for the 'Battle of Geneva,'" *China Weekly Review*, October 22, 1932, 318.
7. "Mr. Henry W. Kinney's 'Strictly-Confidential' Document," *China Weekly Review*, May 21, 1932, 391.

Edwin S. Cunningham to solicit Cunningham's support for his tour. Rea justified the Japanese military action as a way of protecting Japan's huge investments and the large number of Japanese citizens from the absence of law and order in China. He intimated to Cunningham that Japan established Manchukuo not as a base for further expansion into China but, rather, to reach out to Mongolia. He also promised that he would advise Japan's foreign minister Matsuoka Yōsuke to redirect Japan's interests from Shanghai to Manchuria, so as to leave the administration of Shanghai entirely to Britain and the United States. Although Cunningham disliked Rea's abuse of his American citizenship in the Manchurian crisis and found his statement unconvincing, he was impressed with Rea's ability to "advance his argument logically and with apparent sincerity."[8] Indeed, Rea's US background and his eloquence were what the Manchukuo government paid him for. The government generously offered him 60,000 silver yuan per year and allocated an additional 20,000 silver yuan to cover his office, furnishings, assistants, residence, and travel.[9] The handsome salary to Rea together with the series of propaganda activities indicated the importance Japan placed on propaganda after the Manchurian crisis.

In response, the Nanjing government organized its own international propaganda activities during the tour of the Lytton Commission. It sought to influence the commission via the Chinese assessor of the League, Wellington Koo. While traveling with the commission from April to August 1932, Koo frequently sent memoranda to its leaders, offering them background information on the Sino-Japanese conflict. The memoranda covered a wide range of topics. Apart from basic facts regarding the development of the Mukden and Shanghai Incidents, Koo also reported on Japan's provocative activities in other parts of China, the anti-Chinese riots in Korea, Chinese construction in Manchuria, Manchurian currency and its relation to the soybean industry, and issues of Outer Mongolia.[10] He dated Japan's encroachment on China back to the 1870s and accused Japan of intending to perpetuate China's internal political struggles by intervening in Chinese affairs.[11] Clearly, Koo's goal was to establish a broader historical context for the Manchurian crisis. He argued that Japan's seizure of Manchuria was a long-planned scheme and that the Mukden and Shanghai Incidents were the beginning of its invasion of the whole country.

Disturbed by Koo's overt anti-Japanese view, the Manchukuo leaders tried to separate Koo from the commission by rejecting his entry into Manchuria.[12] Upon

---

8. Edwin Cunningham to the Secretary of State, August 8, 1932, 893.01-A-MANCHURIA/3, Confidential US State Department Central Files, China, Internal Affairs 1930–1939 (hereafter SDCF).
9. Hsieh Chieh-shih to George Bronson Rea, August 17, 1932, 893.01-A-MANCHURIA/14, SDCF.
10. V. K. Wellington Koo, *Memoranda Presented to the Lytton Commission* (New York: Chinese Cultural Society, 1932).
11. "General Memorandum on the Sino-Japanese Dispute," "Memorandum on Japan's Plots and Schemes against China's Unification," in Koo and League of Nations, *Memoranda Presented to the Lytton Commission*.
12. "League Commission on the Eve of Its Manchurian Journey," *China Weekly Review*, April 16, 1932, 210.

Lytton's insistence that Koo joined the tour, they eventually allowed Koo to travel to Manchuria but only by sea instead of by rail. As a result, the commission entered Manchuria in three groups. One, led by Schnee and Claudel, traveled in a Japanese destroyer; another, led by Aldrovandi, entered by rail via Shanhaiguan; a third, in which Koo was escorted by Lytton himself, traveled in a Chinese cruiser. Immediately after Koo's arrival, he received a warrant of arrest should he venture out of the Japanese railway zone. This implied that Koo would not be able to accompany the group to north Manchuria, where the Japanese railway was much less developed.[13] The attempt of the Manchukuo leaders to undermine Koo's involvement in the investigation drew international protests. A Reuters' telegram from Geneva complained that Japan's intervention "produced the worst possible impression in League circles."[14] Members of the League also warned the Manchukuo leaders against rejecting Koo any further, which would have complicated the situation even more.[15]

The Nanjing government sought to influence the commission's investigation of treaty-port opinions. The Lytton Commission regarded Westerners living in China as the most credible sources for their investigation and interviewed "as many as possible" of the correspondents who had been in Mukden at the time of the incident or had visited the scene soon afterward.[16] Keenly aware of the importance of the testimonies of Western expatriates, Nanjing paid special attention to shaping Westerners' view of the Sino-Japanese conflict. It supported Sun Ruiqin, an official propagandist, to compile English pamphlets on China's versions of the Mukden Incident. The pamphlets were then sent directly to the commission and distributed widely in treaty ports and in Beijing.[17] In June 1932, before the commission settled in Beijing to draft its final report, the government launched an English-language daily, the *Peiping Chronicle*, in the hope of creating a favorable public opinion among Western communities in the city. The paper was established based on the asset of the *Leader*, which had been forced to close before the Shanghai Incident under pressure from the Japanese military. To conceal its connection with Nanjing, the paper installed a British national, William Sheldon Ridge, as its chief editor. Yet most of the reporting and editing was done by the paper's Chinese staff.[18]

---

13. Ian Hill Nish, *Japan's Struggle with Internationalism: Japan, China, and the League of Nations, 1931–33* (London: Kegan Paul International, 1993), 125.
14. See the summary of the Reuters' telegram in "League Commission on the Eve of Its Manchurian Journey," 210.
15. Ibid.
16. League of Nations, *Report of the Commission of Enquiry of the League of Nations*, signed at Beijing, September 4, 1932, 133.
17. Zhang Weiying, ed., *Yanjing daxue shigao, 1919–1952* [A history of Yenching University, 1919–1952] (Beijing: Zhongguo renmin chubanshe, 1999), 776.
18. Israel Epstein, *My China Eye: Memoirs of a Jew and a Journalist* (San Francisco: Long River Press, 2005), 61; Wang Wenbin, *Zhongguo xiandai baoshi ziliao huiji* [Historical records on the Chinese press] (Chongqing: Chongqing chubanshe, 1996), 158.

The *Peiping Chronicle* together with other pro-Nanjing papers in Shanghai formed an alliance to expose Japan's suppression of information in the occupied region. They denounced the Japanese military for trying to prevent Koo's travel to Manchuria and to interfere with the commission's interview of Ma Zhanshan, a Chinese general who resisted Japan after the Mukden Incident.[19] "Every movement of the Commission so far," commented the paper, "has been hampered directly or indirectly by Japan."[20] The *Chronicle*'s view was strengthened by the *China Weekly Review*'s reports on similar experiences of Western journalists.[21]

While the Lytton Committee's investigation caught the attention of international media, the Nanjing government took the opportunity to distribute Koo's memoranda to the Lytton Commission widely in the United States and Europe. Within two months after Koo submitted his last memorandum to the commission, more than forty thousand copies of the complete collection of his memoranda were printed and distributed abroad.[22] After arriving in Paris, Koo organized the reprinting of the French translation of his memoranda himself and appointed Shi Zhaoji (also known as Alfred Sze), Chinese minister to Washington, to supervise the distribution of the collection in the United States.[23]

However, China's anti-Japanese propaganda waned quickly after the publication of the Lytton Report. The trend reflected Nanjing's change of direction in diplomacy—from appealing for international assistance to appeasement of Japan. By early 1933, Japan's defeat at Geneva was certain, yet China's victory in the League neither brought about economic sanctions against Japan nor ended its military aggression. In March 1933, the Japanese army crossed the Great Wall, expanding its invasion to the Beijing-Tianjin area. Unable to afford to lose more territory, which would lead to the demise of Chiang's regime, the Nanjing government instead abandoned its reliance on Western powers' mediation and sought a direct settlement with Japan. Accordingly, the Tanggu Truce was signed in May 1933, which marked the beginning of the government's appeasement approach. To further strengthen this strategy, Chiang Kai-shek replaced the overtly anti-Japanese foreign minister Luo Wengan with Wang Jingwei, who was in complete accord with Chiang in seeking reconciliation with Japan.[24] During a conference in October, T. V. Soong, another proresistance leader, was removed from the position of minister of finance and vice president of the Executive Yuan.[25]

---

19. "Frank Avowals," *Peiping Chronicle*, June 8, 1932; "The Weekly in China," *Peiping Chronicle*, June 12, 1932.
20. "Frank Avowals."
21. "Japan's Interference with Foreign Journalists in North Manchuria," *China Weekly Review*, July 9, 1932, 196.
22. V. K. Wellington Koo, *Gu Weijun huiyilu* [Memoir of Wellington Koo] (Beijing: Zhonghua shuju, 1983), 64.
23. Ibid.
24. So Wai Chor, "The Making of the Guomindang's Japan Policy, 1932–1937: The Roles of Chiang Kai-Shek and Wang Jingwei," *Modern China* 28, no. 2 (April 2002): 215.
25. Coble, *Facing Japan*, 137–141.

Facing Dilemmas

The Nanjing government did not, however, abandon its efforts to seek Western assistance entirely. Instead of openly identifying itself with Western powers, it pursued "quiet" diplomatic interactions with them, aiming to obtain economic assistance. Chiang believed that "accommodation with Japan should serve as a smokescreen for diplomacy (seeking assistance from Western powers)."[26] This required China's propaganda to tone down its anti-Japanese voice and to avoid direct confrontation with Japan in the press. Meanwhile, the government was also keen to suppress pro-Manchukuo reports. In 1933, it suspended postal services for the Japanese-subsidized *Far Eastern Review*. It banned *Oriental Affairs* the next year because of the pro-Manchukuo stance of its editor H. G. W. Woodhead and restricted the circulation of two US magazines, *Asia* and *Time*, in 1935 and 1936, because of their "derogatory" comments on China's leaders.[27]

Registration of the Foreign Newspaper: A Battleground for Extraterritoriality

The period between 1932 and 1941 is generally considered a breaking point for negotiations about the overall abolition of extraterritoriality.[28] Yet behind China's seemingly dormant efforts to relinquish extraterritorial rights were its continuous attempts to restore its legal sovereignty in specific areas. Regulating the foreign press was one of the fronts. Indeed, the Nanjing officials were in a quandary about how to deal with extraterritoriality. Despite their desire to abolish the system, they were also aware of the benefits it could bring to the Chinese government in forming an alliance with Western powers against Japan's military threat. The complexity of the dilemma compelled the government to adopt a more accommodating approach toward the extraterritoriality-related negotiations.

Foreign newspapers in China had long been a vexation in the eyes of the Guomindang officials. The Ministry of Information openly criticized them as rumor mongers, "trying their best to insult China and agitate anti-Chinese sentiments."[29] As early as 1930, before the Publication Law was promulgated, the Ministry of Information had issued the Guidelines for Registration of Foreign Papers to regulate the foreign press. Yet the guidelines were not actively enforced because of extraterritoriality. In October 1932, the Ministry of Communications reopened the registration

---

26. "Yihe yi yanhu waijiao," Chiang Kai-shek diary, July 14, 1933, quoted in Youli Sun, *China and the Origins of the Pacific War, 1931–1941* (New York: St. Martin's Press, 1993), 44.
27. Memorandum by the Assistant Chief of the Division of Far Eastern Affairs (Hamilton), June 6, 1935, Papers Relating to the Foreign Relations of the United States (hereafter PRFRUS), 1935, 817; Meiguo Yaxiya yuekan bushi baodao, 1936–1937, Ministry of Foreign Affairs, 303000000B, 1400.10/8060.02–01, Academia Historica (hereafter AH).
28. Wesley R. Fishel, *The End of Extraterritoriality in China* (Berkeley: University of California Press, 1952), 188.
29. *Zhongyang dangwu yuekan* 19 (March 1930): 68–69.

issue. On the basis of Article 7 of the Law of Publication, which required all publications to be registered with the government, it sent instructions to foreign newspapers in China, requesting that they register with both the Ministry of the Interior (state) and the Ministry of Information (party). Periodicals that failed to comply with the article would lose their access to postal services.[30] Determined to control the foreign press, the government was also careful to separate the registration order from extraterritorial disputes. It explained that the registration was a "mere formality"[31] to deprive Chinese publications of their excuse for not registering.[32] The government had no intention of intruding on the paper's independence.

The Japanese legation ignored the order. It neither replied to Nanjing's request nor communicated with other legations for a solution.[33] Legations of the other Powers, however, quickly lodged their protests, considering the order to be an infringement of the extraterritoriality principles. The legations were also irked by the need for dual registration. They believed that if registration to the Ministry of Interior was already an impingement on the papers' exterritorial rights, registration to a party organ, the Ministry of Information, was not only redundant but also a violation of the principle of freedom of speech, since it indicated an endorsement of the party's view.[34]

The American, British, and French legations, therefore, sought a coordinated effort to boycott the registration. They advised papers of their respective nationalities to ignore Nanjing's demand temporarily and see how things would develop.[35] They also took concerted efforts to exert diplomatic pressure on Nanjing, demanding that the government exempt foreign papers from the Chinese Publication Law. The legations kept close correspondence with each other to formulate a consensus before replying to the Chinese government. They even tried to synchronize the time of their replies so as to avoid inconsistency and to enhance their pressure.[36]

The foreign legations nevertheless knew their limits. The Chinese government had restored its postal control outside of treaty ports. Even if extraterritoriality protected foreign papers from Chinese penalties, Nanjing could still subject unfriendly papers to severe economic loss by imposing a postal ban or even impounding publications

---

30. Edwin S. Cunningham, American Consul General, to Nelson T. Johnson, American Minister in Beijing, October 1, 1932, 893.918/75, SDCF.
31. The Charge in China (Gauss) to the Secretary of State, November 20, 1934, PRFRUS, 1934, the Far East, vol. 3, 619.
32. The Minister in China (Johnson) to the Secretary of State, March 7, 1933, PRFRUS, 1933, the Far East, vol. 3, 683.
33. The Minister in China (Johnson) to the Secretary of State, April 5, 1933, PRFRUS, 1934, the Far East, vol. 3, 687.
34. Ingram to Luo Wengan, October 26, 1932, in Waiguo xinwenzhi zazhi shiyong chubanfa wenti'an, October 1932–December 1934, 172–1, 3138–(1), files of the Ministry of Foreign Affairs, AH.
35. Edwin S. Cunningham, American Consul General, to Nelson T. Johnson, American Minister in Peiping, October 1, 1932, 893.918/76, SDCF.
36. The Secretary of State to the Minister in China (Johnson), April 1, 1933, PRFRUS, 1933, the Far East, vol. 3, 686.

outside the treaty ports.[37] Western powers also faced a moral dilemma in denying the binding force of China's Publication Law. Sir John Brenan, British consul general, confessed that the registration was "a difficult matter to deal with." "The foreign powers had been continually urging the Chinese to enact modern laws, codes, etc.," stated Brenan. "Now the Chinese had brought forth a law of publications. . . . It would be difficult for a foreign publication to refuse to comply with the law."[38] Brenan also admitted that similar registration orders were common in Western countries and that all publications within their borders had to live up to the orders. The Chinese government was justified, therefore, in setting reasonable standards to regulate publications.[39] Confined by these limitations, the foreign legations understood well that they could not seek an entire abandonment of the registration order from Nanjing. The practical goal was to "satisfy the government half-way" so as to continue using the postal facilities.[40]

Nevertheless, this coordinated effort could not obscure the disunity among Western powers. It should be noted that the American legation, which merely followed Britain in the negotiations over the abolition of extraterritoriality in 1930, took a more radical attitude toward the registration issue. The British legation, instead, appeared to have lost interest in defending its extraterritorial rights regarding publications and became a passive follower.

Members of the American legation believed that the order posed a serious encroachment on Americans' extraterritorial rights. They protested that China's postal ban was a misuse of the post office, which violated the resolution reached at the Washington Conference,[41] and insisted that American newspapers and periodicals should not register with the Ministry of Interior before Chinese authorities provided a written assurance to exempt the papers from Chinese penalties, censorship, and registration with the Nationalist Party.[42]

The British legation, in contrast, viewed this matter much less seriously.[43] It tended to ignore Nanjing's demand and deal with the issue through informal negotiations, which Ingram had been carrying out with China's Ministry of Foreign Affairs.[44] It also

---

37. The Minister in China (Johnson) to the Secretary of State, 5 April 1933, PRFRUS, 1933, the Far East, vol. 3, 688.
38. Memorandum of conversation, October 20, 1932, 893.918/76, SDCF.
39. Ibid.
40. Edwin S. Cunningham, American Consul General, to Nelson T. Johnson, American Minister in Peiping, October 1, 1932, 893.918/75, SDCF.
41. Nelson T. Johnson to Luo Wengan, February 2, 1933, in Waiguo xinwenzhi zazhi shiyong chubanfa wenti'an.
42. The Acting Secretary of State to the Minister in China (Johnson), July 13, 1933, PRFRUS, 1933, the Far East, vol. 3, 690.
43. The Minister in China (Johnson) to the Acting Secretary of State, December 7, 1933, PRFRUS, 1933, the Far East, vol. 3, 692.
44. The Minister in China (Johnson) to the Secretary of State, April 5, 1933, PRFRUS, 1933, the Far East, vol. 3, 687.

believed that the case was not closely pertinent to the preservation of extraterritorial rights since "there was no question of relinquishment."⁴⁵ Issues concerning penalty clauses in the Publication Law that contravened extraterritorial rights "should be dealt with as they arise."⁴⁶ The weakest link of the alliance, nevertheless, was the French legation, which was much less confrontational to the Nanjing government on this matter.

The Nanjing government maintained a flexible and compromising attitude, which was not only the result of the foreign legations' pressure but also because of the relevant ministries' lack of communication and consensus. The Ministry of Communications and the Ministry of the Interior, the two offices that initiated the registration, did not consult with the Ministry of Foreign Affairs before the registration order was sent to the foreign papers. Luo Wengan, then the Foreign Minister, had to learn the "facts of the case" from complaints lodged to his ministry by various legations.⁴⁷ Yet Luo was much less willing to cause a rift between Nanjing and the foreign press when the propaganda battle against Japan was at its height and a favorable portrayal of China by the foreign press was desperately needed. A memorandum for Luo cogently reflected the ministry's concern over the timing of the imposition of the registration order:

> The time seems most inappropriate to extend to the foreign press of China the restrictions of the Chinese press law. The British, American and French papers of Shanghai and of the main open ports of China are at present, on the whole, supporting the Chinese case against Japan. They are contributing to the formation of a general current of opinion favorable to China's claims. It would be impolitic to antagonize them just now and to give to Japanese propagandists a weapon which they will not fail to use against the Chinese government.⁴⁸

The ministry therefore tried hard to temper the conflict. Luo even orally promised Ingram that "the [Chinese] legislation would not be applied to British publications which accordingly would not be required to register."⁴⁹ Although he refused to support his oral promise with a written assurance when Ingram asked, the promise at least indicated his eagerness to quell the unrest and to what degree his ministry was willing to concede. While the Nanjing government was seeking amendments to the registration order, Luo repeatedly advised the Ministry of the Interior to temporarily suspend it before new terms were settled on.⁵⁰

---

45. Memorandum of conversation, October 20, 1932, 893.918/76, SDCF.
46. Edwin S. Cunningham to Nelson T. Johnson, December 6, 1932, 893.918/76, SDCF.
47. Ingram to Luo Wengan, 26 October 1932, in Waiguo xinwenzhi zazhi shiyong chubanfa wenti'an.
48. Memorandum for Luo Wengan, 1932 (estimated), in Waiguo xinwenzhi zazhi shiyong chubanfa wenti'an.
49. Ingram to Luo Wengan, December 17, 1932, Waiguo xinwenzhi zazhi shiyong chubanfa wenti'an.
50. The Ministry of Foreign Affairs to the Ministry of the Interior, November 25, 1932; International Department of the Ministry of Foreign Affairs to the Mayor of Shanghai, November 23, 1932; the Ministry of Foreign Affairs to the Secretary Department of the Executive Yuan, November 26, 1932, Waiguo xinwenzhi zazhi shiyong chubanfa wenti'an.

The Ministry of the Interior was eager to activate the registration order so as to "gain face."⁵¹ "Should those foreign papers refuse to register," commented an official of the ministry, "the order would be issued in vain."⁵² However, the intransigent policy met with foreign newspapers' noncooperation. Most of the papers, upon their legations' advice, chose to ignore the order and await further amendments. The Ministry of the Interior, as discussed above, also received little support from officials of the Ministry of Foreign Affairs. The lack of cooperation eventually forced it to soften its stance so as to make the order effective. First, instead of exempting the foreign papers from the Chinese Publication Law, as Luo orally promised to the British legation, the ministry agreed to temporarily suspend the penalties of the press law for the foreign papers. Second, the ministry relinquished the requirement to register with the party headquarters. Third, discounts on postal services were offered to reward registered papers. The ministry insisted that the purpose of the registration "was to collect statistical information about the foreign press,"⁵³ rather than to regulate its content. These favorable terms were to "eliminate suspicion of China's intention on the registration order and show respect to the friendly nations."⁵⁴ No matter how many concessions Nanjing made to the Western legations, the bottom line was clear: China would not forfeit its right to punish unfriendly papers. T. V. Soong, then the deputy president of the Executive Yuan, reaffirmed that the Nanjing government would withdraw postal privileges from "any foreign papers that failed to abide by the Chinese press law."⁵⁵

China's concession as well as the threat of a postal ban dissolved the foreign legations' antiregistration alliance. In April 1933, the French legation advised papers operating in the French Concession to register.⁵⁶ Satisfied with not having to register to the party, the British legation acquiesced to the registration order in December 1933.⁵⁷ This left the US legation alone in the battle. Its position was further challenged when the US journal the *China Weekly Review* voluntarily lodged its registration despite the legation's advice to ignore the order. After the Nanjing government issued an ultimatum to foreign papers in 1934, threatening to cancel postal services to unregistered papers, the American legation withdrew its objection. It adopted a hands-off policy, refusing to compel periodicals or publications to register if a paper

---

51. C. E. Gauss quoted Gan Naiguang, Vice Minister of the Interior, in The Charge in China (Gauss) to the Secretary of the State, November 20, 1934, PRFRUS, 1934, the Far East, vol. 3, 619.
52. Correspondence of the Ministry of the Interior, November 1933 (estimated), in Waiguo xinwenzhi zazhi shiyong chubanfa wenti'an.
53. Ibid.
54. Documents on foreign press registration, May 19, 1933, Waiguo xinwenzhi zazhi shiyong chubanfa wenti'an.
55. T. V. Soong's order, 1932–1933 (estimated), in Waiguo xinwenzhi zazhi shiyong chubanfa wenti'an.
56. The Minister in China (Johnson) to the Secretary of State, April 5, 1933, PRFRUS, 1933, the Far East, vol. 3, 688.
57. The Minister in China (Johnson) to the Acting Secretary of State, December 7, 1933, PRFRUS, 1933, the Far East, vol. 3, 691.

decided not to.⁵⁸ But without strong support from the legations, foreign papers began to give ground and lodge applications to the Ministry of the Interior in 1934.

Unifying the Voice, Unifying the Control

International propaganda in the mid-1930s was not only a means of diplomacy but also a way to acquire political supremacy in domestic struggles. In 1932, Chiang Kai-shek had only limited control over international propaganda. Most of the resources were held by the Guomindang leftists. The Guomin News Agency and the *Peking Leader / Peiping Chronicle*, for instance, were operated by the Ministry of Foreign Affairs, a ministry dominated by the Anglo-American faction (*Yingmei pai*) that leaned toward the left. The *People's Tribune*, a "mouthpiece of Wang Jingwei,"⁵⁹ was edited by Tang Liangli (also T'ang Leang-li), Wang's personal secretary and foreign propagandist.

Tang poses something of a mystery to historians. He was born into a Chinese family in Java and received degrees from the London School of Economics and Vienna University. During his stay in London, he established connections with the staff of the Guomindang Ministry of Foreign Affairs led by Chen Youren. Around 1928–1929, he met with Wang Jingwei on the recommendation of Gan Naiguang.⁶⁰ His connection with the left-wing Guomindang won him the position of chief of the Communication Office to Europe of the Central Executive Committee in 1929.⁶¹ Tang's English was much better than his Chinese. He later served as Wang's private English-language secretary and his personal English propagandist.⁶² Meanwhile, he also worked as a reporter for several foreign news organizations, including the News Agency of the Social Democratic Party of Germany, the *Daily News* (London) and the *Batavia Newspaper*.⁶³ In March

Figure 8
Tang Liangli. From *Liangyou*, no. 34 (1929): 32.

---

58. The Acting Secretary of State to the Minister in China (Johnson), January 18, 1934, PRFRUS, 1934, the Far East, vol. 3, 618.
59. C. E. Gauss to the Secretary of State, Washington, February 18, 1935, 893.91/18, SDCF.
60. Gan Naiguang served as English secretary and political instructor in the Huangpu Military Academy in the mid-1920s. He was one of the principle architects of China's administrative reform during the 1930s and 1940s. For details of Gan's profile, see Morris L. Bian, "Building State Structure: Guomindang Institutional Rationalization during the Sino-Japanese War, 1937–1945," *Modern China* 31, no. 1 (January 2005): 35–71.
61. Files on Tang Liangli's case, 4187-2-119, the Shanghai High Court, Shanghai Municipal Council Archives.
62. See Liangli Tang, *Wang Ching-Wei: A Political Biography* (Beijing: French Book Store, 1931).
63. Huaqiao huaren baike quanshu bianzuan weiyuanhui, *Huaqiao huaren baike quanshu, renwu juan* [An encyclopedia of overseas Chinese, personnel] (Beijing: Zhongguo huaqiao chubanshe, 2001), 483–84.

1931, he founded the *People's Tribune* with funding from Sun Ke and became chief editor of the journal, voicing the opinions of the left wing of the party. In 1931, Tang published an English biography of Wang, applauding his achievements in politics. He gained fame by editing The China Today series in the 1930s, in which he attributed China's construction to the leadership of Wang Jingwei. Tang stuck with Wang throughout the latter's political maneuvering, from setting up a rival government to Chiang Kai-shek in 1930, to joining forces with Chiang in 1932, and finally to collaborating with the Japanese after 1938.[64]

Despite Wang and Chiang's alliance in 1932, the power sharing between the two was unequal. Wang was excluded from military and financial decisions. He had no access to Chiang's intelligence machinery and was undermined in party affairs by the C. C. Clique led by Chiang's protégés.[65] This insecurity pushed Wang to focus more on elevating his position in the party. The *Tribune* thus was exploited to enhance Wang's personal prestige. It frequently carried articles critical of Chiang's policy, despite such a stance undermining China's general reputation abroad. Perceiving the *Tribune* as the proper representative of the government, Tang was intolerant to criticism of government policies leveled by independent treaty-port elites and journals. After the prominent writer Lin Yutang released his novel *My Country, My People* in the United States, the *Tribune* condemned Lin as a traitor who exposed China's defects and failings simply to please foreigners and the foreign media in China. In Lin's correspondence with his American publisher Richard Walsh, he also intimated that over the years the *China Critic* was operating under the pressure of Tang and his journal.[66]

Chiang also faced Hu Hanmin's challenge from South China. Hu was one of the most senior members of the Guomindang after Sun Yat-sen's death in 1925. He supported Chiang Kai-shek's purge of the communists in 1927 but split with him in 1931 because of disputes over the provisional constitution. Hu was placed under house arrest by Chiang in 1931. After his release, he traveled to South China and allied with other anti-Chiang factions to form a political power against the Nanjing government. Tapping into the unpopularity of the Tanggu Truce of May 1933 and Chiang's nonresistance policy, Hu vehemently criticized Nanjing's appeasement of Japan as "humiliating" and constantly pressed Chiang to go north to confront the Japanese troops.[67] Hu's policy was characterized as "anti-Chiang," "anti-Japanese,"

---

64. Lawrence Kessler, "Reconstructing Zhou Enlai's Escape from Shanghai in 1931: A Research Note," *Twentieth-Century China* 34, no. 2 (April 2009): 119.
65. So, "The Making of the Guomindang's Japan Policy," 218–19.
66. Qian Suoqiao, "Gentlemen of *The Critic*: English-Speaking Liberal Intellectuals in Republican China," *China Heritage Quarterly*, nos. 30/31 (June/September 2012), http://www.chinaheritagequarterly.org/features.php?searchterm=030_league.inc&issue=030.
67. Hu Hanmin to the party headquarters in the United States, in Chen Hongmin, *Hu Hanmin weikan wanglai handiangao* [Hu Hanmin's unpublished correspondence] (Guilin: Guangxi shifan daxue chubanshe, 2005), 3:573.

and "anti-Communist."[68] It was clear that challenging Chiang's rule was the ultimate objective, while opposing Japan and the Communist Party were means to garner public support for his rivalry with Nanjing. In fact, Hu only paid lip service to his anti-Japanese agenda. He was found secretly receiving Japanese military and political visitors, who were sent to South China to win over Hu's support in attacking Chiang.[69]

Hu Hanmin built his own international propaganda machinery to win foreign support. He established an English-language news agency in Guangzhou to transmit news about southwestern China—the region he controlled—to the outside world. The agency not only networked with British, US, Russian, and German news agencies but also connected with the *China Press* in Shanghai, *South China Morning Post* in Hong Kong, and key newspapers abroad.[70] In the latter half of 1934, the agency transmitted 609 short reports (300–1,000 characters) and 723 long articles (1,500–3,000 characters). It was estimated that more than thirty newspapers in and outside China frequently quoted reports from Hu's news agency.[71]

As one of the main party leaders, Hu also used the Guomindang headquarters overseas to influence the foreign public. After the Tanggu Truce, Hu sent Cheng Tiangu to the Guomindang headquarters in San Francisco to organize international propaganda in the United States.[72] According to Cheng's correspondence with the headquarters, the goal of Cheng's trip was to interpret China's domestic situation from Hu's perspective and instigate protests against Chiang's policy. Hu criticized the Nanjing government's acceptance of the Tanggu Truce and the nonresistance policy. He also condemned the suppression of popular anti-Japanese activities by Nanjing. T. V. Soong, despite his disagreement with Chiang's appeasement policy and his efforts in obtaining financial support from Western powers to aid China's economic development, was not immune to Hu's attacks. Hu regarded the US cotton and wheat loan obtained by Soong as something that would fuel Chiang's rivalry with the leftists.[73]

The marked difference between Hu's and Chiang's interpretations of Chinese affairs created confusion among foreign audiences, thus undermining China's diplomacy and prestige abroad. Wellington Koo complained that the split between the central government and regional forces as well as the struggles within the Nanjing regime wreaked havoc on his propaganda efforts in the League of Nations. Delegates from

---

68. Chen Hongmin, "Hu Hanmin nianbiao (1931.9–1936.5)" [Chronicles of Hu Hanmin], *Minguo dang'an*, no. 1 (1986): 126.
69. Chen Hongmin, *Handian lide renji guanxi yu zhengzhi: Du Hafo-Yanjing tushuguan cang "Hu Hanmin wanglai handian gao"* [An analysis of Hu Hanmin's interpersonal relations through his correspondence] (Beijing: Shenghuo, dushu, xinzhi sanlian shudian, 2003), 281–82.
70. Xi'nan zhixing mishu chu, *Xi'nan dangwu niankan* [Yearbook of the southwestern Guomindang affairs], 1932, 91–93.
71. Chen Hongmin, *Handian lide renji guanxi yu zhengzhi*, 276.
72. Hu Hanmin to the party headquarters in the United States, in Chen Hongmin, *Hu Hanmin weikan wanglai handiangao* 3:573–574.
73. Ibid.

Facing Dilemmas 139

France, Britain, Australia, and other countries had repeatedly expressed their dissatisfaction with China's chaotic political situation, intimating to Koo that a unified voice from the Chinese government was the prerequisite to win their support.[74] China's disunity was also exploited as a pretext for Japan to denounce the Lytton Report, which requested that Japan negotiate directly with the Chinese government for a settlement of the Manchurian issues. Japanese prime minister Saitō Makoto openly complained to the media that negotiating with China was difficult: "We simply do not know where the Chinese government is, who the leader is and how we should negotiate."[75]

The Communists nevertheless were not bystanders in this rivalry in the treaty-port press. They challenged Guomindang's voice with the English journal *China Forum*, edited by Harold Isaacs in Shanghai. Launched in early 1932, the journal was supported by Soong Qing-ling as an organ of the underground Communist Party. Despite the party sponsors' wish to keep a moderate stance for the paper, Isaacs was unwilling to tone down his rage against Guomindang and imperialism. The "Ninpo [Ningbo] Napoleon," "the bastard," and "the son of a bitch," which he used to refer to Chiang Kai-shek, suggested that he had little interest in mincing his words when it came to attacking Guomindang leaders.[76] His bold and provocative approach irritated the Guomindang censors. Upon Nanjing's complaint, the consulate general of the American legation changed its conventional noncooperative attitude but promised Chinese leaders that the legation would not object to the suppression of the *Forum* by Chinese authorities.[77] Apparently, the support for "freedom of speech" was conditional. The legation would not enforce the use of an American identity as protection to practice communist activities. Nevertheless, what eventually led to the demise of the paper was Isaacs's split with the Communist Party. Isaacs increasingly departed from the Comintern and the Chinese Communist Party's line by turning toward Trotskyism during his years with the *Forum*. His unwillingness to submit to the CCP's guidance and restrictions precipitated the party's decision to drop him. The paper disappeared from the market in Shanghai in 1934, which was good news for the Guomindang government. Yet the various domestic and international interest groups behind the *Forum* and their eagerness to penetrate the English news market also warned the Nanjing leaders that this medium was far more complex than they had expected.

In May 1932, the Central Executive Committee initiated the creation of an ad hoc propaganda committee to organize international propaganda. It was the government's

74. Koo, *Gu Weijun huiyilu*, 71.
75. Ibid., 72.
76. Jinxing Chen, "Harold R. Isaacs' Trotskyist Turn in the *China Forum* Years," in *Twentieth-Century China* 24, no. 1 (November 1998): 41.
77. Correspondence between the Consulate General at Shanghai and the Secretary of the State, September 8, PRFRUS, 1932, the Far East, vol. 4, 660–61.

first attempt to build a supraministerial office to centralize its international propaganda resources. The committee was designed to incorporate the services of various ministries. Gu Mengyu, minister of railways, was appointed as its leader. Zhu Jiahua, minister of education; Shao Yuanchong, deputy president of the Legislative Yuan; Luo Jialun, president of the National Central University; and Luo Wengan, minister of foreign affairs were invited to join the board.[78] This was the government's clear move to centralize propaganda resources. Grand as the plan was, the office was dysfunctional. A report by Shao Yuanchong revealed that communication among the designated ministries was absent.[79] Given the structure of the committee, such a result was not surprising: the officials involved in the propaganda project were of equal executive rank. There was no higher institution to supervise their cooperation. In a patrimonial political system where officials were responsible for the upper levels of leaders and the source of power was defined by concrete purpose and personal trust, the lack of vertical hierarchy and a powerful leadership in the committee reduced the incentive of various ministries to be committed to the propaganda tasks that were in addition to their daily responsibilities.

Troubled by the lack of a unified voice, Chiang Kai-shek resolved to strengthen his control over international propaganda. For him, winning a favorable international reputation was a crucial part of his struggle for power against his political rivals and factional challengers. Keenly aware that centralization of the propaganda institution would be premature before a political unity was formed, he chose to strengthen his control on specific resources, including reorganizing the Central News Agency, subsidizing the *China Press*, and creating a censorship system for outgoing news.

Reorganization of the Central News Agency

The Central News Agency was launched in 1924 in Guangzhou under the supervision of the Central Party Headquarters. Unlike other commercial news agencies that focused on expanding news supply in the market, it was motivated by the political mission to disseminate messages of the party.[80] The agency did not have its own correspondents in the early years. Every local party member was in theory its correspondent, responsible for feeding the agency with reports.[81] Yet few were keen to

---

78. Minutes of the Eighteenth Standing Conference of the Central Executive Committee, May 10, 1932, 4.3/37.42, Guomindang Archives.
79. Chiang Kai-shek to Ye Chucang and Shao Yuanchong, December 2, 1933, 002010200099011, Chiang Kai-shek archives, AH.
80. Notice no. 29 of the Central Executive Committee, quoted in Xiao Tongzi, "Zhongyangshe ershi zhounian jinianhui jiangci," in Changning weishi ziliao weiyuanhui, *Changning wenshi ziliao disiji: Xiao Tongzi he Zhongyang tongxunshe* [Materials about Changning, vol. 4, Xiao Tongzi and the Central News Agency] (Changning: Wenshi ziliao weiyuanhui, 1988), 121–22.
81. Zhongyang tongxunshe, *Zhongyangshe liushi nian* [The Central News Agency in the past sixty years] (Taipei: Zhongyang tongxunshe, 1984), 2.

maintain a regular service, since there was no efficient mechanism to foster commitment. The agency ended up distributing news only once a day, comprising reports of 2,000 words at most.[82] Staffed by party administrators with no journalistic training, most news concerned party-related issues, which hardly attracted attention from the press.[83]

The agency moved its headquarters from Guangzhou to Nanjing after Chiang Kai-shek founded the Nanjing government in 1928. Hu Hanmin, then the minister of information, placed the agency under his wings.[84] He created editing and news offices, established branch offices in Wuhan, Beijing, and Shanghai, and hired local correspondents in these cities. With the support of local cable companies, the agency greatly expanded its news network. Apart from disseminating news, it was also in charge of censorship, blocking or editing news reports unfriendly to the Guomindang government.[85] Although the agency received sufficient funding from the government, its impact remained limited, little known among foreign correspondents in the late 1920s and early 1930s.[86]

The agency achieved a marked development after Xiao Tongzi's reorganization in 1932. As a secretary of the Ministry of Information, Xiao was a close ally of Ye Chucang and Wu Tiecheng, cabinet officials of Chiang Kai-shek. Xiao gained Chiang's trust in 1930 when he, together with Wu, assisted Chiang to win over Zhang Xueliang's military support against the warlord rebellion in Beijing.[87] In 1932, Xiao was appointed head of the Central News Agency upon Ye's recommendation. Unlike some of the conservative party propagandists, Xiao believed that the agency should be a public institution, independent of party control. Xiao's vision translated into three principles in his plan for reorganization: the agency should be independent from the Ministry of Information; it should establish its own wireless news networks; and it should enjoy sufficient discretion in deciding what to report on and whom to recruit.[88] Xiao's "three principles" were endorsed by Chiang Kai-shek, who saw the separation of the agency from the party as an opportunity to weaken the leftists' control of information. Chen Guofu also favored Xiao's plan, partly because it coincided with his own nationalistic passion and partly because the plan would bring in

---

82. Ibid.
83. "Liushisannian jiuyue shi'er ri zoufang Luo Xuelian xiansheng bilu" (The visit to Luo Xuelian on 12 September 1974) quoted in Changning weishi ziliao weiyuanhui, *Changning wenshi ziliao disiji: Xiao Tongzi he Zhongyang tongxunshe*, 247.
84. Zhongyang tongxunshe, *Zhongyangshe liushinian*, 2.
85. See quotes on the Guomindang government's order, ibid., 4.
86. Thomas Ming-heng Chao, *The Foreign Press in China* (Shanghai: Institute of Pacific Relations, 1931), 6.
87. Feng Zhixian, *Xiao Tongzi zhuan* [A biography of Xiao Tongzi] (Taipei: Zhuanji wenxue chubanshe, 1975), 125–36.
88. Xiao Tongzi, "Zhongyangshe ershi zhounian jinianhui jiangci," in Changning weishi ziliao weiyuanhui, *Changning wenshi ziliao disiji: Xiao Tongzi he Zhongyang tongxunshe*, 247; Feng Zhixiang, *Xiao Tongzi zhuan*, 154–55.

more funding for the construction of a nationwide wireless network in which he was then engaged.[89]

The first thing Xiao did after his inauguration was to move the agency's offices out of the compound of the Ministry of Information. This amounted to an open declaration of the agency's autonomy. Yet the independence was symbolic: it still relied on the ministry for funding and refrained from filing reports unfriendly to the central government.[90] Xiao's gesture to keep the agency at a distance from the party-dominated information system nevertheless won acclaim from private news entrepreneurs. They welcomed Xiao's leadership and expressed interest in cooperation.[91]

Recognizing the importance of a news infrastructure, Xiao launched a project to construct a wireless news network that sought to connect Beijing, Tianjin, Xi'an, Nanjing, Shanghai, Hankou, and Hong Kong. The project was completed within a year, thanks to the support of the government. The project received funding from various ministries and local party organs.[92] Even Chiang Kai-shek was occasionally involved in fund-raising for the agency when the project was in urgent need of capital.[93]

The Central News Agency started expanding its international presence by exchanging news with Reuters. Through the exchange, it also broke the latter's news monopoly in China. As early as October 1931, the Central News Agency, with the assistance of Reuters' chief correspondent Zhao Minheng, had withdrawn Reuters' rights to operate a wireless service as well as to supply the local press with Chinese-language dispatches.[94] Most of Reuters' profit in China nevertheless came from subscribing to English-language papers, and the agency did not have much interest in investing further in its Chinese service.[95] The agreement was Reuters' attempt to maintain strategic presence in China's news market by riding on the growth of the Central News Agency.[96]

Yet the agency back then was too weak to take over Reuters' Chinese service.[97] Significant acquisition took place only after the reorganization in 1932. In June that year, the agency acquired Reuters' cable assets in Shanghai and Nanjing.[98] Two years

---

89. See Fang Zhi's account on Chen's support of the independent operation of the Central News Agency in Feng Zhixiang, *Xiao Tongzi zhuan*, 154–155.
90. Changning weishi ziliao weiyuanhui, *Changning wenshi ziliao disiji: Xiao Tongzi he Zhongyang tongxunshe*, 161.
91. Feng Zhixiang, *Xiao Tongzi zhuan*, 253.
92. Changning weishi ziliao weiyuanhui, *Changning wenshi ziliao disiji: Xiao Tongzi he Zhongyang tongxunshe*, 161, 107.
93. Ibid., 161.
94. Zhao Minheng, *Caifang wushi nian* [Fifty years of interviews] (Taipei: Longwen chubanshe, 1994), 22–23.
95. FO371/6668 [F3934/3934/10] reports on Reuters in China, October 1921, FOFC.
96. Sheng-chi Shu, "Managing International News-Agency Relations under the Guomindang: China's Central News Agency, Zhao Minheng, and Reuters, 1931–1945," *Frontier History of China* 10, no. 4 (2015): 606.
97. Feng Zhixiang, *Xiao Tongzi zhuan*, 190.
98. Zhongyang tongxunshe, *Zhongyangshe liushi nian*, 14; Changning weishi ziliao weiyuanhui, *Changning wenshi ziliao disiji: Xiao Tongzi he Zhongyang tongxunshe*, 254.

Facing Dilemmas 143

later, it renewed its news exchange contract with Reuters. Beyond Shanghai, Reuters lost the right to distribute news to Chinese newspapers. Its reports were required to be sent to the headquarters of the Central News Agency in Shanghai, where further selection and distribution would be made.[99] Reuters nevertheless insisted in maintaining independence of its news service in Shanghai, until it had to further abandon its news privilege in 1937.[100]

Reuters did not give up its Chinese service for free. It requested that the Central News Agency allocated 10,000 yuan every month as a differential payment to cover the loss of news exchange as well as the use of its facilities.[101] Both the Central Executive Committee and the Ministry of Finance, two financial providers of the Central News Agency, helped to collect the funds. Yet because of a misunderstanding and a lack of coordination, double payment occurred. The mistake was rectified by Chiang Kai-shek in August 1934, who ordered the allowance be paid by the Central Executive Committee alone.[102] However, the news exchange did not markedly increase the visibility of the Central News Agency in the international news market. And the monthly payment to Reuters had placed a heavy burden on the government.[103] The deal also tarnished Reuters' reputation. Rumors began to spread among treaty-port journalists that Reuters was receiving subsidies from Nanjing.[104]

To further extend the influence of the agency globally, Xiao in 1934 established an English-language department. Having no experience with English-language publications, he turned to his friend Zhang Mingwei, editor of the *Peiping Chronicle*, for advice.[105] Together, they worked out criteria for the recruitment of department personnel: they had to be Chinese nationals with high English-language proficiency and professional training in journalism.[106] While appointing people with the right factional connections was a common practice in the Guomindang officialdom, Xiao was keen to recruit a team based on professional qualifications. To secure the assistant editor of the *Chronicle* Ren Lingxun to lead the English department, Xiao

---

99. Agreements between the Central News Agency of China, Nanking, and Reuters Limited, December 16, 1933, LN 229 [8712625], Reuters Archives, London.
100. Agreements between Reuters Limited and the Central News Agency of China, Nanking, January 1, 1937, LN 243 [8714811], Reuters Archive, London.
101. Shu, "Managing International News-Agency Relations under the Guomindang," 607.
102. Correspondence between Shao Yuanchong and Chiang Kai-shek, August 6, 1934, Chiang Kai-shek archives, 002-080200-00173-064, AH; Ministry of Finance correspondence, January 1936, Hong Jiaguan, *Zhongyang yinhang shiliao, 1928.11–1949.5* [Materials of the Central Bank of China, November 1928–May 1949] (Beijing: Zhongguo jinrong chubanshe, 2005), 133; Zhou Peijing, *Zhongyangshe de gushi: 1932–1972* [The story of the Central News Agency] (Taipei: Sanmin shuju, 1991), 17–18.
103. Shu, "Managing International News-Agency Relations under the Guomindang," 607.
104. News agencies, confidential office memorandum, 893.91/15, SDCF.
105. Xu Zhaoyong, "Xiao xiansheng chuangban zhongyangshe yingwenbu de qingxing," in Changning weishi ziliao weiyuanhui, *Changning wenshi ziliao disiji: Xiao Tongzi he Zhongyang tongxunshe*, 14.
106. Ibid.

offered Ren a wage higher than his own.[107] Yet what ultimately won Ren's loyalty to the agency was Xiao's charismatic leadership. As Ren recalled, working under Xiao was an "inarticulate pleasure." "Nowhere else can one find a more sympathetic and considerate leader."[108]

The English department established its headquarters in Tianjin. Ren's first challenge was to win contracts from the two English-language newspapers in the city, the *North China Star* and the *Peking and Tientsin Times*. With better access to news sources after taking over Reuters' domestic service, Ren's office managed to report China's domestic events faster than its competitors. The American-owned *North China Star* signed a contract with the Central News Agency immediately after the trial expired. The British paper *Peiping and Tientsin Times*, however, refused to pay for the service under the pretext that the agency was a government organ and that the material it supplied was pure propaganda. It turned out the paper's complaint was an opportunist claim to obtain free service. Within a month after Ren terminated the news supply, the paper began to approach Ren, inquiring about the possibility of signing a contract. In the following years, the *Peiping and Tientsin Times* quoted more Central News Agency's reports than did the *Star*.[109] Following the success in Tianjin, Xiao expanded the English-language service to Nanjing, Shanghai, and Hong Kong.

The English department of the Central News Agency benefited from its connections with the Yenching University, an American-operated Christian university established in 1919. Most of the staff of the department were graduates of the School of Journalism of the university. The school was launched in 1924. It was modeled on the School of Journalism at the University of Missouri, whose alumni, including Thomas F. Millard and his followers John B. Powell, Edgar Snow, and Hollington Tong, deeply influenced China's modern journalism. The Missouri-China network become further institutionalized in 1928 when Walter Williams, the dean of the School of Journalism, University of Missouri, obtained funds for the five-year operation of the faculty of Journalism at Yenching University. The two institutions exchanged professors and visiting lecturers. They also established reciprocal graduate fellowships to promote student exchange. Curriculums and textbooks of the journalism school of the University of Missouri were widely used in its counterpart at Yenching University. As Volz and Lee pointed out, the reason that the Missouri model could conquer China without much resistance was partly because of America's neocolonial ideology that promoted democracy and an open-door policy. Missouri's down-to-earth, learning-by-doing approach was also timely in providing Chinese intellectuals with

---

107. Yu Heng, "Xianghe, aicai, xiaosa, lianjie," in Xiao Tongzi wenhua jijinhui choubeichu, *Zaiziji* (Taipei: 1974), 10.
108. Ren Lingxun, "Mofan shangsi," in Xiao Tongzi wenhua jijinhui choubeichu, *Zaiziji*, 33.
109. Changning weishi ziliao weiyuanhui, *Changning wenshi ziliao disiji: Xiao Tongzi he Zhongyang tongxunshe*, 277.

an example to emulate when the pressing national crisis allowed no time for them to devise a model of their own.[110]

Yet the high level of English competence and journalistic skills were not the only reasons that make Yenching graduates attractive to the Central News Agency. International propaganda was nevertheless a highly nationalist cause driven by the desire to achieve national independence. It required deep understanding of local conditions beyond general professional training. Despite Yenching's Christian background, it had broken free from its missionary-oriented and Eurocentric models of civilizing approach and had indigenized its education with a strong focus on local context.[111] After 1931, Chinese educators Huang Xianzhao and Liang Shichun succeeded Vernon Nash to lead the journalism faculty. While American instructors taught survey courses, local newspaper editors and publishers were invited to give talks about their work experience.[112] Courses about the development of Japanese journalism were also introduced in response to the Sino-Japanese crisis.[113] Yenching's adaptation to Chinese conditions made it a popular program among the Chinese community. Xiao Tongzi joined the school's advisory committee to attract funding for the school after the Missouri fund was exhausted. Military leader Zhang Xueliang was found to be one of the biggest donors who was eager to support training of propagandists against Japanese aggression.[114]

Xiao recruited outstanding Yenching graduates into his team. Wang Jiasong, then teaching assistant at the School of Journalism of Yenching University, was hired to take charge of the department's Nanjing office. Xu Zhaoyong, a Yenching graduate who was then working as head of the translation office of the Longhai Railway Bureau, was employed to assist the department's news reporting.[115] In the Shanghai office, Xiao appointed Tang Dechen and Shen Jianhong, two Yenching University alumni with exchange experience at the University of Missouri.[116] Xiao nevertheless had never recruited an English native into the English department, not even as a proofreader. This might have been because of his belief that a deep understanding of

---

110. Yong Z. Volz and Chin-Chuan Lee, "American Pragmatism and Chinese Modernization: Importing the Missouri Model of Journalism Education to Modern China," *Media Culture Society* 31 (2009): 711–30.
111. Arthur Lewis Rosenbaum, "Introduction: Revisiting Yenching's Experience of Biculturalism," in *New Perspectives on Yenching University, 1916–1952*, ed. Arthur Lewis Rosenbaum (Chicago: Imprint Publications: 2012), 2.
112. Yong Z. Volz and Chin-Chuan Lee, "American Pragmatism and Chinese Modernization," 724.
113. Yenching University, *Zhongguo baojie jiaotong lu* [Newspapers in China] (Beijing: Yanjing daxue xinwenxi, 1933).
114. Yong Z. Volz and Chin-Chuan Lee, "American Pragmatism and Chinese Modernization," 724.
115. Changning weishi ziliao weiyuanhui, *Changning wenshi ziliao disiji: Xiao Tongzi he Zhongyang tongxunshe*, 277.
116. Xu Zhaoyong, "Xiao xiansheng chuangban zhongyangshe yingwenbu de qingxing," in *Changning wenshi ziliao disiji: Xiao Tongzi he Zhongyang tongxunshe*, 15.

Chinese culture was the prerequisite for the job. It also reduced the risk of information leakage, since the agency often dealt with political or military intelligence unfit for publicity.

However, the English department maintained close ties with the *China Press* and Hollington Tong. Before joining the Central News Agency, Shen Jianhong and Tang Dechen served the *China Press* under Tong's leadership. Tong then recommended Tang to the Associate Press to become its Nanjing correspondent for a year. Despite Tang's move to the Associate Press and later the Central News Agency, he remained loyal to the *China Press* team, continuing to contribute two reports to the *Press* every week until the outbreak of the Sino-Japanese War in 1937.[117]

The Control of the *China Press*

Chiang Kai-shek was eager to acquire a prestigious treaty-port English-language paper to strengthen his influence in the English-language media. The paper he chose to subsidize was the *China Press*, one of the most distinguished English-language dailies in Shanghai in the 1930s. The circulation of the paper reached eight thousand in the mid-1930s, just next to its British competitor the *North China Daily News* to become the second largest English-language paper in Shanghai.[118] Chiang gained access to the *China Press* through Hollington K. Tong, the managing director of the paper from 1930 to early 1935.

Hollington Tong was undeniably the most important person linking Chiang Kai-shek with the treaty-port press. His professional ability and his extensive social networks in both the treaty-port press and politics (see Chapter 3) made him an ideal contact for Chiang. Chiang approached Tong via his secretary Yang Yongtai in 1932, inviting him to assist with the government's propaganda in Shanghai.[119] Unlike some of the members of the *China Critic* group, who tried to distance themselves from governmental influence so as to maintain editorial independence, Tong was more accessible to Chiang. He was Chiang's English teacher in 1906 when Chiang was a student of the Longjin high

Figure 9
Hollington K. Tong. From the author's collection.

---

117. Tang Dechen's documents, Office of Aide-de-Camp for Chiang Kai-shek, AH.
118. Tzu-Hsiang Ch'en, *The English-Language Daily Press in China* (Beijing: Collectanea Commissionis Synodalis, 1937), 12.
119. Yang Yongtai to Chiang Kai-shek about Hollington Tong's plan on foreign propaganda, September 24, 1932, Chiang Kai-shek archives, 002080200057017, AH.

school.[120] After that, Tong pursued a degree in the United States and started his career in journalism in the treaty ports, while Chiang received his training in military schools and quickly ascended to top-level leadership in the government. Chiang met Tong again in 1929 when Tong was invited by his friend Du Xigui, general of the navy, to accompany him on a tour of Japan, the United States, Britain, France, and Italy to gain experience in naval operations. Chiang then invited Tong to visit his hometown, Xikou village. The private trip greatly deepened their mutual trust and enhanced Tong's loyalty to Chiang.[121] Their teacher-student experience, as Tong observed, paved the way for "a strong personal friendship besides the working relationship" and strengthened their ties in politics in the following years.[122]

Their friendship was based not only on the native-place and teacher-student relationship but on their common vision of the importance of militarism to China's national salvation. Unlike other protagonists of the New Culture Movement who detested militarism and perceived China's backward culture as the primary reason for its weakness, Tong believed that building a strong army was key to reviving the Chinese nation. Indeed, his primary career plan was to become a military leader rather than a journalist. Before joining the School of Journalism at University of Missouri, he wrote several letters to the Chinese minister in Washington to obtain a recommendation for his application for admission to West Point. Receiving no reply, he pursued a journalism career as a "second choice."[123] Yet the road not taken continued to attract him. He maintained a good relationship with military leaders and offered them advice on publicity issues whenever he was approached.

Tong agreed to work as a contact for Chiang on the condition that his connection with the government was concealed. Trained in the United States, he understood the Anglo-American audience's distrust of propaganda after World War I. He believed that China's international propaganda was more plagued by unsophisticated techniques than the underdevelopment of the news infrastructure and network. "The propaganda material used by the *Chinese Nation* and the Guomin News Agency," Tong criticized, "is either too dry to arouse people's interest or smacks too strongly of propaganda."[124] He believed that indirect propaganda was the best way of spreading information, in which the true source and intention were concealed and messages were transmitted to audiences via an independent outlet. He therefore strongly encouraged the Nanjing government to use the better-trusted foreign newspapers

---

120. Hollington Kong Tong, *Dong Xianguang zizhuan: Yi ge nongfu de zishu* [Hollington Tong's autobiography: A self-introduction of a farmer] (Taipei: Taiwan xinsheng baoshe, 1973), 53–54.
121. Ibid., 48–54.
122. Ibid., 53.
123. Hollington Kong Tong, *Chiang Kai-shek's Teacher and Ambassador: An Inside View of the Republican China-General Stilwell and American Policy Change towards Free China* (Indiana: Authorhouse, 2005), 15–16.
124. Yang Yongtai to Chiang Kai-shek about Hollington Tong's plan on foreign propaganda, September 24, 1932, Chiang Kai-shek archives, 002080200057017, AH.

and agencies to fulfill its propaganda agenda. Assenting to Tong's vision, Chiang subsidized Tong with 5,000 yuan each month to advance Chinese propaganda via the *China Press*. Tong's responsibility was threefold: to publish progovernment information in the *China Press*, to establish a professional and social network in treaty ports, and to collect propaganda material for the government.[125]

The *China Press* was an ideal platform for Tong to strengthen his connections with foreign journalists. As an English-language paper ostensibly operated as a Sino-American joint venture, the paper attracted many young Americans who were enthusiastic about East Asian affairs. While Tong was editor of the *Press*, "a surprisingly large number of American newspapermen . . . drifted in and out of the staff."[126] The paper became the first stop for most foreign journalists to China. It was practically an "incubator" that trained "newly-coming western journalists to develop better knowledge of this country and establish personal networks."[127] As Tong recalled:

> The *China Press* was to the Far East what the *Paris Herald* was to Europe. Newspapermen and women on their way around the world would stop over in Shanghai, work for the *Press* for a few months to earn passage money to the next port, and then moved on. Others who held permanent interest in China and the Far East would stay longer and then took positions as correspondents with home-based papers and agencies.[128]

The *China Press* nurtured a significant number of foreign correspondents who would later work for mainstream media in the United States and Britain. Tillman Durdin, who worked for the *China Press* in the mid-1930s, for example, became a Far Eastern correspondent for the *New York Times* after 1937, while Harold Isaacs later moved to *Newsweek* to cover wartime China.

The managing team led by Tong paid special attention to maintaining the paper's "liberal" stance despite the government's secret subsidies. Tong therefore had to mediate between the government and the paper to ease tensions when the paper's independent position aroused the government's ire. During the Shanghai Incident in 1932, Chiang repeatedly requested that Tong hold back reports on the Nineteenth Route Army's disregard of the order from the central government, believing such reports would expose the disunity within the government. Tong followed Chiang's advice, but the paper's reticence to cover issues relating to the Nineteenth Route Army received heavy complaints from his American colleagues.[129] In late 1933, when Chiang sent troops to Fuzhou to break the rebellion launched by the leaders of the

---

125. Ibid.
126. Hollington Kong Tong, *Dateline: China; the Beginning of China's Press Relations with the World* (New York: Rockport Press, 1950), 4–5.
127. Ibid.
128. Ibid.
129. Tong, *Dong Xianguang zizhuan*, 61.

Nineteenth Route Army and the Guomindang leftists, a photo depicting the Nanjing government's air bombing of a high school in Fuzhou published by Harold Isaacs in the *Press* infuriated Chiang. As a result, Tong had to travel from Shanghai to Nanjing in person to apologize for the "mistake."[130]

Tensions also arose between the owner of the press syndicate, Zhang Zhuping, and the Nanjing leaders. Zhang was a graduate of St. John's University, an American-operated missionary university in Shanghai. He was also a member of the Green Gang, an influential underground society in Shanghai led by Du Yuesheng.[131] He joined *Shen bao* in 1914. Together with Shi Liangcai, they turned *Shen bao* into the most popular newspaper in China, with a daily circulation of 150,000 in the early 1930s.[132] While working under Shi, Zhang started his own news agencies and newspapers. In 1928 he established the Shenshi News Agency and purchased the *Shishi xin bao*. In late 1930, he obtained control of the *China Press*, and in early 1932 he founded a native evening paper *Da wanbao*. With a Chinese-language daily and evening paper, an English-language daily, and a news agency in hand, Zhang began

Figure 10
The *China Press* staff party, probably Chinese New Year 1934. Seated: left three, Shen Jianhong, middle, Zhang Zhuping. Back row: left four, Tillman Durdin, left five, Hawthorne Cheng, left seven, Hollington Tong. From *The Press Corps of Old Shanghai*, 12.

---

130. Ibid., 59–60.
131. Huang Zhuoming and Yu Zhenji, "Guanyu *Shishi xin bao* de suojian suowen," in *Xinwen yanjiu ziliao* [Research materials on Chinese journalism] 19 (1983): 184; about Du Yuesheng and the Green Gang's relations with the Nanjing regime, see Brian G. Martin, *The Shanghai Green Gang: Politics and Organized Crime, 1919–1937* (Berkeley: University of California Press, 1996), chapters 7 and 8.
132. According to statistics on press circulation assessed by the Ministry of Information in 1931, quoted in Yao Fushen, "Sishe—jiu Zhongguo baoye jituanhua jingying de yici changshi" [Four Agencies—a trial of press syndicate in Republican China], *Xinwen daxue* (Winter 1997): 59.

to build his long-planned press syndicate.¹³³ He created a general managing team to supervise the operation of the Shenshi agency, *Shishi xin bao*, the *China Press*, and *Da wanbao*, and named the alliance the Four Agencies (Si she). The alliance was the first commercial press syndicate in China. Its network greatly facilitated the flow of information, and Zhang was frequently referred to in the West as the "Chinese Lord Northcliffe or Hearst."¹³⁴

The intervention of the Guomindang government undermined the development of the press syndicate before Zhang was able to fully integrate the Four Agencies. Chiang Kai-shek was unwilling to see a large press syndicate operated by a private media entrepreneur beyond his control, especially during the mid-1930s when his supremacy was challenged by both an international and a domestic crisis. Chiang and Zhang's dispute lay mainly in the editorial policy of the *Shishi xin bao*. As the third-largest native paper, circulating about fifty thousand copies daily, the paper was the backbone of Zhang's Four Agencies. It adopted a critical and sometimes unfriendly attitude toward Chiang's clique. After the Shanghai Incident, for example, *Shishi xin bao* was the only paper that objected to the signing of the Shanghai Truce.¹³⁵

The tension between Chiang and the paper reached breaking point when Chiang found that the paper was involved in the Fujian rebellion. In 1933, the Nineteenth Route Army was deployed to Fujian to suppress a Communist rebellion. Instead of confronting the Communists, the leaders of the army, including Cai Tingkai, Chen Mingshu, and Jiang Guangnai, entered peace negotiations with them. Allied with the Guomindang leftist forces led by Li Jishen, they formed an anti-Chiang group in Fujian and proclaimed a new government in the area in November 1933. Meanwhile, Jiang Tingkai secretly approached Zhang, asking him to promote the legitimacy of the Fujian government via his Four Agencies. In return, Jiang promised to invest 400,000 yuan in Zhang's media enterprise, a fund Zhang urgently needed to strengthen his fledgling syndicate.¹³⁶ After Chiang suppressed the Fujian Rebellion in January 1934, its connection with the Four Agencies was revealed.¹³⁷ In response, Chiang placed a postal ban on the *Shishi xin bao* in late 1934. Upon learning that Zhang secretly inserted banned *xin bao* pages in the *China Press*, Chiang not only ceased subsidy to the *Press* but also suspended postal services for the paper.¹³⁸

---

133. Zhang Zhuping, "Shenshi dianxunshe zhi huigu yu qianzhan" [The past and present of the Shenshi News Agency], in Shenshi dianxunshe, *Shinian: Shenshi dianxunshe chuangli shi zhounian jinian* [Ten years: The tenth anniversary of the Shenshi News Agency] (Shanghai: Shenshi dianxunshe, 1934), 11.
134. Douglas Jenkins to Nelson T. Johnson, February 24, 1931, 893.911/266, SDCF.
135. Chiang Kai-Shek archives, 00202020000015119, AH.
136. *Xinwen yanjiu ziliao*, 187; Yao, "Sishe—jiuzhongguo baoye jituanhua jingying de yici changshi," 61; Fang Hanqi, *Zhongguo xinwen shiye tongshi* [General history of Chinese journalism] (Beijing: Zhongguo renmin daxue chubanshe, 1992), 458.
137. *Xinwen yanjiu ziliao*, 187; Yao, "Sishe—jiuzhongguo baoye jituanhua jingying de yici changshi," 61.
138. Chiang Kai-shek ordered Zhu Jiahua to cease postal services for the *China Press* and *Shishi xin bao*, September 13, 1934, Chiang Kai-shek archives, 002080200179076, AH.

Facing Dilemmas   151

The postal ban on two of Zhang's major papers dealt a heavy blow to his syndicate. Zhang was already deeply indebted to Du Yuesheng for his help with establishing the syndicate. The postal ban further exacerbated his financial difficulties. Under pressure from Du, Zhang had to mortgage the properties of the Four Agencies to Du and appointed Du as temporary managing director. During Zhang's semiretirement, he was approached by Minister of Finance Kong Xiangxi, possibly on behalf of members of the Soong family,[139] to purchase his shares of the Four Agencies at the low price of 200,000 yuan.[140] Zhang had to accept the deal since it was supported by his creditor Du, who cared more about his monetary interests in the paper than its ownership and editorial policies.[141] Yet Zhang was even denied the 200,000 yuan on the pretext that he had not cleared his debt.

To further oust Zhang from the Shanghai press, the Guomindang officials sought to isolate him from his *Shishi xin bao* colleagues, creating the impression that Zhang's political disorientation was the sole reason for the current difficulties of the paper. In March 1935, Ye Chucang, vice minister of the Legislative Yuan, and Tang Youren, vice minister of foreign affairs, lodged a joint petition to Chiang Kai-shek's secretary Chen Bulei, in the hope he would help with recruiting the current *Shishi xin bao* editor Pan Gongbi to the Legislative Yuan. By doing so, Ye and Tang sought to disassociate their friend Pan from the scandal and further ostracize Zhang from the managing team.[142] Meanwhile, Hollington Tong resigned from the *China Press*. Although he claimed that he was obliged to leave the *Press* because of health problems, it was possible that his resignation was related to the Four Agencies case. Having sensed the political danger involved in the crisis, Tong sought to disentangle himself from the *Press* so as to avoid further political implications.

None of the pressure was as compelling as the Guomindang's threat of assassination. In November 1934, Shi Liangcai, the owner of China's largest newspaper, *Shen bao*, was shot dead on his way back to Shanghai from Hangzhou. Shi was a long-term critic of Chiang's policy. His connection with the underground Communists eventually made him the target of assassins of Chiang's intelligence office.[143] Although Zhang split with Shi to start his own press business in the late 1920s and became one of Shi's major competitors, their rivalry was purely business related. Shi's death dashed Zhang's last hope for Chiang's regime. It dawned on him that the current government would become only more intolerant of political dissent as the government's insecurities increased and the national crisis deepened. Shortly after Shi's death, Zhang

---

139. Edwin S. Cunningham to the Secretary of State, Washington, June 10, 1935, 893.911/311, SDCF.
140. Yao, "Sishe—jiuzhongguo baoye jituanhua jingying de yici changshi," 61.
141. Edwin S. Cunningham to the Secretary of State, Washington, June 10, 1935, 893.911/311, SDCF.
142. Ye Chucang and Tang Youren to Chen Bulei via Yang Yongtai, March 27, 1934, Chiang Kai-shek archives, 002-080200-00217-042, AH.
143. Shen Meijuan, *Shen Zui huiyi zuopin quanji* [Complete collection of Shen Zui's memoir] (Beijing: Jiuzhou tushu chubanshe, 1998), 78–80.

received a letter with a bullet and a note inside, threatening that if Zhang remained uncooperative, he would face the same fate as Shi.¹⁴⁴ With all this pressure, Zhang eventually gave up his press career in Shanghai, a career in which he had invested fifteen years of his life. He left Shanghai for Hong Kong, with a merciful 50,000 yuan "gift" from Kong Xiangxi, and never returned to the press business.¹⁴⁵

With the government's purchase of the Four Agencies in early 1935, Kong obtained full control of the *Press* and turned the paper into "an organ of propaganda for the National Government."¹⁴⁶ Kong assigned Yang Guangsheng (also known as Kwangson/Kuangson Young) as managing director, assisted by the Australian F. L. Pratt and the American John B. Penniston.¹⁴⁷ Yang was a graduate of Tsinghua College with a PhD from Princeton University in international law and political science. On his return to China, he joined the Ministry of Foreign Affairs to work as director of the intelligence and publicity department.¹⁴⁸ Yang maintained the paper's registration in the United States and kept hiring American reporters. Experienced in the diplomatic field, he established a good relationship with US journalists. Malcolm Rosholt, an American journalist working for the *China Press* between 1932

Figure 11
Yang Guangsheng. From *The Press Corps of Old Shanghai*, 22.

and 1937, commented that "of all the people with whom we worked in Shanghai, not one was better liked than Kuangson Young."¹⁴⁹ But Yang's true identity remained a mystery to many of his foreign colleagues. Rosholt, who accidentally met Yang on his trip to Paris, was "surprised to hear Kuangson speak French" and was even shocked when he learned that Yang was in Paris to purchase arms for Chiang Kai-shek.¹⁵⁰ Although Yang claimed to be a full-time manager of the *China Press*, it was clear that his connection with Chiang and the Ministry of Foreign Affairs was close. Yang's service to the *Press* was cut short after the outbreak of the Sino-Japanese War. In 1940, he was sent to Manila to replace the Chinese consul and was killed during Japan's occupation of the Chinese consulate. His body was identified by the gold-rimmed glasses he usually wore.¹⁵¹

---

144. Yao Fushen, "Zhang Bao'an jiaoshou hua xianfu Zhang Zhuping yishi" [Professor Zhang Bao'an's reminiscence about his father Zhang Zhuping], *Xinwen daxue* [Journalism], no. 1 (2008): 43.
145. Ibid., 61.
146. Edwin S. Cunningham to the Secretary of State, Washington, June 10, 1935, 893.911/311, SDCF.
147. Malcolm Leviatt Rosholt, *The Press Corps of Old Shanghai* (Rosholt, WI: Rosholt House, 1994), 22.
148. Edwin S. Cunningham to the Secretary of State, Washington, June 10, 1935, 893.911/311, SDCF.
149. Malcolm Leviatt Rosholt, *Press Corps of Old Shanghai*, 22.
150. Ibid.
151. Ibid.

Censorship on the Outgoing Dispatches

The Nanjing government did not enact effective censorship on international dispatches until 1934, when new contracts with the Great Northern Telegraph Company, the Eastern Extension Telegraph Company, and the Commercial Pacific Cable Company were eventually signed after two years of delay. The new contract allowed the Nanjing government to install censors in each of the foreign cable companies. The Main Cablegram Acceptance and Delivery Office attached to the Ministry of Communications was established to supervise the censorship.[152]

Facing this newly acquired censorship power, Nanjing officials were left in a quandary about how to exercise it. The government lacked a clear protocol and mechanism for how to censor outgoing dispatches. As a result, international messages were subjected to the same regulations that were applied to domestic reports:

> No reports should contain words that cause danger to the Guomindang, the nation and social security. Apparent rumours as well as information that reveal military and diplomatic secrets are prohibited.[153]

The regulation indicated that information was censored not only based on its content but also on its potential outcome. The vague definition offered censors excessive jurisdiction to withhold any views they deemed unfit for publication. Without a clear definition of "secret," any military or diplomatic information from private sources could be subjected to the highest level of scrutiny. Staff members of the office usually took the most conservative censorship standard so as to avoid "mistakes."

The Nanjing government's censorship machine had drawn heavy protests from the foreign press in Shanghai and abroad. They frequently blamed Chinese censors for their lack of general journalistic knowledge and appreciation of newspaper operations. In May 1935, the *Journal de Shanghai* commented:

> These sorry gentlemen [censors] who, without any preparation, have been in one day placed with the various foreign telegraph offices are too ignorant of their new work to be able to discern what "Article 26 of the International Telegraph Agreement" permits them to cut out from the telegrams handed in by the correspondents of the foreign newspapers and news agencies. They tremble unceasingly at the thought lest a phrase which they very often do not understand or a comment the meaning of which is generally unintelligible to them should attract the attention of one of the officials of their Legations in Paris or London or Washington or Rome or Moscow and who may report the matter to Nanking, resulting in a reprimand being brought upon them.[154]

---

152. Negotiation of the contract with the Great Eastern and Great Northern companies, February 1933–June 1934, 020000003139, AH.
153. Procedure of the Ministry of Communications Governing Censorship of Telegrams, 893.918/91, 11–16, SDCF.
154. "Required: A School for Censors," *Journal de Shanghai*, May 30, 1935, no. 2398, Shanghai Municipal Police Files (hereafter SMP).

Hollington Tong, in his autobiography, also cited a notorious example of the government's abuse of censorship: the New York Times once received a dispatch from its China correspondent which read, "TIMES NEW YORK STOP STOP STOP STOP STOP STOP SIGNED JAMES WOOD."[155] Randall Gould, editor of the Shanghai Evening Post and Mercury, complained, "No one could tell when some particular enterprising censor might write in a whole essay of his own, to go to some American newspaper over the signature of its unsuspecting correspondent."[156] Even the Australian journalist H. J. Timperley, who was sympathetic to the Guomindang government, denounced the inconsistency of the censorship:

> In China the censoring of foreign telegrams has been marked both by extreme severity and by a lack of consistency which makes it virtually impossible for the bewildered correspondent to work out any sort of guiding principle, no matter how anxious he may be to accommodate himself to official requirements.... What is permissible today may be blue-pencilled tomorrow. Regional interpretation of the censorship rules add to the confusion. A news item which is suppressed in Peiping may pass the Shanghai censor without difficulty, and vice versa. In practice the system is haphazard, erratic and, on occasion, irresponsible.[157]

Inadequate censorship not only affected China's outgoing dispatches but also plagued domestic news transmissions. Complaints about censors' lack of professionalism and their arbitrary deletion of information were commonly heard.[158] Protests against censorship ran high in 1935, especially after the government forbade newspapers to distribute any news "relating to military or diplomatic secrecies."[159] The policy became so unpopular that even the party organ, Zhongyang ribao, turned against it, believing "such an irrational system" of censorship was "completely demoralizing." The paper warned that the censorship would turn the nation into a place full of deaf and dumb people and questioned, "How can a deaf and dumb nation organize a [s]tate and exist on earth?"[160]

Fearing the suppression of diplomatic information would give rise to secret diplomacy between the Nanjing government and the Japanese army, Chen bao, a semiofficial paper, urged officials to relax their censorship and keep the public fully informed.[161] Meanwhile, the departments of journalism at several prestigious universities in Shanghai, Beijing, and Guangzhou submitted a joint petition to the

---

155. Tong, Dateline: China, 6.
156. Randall Gould, China in the Sun (Garden City, NY: Doubleday, 1946), 308.
157. H. J. Timperley, "Makers of Public Opinion about the Far East," Pacific Affairs 9, no. 2 (June 1936): 225.
158. Lee-hsia Hsu Ting, Government Control of the Press in Modern China, 1900–1949 (Cambridge, MA: Harvard University Press, 1974), 87.
159. "Censorship of Telegraphic Messages in China: The Chinese Telegraph Administration," April 19, 1935, 893.918/92, SDCF.
160. Quoted in "Censorship System Has Evil Effects," Shanghai Times, November 29, 1935.
161. "Censorship Policy Criticized, Chen Bao Points Out Three Points to Be Kept," Shanghai Times, December 6, 1935.

government, appealing for abolition of the censorship. They argued that censorship was conducted by local officials who often attempted to suppress news harmful to their personal reputation. "If the control over the press is not concentrated, or if no definite standards of censorship are established and followed," warned the petition, "not only will press censorship be ineffective, but it may also be abused by the local authorities."[162]

The absence of censorship on Japanese telegrams was often cited by the treaty-port journalists to oppose the government's suppression of news. Japan had its own cable linking Shanghai and Nagasaki, over which the Nanjing government had no control. It was open to all pro-Japanese correspondents, provided their messages were sent in Japanese. European or American correspondents who wished to use Japanese cables could easily arrange retranslation in Tokyo and transmit their dispatches to their final destinations.[163] While pro-Japanese messages would suffer only the minor inconvenience of retranslation and a short delay, some of the balanced accounts provided by neutral observers were completely suppressed.[164] Treaty-port journalists considered China's incomplete censorship as the cause of the "most serious discrimination" that deeply damaged their credibility.[165]

Western correspondents worried that Tokyo would replace Shanghai as the news center for Chinese issues. Their concern was justified. In the mid-1930s, Tokyo dominated dispatch transmissions in East Asia. Among the 33,204 press dispatches, containing 1,385,974 words filed by various news services around the world in 1934, 525,001 words—more than one-third of the total—were transmitted to Japan.[166] With a steady flow of information abroad, Japan became the interpreter of East Asian politics. A semiofficial report from Washington attested to the anomaly:

> The public, as well as Washington officialdom, has been beclouded about events in the Far East. We are uncertain about what has happened lately in regard to Japan's moves *vis a vis* China and the reported disposition of the Nanking government to accept Japan's tutelage. Practically all the news published in the Washington newspapers about this important matter has come from Tokyo; there have been only two or three short dispatches from China.[167]

Journalists in Shanghai offered different suggestions to solve the problem. Some urged the Nanjing government to subject Japanese cables to the same level of control as that applied to foreign cables;[168] others demanded a complete abolition of cable

---

162. "Petition for Improvement of Press Censorship," *Shanghai Times*, December 28, 1935.
163. Timperley, "Makers of Public Opinion about the Far East," 226.
164. "Tokyo Defies Nanking on News-Commercial Censorship," *China Weekly Review*, April 20, 1935, 240.
165. J. B. Powell to Willys R. Peck, American Consulate General, March 15, 1935, 893.918/91, SDCF.
166. Ibid.
167. Quoted in "Lack of Censorship on Jap Cable Cause of Distorted News," *China Weekly Review*, April 27, 1935, 274.
168. Ibid.

censorship.[169] Yet one message was clear: actions needed to be taken by the Nanjing government to modify its censorship policy.

To redress the inconsistency in censorship, the government sought to centralize its censorship apparatus. It abandoned censorship branches at local telegram companies and established offices in five key cities: Beijing, Tianjin, Shanghai, Nanjing, and Hankou.[170] All outgoing dispatches were censored at these five branches before further transmission. Although the branches were ostensibly organized by the Ministry of Information (party), the Executive Yuan (state), and the Military Affairs Commission (military), the actual operation was exercised by the military sector under Chiang Kai-shek's control.[171]

Chiang hoped to install his follower, Hollington Tong, to lead the key office—the Shanghai censorship bureau. After leaving the *China Press*, Tong received a telegram from William H. Donald, asking him "in the interest of patriotism" to consider accepting the position as chief censor of all outgoing foreign press telegrams. Tong had known Donald for more than twenty years. They exchanged news items when Tong worked for newspapers in Beijing and Donald served for the London *Times* as a Beijing correspondent. Their cooperation continued in 1931 during the reorganization of the *China Press* when Donald was a member of the board and Tong was the managing director of the paper. Donald resigned from the board in 1932 and became an unofficial advisor to Chiang Kai-shek. Given Donald's position, it was clear that the invitation offered to Tong came from Chiang and that Donald was the messenger to test Tong's response.

Donald's invitation presented Tong with a dilemma. As a former journalist who had long been a victim of the government's censorship, Tong disliked censorship as much as any journalists.[172] Although working for the government was not an entirely new experience for him, becoming a censor would make him the adversary of his former colleagues in the press. Joining a government that was notorious for its abuse of censorship power would inevitably estrange him from his treaty-port press cohort and tarnish his reputation of being independent and professional, two principles he had adhered to throughout his two-decades-long career in journalism. Moreover, Tong might put himself in an insecure position by throwing himself pell-mell into the Guomindang bureaucracy, where seniority in the party was valued more than

---

169. "An Inefficient and Illegal Censorship," *Journal de Shanghai*, May 2, 1935; "Required: A School for Censors," *Journal de Shanghai*, May 30, 1935, no. 2398, SMP.
170. Zhongyao dushi xinwen jiancha banfa huibian [Guideline for censorship in key cities], January 19, 1933, in Liu Zhemin, *Jinxiandai chuban xinwen fagui huibian* [Press regulations in modern China] (Shanghai: Xuelin chubanshe, 1992), 513.
171. The Central Executive Committee to Chiang Kai-shek, August 6, 1934, Chiang Kai-shek archives, 002080200439034, AH; Division of Far Eastern Affairs correspondence, May 13, 1935, 893.918/91, 11–1, SDCF.
172. Tong, *Dateline: China*, 7.

professional capability. Apart from an informal connection with Chiang Kai-shek, he had no political involvement in the Nationalist Party. Although Chiang's support could provide him the authority to offset his lack of party experience, the association with Chiang could also backfire by making him the target of Chiang's political rivals or incurring attacks from Chiang's own cliques.

Yet Donald struck the right chord with Tong by citing patriotism. With the Japanese threat becoming more frightening, Tong, together with many other liberal treaty-port elites, began to increasingly feel morally obliged to cooperate with the government, even though this might indicate a sacrifice of his liberal principles. Liberalism and independence were, after all, an extravagance during a national crisis when individuals' fate was hinged upon the survival of their nation. Although Tong disagreed with many of the government policies and abhorred the stifling political culture, he still recognized Chiang as the main power who had the ability to mobilize the national resources necessary for an eventual war with Japan. When the heightened crisis no longer allowed time for a gradual reform, the most efficient way of revamping the ineffective censorship system was to partake in its operations and make changes from within. The suppression of Zhang Zhuping's media syndicate also warned him of the painful reality that the pursuit of journalism beyond the government's control became increasingly difficult as political struggles intensified. Complete independence to political penetration was not an option. Instead, it was a question of which faction to ally with as a patron. As the national crisis deepened, cooperation with Chiang was just a matter of time. After an agonizing deliberation, Tong accepted Chiang's offer and perceived it as "an opportunity to contribute his share toward building foreign goodwill through the press,"[173] albeit in a new direction.

Tong immediately organized a new censorship team after his inauguration. His office was attached to the Military Affairs Commission and received 12,000 yuan funding from Chiang Kai-shek.[174] The office included six people, most of whom were his old colleagues from the treaty-port press, with extensive experience in journalism. Zeng Xubai had been Tong's colleague at *Yong bao* and the Four Agencies; Dong Shoupeng (Z. B. Tong) used to work under Tong's supervision at the *China Press*; Wei Jingmeng (known as Jimmy Wei) was Tong's assistant at the Four Agencies; F. L. Pratt, once an employee of the *China Press*, was now Tong's advisor in the censorship office; and Zhu Shuqing (also S. T. Chu) was responsible for censoring Russian materials.[175] As soon as Tong's censorship office was established, the government accelerated the centralizing process. In August 1935, Minister of Communications

---

173. Tong, *Dateline: China*, 7.
174. Confidential spending regarding military affairs, February 1936–February 1937, Chiang Kai-shek archives, 00208010200031001, AH.
175. Tong, *Dateline: China*, 10; Zeng Xubai, *Zeng Xubai zizhuan* [Autobiography of Zeng Xubai] (Taipei: Lianjing chuban shiye gongsi, 1988), 1:179–180.

Zhu Jiahua, also a close ally of Chiang, ordered the censorship branches in the other four key cities to transmit foreign-language dispatches to Tong's Shanghai office for a final check.[176] This made Tong's office the pivot of censorship for China's outgoing news.

As an experienced journalist in Shanghai, Tong was fully aware of the government's inadequate censorship policies. Without delay, he set down new rules. He pursued a relatively liberal censorship policy, insisting that messages should be held up only because of wrong facts.[177] He believed that, except for information that concerned China's "national security," the censorship office "must give the writers free rein."[178] Accountability was another aspect he tried to improve. He required his staff to notify correspondents of any changes made to their reports prior to transmission. And correspondents reserved the right to refuse changes.[179] Tong kept in close communication with foreign journalists. When serious disputes occurred, Tong would "reason with" them, so as to avoid any misunderstanding that might translate into negative portrayals of China in their reports.[180]

Tong markedly improved the censorship system. Randall Gould praised Tong for having finally "developed a censorship as nearly ideal as any censorship could be":

> It was usually him [Tong] rather than a subordinate who phoned the correspondent in case of a projected deletion. If necessary he would meet the correspondent personally. Sometimes the correspondent was able to convince Holly [Hollington] that facts were as stated, in which case the message went off unchanged. Sometimes Holly convinced the correspondents that he had fallen for a rumour, in which case the correspondent was saved from consequences unpleasant to himself.[181]

Tong's censorship office was severely tested during the Xi'an Incident, though. In December 1936, Chiang Kai-shek visited Xi'an to promote a new anticommunist campaign. During the trip, he was arrested by his own generals Zhang Xueliang and Yang Hucheng, who opposed his policy of suppressing the communists before resisting Japan. After two weeks of intensive negotiation, Chiang was released on December 25, and he agreed to form the second Nationalist-Communist United Front against the Japanese. The incident was a nerve-racking experience for Tong. As chief censor, Tong was responsible for blocking all false information and rumors about Chiang's death from transmitting abroad. He maintained a twenty-four-hour watch over the events and sometimes communicated with Madam Chiang to verify

---

176. Zhu Jiahua to the Military Affairs Commission, August 21, 1935, Chiang Kai-shek archives, 00207020000006064, AH.
177. Gould, *China in the Sun*, 309.
178. Tong, *Dateline: China*, 10.
179. Gould, *China in the Sun*, 309.
180. Tong, *Dateline: China*, 10.
181. Gould, *China in the Sun*, 309.

facts. As he recalled, he was "trembling throughout the fortnight." Even when he slept, a telephone was placed under his pillow to connect him with his assistant.[182] By the end of the incident, no false report was sent to the world from Shanghai. Misleading information was mostly received by way of Japan. Indeed, Japanese correspondents had misreported Chiang's death at least ten times, which severely damaged their reputation.

However, Tong's vision of censorship was not shared by some of the conservatives in the government. In mid-1937, he was temporarily squeezed out by Zhang Xinhai (H. H. Chang), a Harvard graduate and former ambassador to Portugal and Poland. Although he was highly competent in diplomacy, his tenure in the censorship office was brief and troublesome. Without much experience in the press, Zhang had little understanding of the importance of timeliness in journalism. He replied to foreign correspondents in a dilatory manner, which often drew heavy complaints from them. Zhang's fatal mistake that brought his censorship job to an end was his arbitrary restriction of news on the Red Army's reorganization into the Chinese National Army in September 1937. When the foreign correspondents quoted the reports about this reorganization by the Central News Agency, Zhang saw it as just another reference to the Communists and ordered deletion of all such items. Later he explained that, "having killed so many previous references to the Chinese Communists, he might just as well kill this one also."[183]

Zhang's words mirrored the mind-set of many of the Chinese politicians who failed to value modern journalism. The contention between liberal publicists and Guomindang bureaucrats was long lasting, and Tong's return to the censorship office did not mean Nanjing officials in general gained any clearer concept of the meaning of free press and credibility of sources. As Tong recalled:

> All through my years in the government service I faced this continuing problem of Chinese incomprehension of American journalistic methods and standards. It vastly complicated at times my task as China's intermediary with the Western Press. Part of my difficulties stemmed from the wide differences between Chinese and American newspapers. . . . Pre-war Chinese newspapers, with rare exceptions, were partisan and one-sided organs of particular factions or interests. The idea that a publication should present more than one side of a story in its columns was almost unthinkable to Chinese engaged in politics. Few of the government officials with whom I worked cared to read a newspaper pursuing an independent policy. It was difficult for many of them to understand my prolonged efforts to win the goodwill of free American publications. . . . The other angle of my problem was psychological. Chinese habitually dislike open disputations. They shrink from the kind of controversial plain-speaking journalism which is popular in America. Their most embittered controversies are invested in an atmosphere of

---

182. Tong, *Chiang Kai-shek's Teacher and Ambassador*, 63–64.
183. Tong, *Dateline: China*, 8–9.

deceptive calm.... They prefer to handle their disputes by innuendo rather than through direct collision.[184]

Indeed, Tong was not the only person disturbed by the misunderstanding of international propaganda among conservative officials. Yan Huiqing, China's delegate to Geneva also complained that many Guomindang officials were reluctant to present China's case abroad, regarding such an activity as not "dignified and worthwhile."[185]

In an age of uncertainty, disunity and ambiguity characterized by the way rhetoric flowed in the press. Despite all the progress Nanjing had made in improving news infrastructure and administration, the government faced enormous challenges in devising a consistent news policy. The dilemma between resistance and appeasement prevented the treaty-port papers from forming a unified voice. The Amō case discussed in the following chapter reflects this complexity in detail.

---

184. Ibid., 9.
185. W. W. Yen (Yan Huiqing), *East-West Kaleidoscope, 1877–1946: An Autobiography* (New York: St. John's University Press, 1974), 196.

Figure 12
Sapajou, "A Damsel in Distress," *North China Daily News*, June 3, 1933.

6
Friend or Foe
The Amō Doctrine

On April 17, 1934, Amō Eiji, head of the Department of Information of the Japanese Ministry of Foreign Affairs, issued an "unofficial" statement in response to questions about the Japanese government's attitude toward foreign assistance to China. The statement was later summed up as a "hands-off China" policy. Some Japanese and foreign papers also referred to the policy as the "Monroe Doctrine of Asia." The statement declared that Japan had a special responsibility to maintain peace in Asia and that it opposed any foreign assistance to China that could be exploited as a means of countering Japan's influence in the country:

> Owing to the special position of Japan in her relations with China . . . Japan is in a position to do her best to carry out her mission in the Orient, and though there may be a divergence of opinion between the position of Japan and that of other nations towards China, [which] led to Japan's withdrawal from the League of Nations, nevertheless Japan deems it natural to maintain peace in the Orient by herself, and on her own responsibility. . . . Furthermore, Japan will be forced to object to any measures on the part of other powers, which are likely to lead to disturbance of peace in the Orient. For example, the providing of China with military aeroplanes and military instructors, and the giving of political loans are among the measures which are doomed to be met with opposition from Japan.[1]

The Amō case took place when Japan's international reputation was on the wane and the country was in the middle of disputes with Western powers on various fronts. Its image was tarnished by Chinese propagandists' skillful reference to the existing controversies Japan was involved in, a strategy China quickly learned from Japan in its previous battles in the press. Yet papers representing different political interests in China failed to form a unified anti-Japanese line. Japanese propaganda was also plagued by its own indecisive attitudes. While Chinese government was caught in a dilemma between its antiforeign tradition and appeasement of Japan, Japan was in

---

1. Quotes from the *New York Times* translation of the Amō statement in Westel Woodbury Willoughby, *The Sino-Japanese Controversy and the League of Nations* (Baltimore: Johns Hopkins Press, 1935), 629–30; see also quotes of Reuters' translation of the Amō statement in "Tokyo Opposes Aid to China," *North China Daily News*, April 18, 1934, 9.

an equally difficult situation. The disagreement between the civil government and the military sector led to conflicting interpretations of the Amō's statement. Japan was struggling to balance its national interests in East Asia with its international reputation.

The Context

The year 1934 was not a fruitful time for Japan to assert its "hands-off China" policy. The policy undermined its promise for international cooperation. After the occupation of Manchuria, Japanese officials were keenly aware of the harm the military aggression had brought to Japan's international image. Since the latter half of 1933, the Japanese government had made efforts "in every direction possible" to ameliorate international antagonism toward Japan.[2] Hirota Kōki was appointed foreign minister with this specific task.[3] As US ambassador in Japan, Joseph Grew observed, Hirota came into office at a moment when the pendulum of public sentiment was tending to swing away from a militant policy toward a desire to normalize relationships with the outside world. The resignation of Uchida Yasuya was in itself a blow to military influence. In the Diet, members openly expressed their dismay at the size of the military budgets and accused the army of leading the nation into the unnecessary and dangerous state of agitation. Meanwhile, businesspeople wished to break the shackles of political and military control and reap the profits of the export boom. Hirota, after coming into office, answered those calls by restraining military influence over diplomacy and actively repairing Japan's relations with China, Soviet Russia, Great Britain, and the United States. He tried to tone down Japan's antiforeign rhetoric in the press, solve disputes with Russia, and improve American-Japanese relations. The appointment of Hirota suggested a shift in Japan's foreign policy—from what the Japanese press called the "desperate diplomacy" of Uchida to Hirota's "national defence by diplomacy."[4] However, at a time when Japan's relations with other Powers appeared to be improving, the Amō statement pulled Japan back into diplomatic isolation.

The doctrine was issued when Japan was involved in various disputes with China and the Western powers. After the Tanggu Truce, Japan had been pushing the Nanjing government to restore railway and postal links between China proper and Manchuria. For Nanjing, restoration of communications with Manchuria equaled recognition of Manchukuo, yet denying Japan's demands would incur military confrontation. The

---

2. Ambassador in Japan (Grew) to the Consul at Geneva (Gilbert), May 17, 1934, PRFRUS, 1934, the Far East, vol. 3, 182.
3. Ian Hill Nish, *Japanese Foreign Policy, 1869–1942: Kasumigaseki to Miyakezaka* (London: Routledge, 2002), 198–99.
4. Ambassador in Japan (Grew) to the Consul at Geneva (Gilbert), May 17, 1934, PRFRUS, 1934, the Far East, vol. 3, 182.

Nanjing leaders had managed to delay responding to Japan in late 1933 on the pretext that the government had to pacify the Fujian Rebellion first. With the successful suppression of the rebellion in early 1934, the government was running out of excuses to postpone facing this thorny issue. Publicly, both Zhu Jiahua, the minister of communications, and Sun Ke, president of the Legislative Yuan, repeated that Nanjing had no intention of restoring rail and postal connections with Manchukuo. This intransigence drained the patience of the Kwantung Army. On April 13, 1934, the army reinforced troops along the Beijing-Liaoning Railway and held military maneuvers in Fengtian and the eastern suburbs of Beijing. Under such duress, Chiang Kai-shek sent Huang Fu to Shanghai on April 16 to discuss with Japanese minister Ariyoshi Akira the possibility of resuming negotiations over communications with Manchukuo.[5] On the following day, the Amō Doctrine was announced. Even though the statement may not have had anything to do with the rail and postal negotiations, as Japan claimed, the timing of the statement made the case fairly easy to be perceived as Japan's effort to push for the restoration of communications with Manchuria.

With the United States and Britain, the statement of the Amō Doctrine cast a shadow over the 1935 naval conference. Determined to achieve parity in naval power, Japan sought to abandon the 1930 London Naval Conference Treaty that set Japan's battleship tonnage at 70 percent of that of the other two countries. Since a new round of naval talks was to be held in 1935, the year 1934 had seen a rise in tensions over the arrangement of naval power between Anglo-American powers and Japan. In the spring of 1934, the British government invited the United States and Japan to London for a preliminary discussion. Both sides refused to give ground. Japan argued that the progress of naval science that increased the radius of action of vessels had altered the environment of security in the Pacific. The United States was determined to maintain the status quo, claiming that Japan had neither the length of sea lanes to defend as Britain did nor two fronts to guard as did the United States. Moreover, Japan had met no naval challenge in the past half century.[6] While the United States was on high alert regarding Japan's naval expansion, the Amō Doctrine, which reinforced Japan's desire to challenge the existing order in East Asia, heightened America's caution over Japan's naval demands. Grew considered it "highly probable that the (Amō) statement has been made with a view to building up Japan's position in the eventual conversations preliminary to the coming Naval Conference."[7]

The Amō statement continued to sour relations between Japan and the League of Nations. The league had sent various experts to assist China with economic

---

5. Parks Coble, *Facing Japan: Chinese Politics and Japanese Imperialism, 1931–1937* (Cambridge, MA: Harvard University Press, 1991), 166–68.
6. Linden A. Mander, *Foundations of Modern World Society*, revised edition (Stanford: Stanford University Press, 1947), 129.
7. The Ambassador in Japan (Grew) to the Secretary of State, April 20, 1934; and the Ambassador in Japan (Grew) to the Consul at Geneva (Gilbert), May 17, 1934, both in PRFRUS, 1934, the Far East, vol. 3, 182.

Friend or Foe

development since 1931. Japan had been opposing such assistance, and this tension was intensified in the spring of 1934 when Ludwig W. Rajchman was appointed as head of the League's mission to China. Having been closely associated with T. V. Soong, Rajchman was in Nanjing when the Mukden Incident happened and was believed to be the one who helped Chiang Kai-shek appeal to the League for a solution to the Manchurian crisis.[8] Japanese leaders distrusted Rajchman's activities in China, believing that his programs were "either implicitly or explicitly politically antagonistic to Japan."[9] Amō's statement, which directly targeted foreign assistance to China, further estranged Japan from the League.

The unfavorable context of opinion was not only created by contemporary international disputes but also by the anti-Western message implied in Amō's statement and the way Japan proclaimed it. Japan's overt claim to a special position in East Asia and its opposition to foreign aid to China contained a strong Asia-centric flavor. It maintained that East Asia was a distinctive community in itself and that the peace and order of this region were of utmost concern to Asian members. Western powers, as outsiders of the region, would only complicate its difficulties by involving themselves in the region's affairs. The doctrine also emphasized Japan's leadership role, stressing that it was Japan's duty to police the region without interference from Western powers. Amō even acted as a representative of China, arguing that China's unification could be attained "through no other means [foreign assistance] than the awakening and voluntary efforts of China herself."[10]

Amō's claim signified that Japan was ready to openly challenge the current order in East Asia. Considering the implication of the statement, Western powers, especially the United States, insisted that the statement should not be permitted to pass without resistance from the West.[11] Although neither the United States nor Britain was willing to confront Japan by military and diplomatic means, they were ready to denounce Japan's ambitions in the press.

Japan's Response

Japan's official statement concerning the doctrine failed to follow a unified line. The attitude of Tokyo officials alternated between endorsement of the statement and denial of its authority. On April 18, a day after Amō issued the statement, Japan's

---

8. Coble, *Facing Japan*, 156; Wen-Hsin Yeh, *Becoming Chinese: Passages to Modernity and Beyond* (Berkeley: University of California Press, 2000), 143.
9. See quotes in Arthur Nichols Young, *China's Nation-Building Effort, 1927–1937: The Financial and Economic Record* (Stanford: Hoover Press, 1971), 344.
10. Quotes from the *New York Times* translation of the Amō statement, *New York Times*, April 21, 1934, in Willoughby, *Sino-Japanese Controversy and the League of Nations*, 629–30.
11. The Counselor of Legation in China (Gauss) to the Secretary of State, April 27, 1934, PRFRUS, 1934, the Far East, vol. 3, 143.

foreign minister, Hirota, modified the anti-Western tone of the Amō speech, emphasizing that "Japan will not ignore her treaty obligations." He also ensured that "the principle enunciated in the statement will be applied with such effect as not to conflict with existing treaties."[12] Meanwhile, the Ministry of Foreign Affairs delayed providing the translation of the document for two days. The belated translation was carefully labeled as "unofficial," so as to leave room for further retraction when necessary.[13]

On April 20, however, another announcement made by the official spokesperson of the Japanese Ministry of Foreign Affairs to foreign newspaper correspondents in Tokyo offset the moderate attitude. The spokesman claimed that Japan, despite its respect for the "Open Door principle" and existing treaties, would not tolerate "any action [by the Powers] which may lead to disturbance of the peace of East Asia, regardless of the form or pretexts."[14] "The time has passed," the spokesperson said, "when other Powers or the League of Nations can exercise their policies for the exploitation of China."[15] The announcement reinforced the anti-Western attitude voiced by Amō and spread the view that Japan was the protector of China from Western "exploitation."

On April 22, before the world media knew of Japan's intention to make such a radical announcement, Saitō Hiroshi, Japanese ambassador to the United States, recapitulated Japan's leading role in Chinese affairs in an interview with the *Washington Star*. He asked the foreign powers to consult with Japan before any important transactions between the Nanjing government and foreign interests were concluded. The Japanese government would consider noncooperation as an "unfriendly act," and "the responsibility will fall on the Chinese government for having overlooked [the] warnings."[16] The interview not only reinforced the Amō statement but extended it. It indicated that China no longer had the right as a sovereign state to decide on commercial and financial matters with other countries; the same was true for other countries hoping to establish any form of cooperation with China. Britain and the Unites States began to feel uneasy about Japan's overt claim of dominance. On April 24, British ambassador to Japan Francis Lindley sent a memorandum to Hirota expressing the discontent of the British government on this issue.[17] The United States also gathered envoys of the foreign powers and members of the State

---

12. "Mr. Hirota's Policy Explained," *North China Daily News*, April 19, 1934, 9.
13. The Ambassador in Japan (Grew) to the Secretary of State, April 26, 1934, PRFRUS, 1934, the Far East, vol. 3, 138.
14. "Tokyo Statement Gives Rise to Anxiety," *North China Daily News*, April 21, 1934; Quotes of an announcement by the spokesman of Japan's Ministry of Foreign Affairs, in Willoughby, *Sino-Japanese Controversy and the League of Nations*, 629–30.
15. "Tokyo Statement Gives Rise to Anxiety," *North China Daily News*, April 21, 1934.
16. Saito Hiroshi's interview by the *Washington Star* on April 22, 1934, quoted in Willoughby, *Sino-Japanese Controversy and the League of Nations*, 629–30.
17. "Special Position Emphasized," *North China Daily News*, April 26, 1934, 9.

Department to discuss how the signatories to the Nine Power Treaty should treat Japan's hands-off policy.[18]

Under such pressure, Japan shifted its attitude again. On April 28, Hirota retracted the Amō statement entirely, declaring that the informal Amō statement was "officially non-existent."[19] The setback spared Japan the risk of offering more inconsistent explanations. It also provided an opportunity for Britain, which was eager to minimize tensions with Japan, to bring an end to the public debate over the case. Immediately after Hirota's denial of the authority of the Amō Doctrine, the British government declared that it considered the "hands-off China" incident "closed."[20]

The ten-day Amō Doctrine drama was more a propaganda incident than a diplomatic one. Amō's statement primarily targeted the world press. The *Japan Advertiser* revealed that Amō's declaration was not issued at a regular press conference, which was held at eleven o'clock on Mondays, Wednesdays, and Fridays, but was distributed to the newspapers and press associations through the Rengō service and was carefully labeled as "unofficial."[21] This ensured the statement appeared in the press before it was circulated among diplomatic offices. Furthermore, Japan's various explanations about the statement differed only in rhetoric without altering the basic stance. No matter how Japan modified the original wording of the Amō statement, none of the ensuing versions denied Japan's claim of its special position in East Asia and its fundamental rights in China. The various explanations merely restated Japan's East Asian policy, with some minor adjustments to its relationship with the Western powers.

The reason that Amō announced the doctrine remains a mystery. Grew learned from a "reliable authority" that the announcement was made without the authorization or knowledge of Hirota. Hirota was reported to be angry and distressed at Amō's action, which was considered to have been taken to please the military with whom Amō was then working in an endeavor to emulate the former spokesman, Shiratori Toshio.[22] Knowing that rejecting the statement would endanger his position, Hirota tried to modify it in the hope of reducing its negative impact.[23] Yet his moderation was constantly in conflict with the hard line pursued by promilitary officials in the government and sections of the Japanese public that favored Amō's radical line.[24] Grew's "reliable" explanation of Hirota's role in the Amō case was nevertheless

---

18. "Nanking Opposed to Domination," *North China Daily News*, April 27, 1934, 11.
19. "Japanese Retraction of Statement," *North China Daily News*, April 29, 1934, 11.
20. Ibid.
21. "Japanese Hands-off Declaration Precipitates Far Eastern Crisis," *China Weekly Review*, April 28, 1934, 319.
22. The Ambassador in Japan (Grew) to the Secretary of State, April 20, 1934, PRFRUS, 1934, the Far East, vol. 3, 115.
23. The Ambassador in France (Straus) to the Secretary of State, April 20, 1934, PRFRUS, 1934, the Far East, vol. 3, 162.
24. "Latest Threat from Tokyo," *North China Daily News*, April 20, 1934.

not commonly shared by his colleagues. Another version popular among US diplomatic circles was that the Amō announcement was a carefully considered step taken with the full approval of Hirota, who later was obliged to make Amō the scapegoat.[25] Nonetheless, both versions, together with Japan's inconsistent reaction to the Amō statement, reflected the lack of unity between civil and military powers in the Japanese government.

Japan's inconsistent explanations of Amō's declaration were also a result of its dilemma between maintaining an international reputation and pursuing national interests. The Amō Doctrine was a disclosure of Japan's policy rather than a declaration of it. As Stanley Hornbeck, chief of the Division of Far Eastern Affairs commented, the statement "simply shows what Japan's 'China policy' is; it confirms estimates long since made by unprejudiced outside observers of what it has been."[26] To keep foreign powers' hands off China was what Japan's national interests required, and it was hard to deny Japan's intention to pursue it. Yet disclosing it would inevitably draw foreign protests and thus further isolate Japan from Western powers. Japan's alternation between endorsement and denial of the statement in the press reflected such a dilemma.

The Japanese-controlled paper, the *Far Eastern Review*, was keen to defend Japan's national interests in the Amō case. Its argument mainly followed two lines: self-preservation and the necessity to change the order in Asia. The paper tried to appeal to the Powers' sympathy by arguing that each nation had an instinct for survival and that Japan's expansion in China was propelled by such a natural response. It emphasized that Japan had to feed its huge population with scarce natural resources. While Europe was able to move its excessive population to colonies like America, Canada, and Australia, Japan, victimized by strict immigration policies crafted by Western countries, was deprived of such a choice. Moreover, China's boycotts and tariffs burdened Japan's sale of cotton textiles, an industry crucial for Japan's economic growth.[27] The expansion in China was therefore a matter of life and death for Japan.[28]

The editor of the journal also argued that Japan had been unfairly treated internationally and that the injustice should be corrected by a change of rules. Japan won the war with China in 1894, beat Russia in 1905, and contributed immensely in World War I, "yet at the end," stated George Bronson Rea, "we see Japan practically stripped of the gains of her three wars, caught and held fast in the treaty trap."[29]

---

25. Grew's summary of an alternative explanation of Hirota's role, in the Ambassador in Japan (Grew) to the Secretary of State, May 4, 1934, PRFRUS, 1934, the Far East, vol. 3, 161.
26. The Chief of the Division of Far Eastern Affairs (Hornbeck) to the Secretary of State, April 26, 1934, PRFRUS, 1934, the Far East, vol. 3, 142.
27. "Responsibility for Peace and War in the Pacific," an address delivered by Dr. Angus at the Vancouver Institute, *Far Eastern Review*, January 1934.
28. "Must America Fight Japan?" *Far Eastern Review*, May 1934, 193.
29. Ibid.

He complained that the current treaty system, particularly the Nine Power Treaty, had deterred Japan's progress as well as its attempts to achieve justice and liberty:

> The Nine Power Treaty may have been politically sound when the Treaty was signed, but from the viewpoint of humanity it has developed into the most immoral and wicked policy of modern times, handing over to one war-lord [Chiang Kai-shek] the right to consolidate his rule over the whole country by the sword.[30]

Considering that his position as adviser to Manchukuo might arouse suspicion from the readers, Rea emphasized his US citizenship, claiming his loyalty to his home country. He explained that his defense of Japanese rights was to help the United States understand the situation better and to avoid the agony of war with Japan:

> I retained all my rights, privileges and duties as an American citizen. In this capacity, as one American speaking to another, I can express my views and interpret those of the Government and people of Manchukuo with greater clarity and frankness than as a duly accredited diplomatic agent. If my opinions convey to you the impression that I am not in full sympathy with the policies of our State Department, there are weighty reasons which have influenced me to take this stand. The trend of American diplomacy in the Far East will inevitably lead the nation into war.[31]

China's Response

The Amō Doctrine was of benefit to China's propaganda. The tension it created allowed China to further isolate Japan from the international community. Yet the Chinese-operated English-language periodicals failed to form a unified line. In the mid-1930s the Nanjing government as well as public elites remained torn between resistance and appeasement. This dilemma gave rise to various interpretations of the doctrine.

The *China Press* pursued an anti-Japanese stance. Instead of viewing Amō's statement as a diplomatic accident, the paper saw it as another step of Japan toward its long-harbored plan to dominate China. The *Press* traced Japan's hegemonic ambitions back to 1915 and argued that the doctrine "revived the spirit and substance of the Twenty-One Demands."[32] To reinforce the Amō Doctrine's connection with the Twenty-One Demands, the paper reviewed the profile of Hirota, arguing that the recent moderate Sino-Japanese policy pursued by him was only a guise for his true intention of reviving the demands. As a member of the political affairs bureau of the Ministry of Foreign Affairs in 1915, claimed the paper, Hirota was involved in draft-

---

30. "The Independence of Manchukuo," *Far Eastern Review*, February 1934, 51.
31. Ibid.
32. "Twenty-One Demands Revived," *China Press*, April 21, 1934, 10.

ing both the demands and the Tanaka Memorial.³³ Meanwhile, Hirota was a member of the Black Dragon Society, a Japanese right-wing group supporting Japan's expansion in China. He was also "intimately" associated with the army clique.³⁴ The paper sought to create the impression that the Amō Doctrine, which "revived the worst features of the Twenty-One Demands," was another attempt by Hirota to dominate China.³⁵ When diplomatic circles were unclear about Hirota's role in the Amō case, the *China Press* was keen to emphasize his connection with the case and used it to attack his foreign policies in general.

The paper continued to explore the international implications of the statement, arguing that the Amō Doctrine was more a crisis between Japan and Western powers than a Sino-Japanese conflict. Instead of calling the Amō Doctrine the "hands-off China policy," a name widely used by Western papers, the *China Press* referred to the doctrine as "Asian lordship" and "overlordship."³⁶ The choice of words clearly displayed the editors' efforts to emphasize Japan's political ambition. Japan's "lordship," stated the *Press*, equaled a "closed-door" policy toward this region. It was a direct "embargo on any attempt by this country [China] to prepare to defend itself and a challenge to the rest of the world to dare to afford any sort of help to that end."³⁷ The *Press* deliberately downplayed China's role in the dispute, trying to create the impression that the doctrine, although it revolved around Japan's interests in China in discourse, did not have much to do with the Sino-Japanese relations. It fundamentally concerned the conflict between Japan and Western powers, with China being a victim in this struggle among the Powers.

The *China Press* drew linkages between the Amō Doctrine and Japan's specific disputes with the United States and Britain, with the goal of urging the Anglo-American countries to take immediate action to curb Japan's expansion. The paper argued that Japan's claim to a special position in East Asia served as leverage to achieve naval parity in the forthcoming naval conference. Hollington Tong commented in one of his editorials that Hirota, by announcing the Amō Doctrine, was attempting to see whether global public opinion would view Japan's domination of Asia in a favorable light. Japan would then decide how far it could go in negotiations with Western powers.³⁸ Tong also warned that if the United States allowed Japan to advance its Amō Doctrine unchallenged, it would fall into Japan's trap and lose ground in the naval negotiations.³⁹

---

33. Hollington Tong, "Hirota Making Bid for Eastern Power," editorial, *China Press*, April 21, 1934, 9.
34. "Hirota's Role in Policy of Japan Revealed," *China Press*, April 21, 1934, 14.
35. "Twenty-One Demands Echo," *China Press*, May 10, 1934, 10.
36. "Japan Seeks Okeh on Asian Lordship," *China Press*, April 18, 1934, 9; "Japan's Bid for Overlordship," *China Press*, April 22, 1934, 10.
37. "Japan's Bid for Overlordship," 10.
38. "Hirota's Error Stirs Capitals of World," *China Press*, April 22, 1934, 9.
39. "Another Warning by Japan," *China Press*, May 12, 1934, 10.

Such an interpretation struck a chord with American diplomats. The United States saw a large Japanese navy as a direct threat to its national security and a challenge to its authority in the Pacific region. As Stanley K. Hornbeck acknowledged, Japan's comparative naval strength was "of most and vital concern to us than to any other of the powers." Whereas Britain, France, and the Netherlands had little reason to fear an assault by the Japanese upon their home territories, the concern was real for the United States. "They are powers in but not powers on the Pacific Ocean. We are a power both in and on that ocean."[40]

Editors of the *China Press* also saw the Amō case as an opportunity to estrange Britain from Japan, particularly over international trade. By 1934, Japan's cotton textile business had made serious inroads into a market that had long been monopolized by British manufacturers. It threatened British business not only in Manchuria and South America but also in colonies of the British Empire. Hungry for more open markets for Japan's cotton textile trade, the Japanese ambassador in London appealed to the British government to modify the existing quota system. The *China Press* took advantage of the trade dispute, arguing that Japan sought to acquire a new quota by challenging the treaty system in East Asia.[41] The paper portrayed Japan as a country ready to betray any friend who might stand in the way of its development. It insinuated that Japan, lacking both respect for rules and loyalty in partnerships, was by no means a trustworthy friend of Britain.

The *China Press* pointed out that the statement was not the misrepresentation of some hot-headed politicians but a reflection of the anti-Western mentality of the general Japanese public. It implied that the doctrine was based on Japanese suspicion of the West and excessive self-regard. Editors of the *Press* complained that Japan lacked evidence that foreign assistance to China was being used for political purposes and assumed that all Western assistance was targeted against Japan. Although Japan complained that other non-Asian countries were disturbing stability of the region, its oversensitive reaction to foreign goodwill was in fact the very factor that threatened the peace in East Asia.[42]

> [Japan] remained stubborn in her belief that she was right and the rest of the world wrong. In other words she claimed the right to be a kind of supernation, whose interpretation of treaties must be meekly accepted by the rest of the world. Instead of showing contrition she withdrew from Geneva in high indignation, and has since steadily aggravated her original offence.[43]

---

40. Memorandum by the Chief of the Division of Far Eastern Affairs (Hornbeck), May 24, 1934, PRFRUS, 1934, the Far East, vol. 3, 192–93.
41. "Equal Favors to All Nations," *China Press*, May 18, 1934, 10.
42. "Japan's Chiefs Hurl Defiance to Powers in New Challenge," *China Press*, April 20, 1934, 9.
43. "Equal Favors to All Nations," 10.

Such arrogance, explained the paper, was derived from Japan's contempt for the treaty system. It considered an international treaty as "a scrap of paper"[44] and was ready to neglect it when it contradicted Japan's "heaven-sent mission to dominate Asia."[45]

The *Press*'s outspoken anti-Japanese view stood in contrast to its reticence in domestic politics. Popular topics in vernacular papers, such as criticism of the Guomindang government's docile reaction to the Amō Doctrine, the political rupture between Chiang Kai-shek and Hu Hanmin, and appeals for an end to the anti-Communist campaign in the interest of uniting the Communists for joint resistance to Japan, were completely absent. The lack of dissension against the Nanjing government was likely to have been the result of Chiang's penetration of the *Press*. As mentioned in the previous chapter, the *Press* had secretly become a semiofficial organ; Chiang directly communicated with Tong to set the editorial line. Chiang played a double game in the Amō case: while secretly using English-language propaganda as a way to resist Japan, he also displayed a preference for diplomatic compromise with Japan to avoid giving Japan ammunition for further military attacks. Indeed, concealing Chiang's connection with the *Press* was of strategic importance. Its anti-Japanese propaganda helped the Nanjing government form an alliance with the other Powers in their common defense against Japan's offensive policy. Chiang could, however, conveniently distance himself from its editorial line when challenged by the Japanese government, claiming that its anti-Japanese attitude was evinced by a nonofficial paper beyond his control.

Like Japan, China also lacked a unified propaganda policy. On April 19, the Chinese Ministry of Foreign Affairs issued an official response to the Amō declaration. It denied Japan's charge that China intended to use international aid as a resource to resist Japan. It rejected Japan's request for the termination of foreign assistance and appealed to Japan to handle Sino-Japanese issues with "goodwill and mutual understanding."[46] The reply was mild and defensive. Unlike the *Press*, which denounced the Amō Doctrine as Japan's attempt to control China and to challenge the existing order, the reply interpreted the statement as a minor dispute between the two countries over foreign assistance. The Nanjing government made a further compromise by reducing support for T. V. Soong's bid for foreign funds and showing less interest in seeking assistance from the League of Nations.[47]

The intensity and specific lines of argument were different even among the Chinese-operated English-language periodicals that shared the anti-Japanese stance. Compared with the *China Press*, the *China Critic* devoted much less attention to the Amō case. There was no editorial directly related to the Amō statement in the

---

44. "Powers Interests in China Now Menaced," *China Press*, April 25, 1934, 9.
45. "Japan Told to Keep Hands Off," *China Press*, April 24, 1934, 10.
46. See quotation of Chinese official reply to the Amō statement in Willoughby, *Sino-Japanese Controversy and the League of Nations*, 633–44.
47. Coble, *Facing Japan*, 156–58.

issue published on April 19, two days after the statement was made. The most pertinent article was about Rajchman's trip to Geneva, in which the editor expressed his concern over Japan's interference in the League of Nations' aid to China.[48] If two days were not enough for a weekly to react to the statement, the ensuing issues had well testified that the lack of reference to the case was not a matter of time but a lack of interest. In the following issue, published on April 26, only one out of the ten articles in the *Critic*'s editorial section discussed the Amō statement.[49] That single article even appeared toward the end of the section, an inconspicuous position that might easily escape readers' attention. The Amō case was again missing in the May 3 issue. Although the *Critic* discussed the Manchukuo problem and Rajchman's assistance to China, two cases highly relevant to the Amō Doctrine, the journal made no effort to link them to the Amō statement.[50] The May 17 issue continued to downplay the Amō case even though topics that it discussed—the League of Nations' assistance and the British-Japanese trade war—were highly pertinent to the statement.[51] The journal's first strong condemnation of the Amō Doctrine came belatedly on May 24, when the editor denounced the policy as a "blunder" of Japanese foreign policy.[52]

Whereas the *China Press* established the Amō case as a conflict between Japan and Western powers, the *Critic* saw the Amō Doctrine as a Sino-Japanese dispute. The *Critic* believed that Japan had planned the Amō statement to press Nanjing to concede its demand on rail and postal connections with Manchukuo. It was a scheme to delay China's construction process, a warning against China's use of the American cotton and wheat loans, an effort to discredit T. V. Soong in the eyes of the American public, and an attempt to impede Rajchman's technical aid to China endorsed by the League of Nations. The *Critic* did not regard the case as an urgent matter. "The threat," it noted, "does not appear to be designed for immediate action. Japan is merely playing the part of a bully, and it goes without saying that neither China nor the League is prepared to run counter to her wishes."[53]

Indeed, the *Critic*'s attitude reflected a mixture of complicated feelings shared by Chinese elites. The journal's lack of interest in the Amō case testified to the elites' suspicion of the treaty system's capacity to maintain order in East Asia. Previous Sino-Japanese conflicts had shown clearly that the League and the other Powers were incompetent in checking Japan's aggression and that the international harmony promoted by the Powers was merely a political "ideal" that fell into "the realm of

48. "Dr. Rajchman's Trip to Geneva," *China Critic*, April 19, 1934, 369.
49. "The Latest Threat from Tokyo," *China Critic*, April 26, 1934, 392.
50. "Japan Chronicle Editor Speaks Out," *China Critic*, May 3, 1934; "Will Dr. Rajchman Be Dismissed?" *China Critic*, May 3, 1934; "'Manchukuo' Athletes Attacking Japan," *China Critic*, May 3, 1934, 414–15.
51. "Dr. Rajchman's Report," *China Critic*, May 17, 1934, 462; "British-Japanese Trade War?" *China Critic*, May 17, 1934, 464–65.
52. "Japan's Diplomatic Blunder and After," *China Critic*, May 24, 1934, 489–90.
53. "The Latest Threat from Tokyo," *China Critic*, April 26, 1934, 392.

Utopianism."[54] In addition, the elites were cautious of the Western powers' intentions in China. In its official reply to the Amō Doctrine, Britain openly acknowledged Japan's "special rights" in China. This kept the elites alert to the possibility of an alliance formed by imperialist countries to preserve their common interests. Meanwhile, France kept encroaching on Yunnan, and the British were making inroads into Tibet.[55] While the elites perceived Japan as their most urgent enemy, they identified no friends among the other empires, fearing the efforts to ally with other Powers for a joint resistance against Japan would end up inviting in more avaricious foes.

The *People's Tribune*, an organ of the left wing of the Guomindang, considered the Amō statement to be Japan's version of Monroe Doctrine. Yet, instead of denouncing the statement, it welcomed Japan's idea of excluding the exploitation of China by Western powers and supported Japanese hostility toward non-Asians. What Japan needed to modify, indicated the *Tribune*, was not Japan's Asiatic vision but its means in pursuing it.

> This is not to say "Asiatic Monroe Doctrine" is not permissible in any form whatsoever, but the only right form is that which is in full harmony with the original [American Monroe Doctrine]; that is, to prevent non-Asiatic nations from infringement of the political independence of existing sovereign States in Asia, and from securing new acquisitions of territories. If, under these principles, Japan should oppose the activities of non-Asiatic nations by formulating an "Asiatic Monroe Doctrine" . . . such a Monroe Doctrine would be proper and righteous; it could be applicable not only to Asia or America, but to the whole world.[56]

Opinion of the Treaty-Port Press

The *North China Daily News* conveyed an ambiguous attitude toward the Amō case. On the one hand, it tried to downplay the significance of the case so as to prevent public tension from escalating into a larger crisis; on the other hand, it was critical of Japan's policy in Asia, fearing that British interests would be in danger if Japan's hegemony in Asia was allowed to pass without denunciation. The paper denied the allegation that the Amō statement targeted Western interests. "There seems to be so much of wrong presumption," argued the paper, "that settlements and understandings and arrangements made between countries other than the two principals—China and Japan—can resolve the issues between them."[57] It believed that the Amō Doctrine was announced to resolve the deadlock in the negotiations over China's postal and

---

54. "The Prospect of Disarmament," *China Critic*, April 26, 1934, 394.
55. "What about the Back Door?" *China Critic*, April 26, 1934, 396.
56. "Japanese Exposure of the 'Asiatic Monroe Doctrine,'" *People's Tribune*, May 1, 1934, 467.
57. "A Grave Issue: A Reply to Taira," *North China Daily News*, April 27, 1934, 2.

rail connections with Manchukuo, which was a crucial step ahead in the process of obtaining recognition of its new state.[58]

The paper was ready to accept Japan's moderation of the original Amō statement and considered such an attempt to be "extremely gratifying." It expressed sympathy for Japan's concern over China's misuse of international aid. In a letter to the editor, the paper quoted:

> The publication of the "hands-off China" statement may have been inopportune in time, or clumsy in its manner of presentation, yet the fact remains that the declaration was the logical outcome of the political events of the last three years. The League of Nations, it will be recalled, intervened between China and Japan, passing against Japan a verdict which had the effect of stiffening the Chinese attitude. Thus the League functioned not as a mediator, but as an interventionist taking sides with China. . . . Japan has every reason to be sceptical and suspicious when a man like Dr. Rajchman would act as a liaison agent, his appointment being considered as a "colossal blunder" in some quarters; also when China itself is desperately seeking political aid from Europe and America in order to offset Japan, as evidenced in the recent Chinese outcries of the fabled "wolf! wolf!," if not in its traditional tactics of playing off one enemy against another.[59]

Despite the *Daily News*' sympathy, it did not soften its words of caution against Japan's hegemonic plans in Asia. Perturbed by the anti-Western sentiment shown by the Amō Doctrine, the paper feared that Japan might exclude other Powers from China after securing control over it.[60] It warned that Japan aimed to control not only China's foreign policy but also its domestic affairs. It claimed that, after conquering China, Japan would manipulate the Chinese market and "reduce the country to a scantily concealed vassalage."[61] Although editors of the paper doubted whether Japan had the capacity to put the Pan-Asian framework into practice, they still worried that Japan's current policy might lead to a united Asian "crusade for elimination of every 'white' influence from these shores of the Pacific."[62] Such fears gave rise to the paper's revision of its traditional pro-Japanese sentiment:

> Those who professed to see everything good in Japan's actions regarding China during the past three years, have now been given an opportunity to realize that not only are the Japanese injuring the interests of China alone, but that a very definite threat has been made against the interests of those who so unthinkingly have given their moral support to the aggressions that have occurred since the Mukden Incident.[63]

---

58. "A Suggestion," *North China Daily News*, April 23, 1934; "A Grave Issue," *North China Daily News*, April 21, 1934; "Britain Adheres to Nine-Power Pact," *North China Daily News*, April 25, 1934.
59. "A Grave Issue: The Japanese Case," *North China Daily News*, May 1, 1934, 2.
60. "Press Reactions: Tokyo Doing the Talking," *North China Daily News*, April 25, 1934.
61. "A Grave Issue," *North China Daily News*, April 21, 1934.
62. "The Far East: A New Policy Wanted," *North China Daily News*, May 3, 1934.
63. "A Grave Issue," *North China Daily News*, April 21, 1934, 4.

Furthermore, the paper was especially discontent with Japan's claim to "special rights" in Asia and was particularly impatient with the claim that Japan was to surpass Britain to become the leading empire in China. The paper argued that Britain, given the size of its interests in the country, also had a valid reason to claim a "special position." Yet Britain refrained from doing so for the sake of peace and stability in East Asia. Japan should follow Britain's example and withdraw its claim.[64] To further deny Japan's "special interests" argument, the *Daily News* invoked the Nine Power Treaty. It pointed out that Japan had no more right than the other seven non-Chinese signatories to the treaty, thus having no legal advantage to claim a "special position."[65] Here, the paper once again split with the official line of the British government, since British Foreign Secretary John Simon had openly recognized that Japan enjoyed "special rights in China which were not shared by other Powers."[66] The *Daily News* severely criticized the British response as a "submission" to Japan and warned that such a policy would "bring an unfortunate effect upon the entire world."[67]

In contrast to the *North China Daily News*' ambiguity toward the Amō Doctrine, the *China Weekly Review*'s stance was decisively anti-Japanese. The *Review* believed that the Amō Doctrine not only infringed on China's sovereignty but also threatened US and British interests. It referred to the statement as Japan's declaration of a "protectorate over China"[68] and condemned the policy as amounting to "telling China that she cannot take any steps in the direction of reconstructing her national life without the consent of Imperial Japan."[69] It believed that Japan, by issuing the statement, aimed to force China into some form of military alliance against Soviet Russia that would legitimize Japan's use of North China as a base for military activities through Chahar, Inner Mongolia, and Xinjiang. After China breached its neutrality, it would bear the brunt of a Russian attack, and the heightened crisis could easily give rise to large-scale military clashes. The *Review*, therefore, portrayed the case as "much more serious than the mere matter of cutting China off from financial and economic contact with other nations." It was nothing less than war provocation.[70]

The *Review* was critical not only of the Amō case itself but also of the way in which it was handled by Japan. Japan timed the statement deliberately, argued the journal, because it planned to seize control of China while Western powers were busy solving problems in Europe. Moreover, the unofficial way in which Japan released

---

64. "Happy Ending?" *North China Daily News*, April 30, 1934, 4.
65. Ibid.
66. "More Decided Policy Urged," *North China Daily News*, May 9, 1934, 9.
67. Ibid.
68. "Japan Declares 'Protectorate over China,'" *China Weekly Review*, April 21, 1934, 277.
69. Ibid.
70. "Japanese 'Hands-off' Declaration Precipitates Far Eastern Crisis," *China Weekly Review*, April 28, 1934, 318; "Will China Cooperate with Japan against Russia?—the Situation in the North," *China Weekly Review*, April 28, 1934, 330–31.

the document was also a well-planned scheme to fool international audiences.[71] The journal criticized Japan for presenting its presumptuous policy without courage and honesty. Lacking the resolution to denounce international treaties, Japan resorted to hypocrisy, borrowing the name Monroe Doctrine to cover things up.[72]

Indeed, the *Review* had become a close ally with the *China Press* in the Amō case. Yet the two papers united only behind the anti-Japanese line. Contrary to the *Press'* reticence about the Nanjing government's appeasement of Japan, the *Review* criticized the government's submissive reply to Amō's declaration and pressed it for a firmer action against Japan's pressure. While blaming Japan's "lordship" over China, the journal also challenged China's appeasement policy, warning that "those who apparently thought Japan could be conciliated or circumvented by soft diplomatic words are likely to be disillusioned."[73] "China should take far more substantive action than the mere issuing of telegrams or 'answers' to the Japanese declaration," the *Review* declared. "Unless China herself makes up her mind to make a firm stand against the Japanese aggression, no other power would come to her help."[74]

The *Review* did not refrain from criticizing China's political chaos either. After the Amō statement, both the Nanjing government and Hu Hanmin's clique in Guangzhou responded to the situation. While Nanjing's reply was mild, Guangzhou strongly condemned Japan's policy, criticizing Japan as being intent on "nothing short of complete domination in the Far East."[75] The *Review* quoted Hu's address in full as a contrast to Nanjing's moderation. It also cited Wang Jingwei's warning to the Southwest Political Council controlled by Hu, in which he advised Hu "not to issue further statements so as not to create a bad impression among the Powers."[76] By doing so, the *Review* once again exposed the rupture between Guomindang leaders in front of the treaty-port papers' readers. Indeed, editors of the *Review* were watching the activities of the government with a mixture of hope and discouragement. While they sympathized with China's tragedy in facing Japan's coercion, they were also frustrated with the infighting among political factions.

Metropolitan Opinions

While the treaty-port papers closely followed the development of the Amō case, the metropolitan papers paid only perfunctory attention to the affair. The *Times* of

---

71. "Japanese 'Hands-off' Declaration Precipitates Far Eastern Crisis," 318–19.
72. "Tokyo Withdraws Note Which Now Regarded as 'Irreparable Blunder,'" *China Weekly Review*, May 5, 1934, 361.
73. "Japan Declares 'Protectorate over China,'" *China Weekly Review*, April 21, 1934, 277.
74. "China, the Foreign Powers and Tokyo's 'Hands off' Declaration," *China Weekly Review*, May 5, 1934, 380.
75. For a quote of Hu Hanmin's address, see "China Declares Opposition to International Control or Domination by Any Country," *China Weekly Review*, May 5, 1934, 366.
76. Ibid.

London, for example, first mentioned the Amō statement on April 19, two days after the statement was issued. Within the first week after Amō's declaration, only four reports were devoted to investigating the background to the announcement, without any editorial reference to it. Discussion of the Amō statement did not appear in the *Times*' editorial page until more than one week later, on April 26. In the following month only three editorials focused on the case. The *Times*' lack of interest in the statement could be explained by its preoccupation with the growing complex situation in Europe, particularly the Nazi's arms expansion. Part of the British aloofness, however, also came from the general realization after the Tanggu Truce and Japan's withdrawal from the League of Nations that nothing effective could be done about the Sino-Japanese conflict.[77] Indeed, none of the Western powers were interested in taking the lead in challenging Japan in the mid-1930s. After the Amō statement was issued, Sir John Simon had intimated to the US State Department that Anglo-American cooperation was desired to cope with Japan's challenge. Yet Chief of the State Department Division of Far Eastern Affairs Stanley Hornbeck replied that the US government had no intention of assuming leadership in any joint action. On learning the United States' reluctance, Britain immediately dropped the proposal, believing a confrontation with Japan would undermine its national interests.[78]

Influenced by inaction in its diplomatic circles, the London *Times* adopted a conciliatory attitude toward Japan in the Amō case. After the statement was released to the press, the paper merely repeated the Japanese version, not intent on interpreting the policy more broadly. Unlike the treaty-port papers, which described the Amō statement as a "hands-off China policy" or "Japan's Monroe Doctrine," the *Times* referred to the statement as "Japan's policy to China" or simply the "statement," so as to avoid any negative connotation. The paper refrained from commenting on the statement or Japan's foreign policy in general under the pretext that Japan's statement was "vague."[79]

Like the *North China Daily News*, the *Times* was receptive to Japan's modification of the statement. While other papers questioned the "unofficial" nature of Amō's statement, believing that Japan's "informal" way of issuing its Asian policy was only a strategy to test the public reaction to its new policy in Asia, the *Times* lent support to Japan's "unofficial" manner. It believed that the Amō statement was an "expression of the official mind but not a definition of official policy."[80] Issuing it "unofficially" indicated that Japan was unsure about its political line and that its policy remained

---

77. Reginald Bassett, *Democracy and Foreign Policy: A Case History, the Sino-Japanese Dispute, 1931–33* (London: Longmans, Green, 1952), 506–7.
78. Dorothy Borg, *The United States and the Far Eastern Crisis of 1933–1938: From the Manchurian Incident through the Initial Stage of the Undeclared Sino-Japanese War* (Cambridge, MA: Harvard University Press, 1964), 78–79.
79. "Japanese Aims in China; Powers Wanted, No Political Interference," *Times*, April 19, 1934, 14.
80. "Japan and China," *Times*, May 1, 1934, 17.

Friend or Foe

open to amendment. After the Japanese ambassador promised to observe the open-door policy and international treaties, the *Times* accepted this fully, believing that Japan would also respect British rights in China. It addressed Japan as an "old ally" and acknowledged that Britain "desired" to remain "on the best of terms" with it.[81] The *Times* welcomed Japan's admission that the Amō statement was "tactless" and was eager to close the case after Japan declared that the statement was officially nonexistent.[82]

Furthermore, the *Times* applauded Japan's promise to maintain peace and stability in East Asia, even though the promise was likely to be unfounded political rhetoric. The British interest, stressed the paper, lay in "promoting, by every possible means peace, security and economic development."[83] It believed that Japan's concern for the disturbance of peace through intervention by foreign powers was legitimate and its attempt to reduce European and American trade in arms and ammunition with China was "desirable."[84] However, the paper also warned Japan of the bottom line—the peace-keeping cause was valid only under the condition that Japan kept the Chinese market open to all Powers.[85]

Dissenting voices nevertheless could still be heard in the paper. The *Times*, for example, quoted a reader's letter criticizing the way Japan handled the Amō case: "It is a pity that matters of such vital importance to the rest of the world should be handled in such a cavalier fashion by Japanese statesmen."[86] The paper also perceived Japan's statement as "arrogant" and suspected that the statement revealed Japan's desire for a "monopoly of influence."[87] Comments like these were nevertheless sporadic and failed to challenge the moderate tone that characterized the paper's general stance.

The *New York Times*, in comparison, was much less moderate. The paper publicized the Amō statement on the front page on April 18, in which it argued that the statement was "aim[ed] at Western nations."[88] The paper repeatedly referred to Japan's policy as intent on "hegemony" over China,[89] which Japan pursued to eliminate the "white peril" from Asia.[90] While the *Times* in London welcomed Japan's modification of its policy, the *New York Times* believed that Japan's various versions failed to

---

81. "The Attitude of Japan," *Times*, April 26, 1934, 17.
82. "Japan and China: Original Statement Tactless," *Times*, April 30, 1934, 14.
83. "Japan and China," *Times*, May 1, 1934, 17.
84. "The Attitude of Japan," *Times*, April 26, 1934, 15.
85. "Japan and China," *Times*, 1 May 1934, 17.
86. "The Far East: Rehabilitation of China," *Times*, May 9, 1934, 15.
87. Ibid.
88. "Japan Warns Powers on China; Threatens Force to Put End to Aid," *New York Times*, April 18, 1934, 1.
89. "Japan Puts Soft Glove on Her New China Policy," *New York Times*, April 29, 1934, E1; "British Challenge Japanese Claims to Control China," *New York Times*, April 24, 1934, 1.
90. "Japan Puts Soft Glove on Her New China Policy," E1; "Again Japan's Policy Agitates the World," *New York Times*, April 29, 1934, XX1.

change its basic massage.⁹¹ The paper echoed the *China Press*' position, tracing Japan's hegemonic plans in China back to the Twenty-One Demands, the claim for special interests in the Lansing-Ishii Agreement and the Manchurian crisis.⁹² It indicated that the Amō statement was only part of a series of Japanese attempts to control China.⁹³

Apart from criticizing Japan's statement in general, the *New York Times* also tied Japan's protest against the foreign supply of airplanes in China to the US aircraft industry. It argued that Japan's policy would damage US aircraft trade with China. "As far as the United States is concerned," the paper pointed out, "aircraft, aircraft engines and accessories valued at $1,762,247 went to China last year. This was out of a total export, in these categories, of $8,827,822." As the US aircraft market was expanding in China, the paper warned that Japan's efforts to curb foreign assistance in China would cut America's gains in China's aircraft market.⁹⁴

Despite the *New York Times*' overt opposition to the Amō Doctrine, it was reluctant to suggest that the other Powers should form an alliance to challenge Japan's hegemonic plan. The paper believed that France, Italy, and other signatories of the Nine Power Treaties exhibited a clear lack of interest in the Amō case.⁹⁵ Besides, none of the fifty-five members of the League of Nations had stood up to protest Japan's challenge to the League's assistance in China. "It seems clearer than ever in Geneva," said the paper, "that the rest of the world has abdicated, at least, temporarily, leadership in the Far East to Britain and the United States."⁹⁶ Acknowledging that "the British and American viewpoints are identical and that Anglo-American consultation at the present stage would only create an 'encirclement' bogy in the Japanese mind," the paper was also aware of British reluctance to ruffle Japanese feathers.⁹⁷ It maintained a traditional isolationist view, suggesting that the United States should follow rather than lead in solving the Amō case. It warned the United States not to repeat what happened during the Manchurian crisis, when Washington took the lead and found no response from London. Furthermore, the paper feared that US entanglement with the issue would invoke two fundamental disputes between Japan and the United States: naval parity and US restrictions on Asian immigration.⁹⁸ Both matters could easily transform from political issues into racial debates, dragging the United States further into the quagmire of the Sino-Japanese conflict.

---

91. "Japan Puts Soft Glove on Her New China Policy," E1.
92. Lansing-Ishii Agreement was a diplomatic document signed between the US secretary of state, Robert Lansing, and Japanese special envoy to Washington, Ishi Kikujirō, in 1917. In the agreement, Japan pledged to uphold the Open Door policy in China, with respect to its territorial and administrative integrity. The US government acknowledged Japan's special interests in areas of China bordering on Japan's own territory.
93. "Again Japan's Policy Agitates the World," *New York Times*, April 29, 1934, XX1.
94. "Open Door and Planes," *New York Times*, April 22, 1934, XX8.
95. "Few Nations Show Concern on China," *New York Times*, May 6, 1934, E1.
96. Ibid.
97. "British Challenge Japanese Claims to Control China," 1.
98. "Again Japan's Policy Agitates the World," XX1.

Figure 13
Sapajou, "A Little Boat May Leave a Big Wash Behind," *North China Daily News*, April 23, 1934.

Part III

Propaganda during the War

7
From Nanjing to Chongqing
International Propaganda in Wartime, 1937–1938

On July 7, 1937, Chinese and Japanese troops clashed near Marco Polo Bridge, southwest of Beijing. Fearing that further concession to Japan would lead to the loss of North China, Chiang Kai-shek reinforced his troops in Hebei. In response, Japan dispatched its Kwantung and Korean armies to the region. When all efforts to negotiate failed, years of tensions finally developed into full-scale war.

The war heightened the need for efficient international propaganda machinery. Despite Nanjing's strong will to end the humiliating "peace," Guomindang leaders were keenly aware that China's chances of successfully withstanding Japan's military aggression were slim. The decision to go to war was in essence a gamble based on Chiang Kai-shek's long-term views on international power politics in East Asia: that a Sino-Japanese war would probably trigger a war between Japan and the Powers, involving either the United States or the Soviet Union.[1] This vision required Nanjing to place greater emphasis on propaganda as a way to appeal for international intervention. Moreover, the war unified China's voice in the media. Although there were disputes between the Nationalist and Communist parties and rivalries among the top Nationalist leaders still existed, the common goal to resist Japan effectively rallied all sorts of political forces behind Chiang's leadership after the outbreak of the full-scale war. This unification eventually generated a unified political line in the press.

Despite these favorable conditions, the lack of a centralized structure continued to plague the propaganda system. Various departments were involved in foreign propaganda, each pursuing its respective objectives. Yet the lack of conformity and centralized control was perhaps inevitable, particularly when the Nanjing government was caught between appeasing and resisting Japan in the mid-1930s. Indeed, the need for a centralized foreign propaganda system was felt well before the outbreak of the Sino-Japanese War. In 1935, Chinese diplomats in Europe had repeatedly urged the government to centralize its foreign propaganda institutions under the leadership of the party headquarters or the Ministry of Foreign Affairs.[2] Yet their appeals

---

1. Youli Sun, *China and the Origins of the Pacific War, 1931–1941* (New York: St. Martin's Press, 1993), 90.
2. Qing zhongyang sushe guoji xuanchuan zongbu [Proposal for the establishment of a central propaganda office], raised by Kang Shipin et al., November 17, 1935, conference papers 5.1/9.16, Guomindang Archives.

were not seriously considered. Fearing that overt propaganda would invoke protest from Japan, the top Nanjing leaders were only halfheartedly committed to the development of international propaganda. Furthermore, the diplomats' plan did not fit Chiang Kai-shek's vision. For years, Chiang had been secretly cultivating his own foreign propaganda network. With his power firmly entrenched in military and financial organizations, he was unwilling to lose this control of information to the party headquarters or to the Ministry of Foreign Affairs.

The Fifth Board of the Military Affairs Commission

The lack of motivation for international propaganda was solved by the start of the full-scale war. The Nanjing leaders, instead of considering international propaganda as an auxiliary instrument in diplomacy, began to see it as part of the military campaigns. A pamphlet produced by the semiofficial Sun Yat-sen Cultural and Educational Publishing House reflected this renewed understanding: news propaganda was portrayed as an "effective weapon," which was "ten times more than what a hundred thousand soldiers could bring."[3]

Chiang Kai-shek appointed his propaganda expert, Hollington Tong, to manage international propaganda. Tong had been solely responsible for the founding of the Guomindang's centralized international propaganda system. He had been secretly collecting materials on war techniques years before the outbreak of the full-scale war. Although he claimed that this research was conducted independently with the hope of providing advice to the government when the war started, it is possible that his activity was supported by Chiang given their close connections after 1932.[4] During the Lushan Conference in July 1937, Tong submitted plans to Chiang for chemical, intelligence, and propaganda warfare against Japan. Chiang took great interest in his plans and initially invited him to organize an intelligence office targeting foreign-related affairs. Realizing that the job would require an extended personal network within the party, which he did not have as a new party member, Tong turned down Chiang's offer. Chiang then appointed him to lead the government's international propaganda office but still put him in touch with Dai Li, the head of the Military Intelligence Service.[5] This connection paved the way for Tong's future cooperation with Dai during the Chongqing period.

In September 1937, a new institution, the Fifth Board of the Military Affairs Commission, was established to supervise all international propaganda activities.

3. Chen Wengan, *Kangzhan junshi yu xinwen dongyuan* [Anti-Japanese war and mobilization by news] (Hankou: Zhongshan wenhua jiaoyu guan, 1938).
4. Zeng Xubai, *Zeng Xubai zizhuan* [An autobiography of Zeng Xubai] (Taipei: Lianjing chuban shiye gongsi, 1988), 172.
5. Ibid., 175.

Tong was appointed vice minister of the board, in charge of international propaganda. The board was a supradepartmental institution, responsible for devising international propaganda policies, coordinating propaganda activities, and building news networks in China and abroad.

Tong revised both the objectives and the techniques of the earlier official propaganda and devised new guidelines. Previously, foreign propaganda offices focused on promoting the Guomindang's prestige. Tong specified that the goal of foreign propaganda in wartime was to form an anti-Japanese alliance with other nations and to engage them in a common war against Japan.[6] This change was conducive to uniting foreign propaganda resources and preventing factional rivals from using foreign propaganda to serve their own political purpose. It also relieved foreign propaganda offices of the duty to disseminate party ideology, a task that had absorbed many resources without producing significant results. While previous propaganda offices tended to follow the Soviet model of exporting revolutionary ideals and the party's ideology to the general public, Tong aimed at influencing the elite groups among the Powers, such as foreign government officials, nongovernmental groups and organizations, and members of the social elite, especially professors and prominent journalists.[7]

Tong stressed the importance of confidentiality and personal networks in propaganda. Acutely aware of the Western audience's distrust of official propaganda, he believed that the government should "erase all traces of propaganda" to enhance the credibility of its information.[8] He suggested that the propaganda office observe the principle that "truth is the best propaganda," ensuring that its factual reports agreed with reality. He also advised the government to recruit foreigners to run propaganda operations for China and emphasized the necessity of concealing connections between the government and the information outlets.[9] These guidelines, based on his decades of experience serving the treaty-port press, were in sharp contrast to the conventional norms of the existing propaganda system, which placed great emphasis on information control, strict surveillance on political background, and personal loyalty.

The reorganization of the foreign propaganda office was an integral part of Chiang's efforts to enhance his authoritarian control after the outbreak of the war. Facing a total war with Japan, Chiang made the Military Affairs Commission the leading office of the Guomindang regime. The commission not only supervised the military but also took over the management of various administrative bodies previously operated by the government and the party.[10] Foreign propaganda activities that had been

6. Ibid., 176–77.
7. Ibid.
8. The Ministry of Information to the Central Secretariat, June 11, 1938, conference papers 5.3/81.6, GA.
9. Ibid.
10. See Ch'ien's discussion of the function of the Military Affairs Commission after the Lugouqiao Incident: Ch'ien Tuan-sheng, *The Government and Politics of China, 1912–1949* (Stanford: Stanford University

organized by the party under the Ministry of Information were taken under Chiang's wing as part of the same reorganization process. Although other departments, including domestic propaganda institutions, moved out of the military during the reorganization in early 1938, the foreign propaganda office remained under Chiang's direct control until the end of the Sino-Japanese War.

The person who shaped Chiang's opinion about the value of international propaganda was his wife, Soong May-ling. Soong had attended a Methodist school in Shanghai from the age of five. She was sent to the United States, where she spent the next ten years—her most formative period—receiving high school and university education. After returning to China, she became heavily involved in foreign affairs–related work. She joined the YWCA, worked as a censor for the National Film Censorship Board, and was a committee member of the industry bureau of foreign concessions. After her marriage to Chiang, she became his secretary and translator, filing documents and receiving foreign guests.[11] Her Christian background and American education provided her with an insight into the importance of public opinion in American politics. She read English-language newspapers, kept abreast of foreign affairs, and was dedicated to obtaining a Western understanding of Chinese issues herself.[12] While Chiang was trained as a soldier in China and Japan, Soong played a key role in linking Chiang to the West, a connection Chiang direly needed when Sino-Japanese relations soured.

Soong shared Tong's vision of the importance of foreign public opinion. It was she who urged Chiang to appoint Tong to lead China's international propaganda. As Tong recalled:

> More perhaps than anyone else in the government orbit, she [Madam Chiang] recognized the extreme importance to China's cause of an understanding foreign press.... Without her insistence, I doubt if we would ever have had an overseas publicity department manned by professionally competent persons. It was not a normal governmental function, by previous government standards, nor was it an undertaking that anyone else would have recognized at that early date as important to China's welfare or to her war effort.[13]

Nevertheless, Chiang's patronage and Soong's support could not protect the new office from factional struggles. Although Tong had engaged in presswork for more than two decades, he had less than two years' experience as a party member. Tong

---

Press, 1970), 185–87; Lloyd E. Eastman, *The Nationalist Era in China, 1927–1949* (Cambridge: Cambridge University Press, 1991), 128–29.

11. Pak-Wah Leung, ed., *Political Leaders of Modern China: A Biographical Dictionary* (Westport, CT: Greenwood Press, 2002), 141–42.
12. Hollington Kong Tong, *Dateline: China; The Beginning of China's Press Relations with the World* (New York: Rockport Press, 1950), 11.
13. Ibid.

often found himself given the cold shoulder by some of the Nanjing officials, who tended to favor cliques and seniority over ability and qualification. Senior party members began a whisper campaign, complaining that Tong, without much experience in party affairs, was unqualified to hold such an important position.[14] The day before Tong took office, Wang Jingwei overtly expressed his dissatisfaction with Tong's appointment, telling Tong that he was "too old to enter official life."[15] Tong's direct superior, Chen Gongbo, Wang's trusted follower, also postponed his inauguration as minister of information in protest. To avoid friction with Chen, Tong moved the headquarters of the Fifth Board to Shanghai while Chen remained in Nanjing to supervise domestic propaganda.

The tension between Tong and Chen was a result of the struggle between Chiang Kai-shek and Wang Jingwei. By 1937, Wang still considered "resisting while negotiating" the best approach to dealing with Japan.[16] His conciliatory attitude, which stemmed from his distrust of China's military capability, deviated from Chiang's ever-growing determination for resistance. Indeed, Wang controlled substantial propaganda resources and enjoyed high prestige in the party. Installing Tong as a direct associate of Chen Gongbo in the propaganda department was Chiang's effort to prevent Wang from disseminating his views, which he feared would eventually affect the morale of the general public.

Apart from political struggles, a lack of competent staff and infrastructure also hindered the development of the Fifth Board. Many of the officers were staff of other ministries who served the board on only a part-time basis. Already overworked with their normal duties during wartime, they often neglected the propaganda tasks that Tong, a junior member of the party, assigned to them. Tong recalled that he seldom saw the chiefs of his departments since they had to give much of their time to duties in other ministries.[17] Even if they had been devoted to propaganda work, they were unlikely to be able to perform up to Tong's high expectations. As a foreign propaganda apparatus, the board required its staff to master foreign languages and have basic journalistic skills. But the staff assigned to Tong's office met neither requirement. Worse than the lack of competent staff was the shortage of office space. Unable to put all his staff in a single building, Tong had to place them in various locations scattered across Shanghai. He ended up using "more than five gallons of gasoline daily" commuting between offices.[18]

14. Ibid., 16.
15. Hollington K. Tong, *Dong Xianguang zizhuan: Yi ge nongfu de zishu* [Hollington Tong's autobiography: A self-introduction of a peasant] (Taipei: Taiwan xinsheng baoshe, 1973), 12.
16. Wang Ke-wen, "Wang Jingwei and the Policy Origins of the 'Peace Movement,' 1932–1937," in *Chinese Collaboration with Japan, 1932–1945: The Limits of Accommodation*, ed. David P. Barrett and Larry N. Shyu (Stanford: Stanford University Press, 2001), 35–36.
17. Tong, *Dateline: China*, 25.
18. Ibid.

Facing what he referred to as "impossible situations," Tong was eager to initiate a thorough reorganization of the board. Yet he was also keenly aware that the change would displease certain senior members of the party and consequently jeopardize his own position: "Had I used my brand new broom for too sweeping a clean-up, both broom and I might swiftly have found ourselves outside the party."[19] Tong therefore turned to Chiang and Soong for help. He repeatedly reported to them on the chaotic situation of the board and suggested the idea of reorganization. Soong responded by sending one of her secretaries, Ilona Ralf Sues, to investigate the situation. Sues's appearance at the board incensed the members, who were annoyed about being instructed by a foreign woman. When their dissatisfaction nearly resulted in a sit-down strike, it further convinced Tong that his current staff, most of whom adhered to the party's conservative nationalist ideology, were unable to cooperate with foreigners effectively. To set foreign propaganda on track, Tong had to either make radical staff changes or create a new organization.

Tong set the board working despite all these difficulties. The board was responsible for censoring outgoing dispatches, providing news materials, and expanding China's news networks. Tong's focus was on the latter two, since the censorship office that he had established two years prior was on track and required only minimal supervision. It seemed that the gathering and compiling of news reports would be the easiest part of Tong's work, since the job was equivalent to running a newspaper, a profession that Tong had held before joining the government. Yet these tasks proved to be the most difficult because of the lack of competent staff and hostile conditions during the war. Fierce battles on the front endangered the lives of the correspondents and greatly limited their activities. The continuous military defeats and retreats resulted in the Nanjing government's further loss of control of media facilities. To redress the situation, Tong turned to Xiao Tongzi, the head of the Central News Agency, for assistance. Despite Xiao's willingness to help, he saw little possibility of lending support to Tong when the agency was having difficulty maintaining its own normal service in the midst of war.[20]

Tong placed great emphasis on distributing human interest stories, which he believed to be effective in evoking readers' sympathies. He was particularly eager to collect stories that exposed Japanese atrocities and reflected the bravery of the Chinese people. Indeed, these two themes were the focus of his propaganda during the early stage of the war. While members of the board were unable to contribute stories that grabbed the reader's attention, Tong turned to his friends and former colleagues in the treaty-port press for support. Hawthorne Cheng was therefore selected to join the news section of the board to write human-interest reports. Cheng was a

---

19. Ibid., 32.
20. Ibid., 29.

long-term member of the *China Press* staff when Tong was in charge of the paper.[21] His sensitivity for news as well as his high level of proficiency in English made him an ideal member of Tong's new office. Another person Tong recruited was Frank Liu. Tong found this Cornell University–trained agricultural specialist had "a flair" for writing features and appointed him as the head of the news section.[22] Immediately after the outbreak of the Sino-Japanese War, Tong also gave telegraph concessions at half price to foreign correspondents who filed reports favorable to China's case.[23]

Tong was keen to strengthen connections with local elites. When the military battle raged in Shanghai in 1937, Tong was active in supplying news updates to foreign communities, whose opinion, according to his assessment, would "importantly affect the attitudes of their people at home and of their governments."[24] While Tong's own staff lacked experience in working with foreign communities, the local Anti-enemy Committee came to Tong's assistance. The committee was a self-organized group that endeavored to inform foreign residents in Shanghai about Chinese positions in the war. Its key members were Xia Jinlin, then president of the Anglo-Chinese Medhurst College and a member of the Legislative Yuan; Wen Yuanning, editor of *T'ien Hsia*, a monthly literary magazine in English that was highly rated among the intelligentsia; Liu Zhan'en (a.k.a. Herman Liu), president of Shanghai University; and H. J. Timperley, then a *Manchester Guardian* correspondent.[25] These members essentially became external agents of the Fifth Board, responsible for communicating with the local communities in Shanghai and editing propaganda materials.[26] With the government's support, Liu organized the Cosmopolitan Club in Shanghai, which gathered foreign consular officials and leading Shanghai bankers regularly to discuss the strategy to deal with the warfare in Shanghai.[27]

After the fall of Shanghai in October 1937, Nanjing came under the spotlight of the world media. The Metropolitan Hotel in Nanjing was packed with curious foreign journalists eager to know what would happen to the capital of China. Tong made great efforts to secure links with European and American correspondents, whom he considered the best third-party observers to report China's position to the world. Tong visited the hotel daily, informing foreign journalists of China's point of view. This contact was deliberately kept informal in order to "erase the trace of

---

21. Paul French, *Through the Looking Glass: China's Foreign Journalists from Opium Wars to Mao* (Hong Kong: Hong Kong University Press, 2009), 159–60.
22. Tong, *Dateline: China*, 28.
23. Yu Feipeng's correspondence, July 16, 1937, 0011200000001, national government archives, Academia Historica (hereafter AH).
24. Ibid., 18.
25. Tong, *Dateline: China*, 21–22; Zeng, *Zeng Xubai zizhuan*, 182; Zeng Xubai, *Zeng Xubai zixuan ji* [Self-selected collection of Zeng Xubai] (Taipei: Liming wenhua shiye gufen youxian gongsi, 1981), 253–54.
26. Zeng, *Zeng Xubai zizhuan*, 182.
27. "Cosmopolitan Club Formed," *North China Herald*, October 13, 1937, 64.

propaganda." Communication was pursued through personal visits, afternoon teas, and private dinners. Tong recalled that, during those days in Nanjing, he had lunch with foreign correspondents almost daily.[28]

Among the Western journalists, Tong built close ties with Tillman Durdin, China correspondent for the *New York Times*. Durdin worked at the *China Press* before joining the *New York Times* in 1937. He met Tong in the early 1930s when Tong was the managing director of the *Press*. In Nanjing, Tong relied on Durdin not only as his source for war updates but also saw him as the most immediate and effective channel to publicize China's perspectives to the world.[29] After the loss of Nanjing, for example, Chiang needed to convince the world that the fall of China's capital did not imply the defeat of the nation. As soon as Chiang drafted an announcement that expressed this position, Tong translated it into English and passed it to Durdin for publication.[30]

Ministry of Information, Wuhan, 1938

With the fall of Nanjing in December 1937, the Guomindang government moved to Wuhan, the economic and industrial center of the central Yangtze River region. Although the move forced the government to abandon the news infrastructure it had built in the lower Yangtze area in the preceding ten years, it also provided Tong with an opportunity to reorganize his office.

Chiang Kai-shek did not wait long to eliminate Chen Gongbo from the propaganda office. In late 1937, when Chen went to Italy to garner sympathy for China from the Mussolini government, Chiang abolished the Fifth Board. As head of the board, Chen naturally lost his leadership role.[31] Chiang then appointed his own man, Shao Lizi, to supervise the Ministry of Information. The foreign propaganda office was reorganized and renamed the International Department, attached to the ministry. Tong was appointed vice minister, in charge of the department. Although the department was ostensibly affiliated with the party, in essence, it was a military institution: it continued to be funded by the Military Affairs Commission and the head of the department reported directly to Chiang. Members of the department were also organized as military staff, holding military rank and wearing military uniforms at work.[32] Indeed, for an unconventional group like Tong's team, the best way to maintain its efficiency was to insulate it from external pressure. Such a peculiar structural design served this purpose. While following the tradition to keep thought control work within the party system, the design ensured Tong's direct contact with Chiang.

---

28. Tong, *Dateline: China*, 38.
29. Ibid., 34.
30. Ibid., 34–35.
31. Chiang took this measure upon the advice of William H. Donald; see J. M. McHugh's memorandum, March 1938, MLMSS 7594 3/10, Winston George Lewis Papers (hereafter WGLP).
32. Zeng, *Zeng Xubai zixuan ji*, 192.

Vice Minister	*Zhongjiang*	Lieutenant General
Head of the International Department	*Shaojiang*	Major General
Chief of Section	*Shangxiao*	Colonel
Section Members	*Shaoxiao–Shangxiao*	Major–Colonel
Clerk	*Shaowei–Zhongwei*	Second Lieutenant–Captain

Diagram 2
The International Department members' military ranks.
Source: Staff members of the International Department, 718 (4)–10, the Second Historical Archives of China, Nanjing

Tong appointed Zeng Xubai, a loyal friend who had followed him since he started *Yong bao* in the mid-1920s, as head of the International Department. Together, they quickly reorganized the new department and created six sections (*ke*) within it, namely the Editing Section (*Bianji ke*), the Public Relations Section (*Duiwai ke*), the Anti-enemy Section (*Duidi ke*), the Photographic Section (*Sheying ke*), the Broadcasting Section (*Chuanyin ke*), and the Section of General Affairs (*Zongwu ke*).

The Editing Section was headed by Tong's loyal follower Shen Jianhong.[33] Shen was Tong's former colleague and fellow Missouri alumnus. He graduated from Yenching University's Department of Journalism in 1932 and joined the *China Press* when Tong was managing director. Between 1934 and 1936, he was sent to the University of Missouri to study journalism. Upon his return, he became an English editor at the Central News Agency.[34] Shen's section operated like a newspaper office. Staff were sent out to collect materials in the morning and returned to write news reports in the afternoon. The section produced written reports at an average rate of twenty-thousand words per day. These pieces were distributed to foreign journalists in Wuhan and sent to the department's overseas branches for further distribution. The section published a weekly called *China at War*, which had a print run of five thousand copies per issue and was distributed to foreign journalists, diplomats, and missionaries in China and organizations overseas.[35] In addition, the section dispatched telegrams to politically prominent foreigners, soliciting their sympathy for China and encouraging them to organize anti-Japanese boycotts or strikes in support. To "erase the trace of propaganda," all such telegrams were sent in the name of China's nonofficial organizations. More than four thousand words were telegraphed every month for this purpose.[36]

The Public Relations Section was created to strengthen China's propaganda network. It received foreign journalists and visitors, arranged interviews with top

33. Tong, *Dateline: China*, 63.
34. Yin Yungong, *Zhongguo xinwenjie renwu* [Important people in China's press] (Beijing: Zhongguo renshi chubanshe, 2002), 382.
35. Work report of the International Department, 1938–1941, GA.
36. Report of the International Department, Ministry of Information, June 11, 1938, conference paper, 5.3/81.6, GA.

officials and military leaders; contacted foreign diplomats, publishers, and news organizations; and convened press conferences. Tong placed great emphasis on providing good service to foreign journalists and visitors to China, trying to satisfy their "needs for all kinds of information" and requests for interviews.[37] This section made particular efforts to put newly arrived Western journalists in touch with government officials. Tong believed that these interviews would provide journalists with an important introduction to Chinese affairs. For newly arrived journalists, interviewing key Chinese officials was an invaluable opportunity. They often wired conversations verbatim despite the high cost of international telegrams.[38] The section resumed press conferences for foreign journalists. It invited military, political, and diplomatic leaders to give talks on the situation at the front. Scholars were also invited to deliver speeches. The department organized more than three hundred press conferences between December 1, 1937, and October 24, 1938, each attracting fifty journalists on average.[39] Tong sought to establish not only working relations with Western journalists but also personal connections, usually by attending to their personal needs. On learning that the British author Freda Utley had arrived in Wuhan in hot weather without enough summer dresses, the section had one made, which Madam Chiang then presented to her as a personal gift.[40] Tong saw this hospitality as good propaganda:

> Running this Public Relations Section is like running a shop and foreign journalists are our customers. Good shop assistants should be ready to satisfy their customers with the idea that the customers are always right. This spirit of service is the most alluring magic of our foreign propaganda. It creates the impression that cooperation with us brings pleasure, both physically and mentally. As a result, they would agree with our ideas and distribute the messages we wish them to send abroad for us.[41]

The Anti-enemy Section was both a propaganda institution and an intelligence organ. Targeting Japanese soldiers in China and the public back in Japan, the section compiled propaganda materials in Japanese and employed Japanese antiwar activists to broadcast antiwar messages to a Japanese audience.[42] Its leader Cui Wanqiu lived in Japan between 1924 and 1933. He served as editor of *Da wanbao*, managed by Zeng Xubai from 1934. While taking on the editorship, he also taught at the Shanghai

---

37. Ibid.
38. Ibid.
39. Work report, the International Department of the Ministry of Information, 1938–1941, general documents 496/294, GA.
40. Tong, *Dateline: China*, 56.
41. Report of the International Department, Ministry of Information, June 11, 1938, conference paper, 5.3/81.6, GA.
42. Barak Kushner, *The Thought War: Japanese Imperial Propaganda* (Honolulu: University of Hawaii Press, 2006), 143–45.

University and Fudan University. He later joined the Bureau of Investigation and Statistics of the Military Affairs Commission (known as Juntong), an intelligence agency under the supervision of Dai Li, and was recruited to Tong's office after it moved to Wuhan, possibly on Dai's recommendation.[43] The section essentially became a branch of Juntong, sharing its intelligence about Japan and its analysis of Japanese affairs. Under the direction of Shao Yulin, a specialist on Japanese intelligence, the committee published the *Report on the State of the Enemy*, *Analysis of the State of the Enemy*, and other journals for the reference of Guomindang's top leaders to help them devise anti-Japanese policies.[44]

The Photographic Section was established with the assistance of the Central News Agency. Tong's first attempt at supplying photographs to the foreign press ended in "dismal failure," due to a lack of trained personnel.[45] Xiao Tongzi came to Tong's aid by sharing the Central News Agency's pictures with Tong's department. One of its key photographers, H. S. Wang, was regarded by Tong as having "both technical skill and a keen news sense."[46] His picture of a lonely baby crying in the ruins of the bombed railroad station in Shanghai became one of the most famous pictures of the war from a Nationalist government source.[47] Indeed, the picture was most likely

Figure 14
A weeping baby amid the ruins of Shanghai railway station. Photograph by H. S. Wang, August 1937.

---

43. Xiong Yuezhi ed., *Shanghai mingren mingshi mingwu daguan* [Shanghai: People, events and relics] (Shanghai: Shanghai renmin chubanshe, 2004), 258.
44. Report of the International Department, Ministry of Information, June 11, 1938, conference paper, 5.3/81.6, GA.
45. Tong, *Dateline: China*, 28.
46. Ibid., 29.
47. The picture is from http://en.wikipedia.org/wiki/Bloody_Saturday_%28photograph%29, accessed December 9, 2013.

to be a directed photo by Wang's photographic team,[48] yet the suffering of civilians featured by the photo was a truthful reflection of the damage and pain the war had inflicted on Chinese society. Apart from taking photos, the section also provided film-developing services to foreign journalists. By doing so, it aimed at strengthening connections with journalists while secretly censoring their pictures.[49]

The International Department established a Radio Section that supervised broadcasts in foreign languages. In December 1937, the section began to broadcast news in English, French, and Japanese, respectively, for ten minutes daily through the Hankou radio station. In May 1938, the Hankou wireless station under the control of the Ministry of Communications agreed to allocate an hour a day for foreign-language programs.[50] While the department lacked outlets for its printed propaganda materials, the international radio station became an important channel to voice China's position in the war. The radio station not only focused on news reports, political comments, and speeches, but also devised cultural programs, including Western music, Chinese operas, and poetry readings. The goal, again, was to minimize its role as propaganda and make the programs more entertaining and acceptable.

At the same time he reorganized the foreign propaganda institutions within the government, Tong was also expanding the external network. He organized a branch office in Hong Kong and appointed Wen Yuanning, organizer of the Shanghai Anti-enemy Committee, as its director. Wen operated the office under the guise of acting as the editor of the *T'ien Hsia* monthly. He had Tong's complete trust. Tong arranged for Wen to be his proxy at the overseas offices in the United States, Britain, and Australia in case he was in danger.[51] With the fall of Shanghai, Hong Kong became the most important city connecting China with the outside world. Propaganda materials were sent overseas from the branch office in Hong Kong. The city was also the first stop for foreign journalists coming to cover the Sino-Japanese War. Wen's office published an English-language monthly named the *Far Eastern Mirror*. Later *China at War* also moved from Wuhan to Hong Kong for the better local printing and transport conditions. The Hong Kong office was the hub that provided other foreign branches with propaganda materials. The office also worked as an intelligence body, investigating the background of foreign visitors to China. Wen kept in close contact with foreign agents through informal gatherings and intentionally exchanged information during banter and raillery rather than at official occasions.[52]

---

48. Tessa Morris-Suzuki, *The Past within Us: Media, Memory, History* (London: Verso, 2005), 72–73.
49. Work report of the International Department, 1938–1941, GA.
50. Ibid.
51. Tong, *Dateline: China*, 50.
52. Work report of the overseas branches of the International Department, 1938–1940, No. 718–917, the Second Historical Archives of China (hereafter SHAC), Nanjing.

The London office was organized by Xia Jinlin, a member of the Ministry of Foreign Affairs, with the help of H. J. Timperley. Both of them were members of the Anti-enemy Committee that had voluntarily assisted with Tong's propaganda during the battle of Shanghai. Xia's cross-appointment greatly facilitated the coordination between the department and the Ministry of Foreign Affairs, which was not the case before the war. Xia was on good terms with Chinese diplomats in Europe and was particularly close to Guo Taiqi, ambassador to Britain, who frequently invited Xia to gatherings at the embassy. At one of the gatherings, Xia met Kingsley Martin, his schoolmate at the Mill High School in London, and Martin's partner, Dorothy Woodman. Both were actively engaged in the China Campaign Committee, a social organization established by a group of progressive Britons at the end of the 1930s to lobby on behalf of China in its war against Japan.[53] Its principal organizers

Figure 15
China Campaign Committee. From the collection of Jenny Clegg and Society for Anglo-Chinese Understanding.

---

53. Xia Jinlin, *Wo wudu canjia waijiao gongzuo de huigu* [A review of my life as a diplomat] (Taipei: Zhuanji wenxue chubanshe, 1978), 58.

were Victor Gollancz, publisher and head of the Left Book Club; Kingsley Martin, editor of the *New Statesman and Nation*; Margery Fry, a feminist and social activist; Harold Laski, the Labor Party theorist; and Arthur Clegg, reporter for the *Daily Worker*.[54] The committee collected funds for medical aid to China, promoted boycotts of Japanese goods, and arranged for Chinese speakers to give talks to organizations in Britain.[55] Xia's personal friendship with Martin and Woodman strengthened his ties with the committee, which became the major platform for the London propaganda branch. For years, the committee had been secretly receiving propaganda materials from Tong's department, perhaps without the knowledge of its British leaders. Xia was particularly careful to keep his connections with the committee informal and out of the public eye so as to "erase the trace of propaganda," as Tong demanded.[56]

Timperley and Earl Leaf, a former United Press correspondent, were sent to New York to open a branch office. Leaf practically lived at the branch office in order to provide timely contact with various local organizations and at the same time save money for the cash-strapped branch.[57] The office was responsible for reporting American trends to the Chinese government and assisting in the spread of news about China in the United States. Hollington Tong particularly advised Leaf to influence opinion in financial and commercial circles in the United States, pushing for an embargo on the shipment of war materials to Japan.[58] Meanwhile, Timperley also extended its US network by securing connections with the Trans-Pacific News Service, headed by Bruno Shaw, the former editor of the *Hankow Herald*, an English-language daily published in Hankou in the 1920s. This new service later developed into the Chinese News Service and became China's major news outlet in the United States.[59]

The branch office led by Leaf paid special attention to distributing propaganda materials through Americans. Frank Price and his brother Harry Price were key contributors to the US network. The Price brothers were born into a Nanjing missionary family. Frank Price was dean of the Nanjing Theological Seminary. He translated Sun Yat-sen's *Three People's Principles* into English in 1929 and was close to Madam

---

54. Xiao Qian (Hsiao Ch'ien), *Traveller without a Map*, trans. Jeffrey C. Kinkley (Stanford: Stanford University Press, 1993), 85.
55. Robert A. Bickers, *Britain in China: Community Culture and Colonialism, 1900–1949* (Manchester: Manchester University Press, 1999), 233; Xiao Qian, *Xiao Qian quanji*, texie juan [A complete collection of Xiao Qian, special volume] (Wuhan: Hubei renmin chubanshe, 2005), 223–28.
56. Work report of the overseas branches of the International Department, 1938–1940, No. 718-917, SHAC. Xia Jinlin, *Wo wudu canjia waijiao gongzuo de huigu* [A review of my life as a diplomat] (Taipei: Zhuanji wenxue chubanshe, 1978), 58.
57. Wen Yuanning to Zeng Xubai, December 7, 1940, no. 718(4)-262, SHAC.
58. Chen Cheng and Hollington Tong to Chiang Kai-shek, February 11, 1938, 00801020200019001, Chen Cheng archives, AH.
59. Tong, *Dateline: China*, 91.

Chiang.⁶⁰ Harry Price was formerly a professor at Yenching University. Together they established a Chinese information service for Tong in the United States, supported exclusively by Americans.⁶¹ The service operated for two years and was regarded by Tong as "extremely helpful" during "the least understood period of war."⁶²

With Leaf's help, the Price brothers organized the Campaign of the American Committee for Non-participation in Japanese Aggression, known as the Price Committee. The committee called for an embargo on American supplies of military materials to Japan. It received warm support from officials in the Department of State, including Stanley K. Hornbeck, chief advisor on far eastern affairs, and such members of Congress as Senator Key Pittman, chairman of the Senate Foreign Relations Committee.⁶³ The executive secretary of the committee, Harry Price, contrived to elicit support from many US political celebrities. The committee was chaired by Roger Greene, former director of the China Medical Board of the Rockefeller Foundation. Walter Judd, a representative from Minnesota, became one of its most effective advocate. In 1939, the committee also successfully recruited former secretary of state Henry Lewis Stimson to be its honorary chairman, with Abbot Lawrence Lowell, Harvard president emeritus, and Harry E. Yarnell, former commander in chief of the US Asiatic Fleet, as honorary vice chairman.⁶⁴ Frederick McKee and Geraldine Fitch, wife of the well-known missionary George A. Fitch, were also important members of the organization.⁶⁵ As Leaf reported, "The home of Harry Price in New York had become a clearing house for editors, writers, research experts, professors, missionaries, boycott organizers and others devoted to the China cause."⁶⁶ Leaf nevertheless left the committee in September 1938 so as not to leave the impression that it was orchestrated or linked to the Guomindang.⁶⁷

Indeed, to win US support for China had become one of the most important tasks of China's foreign propaganda after the war. While most people became aware of Chiang's propaganda efforts in the US in the late 1940s and 1950s through the exposure of the "China lobby" group, it should be noted that a systematic propaganda network had already started in the late 1930s, and news dissemination by Tong's

---

60. Helen Foster Snow, *My China Years* (London: Harrap, 1984), 239.
61. Tong, *Dateline: China*, 95.
62. Ibid., 94.
63. Donald J. Friedman, *The Road from Isolation: The Campaign of the American Committee for Non-participation in Japanese Aggression, 1938–1941* (Cambridge, MA: Harvard University, 1970), 5–6.
64. Akio Tsuchida, "China's 'Public Diplomacy' toward the United States before Pearl Harbor," *Journal of American-East Asian Relations* 17 (2010): 45–46.
65. "The China Lobby—Lobbying Efforts from the 1920s through World War II," *Encyclopedia of the New American Nation*, http://www.americanforeignrelations.com/A-D/The-China-Lobby-Lobbying-efforts-from-the-1920s-through-world-war-ii.html.
66. Tong, *Dateline: China*, 95.
67. Friedman, *Road from Isolation*, 8.

office was an important part of it.⁶⁸ Chiang instructed Kong Xiangxi to allocate US$100,000 a month to support Tong's propaganda in the United States. They especially advised him not to scrimp on spending and "try all means" to find reliable people in the United States to publicize the Chinese cause.⁶⁹ Tong later expanded China's US propaganda branches to Chicago and San Francisco, led by Henry Evans and Malcolm Rosholt, respectively.

In February 1938, Chiang sent Zhang Pengchun to the United States to conduct propaganda.⁷⁰ Zhang was a professor of theater studies at Nankai University, holding a PhD in education from Columbia University. He served as the theatrical adviser and interpreter on Mei Lanfang's successful tour of Beijing Opera performances in the United States and Russia and was experienced in introducing Chinese culture to the West. Within two weeks of his arrival, he had visited more than twenty prominent Americans, including officials in the Department of State and the Department of the Treasury, secretaries of the army and navy, intellectuals, and media practitioners. He intended to collect their views on Chinese issues and inform members of the US elite of China's point of view.⁷¹ Chiang Kai-shek also appointed Hu Shi as ambassador to the United States, hoping his prestige as a scholar would bring about favorable diplomatic and propaganda results. Hu, a Cornell University graduate with a PhD from Columbia University, was warmly welcomed by the Americans. The *New York Times* commended him as one of the few Chinese who were "thoroughly representative of the best of the new and old China" and "well qualified to explain China to the United States and the United States to China."⁷² Hu toured the United States, giving speeches about conditions in China to elicit US public support. His overt diplomatic activities complemented the covert efforts of the propaganda branch office.

Yet China's propaganda activities in the United States also faced many challenges. In 1938, the US government issued the Foreign Agents Registration Act, requiring agents representing interests of a foreign country to disclose their relationship with that foreign government. As a result, many of the elites in the US government and media circles, who used to show sympathy for the Guomindang government, began to keep their distance from China.⁷³ This act required the Chinese government to design its future propaganda activities in a more clandestine manner. Meanwhile, Tong's branch offices in the United States also had to compete with Japanese propaganda agencies that had been successful in instilling Japan's perspectives among the Christian communities and African American groups. Frederick V. Williams,

---

68. Ross Y. Koen, *The China Lobby in American Politics* (New York: Macmillan, 1960).
69. Chiang Kai-shek to Kong Xiangxi, January 16, 1938, 002060100125006, AH.
70. Chen Cheng and Hollington Tong to Chiang Kai-shek, February 11, 1938, 00801020200019001, Chen Cheng Archives, AH.
71. Tsuchida, "China's 'Public Diplomacy' toward the United States before Pearl Harbor," 42–43.
72. "A Welcome Ambassador," *New York Times*, September 20, 1938, 22.
73. Kong Xiangxi to Chiang Kai-shek, 00208010600008001, Chiang Kai-shek archives, AH.

a prominent publicity director for various Catholic organizations, served under Japan's aegis between 1938 and 1939. As Father Charles L. Meeus, who had worked as a missionary in Jiangsu, reported to Tong, he often found Williams sharing "the most absurd things" about Chiang Kai-shek and Madam Chiang with his Catholic audience.[74] The Japanese propagandists also managed to elicit sympathy from African Americans. They emphasized that Japan's goal was to drive the white race out of Asia and to free Chinese people from Western imperialism. This echoed the African Americans' desire to achieve racial equality in the United States.[75]

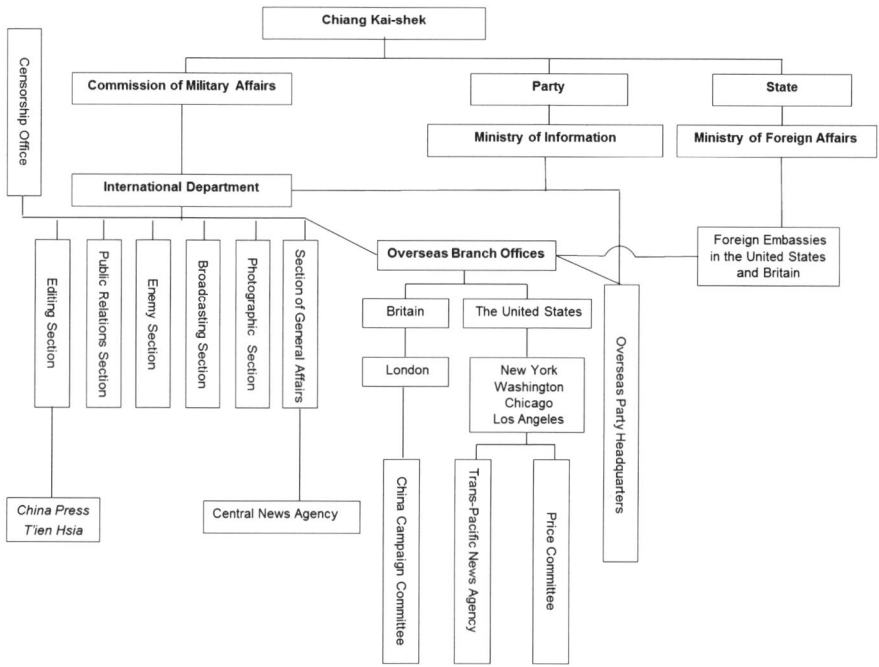

Diagram 3
The structure of the Guomindang international propaganda machinery, 1938

After months in Wuhan, the International Department had created a centralized and coordinated propaganda framework within the government. It also substantially extended its propaganda network abroad. The central office, the International Department of the Ministry of Information, had only twenty-six people on its payroll, yet the total number of people offering services directly or indirectly for the department exceeded two hundred.[76] Straddling the military and party sectors, the

---

74. Tong, *Dateline: China*, 81.
75. Ibid., 85.
76. Report of the International Department, Ministry of Information, June 11, 1938, conference paper, 5.3/81.6, GA.

department obtained support from a wide range of government institutions, including the Ministry of Foreign Affairs, the Military Affairs Commission, the Ministry of Finance, and the Central News Agency. Compared with the disparate foreign propaganda institutions before the full-scale war, the new system was an impressive step forward.

It should be noted that the cohesive force holding the propaganda network together was its network of personal relations. Most of the chiefs and staff members of Tong's department were his former colleagues in the treaty ports or people who shared a similar career path. Similar to Tong, most of the members of his department were inexperienced with the party. They joined the Guomindang a year after being recruited into the propaganda system, perhaps more for the sake of convenience than out of personal belief.[77] Indeed, the long-nurtured treaty-port press network formed the basis for the international propaganda system that Tong was able to establish immediately after the war. Tong was pressured by other party leaders who tried to install their own people in the department. Chen Guofu, an important political client of Chiang Kai-shek and a prominent player in party organization affairs, used to recommend graduates to Tong's office from political training schools that he controlled.[78] Yet the department roster suggested that none of them was hired by Tong.

Indeed, Tong's department almost broke with all the conventions of the Guomindang's party propaganda institution. It introduced new guidelines that downplayed the party's ideology and recruited a team of people most of whom would have had little chance to be recruited into a party-affiliated institution. In fact, Tong tried to create an oasis in the Guomindang officialdom after the model of treaty-port press, where the value of truth and credibility of information were acknowledged, and personal competence was prioritized over nationality, experience with the party, and obedience to bureaucratic rules.

The reason Tong, as a new member of the Guomindang, was able to withstand the pressure of conservative party propagandists and build such an idiosyncratic department was because of Chiang Kai-shek and Madam Chiang's support behind the scenes. They closely supervised the operation of Tong's office and shielded it from external intervention from other factions. Madam Chiang traveled to Tong's Shanghai office from Nanjing twice to arrange propaganda work, braving Japanese bombing along the way.[79] She participated in propaganda activities, delivering speeches and issuing appeals.[80] She even worked as a mediator when Tong and Chiang disagreed on the publication of certain information.[81] For example, when Tong's decision to

---

77. Staff members of the International Department, 718(5)-1, SHAC.
78. Correspondence to Ye Chucang, 718(5)-1, SHAC.
79. Zeng, *Zeng Xubai zizhuan*, 200.
80. May-ling Soong, *War Messages and Other Selections* (Hankou: China Information Committee, 1938).
81. Tong, *Dateline: China*, 57.

withhold a report on Britain's secret agreement with Japan to maintain a neutral zone in Wuhan was overruled by Chiang, he turned to Soong to change Chiang's mind. In fact, Tong was more at ease in dealing with Soong. In great awe of Chiang, he was found visibly trembling in Chiang's presence and stammered on the phone with him.[82] Yet his communication with Soong, according to Chiang's telephone officer, was smooth in both Chinese and English.[83]

William H. Donald's role in China's foreign propaganda also deserves attention. Donald was Chiang and Soong's advisor, who played an important role in mediating with his former patron Zhang Xueliang to have Chiang released during the Xi'an coup d'état in December 1936. Having been a journalist earlier in his career, Donald understood how foreign news organizations worked. He assisted Tong in devising propaganda strategies and secured Timperley's service for the office.[84] It was he who persuaded Chiang to eliminate Chen Gongbo from the propaganda office when Chen was on a goodwill trip to Italy.[85] He also worked as a propagandist himself, informing newly arrived foreign diplomats about the situation in China. When J. M. McHugh, assistant naval attaché to China, first arrived, Donald established a close friendship with him. He explained China's situation to McHugh and later introduced him to Chiang Kai-shek.[86] It is hard to assess how much of a role Donald played in building the foreign propaganda apparatus, but McHugh's claim that Tong was under Donald's direct control overstates his importance.[87] The fact that most of Tong's staff, who were either his former colleagues or fellow Missouri alumni, testified to Tong's independent leadership position in the ministry.

The strategy of covert propaganda was fully developed during the days in Wuhan. Trained at a school of journalism in the United States, Tong understood foreign sensitivity to deceptive propaganda and the harm a forged news item could do to the credibility of its sources.[88] He believed that the audience's trust in Chinese sources was a prerequisite for further acceptance of Chinese views and that presenting balanced reports was the best way to obtain and maintain credibility. Guided by this principle, Tong admitted that Chinese pilots bombed the center of the foreign concessions in Shanghai and the American Dollar Liner *President Hoover* in the Huangpu River by

---

82. Stephen R. MacKinnon, *China Reporting: An Oral History of American Journalism in the 1930s and 1940s* (Berkeley: University of California Press, 1987), 51; Wang Zhengyuan, "Wei Jiang Jieshi jie dianhua shi'er nian jianwen" [Twelve years of connecting phone lines for Chiang Kai-shek], *Jiangsu wenshi ziliao*, vol. 36 (Nanjing: Jiangsu wenshi ziliao chubanshe, 1991), 61.
83. Ibid.
84. J. M. McHugh's report, March 8, 1938, MLMSS 7594/3/10, WGLP.
85. Ibid.
86. J. M. McHugh's report, January 20, 1938, MLMSS 7594/3/5, WGLP.
87. J. M. McHugh's report, March 8, 1938, MLMSS 7594/3/10, WGLP.
88. See comments of Roy W. Howard, president of the Cripps-Howard Newspapers, on Tong's personality, in Tong, *Dateline: China*, vii.

mistake, although foreign correspondents initially speculated that the bombs had been dropped by the Japanese.[89]

Furthermore, Tong adopted a hands-off policy, using foreigners to conduct propaganda for China. His previous connections with the Missouri mafia, St. John's graduates and his colleagues of the *China Press*, helped him to include foreign journalists in his personal network. Being a Christian also helped him secure assistance from foreign missionary groups. As mentioned above, nearly all the leaders of his branch offices overseas were foreigners. Within China, Tong appointed Maurice Votaw, a lecturer from St. John's University who was close to Zeng Xubai, to be his adviser and invited the Oxford-trained Sinologist J. A. MacCausland to assist him with translating conference materials and speeches.[90]

Liberal censorship characterized news policy in the Wuhan days. Censors had the right to delete but not to alter information.[91] They were required not only to inform foreign correspondents about improper content prior to its deletion but also to explain the harm that content might do to China.[92] Such a liberal policy was also a result of China's diminished control of news outlets after the fall of Shanghai. Tong had to admit that "news censorship was doomed to be inadequate with the existence of extraterritoriality."[93] The loss of Shanghai made it even harder for China to control outgoing dispatches. Tong knew very well that foreign journalists had various ways of avoiding censorship. A banned message could be sent by courier or smuggled by travelers from Wuhan to the Japanese-occupied area.[94]

The Wuhan days saw the flowering of free expression. The data on censorship between December 1937 and September 1938 shows that in May, June, July, and September the office deleted 3.11 words from each article on average. Compared with the censorship in the mid-1930s, when foreign journalists often found their articles completely rewritten or rejected, the changes made by the office in Wuhan were minor. The relaxing of censorship not only applied to the English-language press but also to the Chinese press. In 1938 not a single editor or publisher was arrested or assassinated.[95] Foreign journalists in China regarded Wuhan as the "freest" Chinese capital ever.[96]

---

89. Tong, *Dateline: China*, 88–89.
90. Maurice Votaw's reports, no. C3672 f.4, Maurice Votaw's papers, State Historical Society of Missouri.
91. Work report of the International Department, 1938–1941, GA.
92. Report of the International Department, Ministry of Information, June 11, 1938, conference paper, 5.3/81.6, GA.
93. Ibid.
94. Tong, *Dateline: China*, 60.
95. Stephen R. MacKinnon, *Wuhan, 1938: War, Refugees, and the Making of Modern China* (Berkeley: University of California Press, 2008), 63.
96. MacKinnon, *China Reporting*, 38.

Time	Articles Received	Words Deleted
December 1937	78	(only one week)
January 1938	446	
February		
March		972
April		
May	624	2331
June	785	2225
July	558	1614
August		
September	228	861

Diagram 4
Censorship data, International Department, December 1937–September 1938.
Source: Work report of the International Department, 1938–1941, GA.

While the Guomindang government endeavored to strengthen its foreign propaganda forces, the Chinese Communist Party also sought to extend its influence in the English-language media. After the Xi'an Incident in December 1936, the Nationalist and Communist parties formed a united front against Japan. Despite a lack of mutual trust, their cooperation in Wuhan ran relatively smoothly. Zhou Enlai, then the vice minister of the Board of Political Training of the Military Affairs Commission, frequently visited Tong's office and attended foreign press conferences. Tong personally liked Zhou in spite of their political differences. He commended Zhou's cooperation during the period in Hankou, saying that he "helped a great deal to make [the International Department's] relationship with the foreign press cordial."[97] Tong also regarded their cooperation as proof of Chinese unity, which helped to strengthen China's morale.

Zhou's personal charm attracted the attention of many foreign journalists, who believed that he was an official with the ability to "manipulate correspondents' views on China."[98] Peggy Durdin, freelance feature writer for the *Nation*, the *Atlantic*, and the *New York Times*, for example, was impressed by Zhou's "magnetic personality," believing that "nobody on the KMT [Guomindang] side could touch Chou En-lai in persuasiveness or in intellectual charm."[99] Henry Lieberman, editor of the *Foreign News*, while disappointed with Zhou's lack of proficiency in English, still acknowledged Zhou as "one of the greatest people [he had] ever encountered because of his charm, his skills, his mental and dramatic ability."[100] In addition to Zhou's efforts,

---

97. Tong, *Dateline: China*, 51.
98. MacKinnon, *China Reporting*, 82.
99. Ibid.
100. Ibid.

Fan Changjiang, an editor of *Dagong bao* and close associate of Zhou, organized an English-language news agency in Hankou. The agency, which later moved to Changsha, and then Guilin, supplied news reports to the International Department.[101] In Hong Kong, the China Defence League led by Soong Qing-ling became an extension of the Communist Party's foreign propaganda office. After receiving reports from correspondents sympathetic to Chinese Communists, the League distributed these reports as newsletters around the world.[102]

Foreign journalists in Wuhan welcomed the unity between the Guomindang and the Communist Party. They regarded the Wuhan days as the "romantic period of Chinese resistance to the Japanese"[103] and found their journalistic work much easier in Wuhan. They just needed to focus on China's united resistance against the invasion of Japan without wasting unnecessary energy on the complicated struggles between the two parties. Tillman Durdin, then the correspondent for the *New York Times*, reminisced about the experience in Wuhan at a conference in 1982:

> It [the period in Wuhan] was also the height of the united front. . . . The unity tremendously impressed us. Although the Chinese were losing steadily after some very tough battles, their sense of unity as a people seemed to hold. We tried to report this in whatever we wrote.[104]

Into the Lion's Den: Propaganda in Shanghai

Despite the fall of Shanghai, the city's cosmopolitan tradition still made it an important platform from which to disseminate China's point of view. Keenly aware that the attitude of foreigners who lived in Shanghai strongly affected the attitudes of the public abroad and the officials of their home countries, Tong sneaked into Shanghai to organize propaganda activities. Indeed, the morale of foreign and Chinese residents was low. As Tong's colleague reported to him on December 1, 1937, the sense of insecurity was strong among foreigners: "No one knows just how far the Japanese will go or to what extent the powers are prepared to sacrifice their rights."[105] Chinese residents were also war weary. They were disappointed with the Guomindang government's abandonment of the city and complained that little support was offered to the Chinese in the Japanese-occupied regions.[106] Part of Tong's job was to boost public morale in Shanghai.

---

101. Wu Tingjun, *Zhongguo xinwenshi xinxiu* [A new history of news in China] (Shanghai: Fudan University Press, 2008), 314.
102. Israel Epstein, *My China Eye: Memoirs of a Jew and a Journalist* (San Francisco: Long River Press, 2005), 132.
103. MacKinnon, *China Reporting*, 39.
104. Ibid.
105. Quoted in Tong, *Dateline: China*, 71.
106. Ibid.

Tong's trip to Shanghai was also an effort to thwart Japanese propaganda in the region. After conquering Shanghai, Japan occupied the office of the Ministry of Communications and took over the radio station XHQC, then one of the most powerful stations in Asia.[107] The Japanese army muzzled the Chinese press in the International Settlement and assassinated anti-Japanese journalists and activists. On January 6, 1938, the Japanese authorities, claiming to be the successors to the Chinese government in the International Settlement, took over China's censorship office in the Great Northern Telegraph Company, the Great Eastern Telegraph Company, and the Pacific Telegraph Company. Although American and British consulates general verbally challenged Japan's authority to do so, no action was taken to stop it. Unwilling to see this former information center of China slide into Japanese control, Tong considered it imperative to counter Japan's propaganda within the city.

Shanghai was an extremely dangerous place for Tong. The city was in the shadow of wartime terrorism where assassinations were a daily occurrence. Gangsters and members of underground societies affiliated with various political interests vied for power by murdering and kidnapping. Local elites, particularly journalists and opinion leaders, were the target of the terrorist threats.[108] On April 7, 1938, Liu Zhan'en, leader of the Anti-enemy Committee and a key contact for Tong, was shot dead while waiting for a bus with his ten-year-old son. One of the assassins was caught by the police. In court, the twenty-five-year-old suspect declared that he was sent by Lee Yu-pu, leader of a special corps, to kill Liu because Liu had been friendly with pro-Japanese elements in Shanghai and was expected to become the civil governor of Jiangsu Province under the Japanese.[109] The suspect's allegation was clearly an attempt to tarnish Liu's name while legitimizing his murder by citing patriotism during a time of extreme political chaos. In fact, Liu had planned to depart on a trip to the United States to give anti-Japanese lectures. It was possible that his trip was supported by Tong's office. Comments from the Japanese paper *Shanghai nippo* on the day following Liu's death further confirmed Liu's anti-Japanese stance by claiming that Liu had tried to "cause dissention among the higher officials of the so-called reformed Government at Nanking, prior to the organization of the puppet group."[110] Liu's death nevertheless reflected the grave circumstances in Shanghai. It was also a clear warning to Tong's office about the risk in promoting anti-Japanese propaganda in the occupied region.

---

107. Ibid.
108. Frederic E. Wakeman, *The Shanghai Badlands: War Terrorism and Urban Crime, 1937–1941* (Cambridge: Cambridge University Press, 1996), 115–17.
109. "Gunman Story Deprecated by Liu's Friends: Assassinated Educator Said to Have Avoided Political Issues," *China Press*, April 9, 1938, 3; "Herman Liu, Outstanding Chinese Educational Leader," *China Weekly Review*, April 16, 1938, 174; "Dr. Herman Liu Murdered: Third Attempt on Life Succeeded at Corner of Bubbling Well and Majestic Roads," *North China Herald*, April 13, 1938.
110. "Herman Liu, Outstanding Chinese Educational Leader," 174.

Fully aware of the danger in Shanghai, Tong carried out his mission in a highly clandestine manner. Since any transport from Hankou was subjected to the tightest scrutiny by Japanese authorities, Tong flew to Hong Kong first and took an Italian ship bound for Shanghai. Rev. Ronald Rees, then secretary of the National Christian Council, and also Tong's friend, happened to be onboard. Tong declined Rees's repeated offer of help with propaganda activities, so as not to complicate the mission by involving more people than necessary and thereby putting Rees and himself in danger. Learning that other acquaintances were aboard, Tong stayed in his cabin throughout the voyage to keep his trip as secret as possible. During his ten days in Shanghai, he stayed mostly at Timperley's place. He approached the *China Weekly Review*, the *Shanghai Evening Post and Mercury*, the *North China Daily News*, and the *China Press* to arrange intelligence communications with Dai Li's secret agents in Shanghai and for them to receive Chiang's information via the Hong Kong office.[111] Among these papers, the *China Weekly Review* maintained the closest connections with Tong. The inner office of its editor John Powell even kept a secret radio that received message from Tong's office.[112] Tong also sent his remaining Shanghai staff—Dong Shoupeng, F. L. Pratt, and Jimmy Wei—to Hong Kong, since they were too well known in Shanghai as members of his department.[113]

Tong opened an underground office in Shanghai and recruited S. T. Chu and John B. Penniston to operate it. Chu, who had wide connections in Shanghai both among foreigners and Chinese, had worked for Tong in the censorship office. Penniston had been an acquaintance of Tong since their school days at Park College in Missouri. In addition to working for Tong, he also served as chief editorial writer for the *China Press* and was teaching English and logic at Soochow University. Chu and Penniston worked from a tiny office with an entrance down a small alley in the French Concession. They were charged with the task of distributing pamphlets and fliers. Most of the time, materials could be circulated through paper carriers, police officers or vendors, but sometimes they had to do it themselves. By the time of the Pearl Harbor attack, Penniston had a large box in his garage filled with records and publicity materials of the secret Shanghai office. Since burning materials might catch the attention of the Japanese, he calmly waited until the Chinese New Year, joined the Chinese who kept the tradition of burning spirit money for ancestors in New Year and burned the incriminating materials openly for three days.[114] As a double precaution, Tong installed a third underground member of staff—Hubert Freyn, an American—to work more or less as a spy for Tong and to provide him with

---

111. Work report of the International Department, 1938–1939, No. 718–1, SHAC.
112. Maurice Votaw's reports, C3672 f.4, Maurice Votaw's papers, State Historical Society of Missouri.
113. Tong, *Dateline: China*, 69–70.
114. Ibid., 72.

The Nanjing Incident, 1937

The Nanjing Incident tested Tong's international propaganda network. After the Japanese army occupied Nanjing in December 1937, Japanese soldiers committed massacre, rape, looting, and various other inhumane acts against Chinese civilians and unarmed soldiers. Atrocities continued on a large scale for at least the first six weeks and sporadically thereafter.[116] China had a good case to present to the world: its civilians in Nanjing were ruthlessly killed and assaulted in large numbers by the Japanese army. China could easily win foreign sympathy by its victimized position and Japan's inhuman treatment of them in their own territory. If the brutal behavior of the Japanese was successfully publicized, the horror would not only change Western audiences' understanding of Japan's activities in the past but also keep them alert to Japan's future plans.

However, the resources China could use to distribute the information was limited. After the Japanese army occupied Nanjing, all news transmission facilities were tightly controlled by the Japanese. Shanghai, the previous center of information in East Asia, was in no better position. Japan seized the Chinese part of Shanghai and closely supervised activities in the two foreign concessions. The army installed censors in all foreign cable companies and strictly scrutinized China's outgoing information. Indeed, Tong's international propaganda office was faced with two challenges: to collect materials on Japan's atrocities in Nanjing and to transmit them out of the city to the world.

Tong relied heavily on Westerners to conduct propaganda for China. After the fall of Nanjing, the group of Westerners who remained in the city became the eye-witnesses of the events. Most of them later voluntarily offered propaganda services to Tong's office. Some even became China's long-term propaganda agents. The fact that foreign correspondents ended up reporting the Nanjing case abroad was not only because they were the only sources available but also because Tong believed that accounts from "neutral" Western witnesses would be more credible than those from Chinese sources.[117]

The publicity of the Nanjing Incident experienced two phases, divided by the return of international diplomats in January 1938. In December 1937 when the atrocities were at their height, reports on the events were scarce because of the blockade

---

115. Ibid.,72–73.
116. Yuma Totani, *The Tokyo War Crimes Trial: The Pursuit of Justice in the Wake of World War II* (Cambridge, MA: Harvard University Asia Center, 2008), 121.
117. Tong, *Dateline: China*, 46.

on information by the Japanese army. Accounts of the incidents mainly came from the few foreign journalists and missionaries staying in the city. Among them, Archibald T. Steele, correspondent for the *Chicago Daily News*, and Tillman Durdin, correspondent for the *New York Times*, were especially active.

After repeated efforts to leave Nanjing, Steele finally managed to board the *Oahu* leaving for Shanghai on December 15. Once aboard, he wasted no time in trying to cable his reports about the Nanjing atrocities through the ship's radio facilities. He succeeded in bribing the *Oahu* radio operator to send his accounts on the Nanjing Incident to the *Chicago Daily News*, and the messages became the first report on the rape of Nanjing in the Western media.[118] Steele referred to the Japanese killings of Chinese civilians as "systematic extermination," compared their actions to "killing sheep." He also expressed his disgust at the experience of having to drive his car "over heaps of bodies five feet high, over which hundreds of Japanese trucks and guns had already passed."[119] Determined to expose Japan's inhumane act to the world, Steele continued to publish stories about Nanjing on December 17 and 18, each providing graphic descriptions of the Japanese's ruthless treatment of Chinese civilians.[120]

Durdin's first report about Japanese activities in occupied Nanjing came out on December 18. He accurately presented the sharp change of atmosphere within the city:

> A tremendous sense of relief over the outlook for a cessation of the fearful bombardment and the elimination of the threat of serious disorders by the Chinese troops pervaded the Chinese populace when the Japanese took over control within the walls. It was felt Japanese rule might be severe, at least until war conditions were over. Two days of Japanese occupation changed the whole outlook. Wholesale looting, the violation of women, the murder of civilians, the eviction of Chinese from their homes, mass executions of war prisoners and the impressing of able-bodied men turned Nanking into a city of terror.[121]

Durdin not only recorded Japan's brutal treatment of the Chinese but also exposed Japanese soldiers' assaults on American nationals and their property—the staff of the American Mission University Hospital was stripped of cash and watches, and the home of the US ambassador was ransacked.[122] Although Durdin was close to Tong, it was hard to identify him as Tong's propaganda agent. While bitterly condemning the misconduct of the Japanese, Durdin also remained critical of the Chinese military

---

118. Suping Lu, *They Were in Nanjing: The Nanjing Massacre Witnessed by American and British Nationals* (Hong Kong: Hong Kong University Press, 2004), 20.
119. "Japanese Troops Kill Thousands," *Chicago Daily News*, December 15, 1937, quoted in Lu, *They Were in Nanjing*, 20.
120. "War's Death Drama Pictured by Reporter," *Chicago Daily News*, December 17, 1937, 1; "Tells Heroism of Yankees in Nanjing," *Chicago Daily News*, December 18, 1937, 1.
121. "All Captives Slain," *New York Times*, December 18, 1937, 1.
122. Ibid., 10.

defense. In the article, he implied that Chiang Kai-shek himself was responsible for the tragedy of Nanjing. Following the ideas of his German military advisers and his chief military associate, Bai Chongxi, Chiang failed to defend the nation's capital.[123] Durdin portrayed Chinese soldiers as underequipped with munitions and lacking the will to fight. A large number of Chinese soldiers, recorded Durdin, bolted from the front line, threw away their guns, and put on civilian clothes to avoid being captured by the Japanese. Durdin therefore wondered whether the Chinese army "could be rallied again for effective mass resistance against the Japanese military machine."[124]

Although Shanghai was close to Nanjing, its geographical proximity did not provide Shanghai's treaty-port papers any advantage in covering the incident. Reports about the situation from Shanghai came much later than those from the metropolitan papers. The *North China Daily News* first reported the incident on December 25, ten days later than the *Chicago Daily News*. The article was drafted by Miner S. Bates, one of the few Westerners remaining in Nanjing when Japan took over the city. Bates was a professor at the University of Nanjing and the leader of the International Committee for the Nanjing Safety Zone, which was established to offer relief services to the Chinese people. Regarding it as a "moral necessity" to make the atrocities of the Japanese known to the world,[125] he kept a clear record of the events he witnessed, mailed the accounts to his wife, Lilliath Bates, in Shanghai, and asked her to distribute the firsthand accounts to Westerners he trusted, including Steele, Timperley, and Gould of the *Shanghai Evening Post and Mercury*.[126] Bates's article "Rape, Looting Follow Taking of the Capital," which was published anonymously on December 25, 1937 in the *North China Daily News*, was said to have been smuggled out of Nanjing and handed to the American consulate general in Shanghai by Steele.[127] The editor of the *Daily News* commented that although the article was "written with very considerable constraint," a picture of horror was visible between the lines and could be sketched in readers' minds with "terrible vividness."[128] Bates's reports were also used by Steele, Durdin, and Leslie C. Smith, a correspondent of Reuters, in their articles. Hallett Abend, another *New York Times* correspondent in Shanghai, quoted the entire report in his paper on December 24. These examples illustrate how the limited information about Nanjing was secretly shared among the journalists in China.

---

123. Ibid.
124. Tillman Durdin, "Japanese Atrocities Marked Fall of Nanking after Chinese Command Fled," *New York Times*, January 9, 1938.
125. Bates's letter to friends, April 12, 1938, in Kaiyuan Zhang ed., *Eyewitnesses to Massacre: American Missionaries Bear Witness to Japanese Atrocities in Nanjing* (New York: M. E. Sharpe, 2001), 34.
126. Bates to his wife, January 21, 1937, NMP0039, Special Collections of the Yale Divinity School Library (hereafter SCYDSL).
127. Lu, *They Were in Nanjing*, 20.
128. "Nanjing Horror," *North China Daily News*, December 25, 1937, 4.

The *China Weekly Review*'s coverage of the Nanjing Incident came even later. On December 12, the journal published a front-page article relating Mukai Toshiakai and Noda Iwao's competition in killing Chinese. Instead of quoting smuggled accounts by Westerners in Nanjing, the journal cited the *Nichi nichi shimbun*'s report—a legitimate source under the gaze of Japanese censors. Drawing on the killing competition, the journal commented that the report, although "probably exaggerated, shed considerable light on the orgy of looting, murder and rape which took place following the entrance of Japanese soldiers into the Chinese capital."[129] The editor then quoted reports from the *New York Times* on Japanese atrocities to further verify Japanese misbehavior in Nanjing.

It should be noted that the Shanghai treaty-port papers had previously been faster in reporting Chinese affairs and that their comments had often been more radical or progressive; such was the case during the Mukden and Shanghai Incidents. Their slow response and restrained attitude toward the Nanjing Incident reflected Japan's tight control of information in the city. Indeed, Japanese censors strictly controlled all outgoing information regarding Japanese soldiers' misbehavior. Timperley's dispatch to the *Manchester Guardian*, which stated that some three hundred thousand Chinese civilians had been slaughtered by the Japanese soldiers following the occupation of the district, was blocked by censors in the Danish Great Northern Cable Company, since it "was likely to harm the [Japanese] military."[130] Victor Keen, correspondent for the *New York Herald Tribune*, was also asked to withdraw his dispatch about atrocities in Nanjing by censors of the Commercial Pacific Cable Company. The *China Weekly Review* quoted the "unanimous opinion" of international correspondents who opposed the Japanese censorship, saying that "the Japanese system of censoring dispatches is the worst in the world, even worse than censorship in Russia."[131] The *Journal de Shanghai* also pointed out that "when a censorship is instituted in one's country, it is little liked; but when it is instituted in another country it is doubly disliked."[132] These complaints attracted the attention of the British and American consulates. Although both consuls general filed protests with Japanese authorities, they were too weak to exert any meaningful pressure on the censors of the Japanese army, who were bent on seizing control of all reports relating to Chinese issues.

Even if the press had been free to cover the Nanjing Incident, in December 1937 the case may still have received limited foreign attention. Parallel to the Nanjing Incident was the sinking of the USS *Panay*—an event more relevant to American interests. The Japanese air force attacked the US Navy gunboat USS *Panay* and

---

129. "How Lieutenants Mukai and Noda Exceeded Murder Quotas," *China Weekly Review*, January 1, 1938, 115.
130. "Japanese Censor Holds Up All Reports of Atrocities," *China Weekly Review*, January 22, 1938, 199.
131. Ibid., 200.
132. "The Japanese Censorship in Shanghai," *Journal de Shanghai*, January 8, 1938, no. D 2398, Shanghai Municipal Police Files.

three Standard Oil tankers on December 12 while the ships were anchored in the Yangtze River outside Nanjing. The incident immediately appeared on the front pages of major newspapers in China and abroad. The *China Weekly Review*, for example, while keeping reticent about the Nanjing Incident, closely monitored the *Panay* case in late December. Japan's attack on the *Panay*, commented the *Review*, suggested that "the crisis in China has now become an American issue and must be settled by the United States, one way or another—either get out or prepare to fight!"[133] Although the *Panay* case eclipsed the Nanjing Incident in December, it effectively instigated anti-Japanese feelings among the American public. Echoing the *Review*'s position, the *New York Times* denied Japan's explanation that the bombing was an accident. It collected various eyewitness accounts to verify that the Japanese attack was planned.[134] The paper also regarded Japanese guarantees that there would be no repetition of such "mistakes" as fraudulent. It argued that so long as the Japanese troops remained in China, the risk of fire exchanges would always be present, and the conflict would leave American nationals and property at risk:

> The Japanese Government can no more give a convincing assurance that foreigners in China will be safe from the consequences of its aggression than a burglar can give assurance that no innocent bystander will be shot when he sets out to loot a house. The only really valid guarantee that Japan can give in this matter would be the withdrawal of its invading army from the soil of China and the liquidation of this imperialist adventure.[135]

Public emotions instigated by similar comments in the press provided a context for public opinion sympathetic to China. It made the American public more receptive to the Chinese case when details of the Nanjing Incident emerged in the media in early 1938.

It was the return of the diplomats on January 6, 1938, that enabled worldwide dissemination of reports about the Japanese atrocities in Nanjing, and Tong's department played an important role in it. Tong established close connections with Westerners coming from Nanjing and organized various activities to publicize the Nanjing case through his networks abroad. One of the most important contacts was H. J. Timperley. Although Timperley in principle was a correspondent for the *Manchester Guardian*, by January 1938, he had practically become an agent of China's international propaganda office. Timperley had been on good terms with William H. Donald. This personal connection strengthened his ties with the Guomindang government from the mid-1930s. As J. M. McHugh observed, Donald "had always had a particular leaning toward him [Timperley] because he is a fellow

---

133. "Bombing of Anglo-American Ships and Future US Policy," *China Weekly Review*, December 18, 1937, 57.
134. "New Light on Panay," *New York Times*, December 19, 1937.
135. "The Sinking of Panay," *New York Times*, December 14, 1937.

Australian."¹³⁶ At the outbreak of full-scale war, Donald approached Timperley to invite him to join the international propaganda office. Timperley refused at the time, believing that he might be more useful to Donald as a correspondent in Nanjing since most of the other correspondents were stationed in North China or Shanghai. However, he changed his mind after "seeing how the Chinese were pulling in opposite directions and floundering around in their publicity work" after the fall of Shanghai.¹³⁷ He assisted Tong's propaganda in Shanghai as a member of the Anti-enemy Committee and continued to conduct propaganda for China afterward.

Timperley was in Nanjing before the Japanese army occupied the city. He established connections with Christian leaders who later became members of the International Committee of the Nanjing Safety Zone. After leaving Nanjing for Shanghai, he managed to keep in contact with his Nanjing friends. Bates, for example, regarded Timperley as a reliable channel for the distribution of his eyewitness accounts of the Nanjing Incident and frequently asked his wife to relay his reports to him.¹³⁸

Tong approached Timperley immediately after his arrival in Shanghai and proposed to pay him to collect eyewitness accounts of the Nanjing Incident and publish them in a book.¹³⁹ The book project was welcomed by the International Committee in Nanjing. The committee provided Timperley with Bates's correspondence, George Fitch's diary, and John Magee's pictures, all of which recorded Japanese atrocities in the city in great detail. For fear of Japanese retribution, however, the committee had to ask Timperley to edit the information, add accounts from other Japanese-occupied cities, and conceal his sources of information as much as possible.¹⁴⁰ Bates repeatedly demanded that Timperley rely on the facts of their accounts, avoiding unnecessary personalization.¹⁴¹ At one point, the missionaries in Nanjing even asked Timperley to slow down the editing process so as to allow more time for the Westerners in Nanjing to improve their safety conditions or wait for external assistance. Yearning to publish the book as soon as possible, Timperley was reluctant to wait. A letter by Bates suggests that Timperley was not willing to reduce the personal element of their accounts either. Bates believed that both Timperley and "his consultants in Shanghai," who were likely to be Hollington Tong and his associates, felt that personal eyewitness accounts were more direct and authentic.¹⁴² Members of the committee finally allowed Timperley to publish their accounts as soon as possible, hoping "this work in a hurry may result in greater control during later phases of

---

136. J. M. McHugh's report, Chongqing, March 8, 1938, 3/10 MLMSS, WGLP.
137. Ibid.
138. Bates to his wife, January 21, 1938, NMP0039, SCYDSL.
139. Zeng, *Zeng Xubai zizhuan*, 200–201.
140. Bates to Timperley, March 3, 1938, NMP0096, SCYDSL.
141. Bates to Timperley, March 14, 1938, NMP0097, SCYDSL.
142. Bates's letter to friends, April 12, 1938, quoted in Kaiyuan Zhang, *Eyewitnesses to Massacre*, 33–34.

this struggle, and ... heighten attention in the [W]est, both to this particular situation and to the savagery of the whole military game."[143] As a result, Timperley quickly compiled a book entitled *Japanese Terror in China* and published it simultaneously in Shanghai, London, New York, and Calcutta in mid-1938. It took less than five months from the initial plan of the book to its publication. Although Timperley stressed that the idea of producing this book was entirely his own—as an effort to oppose Japanese censorship of his telegrams[144]—it was clear that the International Department was working behind the scenes to provide funding and assistance.[145]

After the Nanjing Incident, Timperley was more and more relied upon as a key agent of the International Department, responsible for linking the Western community in China with the Guomindang propaganda institution. He approached George Fitch and persuaded him to travel to the United States and lecture to American audiences about his personal experiences in Nanjing.[146] Fitch's trip was fully funded by the International Department.[147] Timperley also approached a professor of sociology at the University of Nanjing, Lewis Smythe, who remained in Nanjing during the incident, and assisted him in publishing his eyewitness accounts of the incident with funding from the International Department.[148] Tong and Zeng later invited Timperley to Hankou to discuss plans for expanding China's overseas propaganda network.[149] He was later assigned to supervise the establishment of branch offices in New York and London.

Apart from print media, the International Department sought to publicize the Nanjing Incident through film. In January 1938, George Fitch successfully smuggled out of Nanjing film footage showing the killing and assault of Chinese civilians by Japanese soldiers. On receiving the films, Tong immediately sent Earl Leaf to London to arrange the release of these films with local film companies.[150] In London, Leaf contacted Basil Burton, a movie merchant and a member of the China Campaign Committee.[151] Knowing that most British censors did not bother to examine the

---

143. Bates to Timperley, March 21, 1938, NMP0100, SCYDSL.
144. H. J. Timperley, *The Japanese Terror in China* (Calcutta: Thacker, Spink and Co., 1938), 9.
145. Report of the International Department, Ministry of Information, June 11, 1938, conference paper, 5.3/81.6, GA.
146. H. J. Timperley to Stanley K. Hornbeck, February 16, 1938, NMP0093, SCYDSL; George A. Fitch, *My Eighty Years in China* (Taipei: Mei Ya Publications, 1974), 106.
147. Report of the International Department, Ministry of Information, June 11, 1938, conference paper, 5.3/81.6, GA.
148. Zeng, *Zeng Xubai zizhuan*, 201; Lewis S. C. Smythe, War Damage in the Nanking Area: December 1937 to March 1938 (Shanghai: Shanghai Mercury Press, 1938).
149. Zeng, *Zeng Xubai zizhuan*, 201.
150. Earl Leaf to Hollington Tong, H. J. Timperley and Wen Yuanning, March 7, 1938, London; April 2, 1938, New York, reports no. 21 and 37, Ministry of Information 9/718, SHAC. Translated by Wen Junxiong, in *Minguo dang'an* 4 (2002): 4–12.
151. Confidential report to Chiang Kai-shek, from Hollington Tong, May 6, 1938, no. 5308. Ministry of Information, SHAC, in *Minguo dang'an* 4 (2004): 7.

content on 16mm films because of their small size, Basil transferred the films from 35mm to 16mm format and edited the movies to cater to the interest of British audiences.[152]

In April, Leaf was sent to the United States to supervise film propaganda. He established connections with the supervisor of the Harmon Foundation, Mary B. Brady, who was sympathetic to China's anti-Japanese stance. Brady voluntarily took charge of distributing the film about the Nanjing Incident in the United States and advised Leaf to combine movie propaganda with public lectures to amplify their effect.[153] Meanwhile, Timperley also sent a copy of the film to Stanley K. Hornbeck, a special adviser to Secretary of State Cordell Hull, in the hope of informing him and the secretary of state of the facts of the Nanjing Incident.[154]

Tong also secretly sent his staff to Japan and circulated materials about the Nanjing incident there.[155] They took pamphlets in English and Japanese, films and photographs shot by Western missionaries, and Timperley's manuscript with them. Their target audiences were diplomats of various embassies, foreign correspondents stationed in Tokyo, Christian communities in Japan, liberal business leaders, and government officials. Through this form of what Tong called "whispering propaganda" (*eryu xuanchuan*), the International Department aimed to lay bare Japanese soldiers' misconduct in China so as to stir antiwar sentiment among the Japanese public[156] and demonstrate to the Japanese China's strong will to resist.[157]

Leaving Wuhan

The temporary capital, Wuhan, was under severe threat in October 1938. On October 24, Chiang made the painful decision to abandon the city and move west to Chongqing. Before departure, he ordered Tong to stay in Wuhan till the last minute to prepare for the last press conference the next morning. Having lost another major city along the Yangtze River, the Guomindang government was more eager than ever to explain to Western journalists about China's position and to restore their confidence in the country's will and capacity to resist Japan. Acutely aware of the danger of remaining in Wuhan, Tong had sent all of his staff to Changsha. The only staff member he kept for assistance was his associate and friend Wei Jingmeng, who

---

152. Earl Leaf to Hollington Tong, H. J. Timperley and Wen Yuanning, March 7, 1938, London; April 2, 1938, New York, reports No. 21 and 37, Ministry of Information 9/718, SHAC, in *Minguo dang'an* 4 (2002): 4–12.
153. Ibid.
154. H. J. Timperley to Stanley K. Hornbeck, February 16, 1938, NMP0093, SCYDSL.
155. Report of the International Department, Ministry of Information, June 11, 1938, conference paper, 5.3/81.6, GA.
156. Confidential report to Chiang Kai-shek, from Hollington Tong, May 6, 1938, no. 5308, SHAC.
157. Report of the International Department, Ministry of Information, June 11, 1938, conference paper, 5.3/81.6, GA.

insisted on staying with him. As the Japanese troops approached, any extra minute in Wuhan was a gamble of life and death. At midnight, Zhou Enlai had phoned Tong four times within half an hour, urging Tong to catch the last truck with him at 1 a.m. to avoid being caught by the Japanese.[158] Tong declined and insisted that he would not leave before the press conference was finished.

With the Japanese army on Wuhan's doorstep, telephone communications were interrupted. To inform foreign journalists about the press conference, Tong solicited the assistance of Durdin, who drove his 1925 Ford to collect correspondents and bring them to the conference venue at the American Army YMCA. At 10:30 a.m., the press conference started. The main message was to boost the correspondents' confidence in China's resistance and to persuade them that the loss of Wuhan was part of a strategy to win the final victory:

> We have decided to abandon the Wuhan center as a necessary incident in the course of our all-front warfare.... It must not be mistakenly viewed as a military reverse or retreat. For the key to victorious conclusion of our war of resistance lies not in what happens to Wuhan but in the conservation of our strength for continuous resistance.... [China] is a nation of vast territory, huge population and large resources. The wider the sphere of hostilities extends, the stronger will become our active position.[159]

Before leaving Wuhan, Tong made a last inspection of the telegraph administration and the garrison headquarters to ensure smooth transmissions of foreign dispatches. At 7 p.m., the Japanese cavalry entered the city, and Tong together with other garrison commanders had to leave Wuhan on foot since driving by car would have easily attracted the attention of Japanese soldiers. It took them ten days to reach Changsha, with most of the walking done at night. When Tong appeared before Chiang on November 5, Chiang was surprised and "genuinely moved" to see that his colleague had survived.[160]

---

158. Tong, *Dateline: China*, 63.
159. Ibid., 64.
160. Ibid., 65.

Figure 16
Sapajou, "Double Suicide?" *North China Daily News*, July 28, 1937.

8
Confronting Encirclement
Chongqing, 1939–1941

After the battle of Wuhan, the Sino-Japanese War reached a stalemate. Both sides had failed to win a large-scale victory on the battlefield. Realizing that a quick end to the war was impossible, the Japanese General Staff Office decided to slow down the offensive to ease the strain on the domestic economy. More focus was therefore put on rear area operation, including suppression of Nationalist and Communist guerrillas and collaboration with Chinese officials in the occupied areas.[1] China, in addition to establishing a series of fortress zones across the country to divert Japanese forces, was keen to seek assistance from other Powers.

The period between 1939 and 1941 was the most difficult for the Chiang Kai-shek regime. The government had to abandon the lower Yangtze River region, the base of Chiang's political and financial power, and move westward to a far less developed inland city, Chongqing. On top of the pain of moving was the lack of meaningful foreign support and the Powers' continuous appeasement to Japan. Apart from a limited supply of munitions, the Soviet Union was unwilling to engage in a war with Japan when the conflict with Germany on its western border was imminent. A cease-fire agreement between the Soviet Union and Japan in September 1939 temporarily freed the latter from a military challenge in the north and allowed it to allocate more military resources to fighting in Sichuan Province—the Nationalists' new headquarters in the Southwest. Under Japanese pressure, the British government temporarily closed the Burma Road in 1940, then China's only conduit for foreign aid. Moreover, the defection of Wang Jingwei's clique to Japan further drained the Guomindang's political authority, sapped Chinese morale, and confused the Western powers about the Guomindang's willingness to resist. Meanwhile, cracks began to appear on the united front. Mutual distrust between the Guomindang and the Communist Party intensified and eventually escalated into a large-scale military conflict in the southern part of Anhui Province in 1941. At this critical stage, information control was a matter of survival for the government.

---

1. Hans J. Van de Ven, *War and Nationalism in China, 1925–1945* (London: Routledge, 2003), 233; John Hunter Boyle, *China and Japan at War, 1937–1945: The Politics of Collaboration* (Stanford: Stanford University Press, 1972), 135–66.

The Move to Chongqing

Chongqing was chosen as the capital of the Guomindang government at war for strategic reasons. It was the most important city in Sichuan, a key province in the hinterland, with huge agricultural areas surrounded by high mountains and cliffs. The mountains served as a natural barrier against the Japanese advance. Although the Yangtze River, running through the Sichuan Basin, connects the area with the lower reaches where the Japanese troops were garrisoned, the gorges east of Chongqing drastically narrow the river channel, making attacks by water difficult. In addition to this favorable topography, moisture rising from the Sichuan plain was blocked by the surrounding mountains and created dense fog during winter that hid the city from the enemy's air raids. For the Guomindang government, which had insufficient air force to intercept the large number of Japanese bombers, the mist provided a natural protection for the new capital. Most importantly, the region was self-sufficient. The Sichuan valley, irrigated and nourished by the Yangtze River, produces a wide variety of food crops. The surrounding mountains also contain rich mineral resources, necessary for basic military production.

Nevertheless, Chongqing had its drawbacks as a war capital. While natural barriers shielded the region from Japanese attacks, they also made communications with the outside difficult. The city was connected with Hong Kong by air and with Burma by a few winding and treacherous mountain paths. Neither people nor war materials reached Chongqing easily. Because of its remote location, people from the area were isolated from other parts of the country. They were historically the last to give allegiance to each new central authority. The Guomindang government had only tenuous links with the local leaders who had amassed great power as a result of successive revolts against alien rule. In 1938, the Sichuan people had little consciousness of nationality. Local warlords and native inhabitants considered Chiang Kai-shek's arrival to be another invasion. It took years for Chiang Kai-shek and Zhang Qun to bring the local warlords under temporary control and to convince the native people of the significance of unity against Japan.[2] In addition, Sichuan was separated from central and east China in terms of culture and industrial development. The local Chongqing people, who were little influenced by Western modernization, adhered to old traditions. As Theodore H. White, an American journalist in Chongqing during wartime, observed, local marriages were still arranged by parents. The native Chongqing residents disapproved of the lipstick worn by downriver girls and disliked their frizzled hair; they were even shocked by boys and girls eating together in public restaurants. The coastal people, in return, also expressed contempt for the Chongqing

---

2. Guo Xuyin, ed., *Guomindang paixi douzheng shi* [A history of the Guomindang factional struggles] (Shanghai: Shanghai renmin chubanshe, 1992), 421–44.

locals, regarding them as "a curious species of second-grade inhabitant" who had not even seen a street car.³

If the move from Nanjing to Wuhan did not cause much pain since both cities shared similar natural conditions and were on a par in terms of industrial development, the move from Wuhan to Chongqing was a tough challenge. Propaganda officials who followed the department from the coastal cities to Chongqing found it difficult to adapt to the climate—too chilly and humid in winter. Their physical discomfort often led to forms of depression. Hollington Tong noticed that his staff, as well as the foreign journalists in his department, always underwent a subtle and depressing change under the heavy winter mist.⁴

Worse than the climate was the lack of facilities and daily essentials. Tong's international department took over the Bashan Middle School on the outskirts of Chongqing as its headquarters. The officials, accustomed to modern houses and buildings made of concrete, had to put up with bamboo walls that barely sheltered them from the wind and rain. As Tong recalled:

> It was a large rambling mud and plaster structure, with loose tiles for a roof. The doors did not lock. They did not even close tightly. There was a crack in the door to my office through which every passer-by could peek to see what I was doing or whom I was interviewing. When there was a storm, the tiles of the roof would fly off, and the mud plaster ceilings would soften and fall. Rats gnawed their way through books and papers at night until we learned how to lock the books and papers in closed boxes.⁵

Behind the school, Tong built dormitories for his staff members. While residential compounds close to the office, as was the case for the Bank of China,⁶ were designed to impose corporate discipline onto all aspects of daily life, Tong's plan was partly out of practical concern: staff members could quickly go home and attend to their personal belongings during air raids. Unmarried junior officials were crammed together, with four or more sharing a small room. Each family had only one room, no matter how many members had to be squeezed into the limited space. Most rooms were unheated. Officials were often seen shivering in their overcoats all day during winter, and the same coat would be used for a blanket at night.

Staff toiled away in the office only to find that their paper-money salary lost its value fast, to the point where an entire month's earnings could be spent on a single ordinary party.⁷ People were constantly threatened by hunger. Children were

---

3. Theodore Harold White, *Thunder out of China* (London: Victor Gollancz, 1947), 9.
4. Hollington Kong Tong, *Dateline: China; The Beginning of China's Press Relations with the World* (New York: Rockport Press, 1950), 108.
5. Ibid., 109.
6. Wen-hsin Yeh, *Shanghai Splendor: Economic Sentiments and the Making of Modern China, 1843–1949* (Berkeley: University of California Press, 2007), 88–89.
7. White, *Thunder out of China*, 18.

encouraged to collect whatever they could eat in nearby mountains during the day. Officials often came back from the market empty handed because the government coupons were insufficient and their salary too low to purchase food at market prices.[8] This wartime austerity frequently caused malnutrition. Even high-ranking officials of Tong's department were not exempt from privation. Zeng Xubai once passed out at a gathering at the British embassy from hunger and stress. He was genuinely moved by the British diplomats' offer of milk and eggs, a pure luxury that he had not touched for a long time.[9]

Staff members of the department were not well paid in comparison to other government bureaus. Compared to the top-ranking official of the Salt Inspectorate, who earned 800 yuan during the mid-1930s,[10] Tong's monthly salary at 240 yuan equaled that of a midrank staff from the inspectorate. A large part of their personal income came from additional allowances that depended on their work performance and perhaps the size of the family they had to support. Indeed, Tong had repeatedly appealed to Chiang to raise the wages of his team, complaining that the average income of the department was lower than a typist from the profit sector, such as banks and customs offices. Their income covered only a third of the cost of an average five-member family. Most of his staff had to take loans from the bank or sell their personal belongings to make ends meet.[11] The staff members nevertheless remained loyal to the department. There was no personnel change in the key sections during the war. Indeed, the war situation limited their options for job hopping. Yet, beyond that, a mixture of patriotism, preexisting personal friendships before the war, and Tong's charismatic leadership bound the group together. Ye Gongchao favorably recalled the days working for the International Department under Tong as "the most pleasant experience" of his life. He commended Tong as a leader who trusted his colleagues "like a caring old brother."[12] His sentiments were shared by many who worked with Tong. "Unassuming and easy to approach" (*pingyi jinren*) was the general impression Tong left among his colleagues.[13]

---

8. See Kobayashi Fumio's quote of his interview of an economist living in Chongqing during the war, Kobayashi Fumio, "Kunan zhong de Chongqing" [Wartime hardship in Chongqing], in *Chongqing wenshi ziliao* [Historical materials of Chongqing] (Chongqing: Xinan daxue chubanshe, 1988), 30:85–86.
9. Zeng Xubai, *Zeng Xubai zizhuan* [An autobiography of Zeng Xubai] (Taipei: Lianjing chuban shiye gongsi, 1988), 261.
10. Julia C. Strauss, *Strong Institutions in Weak Polities: State Building in Republican China, 1927–1940* (Oxford: Clarendon Press, 1998), 36.
11. Hollington Tong to Chiang Kai-shek, 718(4)–332, Second Historical Archives of China, Nanjing (hereafter SHAC).
12. Ye Gongchao, "Huainian Dong Xianguang xiansheng," in Dong Xianguang xiansheng zhuisilu bianji weiyuanhui, *Dong Xianguang jiniance* [In Memory of Hollington Tong] (Taipei: Dong Xianguang xiansheng zhuisilu bianji weiyuanhui, 1972), 22.
13. See other articles in *Dong Xianguang jiniance*.

Position	Name	Salary (yuan)	Special Cost	Allowance	Special Allowance	Total
Vice Minister *Fu buzhang*	Hollington Tong	240	320	100		660
Head of Department *Chuzhang*	Zeng Xubai	179.2	192	100	64	595.2
English Editor *Yingwen bianji*	James A. MacCausland			400		400
Head of Section *Kezhang*	Shen Jianhong	153.6	50	50	196.4	450
	Ji Zejin	153.6	50	50	196.4	450
	Chen Yaozhu	153.6	50	50	196.4	450
	Cui Wanqiu	153.6	50	50	126	379.6
Coordinator *Zhuanyuan*	Ni Yuanqing	200		50	100	350
	Zheng Jun	200		35	100	335
	Zhu Xinmin			300	100	400
	Wu Zhuosheng	160		60		220
Commissioner *Tepaiyuan*	Wei Jingmeng	150		95	20	265
	Wang Jiayu	150		65		215
	Lin Zhong	160		65		225
Clerk *Keyuan*	Sun Guodong	140		35		175
Administrator *Banshiyuan*	Qian Binhuan	73		57		130
	Liao Hongyi	48		25		73

Diagram 5
Selected payroll of the International Department.
Source: No. 718 (4)–10, the Second Historical Archives of China, estimated time: 1941.

Despite the primitive conditions, the department managed to resume its daily operation and make some amendments to propaganda policies soon after it had settled in. While the department in Wuhan was keen to expose war atrocities and Japan's brutal treatment of Chinese soldiers and civilians, it retreated from such a position in Chongqing. The International Department instead focused on news about Chinese soldiers' strong will to resist and progress in construction at the rear. The goal was to convince Western audiences that China had not lost the war and was capable of further resistance. As Zeng Xubai explained, China has successfully obtained foreign sympathy by exposing Japanese soldiers' brutality and the trauma of Chinese society in the war. Further elaboration on these aspects would not yield much. It would simply boost the confidence of the Japanese army while sapping the morale of the Chinese.¹⁴ Indeed, at this stage of the war, the department strove harder to win Westerners' confidence in China than their sympathy.

The shift of direction was revealed in the content of department-sponsored publications. Among the sixty pamphlets published by the department in 1939, for example, only *The Bombing of Chongqing* depicted suffering caused by Japanese forces. The rest either elaborated on China's wartime achievements or exposed the harm that the Japanese expansion had brought to the United States and Europe.¹⁵ The department's official journal *China at War* also emphasized China's victory on the front line and the development of southwest China. When the Japanese air raid on Chongqing was most intensive in 1940, the October issue took only a detached position, quoting air raids statistics, including the loss of life and damage to property, instead of graphically depicting the trauma caused by the attacks with personal stories.¹⁶ The goal was to increase the perceived urgency of international assistance while avoiding instigating complaints from domestic audiences who were weary of the war.

The renewed propaganda framework, however, was a hard sell for foreign journalists. While they were eager to assist the Chinese government in exposing Japanese atrocities during the Nanjing Incident, they were not ready to praise the Guomindang as Chiang wished. Their instinctive desire for sensation, conflict, and novelty did not dispose them to report about mundane daily life at the rear. Meanwhile, they remained highly skeptical of the Guomindang's operations. Corruption, graft, endless political treason, and split characterized their understanding of the regime, which contrasted sharply with the materials supplied by Tong's office.

The government's tightening of its censorship after moving to Chongqing further estranged foreign journalists. The change of policy was a result of Tong's loss of censorship power in the cumbersome bureaucratic system. In addition to Tong's department, a news censorship committee and a telegraph censorship office attached to the Commission of Military Affairs and a Censorship Office on Books and Magazines affiliated with the Executive Yuan were all involved in censorship. Each had a powerful party leader behind it to uphold its own censorship guidelines. A message granted a pass by Tong's office may later have been marked by other offices as unfit for publication. As Reuters chief correspondent in China Zhao Minheng observed, Tong's office was "flooded with instructions from various government offices specifically stating that certain news must not be sent or that certain news must not go out without their approval."¹⁷ Yet when Tong sent information to the relevant officials to verify details,

---

14. Zeng Xubai, "Kangzhan zhong de guoji xuanchuan" [International propaganda during the Sino-Japanese War], *Zhongguo xinwen xuehui niankan* [Yearbook of Chinese Press Institute], no. 1 (1942): 16; Zeng, *Zeng Xubai zizhuan*, 233.
15. Work report, the International Department of the Ministry of Information, 1938–1941, general documents 496/294, GA.
16. *China at War* 5, no. 3 (October 1940).
17. Zhao Minheng to C. J. Chancellor, June 9, 1941, 718(4)–87, SHAC.

most of the messages were suppressed not in the interest of Chinese publicity but for fear of causing offense to officials and certain offices. Even if approval could have been obtained, messages were often stalled there for hours or even days, either because censors failed to understand the importance of providing timely public information or because they could not be bothered to reply to Tong.[18]

In October 1940, the department introduced a three-level censorship system. Two junior censors were assigned to check all outgoing dispatches around the clock. Information beyond their judgement would be sent to midlevel censors, with Wei Jingmeng and Ji Zejin in charge. Tong and Zeng were at the top to check information concerning military affairs and activities of the leading officials, to which junior staff had no access. The new system was established at this critical juncture partly to declare the department's authority over censorship. By delegating censorship power to lower officials, Tong also intended to create a buffer between him and his rivals. He hired graduates of the journalism department from the Central Political Institute—a C. C. Clique institution—as junior censors, hoping their connections with the head of the institute, Chen Guofu, would improve coordination. Yet the system proved to make the situation even worse. The junior censors at the bottom of the censorship hierarchy had neither the power nor the interest in resisting external challenges to Tong's authority. Their key priority was to keep their jobs. Trained in a political institute, they were more accustomed to rigidly following established discourses than to approve reports that were closest to the truth. They ended up authorizing only messages already published in the morning papers.[19]

If during the Wuhan days Chiang could shield Tong's office from intervention, he was reluctant to do so in Chongqing. Given the grim international and domestic environment, some dilution of control over information from Tong's office was necessary to recalibrate the political balance among Chiang's factions. Political stability was the priority in a volatile period. Moreover, Chiang did not entirely share Tong's vision of a liberal news policy. He found it preferable to have full authority to curb the spread of certain information that he saw unfit to go public. On September 8, 1940, for example, he forbade the distribution of news about inflation. A month later, he secretly ordered Wang Shijie, then minister of information, to censor news about petitions for a raise in wages.[20]

After a brief idyllic period for the censorship system and for journalists during the Wuhan days, censorship returned to its old ways, where selection criteria remained a mystery and the process continued to be opaque. Israel Epstein, then a correspondent for the London *Daily Telegraph* in Chongqing, recalled that "no mention was

---

18. Plan to improve international propaganda, 718(5)–12, SHAC.
19. Zhao Minheng to C. J. Chancellor, June 9, 1941, 718(4)–87, SHAC.
20. Sichuan difangzhi bianzuan weiyuanhui, *Sichuan shengzhi* (*waishi zhi*) [Sichuan Affairs, foreign-related issues] (Chengdu: Bashu shushe, 2001), 510.

permitted in news dispatches from foreign correspondents about Kuomintang-Communist differences, the existence of cliques or quarrels within the Kuomintang, the movements and personal life of the Generalissimo."[21] Description of the deteriorating economic situation was forbidden. Correspondents were not even allowed to mention that Chongqing's streets were dirty.[22] The censored information was nevertheless not entirely discarded. Tong's department often selected and compiled foreign journalists' reports on domestic issues into pamphlets for internal reference among Chinese leaders.[23] But for journalists who were unable to access these internal reference documents, they had no way of knowing whether their articles would ever see the light of day.

Tong did not give up advocating a liberal news policy. He considered that an effective news policy was to proactively provide counter discourse rather than blocking unfavorable messages.[24] This vision was not shared by traditional party officials, who were uncomfortable with public debate. Keenly aware of the negative effect of the censorship on foreign-targeted propaganda, Tong often hinted to foreign correspondents that they should file dispatches early in the morning before his immediate superior came to the office to decide on the day's censorship guidelines.[25] But his personal belief in liberal journalism could not change the government's increasingly strict control of information as well as the damage to the credibility of Chinese sources that was a result of this excessive control. By the end of the war, people's distrust of the government's censorship system was so strong that the journalists' genuine reports on the government's efforts were commonly regarded as propaganda.[26]

The Press Hotel

Despite these wartime hardships, Tong contrived to provide better conditions for Western journalists in Chongqing. He obtained a 20,000 yuan "personal donation" from Finance Minister Kong Xiangxi and built a Press Hotel near the department headquarters to accommodate them.[27] The hotel had running water and electricity, a luxury unavailable even to Tong himself, who lived in a nearby hut built on the remains of an old pavilion. While people outside were starving, the hotel provided a Western-style breakfast, and Chinese lunch and dinner every day. Servants

---

21. Stephen R. MacKinnon and Oris Friesen, *China Reporting: An Oral History of American Journalism in the 1930s and 1940s* (Berkeley: University of California Press, 1987), 107–8.
22. Ibid.
23. Sichuan difangzhi bianzuan weiyuanhui, *Sichuan shengzhi*, 509.
24. Plan to improve international propaganda, 718(5)–12, SHAC.
25. Israel Epstein, *My China Eye: Memoirs of a Jew and a Journalist* (San Francisco: Long River Press, 2005), 131.
26. White, *Thunder out of China*, 27.
27. Zeng, *Zeng Xubai zizhuan*, 236.

were hired to clean the rooms for the residents regularly. The wholesale service cost the journalists less than five US dollars per month.[28] To facilitate the journalists' correspondence with the outside world, Tong coordinated with the Ministry of Communications to open a post office inside the hotel. In addition, he put the department's car, a rare extravagance in Chongqing, at the disposal of visiting journalists for their official business. As William E. Daugherty, a contemporary scholar commented, "a foreign correspondent is often treated like an official foreign dignitary" while staying in Chongqing.[29] The Press Hotel together with the various forms of support was an application of Tong's "hospitality theory": hospitable service was conducive to a good impression of China, and a favorable impression was likely to translate into friendly reports in the foreign press.[30]

Yet the hotel was not as hospitable as it appeared to be. The activities of Western journalists and correspondences were closely scrutinized. Dai Li, whose Bureau of Investigation and Statistics of the Military Affairs Commission (known as Juntong) controlled mail and telegraphs, monitored the journalists' activities. Any anomalies were reported directly to Chiang Kai-shek.[31] In April 1939, for example, the dispatches and correspondence of Robert P. Martin of the United Press were closely monitored by the International Department after he was charged with leaking confidential military information about the development of China's air force in an article to the Hong Kong–based *South China Daily News*. Although Chiang conceded to Tong's petition to exempt him from deportation, Chiang still requested heightened surveillance of his activities.[32]

In wartime Chongqing, both the International Department and the Juntong were involved in censorship, with the former conducting the job openly and the latter secretly. Tong's belief in liberal journalism at times clashed with Dai's inclination for stricter controls. In August 1939, the Division of Investigations of Chongqing Garrison Command's Guards (Chongqing weishu silingbu jichachu), a key office of the Juntong, proposed a plan to tap the long-distance phone calls of foreign journalists. Zeng Xubai rejected the plan, worrying that such a "daring" activity might undermine the department's international propaganda efforts.[33] Meanwhile, foreign journalists were not entirely ignorant of the surveillance. Emily Hahn, an American

---

28. Ibid., 237.
29. William E. Daugherty, "China's Official Publicity in the United States," *Public Opinion Quarterly* 6, no. 1 (April 1, 1942): 78.
30. Report of the International Department, Ministry of Information, June 11, 1938, conference paper, 5.3/81.6,GA.
31. Frederic E. Wakeman, *Spymaster: Dai Li and the Chinese Secret Service* (Berkeley: University of California Press, 2003), 265.
32. Wu Yanjun, Xu Yiwen, and Liu Chang, "Kangzhan shiqi zai Yu waiguo jizhe huodong jishi" [Activities of the foreign journalists in Chongqing during the Sino-Japanese War], in *Chongqing wenshi ziliao*, 30:152.
33. Ibid., 157.

writer, had refused to live in the Press Hotel during her visit to Chongqing, partly due to its "maddening lack of privacy."[34]

The existence of the Press Hotel, nevertheless, was generally welcomed by journalists of various news organizations, especially in the early days in Chongqing when those who entertained a genuine hope for a united front were commonly impressed by China's resistance. Long-term residents included foreign advisers to the International Department T. J. Timperley, Maurice Votaw, J. A. MacCausland, Melville Jacoby, and Theodore H. White. The hotel also attracted correspondents from Reuters, the Associated Press, the United Press, as well as Israel Epstein and A. T. Steele, China correspondent for the *New York Herald Tribune*, the *Chicago Daily News*, and the *New York Times*.[35] They irreverently referred to the Press Hotel as "Holly's Hotel" (Holly being the nickname for Hollington). Most of them had a favorable impression of the time they spent in the hotel when recalling their Chongqing days decades later, although they used to complain heavily about the broken lights, leaking roofs, lack of running water, and damage by rats.[36]

The competition for news among residents of the Press Hotel was fierce. Rivalry between the two US news agencies, the United Press (UP) and the Associate Press (AP), was especially bitter. Zhao Minheng, Reuters chief correspondent in China, recorded in his memoir that the two agencies kept close watch on each other's activities, each fearing that they would be left behind by the other. When the phone rang in the AP office, the UP staff working next door would immediately call the Central News Agency, inquiring whether the agency had issued any news. After learning that a UP correspondent would be absent at a dinner party for foreign journalists held by a high official, the AP staff also declined the invitation, choosing to wait by the office phone so as not to miss any news that the UP might garner during the party.[37]

In addition to better living conditions, the department also supplied the journalists with information on the war. It resumed the news conference system and increased the frequency of conferences from once a week, as in Wuhan, to twice a week.[38] The most popular official among the journalists was Xu Peigen, a German-trained military officer who always brought fresh news from the front line. Chen Bingzhang and Zhang Pingqun, two associates of Kong Xiangxi, were also well received due to their fluent English and their updates on economic issues.[39] In addition to the press

---

34. Emily Hahn, *China to Me: A Partial Autobiography* (Garden City, NY: Garden City Publishing, 1946), 169.
35. Chen Yunge, "Kangzhan chuqi waiguo jizhe zai chongqing de huodong" [Foreign journalists' activities in Chongqing during the early Sino-Japanese War], in *Chongqing wenshi ziliao*, 30:146–47.
36. Zhao Minheng, *Caifang wushi nian* [Fifty years of interviews] (Taipei: Longwen chubanshe, 1994), 95; Chen Yunge, "Kangzhan chuqi waiguo jizhe zai chongqing de huodong," in *Chongqing wenshi ziliao*, 30:147.
37. Zhao, *Caifang wushi nian*, 89–90.
38. Work report, the International Department of the Ministry of Information, 1938–1941, general documents 496/294, GA.
39. Chen Yunge, "Kangzhan chuqi waiguo xinwen jizhe zai Chongqing de huodong," in *Chongqing wenshi ziliao*, 30:147.

conference, the department actively put journalists in touch with high-ranking Chinese officials for exclusive interviews. On average, twenty such interviews were arranged every month between 1939 and 1940. The figure rose to thirty-four in early 1941.[40] Although Chiang banned exclusive interviews at one point in 1940, fearing that the activity might disturb the government's normal operations, he lifted the ban after the visit of Roy Howard, head of the US Scripps-Howard chain of newspapers, who wrote a series of articles advocating firmer US policies against Japan after returning to the United States.[41] Foreign journalists in Chongqing were also constantly hired as propagandists to defend the position of the Guomindang government. Robert P. Martin of the UP was invited by the International Department to write an article about China's military and financial achievements in Chongqing to counter the anti-Chiang arguments made by the UP's Shanghai correspondent.[42]

The Voice of China

With the move of the capital, Guomindang officials helplessly watched their best cable and wireless infrastructure, which they had carefully built up in the past decades, become effective communication facilities for their enemies. Although the circle of mountains protected them from the Japanese army, it also blocked basic mail delivery and thus separated them from their homeland in the areas of China to which they could not return. Communication conditions were even worse after the Japanese occupation of Guangzhou in October 1938 and the closure of the Burma Road in 1940 by the British government under Japan's pressure. This ruthlessly cut the Guomindang government's already limited channels of communication to the outside and left the regime even more isolated. A new route was urgently needed to ensure undisturbed communications between the International Department and its external networks.

The International Department relied heavily on wireless devices, radio in particular, to disseminate news. Before the fall of Wuhan, the government had already begun to prepare for an international radio station in Chongqing. The station, the Voice of China (call signal XGOY), was completed in November 1938. However, both the Central Broadcasting Administration controlled by the C. C. Clique and the International Department vied for direct control of it. The controversy dragged on for four months despite the urgent need for wireless connections. The International Department eventually secured control of the station with the help of Chiang Kai-shek,

---

40. Work report, the International Department of the Ministry of Information, 1938–1941, general documents 496/294, GA.
41. Tong, *Dateline: China*, 130.
42. Wu Yanjun, Xu Yiwen, and Liu Chang, "Kangzhan shiqi zai Yu waiguo jizhe huodong jishi," in *Chongqing wenshi ziliao*, 30:156.

and the station aired its first foreign-language program in February 1939.⁴³ Like all other offices of the International Department, the radio station was poorly equipped. It even lacked a soundproof studio for broadcasting. Designated listeners in the United States reported that they could hear dogs barking and ducks quacking during news reporting. The complaint finally pushed the Central Broadcasting Administration to install a proper soundproof system.⁴⁴

The station benefited from Tong's foreign staff. Maurice Votaw, who had previously taught journalism at St. John's University and was a good friend of Zeng Xubai, was a regular broadcaster. Melville Jacoby, a postgraduate in journalism from Stanford University, frequently helped edit scripts. James MacCausland, an Oxford-trained Sinologist, was charged with writing broadcasting scripts and translating Chiang Kai-shek's orders and speeches.⁴⁵ These foreign journalists became valuable assets in Tong's office. Tong commented that after Votaw took charge, he "had no worries in connection with the details of editing."⁴⁶ He also considered it "fortunate" to recruit Jacoby to their team and considered it a great loss for the department when Jacoby was employed by *Time* magazine in December 1939.⁴⁷ Meanwhile, Zeng developed a friendship with MacCausland. Although Zeng was sometimes discomfited by MacCausland's complete neglect for his appearance and his primitive way of life, which he deliberately adopted to share the hardship of war with the Chinese nationals, Zeng deeply admired his profound knowledge about China, his dedication to his work, and his genuine personality. More than forty years after the war, Zeng still vividly remembered details of MacCausland's eccentric behavior in Chongqing. He devoted a whole section in his memoir to commemorating MacCausland, who was bitterly ridiculed by other foreign journalists and eventually suffered from a mental disorder and disappeared into the mountains in Chongqing in the mid-1940s.⁴⁸ This emotional attachment between the department members and the foreign journalists was reciprocal. After Melville Jacoby died in an air crash in Australia in 1942, his mother made a donation to rebuild the backyard of the Press Hotel, possibly in accordance with Jacoby's will.⁴⁹

Tong was also keen to extend the influence of XGOY to the United States and strengthen the department's connection with its international network via radio transmission. While broadcasting facilities in Chongqing were not powerful enough

---

43. Central Radio Administration to the International Department, January 31, 1940, 5.3/140.12, GA; Tong, *Dateline: China*, 99.
44. Tong, *Dateline: China*, 121.
45. Ibid., 102–3; Zeng, *Zeng Xubai zizhuan*, 269.
46. Tong, *Dateline: China*, 102.
47. Ibid.
48. Zeng, *Zeng Xubai zizhuan*, 269–78.
49. Zhao, *Caifang wushi nian*, 95.

to transmit the program directly to the United States, the signal of XGOY was relayed in Manila to the US National Broadcasting Company's network.[50] In Ventura, Southern California, Charles Stuart, an American dentist and wireless amateur, was installed to check the quality of the program. Sympathetic to China's resistance against Japan, Stuart conducted his service on a voluntary basis. He received and recorded programs from XGOY every morning at six o'clock, transcribed the recording with the help of his wife, and relayed typewritten copies of the transcripts to the department's New York branch, where the daily news release *Voice of China* was issued via the Chinese News Service.[51] He kept in constant correspondence with Chongqing, reporting about the quality of the wireless signals and offering suggestions for improvements.[52]

Stuart was responsible for receiving not only daily radio programs but also radio mails from the same station. Because of the isolated location of Chongqing, the high cost of press dispatches, and the limited cable facilities, the International Department strove to make the best use of XGOY. Each foreign correspondent was allowed to use it once a week to send up to fifteen hundred words. Journalists who transmitted information unfriendly to the Guomindang government would have their privilege withdrawn for up to two weeks as punishment.[53] On the other side of the ocean, Stuart transcribed between three and ten thousand words daily from XGOY, including both broadcasting and news dispatches, and sent them to the department's various branches in the United States for further distribution.[54] He continued the service for six years until the end of the Sino-Japanese War and practically became a one-man connecting station between Chongqing and its US news network during wartime. His service rendered the continuous flow of war reports from Chongqing to the United State possible. It also saved the Guomindang government a large amount of money on international cable transmissions. After the war, Chiang Kai-shek invited Stuart to Nanjing and awarded him US$100,000 for his contribution.[55] For the first time, Stuart was able to match the voices of the broadcasters with their faces and meet the radio staff members whose signals he had received every day.

The Voice of China broadcast around the clock, targeting audiences in North America, Europe, Russia, South Asia, and Australia. Its programs were in English, French, Japanese, Russian, Dutch, Hindi, and Arabic. The International Department

---

50. Guangbo jiemu, March, 1940, files of the Guomindang Ministry of Information, 062, Chongqing Municipal Archives (hereafter CMA).
51. Daugherty, "China's Official Publicity in the United States," 81; Tong, *Dateline: China*, 121; MacKinnon and Friesen, *China Reporting*, 110.
52. The International Department's correspondence with Charles Stuart, February 20, 1941, files of the Guomindang Ministry of Information, 070, CMA.
53. MacKinnon and Friesen, *China Reporting*, 110.
54. *Radio Amateur's Journal* 3 (1947): 35.
55. Zeng, *Zeng Xubai zizhuan*, 260.

paid special attention to broadcasting to the United States. Compared to the daily program to Britain, which lasted an hour, the station broadcast to the United States for about three hours per day, one hour to the eastern region and about two hours to the western region. The programs included news, speeches, and music. The programs were not only delivered in English but also in Mandarin, Cantonese, and Japanese. The different languages pointed to the multiple audiences it sought to appeal to and the diverse goals it aspired to: to inform US audiences about Chongqing's situation and activities, to invoke patriotic sentiments among Chinese communities in the United States, and to instigate antiwar sentiment among the Japanese audience. XGOY's broadcasting received Soong May-ling's support. She constantly gave speeches via the radio, although this job required her to arrive at the studio before dawn, and technical failures sometimes nullified her efforts.[56]

Chongqing local time	Program	US Eastern Standard Time
7:00 a.m.	Chinese-language news	7:00 p.m.
7:15 a.m.	Chinese music	7:15 p.m.
7:20 a.m.	English-language speech	7:20 p.m.
7:30 a.m.	English-language news	7:30 p.m.
7:40 a.m.	Cantonese-language news	7:40 p.m.
7:50 a.m.	Japanese-language news	7:50 p.m.
8:00 a.m.	National anthem	8:00 p.m.
8:05 a.m.	Stop	8:05 p.m.
		Pacific Standard Time
1:00 p.m.	Cantonese-language news	10:00 p.m.
1:15 p.m.	Chinese music	10:15 p.m.
1:20 p.m.	English-language speech	10:20 p.m.
1:30 p.m.	English-language news	10:30 p.m.
1:40 p.m.	Western music	10:40 p.m.
1:50 p.m.	Stop	10:50 p.m.
9:00 p.m.	English-language news	6:00 a.m.
9:10 p.m.	English-language speech	6:10 a.m.
9:20 p.m.	Western music	6:20 a.m.
9:30 p.m.	Cantonese-language news	6:30 a.m.
9:45 p.m.	Stop	6:45 a.m.

Diagram 6
XGOY's broadcasting timetable to North America, 1940.
Source: Guangbo jiemu, 1940, files of the Guomindang Ministry of Information, Chongqing Municipal Archives.

---

56. Tong, *Dateline: China*, 99.

Outside Chongqing, the Hong Kong branch office became the primary liaison station between the government and the outside world. In February 1939, Chiang Kai-shek allocated special funding to Mao Qingxiang, his confidential secretary in charge of code breaking, to strengthen the international propaganda office in Hong Kong.[57] The office served the Chongqing headquarters in two capacities: it acted as Chongqing's gatekeeper, selecting only suitable visitors to Chongqing, and it served as a distribution center for Chongqing's publications. Before granting visitors permits to enter Chongqing, Tong, with the help of Chiang's intelligence service, would fully investigate their background, the aim of their visit, and their attitudes toward the Guomindang government. Tong received only visitors friendly to Chiang's regime and rejected any who might be connected with the Wang Jingwei government or were enthusiastic about communism. Meanwhile, the Hong Kong office continued to publish English-language journals and pamphlets, and distributed them to foreign readers in Hong Kong and Shanghai who had been identified by the International Department.

Yet the propaganda work in Hong Kong was conducted with great difficulty. In order not to instigate conflicts with Japan, the British government strictly observed a policy of neutrality, preventing any anti-Japanese messages from being distributed.[58] The office had made various attempts to obtain assistance from the Hong Kong government to clamp down on pro-Japanese voices and boycott anti-Chiang activities.[59] Yet after the fall of Hong Kong in December 1941, political tensions put further strain on the already limited propaganda activities organized by Tong's office. Misinformation from Hong Kong also threatened the connections between Tong and his contacts in Shanghai. Agents once reported to Chiang that the *Shanghai Evening Post and Mercury* was purchased by Japan and its editor, Randall Gould, had become a Japanese spy. Tong had to write to Chiang to clear Gould's name and persuade Chiang to accept Gould's visit.[60]

Targeting the United States

The United States became the focus of China's propaganda. On January 17, 1939, Chiang Kai-shek confidentially ordered Hollington K. Tong to pay special attention to approaching the correspondents of the Associated Press in Shanghai and Hong Kong, and ensure that their dispatches were favorable to Chongqing.[61] In September of

---

57. Mao Qingxiang to Chiang Kai-shek, February 1939, Chiang Kai-shek archives, 002080200513048, Academia Historica (hereafter AH).
58. Zeng, *Zeng Xubai zizhuan*, 267.
59. Work report, the International Department of the Ministry of Information, 1938–1941.
60. Hollington Tong to Chiang Kai-shek, 718 (5)–82, SHAC.
61. Chronicle of the Guomindang government's international propaganda activities during the anti-Japanese war, documents in the Second Historical Archives collected by Liu Jingxiu, in *Dang'an shiliao yu yanjiu* [Archives and research] 1 (1990): 84.

the same year, the International Department opened branch offices in Chicago and San Francisco. Their primary task was to promote boycotts against military supplies to Japan from southern and western America. On October 10, Chiang repeated the idea that "propaganda to the United States was of extreme importance to China" and ordered Tong to use various channels—including newspaper, radio, and pamphlets—to encourage US economic sanctions against Japan.[62]

This US-focused propaganda policy was based on Chiang's assessment of the international situation. The years 1939 and 1940 represented a period of extreme uncertainty for China. The Nazi-Soviet nonaggression pact signed in August 1939 and the subsequent war in Europe created fear of a possible British or Soviet appeasement to Japan at China's expense. Chiang's intelligence officers also informed him in November 1939 that Britain was ready to acknowledge Japan's interests in China in exchange for its support in a war against the Soviet Union.[63] Following Britain's endorsement of Japan's ruling in Shanghai and the closure of the Burma Road, Chiang had good reason to fear a revival of the Anglo-Japanese alliance. He clearly sensed that Britain would not assist China without American support. The United States, therefore, became the last and the best hope for China to check Japan's expansion in Asia.

The policy was also a result of the accessibility of US media networks. According to statistics of the International Department, 77 of the 168 foreign journalists visiting Wuhan and Chongqing between the end of 1937 and February 1939 were Americans from key news agencies and newspapers.[64] In 1940, Roy Howard visited Chongqing. In May 1941, Henry Luce, publisher of *Life*, *Time*, and *Fortune*, arrived. In contrast, the British media were much less interested in Chinese affairs. From the fall of Wuhan to late 1940, Britain maintained only one correspondent from Reuters in Chongqing. Tong was disturbed by the fact that the influential organ of British opinion, the London *Times*, "appeared to be pursuing a policy of deliberately playing down Chinese war news."[65] After Tong communicated his concerns to Stafford Cripps, an influential leader of the Labor Party, during his visit to Chongqing in the spring of 1940, Cripps sent C. M. MacDonald of the *Times* to Chongqing for ten days to collect information on the Sino-Japanese War. Yet the brief coverage of Chinese issues was unable to reduce the mutual estrangement between the Chinese and the British public.

---

62. Ibid., 86.
63. Hollington Tong's report on Timperley's investigation of Britain's attitude toward China, November 21, 1939, 00208020000520065, Chiang Kai-shek archives, AH.
64. Liu Jingxiu and Zhang Jian, "Meiguo jizhe yu Zhongguo kangzhan" [American journalists and China's anti-Japanese war], *Minguo dang'an* [Archives of Republican China] 1 (1989): 107.
65. Tong, *Dateline: China*, 132.

Figure 17
W. H. Donald (second left) and H. J. Timperley (first right), 1941. From the collection of Ansie Lee Sperry.

Harold Timperley also experienced the British government's indifference to China's case during his goodwill trip to Britain. Timperley officially joined the Ministry of Information in 1940 to fill the vacancy left by Henry Donald after his resignation. As an Australian-born British subject and a long-term correspondent for the *Manchester Guardian*, his close engagement in China's politics was not much welcomed in British diplomatic circles. Displeased by Timperley's criticism of the closure of the Burma Road in British and US newspapers, B. E. F. Gage, a British representative in China, regarded Timperley as an "unsatisfactory factor in Anglo-Chinese relations" whose publicity greatly jeopardized British relations with China and the United States "at a particularly difficult period."[66] Although A. Clark Kerr, British ambassador to China, was anxious to see a British adviser enjoying Chiang's confidence, he questioned Timperley's ability to do the job as well as his influence on Chiang. Considering Timperley a propagandist for China, Kerr advised the Foreign Office to refrain from leaking information to him, as he believed that Timperley would pretend to be the bearer of confidential messages from the Foreign Office.[67] The Foreign Office's concern was not unfounded. Endeavoring to emulate Donald, Timperley was only to find that he had never acquired Chiang and Soong's complete confidence the way Donald had done. Timperley was eager to step into Donald's shoes after he resigned in 1941. Yet his application was declined. The setback disheartened

---

66. FO 371/24702/9143/ minutes, November 7, 1940, MLMSS 7594/5/9, Winston George Lewis Papers (hereafter WGLP).
67. FO 371/24702/9143/ minutes, December 4, 1940, MLMSS 7594/5/9, WGLP.

him, and he soon showed interest in leaving China. He was then sent to Australia to supervise the department's branch office in Sydney. The mutual trust and loyalty between Tong and Timperley that had developed during the most difficult time of the war started to dissipate. Tong later confessed disappointment at Timperley's performance, particularly with the lack of reports on his expenses. Their relationship did not improve despite Xia Jinlin's mediation.[68] And Timperley became estranged from the department as well as China's cause from this point on.

Surviving the Air Raids

The International Department's work was maintained despite the threat of intensive air raids. Although the thick layer of fog protected Chongqing from bombing during the winter, Japanese bombers came as soon as the fog lifted. Between 1939 and 1941, bombing was part of daily life in the summer.

The bombing began in May 1939, after Chiang Kai-shek rejected the Konoe Fumimaro cabinet's offer of peace on the condition that he resigned.[69] The bombing targeted all major facilities in Chongqing, military and civilian alike.[70] The goal was to cause havoc and thus terror, in order to sap the spirit of the Chongqing government and force it to acknowledge defeat. The first large-scale bombing took place on May 3–4. The Japanese air force sent thirty-six bombers on the first day and twenty-seven on the second day. Residential areas, business centers, schools, and hospitals hit by incendiary bombs were engulfed in flames. It was estimated that on these two days alone more than five thousand Chinese civilians were killed.[71]

Terror seized Chongqing. When the bombing stopped, the trauma continued. As Theodore White described, "A few drifters in the streets would be startled and would run at the imagined sound of an air-raid siren; others would follow, till hundreds of people were racing for the dugouts in terror, although there was not an enemy plane within hundreds of miles."[72] Indeed, the air raid back then was still a novel means of war, especially for Chongqing suburban residents, whose tranquil agrarian life had rarely been disturbed by an aircraft before. Yet when bombing became part of the daily routine in midsummer, the panic gradually passed, and Chongqing settled into a mode of endurance.[73]

---

68. Work reports on the Australian branch, 718(5)–17, SHAC.
69. Boyle, *China and Japan at War*, 155–160.
70. Kobayashi Fumio, "Kangzhan zhong kunan de Chongqing," in *Chongqing wenshi ziliao* (Chongqing: Xinan daxue chubanshe, 1988), 30: 77.
71. Herbert P. Bix, *Hirohito and the Making of Modern Japan* (New York: Harper Collins Publishers, 2000), 364.
72. White, *Thunder out of China*, 22.
73. See Rana Mitter's detailed depiction of air raids in Chongqing, in Rana Mitter, *Forgotten Ally: China's World War II, 1937–1945* (Boston and New York: Houghton Mifflin Harcourt, 2013), 1–2, 176–78.

The Chongqing government in 1939 was unable to offer any meaningful defense against the air raids. They had to rely heavily on an old-fashioned warning system and dugouts to minimize losses. Without radar technology to detect approaching bombers, the government erected towering gallows-like poles on the highest hills in and around the city. Thousands of two-people teams were appointed to watch the sky all over the border between Sichuan and the central Yangtze area from where the Japanese planes came. An enormous paper lantern stocking was the all-clear signal. Meanwhile, Chongqing spies in Wuhan also closely watched the movement of Japanese aircraft and sent warnings to Chongqing via secret radios hidden in the city. The steep cliffs and numerous caves in and around Chongqing also offered the government natural resources for air-raid dugouts. Each bureau had its own dugout nearby to shelter its staff and their families.

Tong developed a systematic safety plan to keep his office running during the air raids. Staff were encouraged to keep their clothing and daily necessities in packs so that they could be whisked to the dugout at any time.[74] Three mat sheds scattered in the compound of the department were also set up to store equipment and the staff's belongings, should the office or living places be destroyed. Each office was provided with boxes for important books and papers. When the siren rang, office assistants assigned to each section would move the boxes either to the mat sheds or to the dugout. Important equipment, such as typewriters and transmitters, would be carried to the dugout first. As the bombers departed, the process would be reversed, and things would be returned to their original places. The frequent raids trained Tong's staff to respond fast. As Tong recalled, they always managed to put valuable equipment in the dugouts before the second round of air raid alarms sounded. The office boys handled the exacting tasks skillfully.[75] Because of the systematic response to the bombings, the office managed to minimize its losses, and most of its facilities remained intact. Tong recalled in his memoir that one of the staff's favorite dugout pastimes was to estimate how much resource-scarce Japan had spent on the bombings which, apart from making the commute between the department and the dugout an unpleasant daily routine, hardly achieved anything.[76] Indeed, three decades after the war, Tong's memory of wartime experiences tended to be more upbeat than what the situation actually merited. With the terror of bombing, any day could be one's last.

The summers of 1940 and 1941 were especially hard for the department. The Japanese upgraded their bombers, increased the frequency of attacks and, most devastatingly, fixed on the department compound as a target.[77] Between June and July, the department suffered nineteen days of raids in a month. Incendiary bombs

---

74. Zeng, *Zeng Xubai zizhuan*, 244.
75. Hollington, *Dateline: China*, 114.
76. Ibid., 125.
77. Kobayashi Fumio, "Kangzhan zhong kunan de Chongqing," 76; Tong, *Dateline: China*, 119.

burned one of the mat sheds, destroyed the department's library and a meeting room, and shattered twelve rooms in a row of residential cottages. In 1941, the Japanese bombed Chongqing for seven days and nights consecutively beginning on August 8. The longest interval between raids was five hours, and the shortest only an hour and a half. Tong's pavilion and Wei Jingmeng's home were bombed several times.[78]

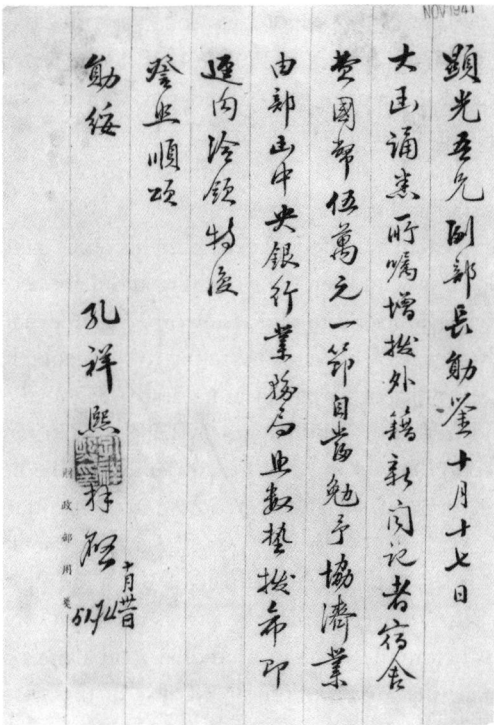

Figure 18
H. H. Kung's financial support to rebuild the Press Hotel, October 1941, 718(4)-332, SHAC.

The biggest loss was the damage inflicted on the Press Hotel. Fortunately, Tong had H. H. Kung's financial support and managed to rebuild it quickly.

Japanese strategy was designed to exhaust Chongqing residents.[79] People sometimes had to be confined to the dugouts for ten to fifteen hours a day for several days in a row and had to suffer through constant hunger and poor ventilation. Tong managed to keep the information flowing despite the severe conditions. His "trump card" was the transmitter he had shipped from his Hankou office. When bombing damaged the telephone service and electricity supply, the six-kilowatt transmitter installed in

---

78. Tong, *Dateline: China*, 119, 124; Zeng, *Zeng xubai zizhuan*, 245–46.
79. Zeng, *Zeng Xubai zizhuan*, 245.

the dugout became the main link between the correspondents in Chongqing and the outside world.[80] It was from the dugout that wireless messages were sent to Hong Kong and to Charles Stuart on the West Coast of the United States.

Time crept by in the dugout, hour after hour, day after day, until the sun disappeared, the chill of winter arrived, and the mist covered Chongqing once again.

Figure 19
Working in the dugouts. From *China at War*, October 1940.

People emerged from the dugouts to enjoy several months of siren-free winter, although a damp cold was facing them and an enormous amount of time had to be spent on expanding the caves to prepare for a new round of bombing in the following year. This process of retreat and reemergence continued for three years, until the lifting of the fog brought only a few Japanese bombers and then none, as the Japanese air force became deeply engaged in the Pacific War from 1942 onward.

Chongqing Versus the New Nanjing

After a few months of respite from political struggles with Wang's clique in Wuhan, Tong had to throw himself into a new round of battles with another pro-Wang superior, Zhou Fohai. After moving to Chongqing, Shao Lizi, the minister of information with whom Tong had cooperated well in Wuhan, was sent to Moscow to obtain Soviet assistance. Chiang initially intended to appoint Gu Mengyu, minister of railways between 1932 and 1935, to fill the vacancy. Yet Gu, who regarded himself as a scholar,

---

80. Tong, *Dateline: China*, 118; Zeng, *Zeng Xubai zizhuan*, 260.

resolved to distance himself from politics during wartime. He stayed in Hong Kong in semiretirement, declining to meet with Tong, who was sent by Chiang to persuade him to take the ministerial position.[81] With Gu's refusal, both Zhou Fohai and Hollington Tong, as vice ministers of the Ministry of Information, were second in line for the post. Although Zhou had by then displayed a strong inclination for peace negotiations with Japan, Chiang still chose to promote him instead of his staunch follower Tong.

Indeed, Tong was unable to match Zhou in his experience with and wide connections in the party. Zhou's career spanned the political spectrum from left to right. During his study at Kyoto Imperial University in his early years, he was heavily involved in radical Marxist socialist politics among the Chinese students, whom he represented at the inaugural congress of the Chinese Communist Party in Shanghai and Hangzhou in July and August 1921.[82] He was later elected vice chairman of the Communist Party and taught at the Whampoa Military Academy during the first united front and from then on developed connections with Chiang Kai-shek who was head of the academy. Under the influence of Dai Jitao, the leading right-wing Guomindang political ideologue, Zhou withdrew from the Communist Party and identified himself more closely with Chiang Kai-shek. Zhou rose rapidly in the ranks of the Guomindang with Chiang's assistance. He was scarcely thirty years old when Chiang appointed him chief political instructor at the newly established Central Military Academy. He was subsequently elected to the Central Executive Committee of the Guomindang and was drawn to the C. C. Clique run by the Chen brothers, who controlled the Central Organization Department on Chiang's behalf. He also participated in the activities of the C. C. Clique's rival organization, Fuxing She, better known as the Blue Shirts, a semisecret organization founded by the Whampoa Clique. Zhou's specialty was in political training and indoctrination. He became an important propagandist for the party in the 1930s, interpreting the party's ideology and editing political journals. This won him the position of vice minister of the Ministry of Information in 1937 and made him a trusted aide-de-camp of Chiang.[83]

However, the appointment was not welcomed by Zhou. By 1938, Zhou shared Wang's pessimistic views about China's resistance against Japan, perhaps because his senior position in the party gave him privileged access to information about the real military situation. He cofounded the Low Key Club, which gathered a group of officials, including Gao Zongwu and Hu Shi, who were opposed to the unrealistic resistance-to-the-death sentiment within the party and instead advocated a rational

---

81. Tong, *Dateline: China*, 109.
82. Brian Martin, "Collaboration within Collaboration: Zhou Fohai's Relations with the Chongqing Government, 1942–1945," *Twentieth-Century China* 34, no. 2 (April 2009): 55.
83. Boyle, *China and Japan at War*, 169.

diplomatic strategy to resolve the Sino-Japanese conflict. The club tied him closer to Wang Jingwei's clique and further strengthened his disapproval of the resistance policy.[84] Zhou confessed in his diary that he suffered insomnia at the thought of being the minister of information. He asked Zhang Qun to persuade Chiang Kai-shek to replace him with Chen Gongbo or Wang Shijie.[85] But Chiang did not change his mind.

As Chiang's wartime propagandist, Zhou's main responsibilities were to justify the resistance policy, boost public morale, and convince the Chinese people that China would eventually win with or without foreign assistance. The contradiction between his tasks and his beliefs tortured him. As he confessed in his diary:

> Supervising Chiang's propaganda organ is the most painful experience for me. I believe that continuous resistance will lead to a total defeat, yet I have to advocate a final victory in the office. I personally suggest keeping the door to negotiation open, but for propaganda purposes I have to promote the spirit of resistance to the end, opposing any compromise. I have tried in vain all means to resign from the post and have to put up with myself telling lies and boasting. I feel extremely guilty doing this to our people. Worst of all are the three meetings held every week. The first is a meeting attended by people from the Propaganda Bureau, the Political Bureau, and all other organizations involved in propaganda; the second is the briefing of foreign journalists, and the third is the briefing of Chinese journalists. In attendance are head of the Political Bureau Chen Cheng, his deputy Zhou Enlai, and head of the Third Department Guo Moruo. Hollington Tong, Xiao Tongzi and I represent the Propaganda Bureau. Every time I am forced to listen to Chen's shallow and awkward political discourses. It pains me greatly to have to sit back and suffer in silence while Zhou Enlai and Guo Moruo make announcements that they had invented.[86]

Tong was displeased with Zhou's leadership. He distrusted Zhou because of his involvement in the Communist Party in the 1920s and his "flirtation" with the Japanese after the outbreak of the full-scale war. He regarded Zhou as a timid man who had flown to Chongqing long before the fall of Wuhan to avoid the air raids. He was also disturbed at Zhou's advocacy of the early cessation of the war and his interference with Tong's international propaganda. The tension between Tong and Zhou escalated. As Tong recalled:

> I was suspicious of his motives, and refused even to see him. If he wanted to replace me, that was his privilege as Minister of Information. But if I did not wish to have my work made entirely ineffective, I could refuse to talk to him, and that was my privilege.[87]

---

84. Ibid., 167–95.
85. Zhou Fohai, *Zhou Fohai riji* [Zhou Fohai's diary] (Beijing: Zhongguo shehui kexue chubanshe, 1986), 1:81.
86. Zhou Fohai, "Huiyi yu qianzhan," in *Zhou Fohai Riji*, 1216.
87. Tong, *Dateline: China*, 110.

Tong's memory of his frustration with Zhou might have been tinged with the label of "traitor" and "collaborator" attached to Zhou ever since his departure from Chongqing. On the margin of Chiang's political center, Tong clearly had no insight into the complexity of Zhou's situation and no access to the information to which Zhou was privy.

The competition with Zhou nevertheless revealed Tong's awkward position in the party. As a mediator between foreign journalists and the Guomindang regime, Tong's rich contacts in foreign circles made him particularly useful to Chiang. Chiang and Soong in return had insulated Tong from external intervention. Indeed, for an idiosyncratic office like the International Department, insulation was the best way to maintain its functionality in the party. As Julia Strauss pointed out, the success of the Ministry of Finance and the Ministry of Foreign Affairs in the 1930s hinged on the government's ability to insulate them from external forces; the same was true for the International Department. Yet the insulation also hindered the department's later development. Tong's office, by nature, required wide and deep engagement with various ministries and institutions across factions. Yet insulation reduced Tong's incentive and ability to nurture such political networks. It also left Tong with the false impression that he was able to climb higher in the party's propaganda system despite his commitment to liberal values. Chiang's decision to promote Zhou as well as his limited support of Tong's censorship policy in Chongqing awakened Tong to the reality that by adhering to the treaty-port style, he was only creating a "lonely island" within the Guomindang officialdom.

Indeed, Tong had never managed to win respect from doyens of the party. He was often regarded disdainfully by senior leaders as the "empress clique" (*hou dang*, here referring to his association with Madam Chiang).[88] Even his supervisor Wang Shijie complained that he had no talent in politics.[89] The political struggles exhausted Tong. During his trip accompanying Soong May-ling's visit to the United States in 1943, he had intimated to his friend that he was fed up with Chinese politics, particularly "sick and tired of those surrounding Madam Chiang with whom he must work closely."[90] He had seriously thought about resigning from government service, a plan he implemented immediately after the Sino-Japanese War.

In late 1938, Wang Jingwei had left Chongqing for Hanoi and announced his support for a negotiated settlement with the Japanese. In March 1940, he established a puppet government in Nanjing, which informally became known as the

---

88. Hollington Tong's files, archives of Aide-de-camp of Chiang Kai-shek, AH; Yang Zhesheng, *Chen Bulei: Guomindang "junji dachen"* [Chen Bulei: the "grand minister of state" of the Guomindang] (Shanghai: Shanghai renmin chubanshe, 1999), 255.
89. Wang Shijie riji, April 28, 1940, Department of Modern History, Academia Sinica.
90. OSS's report on "Madam Chiang and Party," June 25, 1943 [WN#13639], US National Archives and Records Administration.

Wang Jingwei regime. Tong believed that Zhou eventually returned his disrespect by openly appointing him acting minister of information before leaving Chongqing to follow Wang. When Zhou announced the appointment, Tong was on a confidential mission in Shanghai. This open appointment put Tong in the media spotlight and thus endangered his life while he was surrounded by enemies in Shanghai.[91]

In early 1939, Tong sneaked into Shanghai again to improve connections between Chongqing and his secret propaganda office. Much like his first visit in early 1938, Tong's second Shanghai mission was fraught with danger. He twice narrowly escaped capture by the Japanese during his visit to Hallett Abend. As Tong later learned, the admiral commanding the Japanese naval forces in Shanghai was at Abend's place when Tong called in to seek an appointment. After the visit to Abend, Tong also brushed past Horiguchi Yoshinori when stepping out of the elevator.[92] Horiguchi was Tong's fellow alumnus at the University of Missouri and then worked as assistant editor of the Japanese Domei News Agency. He was also a press officer for the Japanese army in Shanghai. If Tong had been seized by Horiguchi, he would not have left Shanghai alive. Fortunately, Horiguchi did not notice him.[93]

Tong's key rival was Tang Liangli, the head of the International Propaganda Bureau of Wang Jingwei's government. Tang was Wang's personal secretary and foreign propagandist. He gained reputation by editing the famous China Today Series and operated the party's journal, the *People's Tribune*. After the start of the war, Liang moved to Hong Kong from Shanghai. Considering him to be an important propaganda asset, Chiang sent Wu Tiecheng to Hong Kong to win him over.[94] Tang worked temporarily for Chiang while remaining in contact with Wang. He did not wait long to split with Chiang and join his old patron. In Shanghai, he assisted Wang in expanding the networks with foreign journalists. He was later appointed director of the International Propaganda Bureau, supervising the foreign publicity of the Wang Jingwei regime.[95] To undermine Tang's propaganda, Dai Li sent two of his agents to Shanghai to keep a close watch on Tang's propaganda activities.[96]

Publications by Tang's department tended to advance the idea that China could not modernize itself single-handedly and that collaboration with imperialist powers was inevitable. Collaboration with Japan, a nation with which China shared a cultural and racial affinity, was far better than collaboration with the "white" races, whose goal was to subdue the yellow people.[97] Such a political vision, according to Tang in

---

91. Tong, *Dateline: China*, 111.
92. Ibid., 77.
93. Ibid.
94. Wang Jingwei government, August 15, 1939, Chiang Kai-shek archives, 002090200023201, AH.
95. Files on Tang Liangli's case, 4187-2-119, 4, the Shanghai High Court, Shanghai Municipal Council Archives (hereafter SMC).
96. Dai Li Archives, 1440101060003016, AH.
97. Files on Tang Liangli's case, 4187-2-119, 1, the Shanghai High Court, SMC.

his deposition during his trial in 1946, was caused by his own unhappy experience with Westerners. Born in Java when it was still a Dutch colony, he remembered being abused by Dutch officials when he was young. His study in Britain, instead of changing his negative impression of the West, intensified his contempt for the British Empire. In a later trip to the United States, he was disturbed by the restrictions and insults inflicted on him by Americans. In contrast, the hospitality he received in Japan left a deep impression and altered his anti-Japanese views. Tang regarded himself as a faithful follower of Sun Yat-sen's idea of a closer cooperation with Japan and claimed that most of his propaganda material constituted translations of Sun's work rather than his own creations.[98]

Tang's confession should not be taken at face value. His line of propaganda was based more on hard-headed calculations of Realpolitik than resistance to racial discrimination. In fact, Tang seriously embraced this pro-Japanese stance only after rejoining Wang in 1940. Before that, he was a staunch supporter of China's independence from Japanese intervention. His book *The Puppet State of Manchukuo* clearly identified Japan as an invader, seeking to control China's resources as well as eroding national sovereignty. The rhetoric in the media was, nevertheless, determined by his political interests. Whichever direction he took, he closely followed Wang, who could guarantee him funding and power. His shift in direction, as with other so-called traitors, also reflected the desperate situation faced by China after the loss of more than half of its territory. When peace with sovereignty seemed unachievable, peace without sovereignty appeared a reasonable compromise.

Outside the propaganda institutions, Tang competed with Tong fiercely for the support of foreign journalists. In early 1940, Tang contrived to establish a news exchange contract with the Reuters services in Shanghai. This dealt a heavy blow to Tong's office since Reuters' worldwide service would inevitably boost the reputation of the Wang Jingwei regime. Tong therefore used his muscle to sabotage this collaboration. He reported the issue to Robert Scott of the British Ministry of Information and pressed him to end the news exchange, warning him that any deal with the Wang Jingwei regime would harm Anglo-Chinese relations. Tong also boycotted Reuters' news from Shanghai and sent protest to the Reuters' headquarters. These acts eventually pushed the agency to send the former head of the Far Eastern division to China in June 1940 to conduct a thorough investigation.[99]

In addition, Tong took preemptive action to prevent further news alliances between international news agencies and the Wang regime. He asked the United Press office in Chongqing to query John Morris, the head of the UP service in Shanghai, about his attitude toward the Wang Jingwei government. He also directed Leaf, who

---

98. Ibid.
99. Wu, Xu, and Liu, "Kangzhan shiqi zai Yu waiguo jizhe huodong jishi," 160.

was working at the department's US branch, to use all of his influence to dissuade responsible people in the UP from approving any agreement with the Wang regime. Meanwhile, Tong sent Roy Howard, who used to be in charge of the UP, a telegraph, warning him of the consequences of the UP's cooperation with Wang:

> Since conclusion [of the] news agreement between Reuters and Tang Liang-li's puppet news agency, Reuters' dispatches formerly used by ninety-five percent of Chinese newspapers reduced more than half. Meantime popularity [of the] United Press [is] increasing by leaps and bounds. This displays Chinese public opinion [for the first] time in fifty years. [We] will appreciate your efforts [to] prevent United Press [from] concluding similar agreement with Nanking puppets so that [the] present happy tendency may continue.[100]

As a result of these efforts, the UP did not establish any connections with the Wang Jingwei government throughout the war.

Tang's bureau, nevertheless, put pro-Chongqing journalists in Shanghai in great danger. Having been involved in the treaty-port press for a long time and having served the Chongqing government in Hong Kong, Tang was privy to the political positions of foreign journalists and the secret connections between Tong and the Shanghai newspapers. As Agnes Smedley learned from John B. Powell, Tang Liangli had helped the Japanese authorities to compile a blacklist of Western journalists holding anti-Japanese views. The list included John Powell, Carroll Allcott of the *China Press*, *Shen bao*'s contributor Norwood Allman, editor-publisher of the *Hua min wanbao* Hal P. Mills, and Randall Gould and C. V. Starr from the *Shanghai Evening Post and Mercury*. They were to be treated as Chinese belligerents if captured.[101] Powell was later arrested and tortured in a Japanese prison. His feet had to be amputated after his release.

Competition with the Chinese Communist Party

Apart from challenges from Wang Jingwei's international propaganda machinery, the Chongqing propaganda office also had to keep an eye on the activities of the Chinese Communist Party. The frustrating reality facing Hollington Tong was that more and more foreign journalists in Chongqing were attracted by the Communist Party. Such a phenomenon was caused much less by the ideological divide between the two parties than by the journalists' growing distrust of the Guomindang government.

Indeed, despite the advocacy of liberal journalism by Tong and other Western-educated elites, the inclination to withhold information was strong among conservative party members, who remained suspicious of the motives of foreign

---

100. Tong, *Dateline: China*, 106.
101. Agnes Smedley, *Battle Hymn of China* (London: V. Gollance, 1944), 359.

journalists. After years of war, they still failed to see the significance of international propaganda. Edgar Snow, for example, initially wanted to interview Chiang Kai-shek before covering communist activities. His trip to Yan'an occurred only after several unsuccessful attempts to reach Chiang. After returning from the trip, Snow tried again to meet with Chiang to gain a balanced view, but his request was turned down once more. Tong later learned that Chiang had never been informed of Snow's requests.[102] It was obvious that some official responsible for foreign liaisons had rejected Snow's requests because of his suspicions around Snow's motivations. In contrast to the Guomindang government's neglect was the Communist Party's warm welcome. Liu Shaoqi, then the head of the northeast bureau of the Communist Party, was himself responsible for making arrangements for Snow to travel to the communist base.[103]

The distrust was also intensified by the Chongqing government's restrictions on visits to the front. Tong banned interviews at the front out of concern for the correspondents' personal safety. He also feared that the journalists' presence at the front might disturb operations since they lacked basic knowledge of the Chinese language and required special care to survive in the primitive conditions of China's rural areas.[104] Another unstated reason was the Chongqing government's lack of confidence in its military capacity, the very reason that prompted Wang Jingwei's defection. The government shared Wang's concern yet disagreed with his solution. To prevent others from adopting a pessimistic view of China's resistance, the government was cautious with news of the war, checking information that might damage sentiments or harm public morale. As a result, the department ordered that all messages about the war should stick to the version provided by the Central News Agency and the briefings given by military staff during press conferences. The ban inevitably drew strong criticism from foreign correspondents who wished to cover the war at the front line after the fashion of correspondents in Europe. Rumors began to circulate that the Guomindang government had issued the restrictions because they were insincere in their intentions to fight the Japanese and were ready to keep negotiations with Japan open, just like the Wang Jingwei clique.[105] Meanwhile, the Communist Party's foreign propagandists tried their best to distribute stories from the front among foreign journalists. They invited Agnes Smedley to cover the guerrilla war in North China, creating the impression that the Communist Party was the most determined to resist the Japanese.

---

102. Tong, *Dateline: China*, 148.
103. Harrison E. Salisbury, "China Reporting: Red Star to Long March," in Chin-Chuan Lee ed., *Voice of China: The Interplay of Politics and Journalism* (New York: Guilford Press, 1990), 219.
104. Tong, *Dateline: China*, 116.
105. Ibid., 116, 149.

Although the friction between the Guomindang and the Communist Party was inconspicuous during the first two years of war, their rivalry to win support from foreign journalists was ongoing. The Guomindang government tried to reduce the Communist Party's influence by prohibiting foreign journalists from visiting communist areas.[106] News regarding the activities of Communists was also censored in an attempt to keep the Communist Party's affairs out of the public eye. However, the blockade was broken from within by Zhou Enlai, the Communist liaison officer in Chongqing. As A. T. Steele, a long-term correspondent recalled:

> [Zhou was] a gold mine of gossip on the Generalissimo [Chiang Kai-shek] and the Kuomintang. Affable, smooth and convincing, Zhou was always prepared to explain in great detail just how Chiang's armies were sabotaging national unity by squeezing the Communists out of this or that area.[107]

Zhou also sought special but secret connections with those interested in the Communists. He approached Anna Louise Strong to give her a confidential briefing about the conflict between the Guomindang and the Communist Party and intimated that she ought to publish the briefing in the United States whenever rivalry between the two parties escalated into military clashes. Similar preparatory information was also conveyed to Edgar Snow.[108] Meanwhile, Zhou repeatedly approached Theodore H. White, a member of Hollington Tong's staff who later served *Time* magazine, to win his sympathy for the Communist Party.[109]

The first open international propaganda battle for the second united front occurred after a military clash in January 1941 between the Communist New Fourth Army and the nationalist troops led by Han Deqin. The clash, which is commonly known as the New Fourth Army Incident, or the Wannan Incident, was the result of an escalation of a series of conflicts between the two sides since 1940. The incident not only dissolved the united front but also brought the competition in international propaganda between the two parties to the surface.

The Communists contrived to distribute their version of the incident to the world press immediately after the incident. Their quick response was attributed to the party's preparation. Before the incident, when friction between the two parties intensified, Zhou Enlai had made several contacts with foreign journalists in Chongqing, persuading them to present the Communist Party's case to the outside world in the event that a larger military conflict occurred. A week before the incident, Zhou had various meetings with Jack Belden, correspondent for the *Time* and *Life* magazines in

---

106. Kenneth E. Shewmaker, *Americans and Chinese Communists, 1927–1945: A Persuading Encounter* (Ithaca, NY: Cornell University Press, 1971), 129.
107. Archibald Trojan Steele, *The American People and China* (New York: McGraw-Hill, 1966), 46.
108. Epstein, *My China Eye*, 132.
109. Theodore Harold White, *In Search of History: A Personal Adventure* (London: Cape, 1979), 118–20.

China, and Hugh Deane, the China correspondent of the *Christian Science Monitor*, at the Communists' city office. He offered them material on the Guomindang's suppression of the Communist army, which helped to instill a view favorable to the Communists.[110] Belden reported on the incident immediately after it occurred, criticizing the Guomindang's assault on the New Fourth Army. To circumvent the Chongqing government's censorship, he typed his principal story twice, made a total of about eight copies, and gave them to several people flying out to Hong Kong.[111] In Hong Kong, the China Defence League led by Soong Qing-ling became an extension of the Communist Party's international propaganda machinery. After receiving reports from Belden, Snow, and other correspondents, the League filed these reports with newspapers around the world.[112] Meanwhile, the progressive leftist editor of the *China Weekly Review*, John B. Powell, also published articles criticizing the Guomindang government's attack on Communist troops. In return, the government banned circulation of the journal in Chongqing. The action prompted strong protests from Powell and soured relations between him and the International Department.[113]

In contrast to the Communist Party's active publicity of the incident was the Guomindang's inaction. The Chongqing government insisted on suppressing all news concerning the incident, and government spokesperson were reluctant to discuss it with foreign correspondents. This policy of silence was justified on the grounds that airing evidence of internal strife would "give aid and comfort to the enemy."[114] Although Tong himself advocated active defense and promotion of the Guomindang's version of events in the world press, he was unable to change the minds of officials who failed to understand the significance of international propaganda and those who attempted to avoid disagreement in the media.

The International Department was not, however, entirely reticent about the incident. Tong secretly passed a message to journalists indicating that their cables would enjoy privileges in the censorship office if they "hinted" in their reports that the Communists had fabricated facts about the incident.[115] On July 19, the department called the foreign correspondents together and asked them to "rectify the Communists' illegal activities through the power of the world media."[116] The department intimated

---

110. MacKinnon and Friesen, *China Reporting*, 103.
111. See Hugh Deane's account on Belden's filing process, in ibid., 103.
112. Epstein, *My China Eye*, 132.
113. Second Historical Archives, Zeng Xubai gongzuo riji xuan 1 [An excerpt of Zeng Xubai's diary 1], *Minguo dang'an*, no. 2 (2000): 27.
114. Tong, *Dateline: China*, 147.
115. Liu Jingxiu, "Kangzhan shiqi Guomindang duiwai xuanchuan jishi (xu 1)" [Chronicle of the Guomindang foreign propaganda activities during the Sino-Japanese War (sequel 1)] *Dang'an shiliao yu yanjiu* [Archives and research], no. 2 (1990): 75.
116. Ibid., 76.

that journalists might use their outgoing cables to condemn the Communists' long-term rebellion against the political direction of the central government.[117] In a confidential cable, Chiang Kai-shek ordered Wang Shijie to collect pro-Communist propaganda materials published in the United States by communist sympathizers, such as Snow and Smedley, for analysis and hire prominent Americans to refute their allegations in public.[118] In addition, the government increased the surveillance of Belden and withdrew Snow's right to practice journalism in China.[119]

This Guomindang-Communist rivalry in the foreign media was the beginning of a larger battle in the 1940s, but in 1941 the strife between the two parties remained irregular. Most of the international propaganda resources were concentrated on winning US support for China's resistance against Japan. In 1941, Tong's effort in engaging the United States in a common war against Japan finally bore fruit.

Pearl Harbor, the End of the Beginning

Step by step, US public opinion moved away from isolationism. In September 1937, when the American Institute of Public Opinion (the Gallup poll) asked Americans whether they sympathized with either China or Japan, 43 percent favored China while 55 percent supported neither side.[120] Nevertheless, the public was unwilling to translate its sympathy into material support: 95 percent of the population surveyed rejected any financial involvement in the Sino-Japanese War.[121] In February 1938, those sympathizing with China grew to 59 percent, and 36 percent of the interviewees supported the United States shipping arms or ammunition to China.[122] In mid-1939, 74 percent showed sympathy for China; 66 percent favored the boycott of Japanese goods, and 72 percent supported an arms embargo on Japan. Despite this approval for material support, the population was still unwilling to confront Japan militarily: only 6 percent of interviewees wished to go to war with Japan.[123] But the situation continued to change quickly. By February 1941, ten months before the Japanese attack on Pearl Harbor, 39 percent of the public were willing to risk war with Japan if necessary.[124]

---

117. Ibid.
118. Liu Jingxiu, "Kangzhan shiqi Guomindang duiwai xuanchuan jishi (xu 1)," 76; Wu, Xu, and Liu, "Kangzhan shiqi zai Yu waiguo jizhe huodong jishi," 169–70.
119. Wu, Xu, and Liu, "Kangzhan shiqi zai Yu waiguo jizhe huodong jishi,"163, 164.
120. September 12, 1937, "Sino-Japanese War," in George Horace Gallup, *The Gallup Poll: Public Opinion, 1935–1971* (New York: Random House, 1972), 1:69.
121. September 19, 1937, "Aid to China and Japan," in *Gallup Poll*, 1:70.
122. February 18, 1938, "Sino-Japanese War," in *Gallup Poll*, 1:90.
123. June 16, 1939, "Japan," in *Gallup Poll*, 1:159.
124. February 24, 1941, "Japan," in *Gallup Poll*, 1:266.

In July 1939, the US government decided to revoke the Japanese-American commercial treaty, thus removing legal obstacles to an embargo on the shipment of materials to Japan. A total embargo on the export of iron and steel to Japan came into effect on October 16, 1941. On November 26, US secretary of state Cordell Hull rejected Japan's demand for the relaxation of the embargo and issued an ultimatum, requesting that Japan withdraw completely from China.

This pressure on Japan resulted in the Japanese attack on Pearl Harbor on December 7, 1941. The news was welcomed in Chongqing. Chiang Kai-shek, for the first time in the war, saw real hope for a victory. He celebrated it by singing an old opera and playing "Ave Maria" throughout the day.[125] The United States finally was at war with Japan! China still faced a long war. Pearl Harbor marked the end of China's lonely resistance. Yet the newly established alliance was not trouble-free. Tensions among the leadership carried on throughout the war, and the growing communist strength began to reshape the political landscape in the 1940s and beyond.

---

125. Youli Sun, *China and the Origins of the Pacific War, 1931–1941* (New York: St. Martin's Press, 1993), 155.

Figure 20
Sapajou, "The Lone Battalion," *North China Daily News*, October 30, 1937.

Conclusion

The period between 1928 and 1941 witnessed two marked trends: the growing sympathy for China's anti-Japanese cause in the English-language press and the development of China's foreign propaganda system. The two processes were closely connected. Even before China became a military ally of the United States and Britain after Pearl Harbor, it had already become an emotional ally. A change in national image is always a complex process. Other elements, such as the conflict of interests between the Western powers and Japan as well as Japanese atrocities in China, may well have contributed to the shift in public opinion. Yet it is undeniable that China's continuous propaganda efforts intensified the existing tensions between Japan and the Western powers and strongly promoted the change. History does not allow "what if" questions. Yet some hypothetical scenarios are useful in urging us toward a reevaluation of the significance of certain stories and events that are absent from current history telling. Would the United States have entered the war in 1941 without any propaganda effort from the Nationalist government? Had the United States delayed confrontation with Japan and stayed out of East Asia, could Chiang Kai-shek's government have survived Japan's encirclement? If the Chiang Kai-shek regime had collapsed in the early 1940s, would World War II have ended with the same result?

The development of China's international propaganda benefited immensely from the treaty-port press, a set of sources long neglected by historians. The press not only provided China with an effective channel to present its case during the deepening Sino-Japanese crisis but also honed the journalistic skills of some members of the Chinese bilingual elite. It nurtured a news network that survived the extreme hardship of warfare, including China's loss of territory and of news facilities, the death of personnel, and the terror of extreme violence. The treaty-port news operations were characterized by a commitment to the norm of the untrammeled flow of information, a respect for credibility, and a skillful use of transnational identities. All of these exerted a strong influence on the government's propaganda policies at the beginning of the full-scale Sino-Japanese War.

However, the path of development of China's international propaganda institution should not be taken for granted. The strong influence of the treaty-port press was a result of the incompetence of the Guomindang government to control it. Operating in these special zones, the press served an audience whose cosmopolitan vision was not restrained by ideological affiliations to nationalism, Marxism, or capitalism. Protected by extraterritoriality, the treaty-port press enjoyed a high level of editorial independence not available elsewhere in the country. This challenged the top-down information order that the Guomindang government sought to establish after the Soviet model and provided a haven where an alternative information order influenced by liberalism could be exercised.

Indeed, the contention between the government and the treaty-port press in part revealed the friction of two propaganda models—the Soviet and the Anglo-American—tested in China during the 1930s. While the former emphasized swamping the public with an all-encompassing ideology through indoctrination and information insulation, the latter focused on persuasion and debate among diverse viewpoints. The former valued the authority of sources, whereas the latter believed that the power of sources lay in their credibility.[1] Yet the two information orders were not always in conflict. Unable to subject the treaty-port press to the control of its party-led propaganda machinery, the government had to play on the field characterized by the intricate power relations of the treaty-port press and adapt to the transnational environment to maximize the chance of broadcasting its voice to the international public. This adaptation also demonstrated the government's compromise with the treaty-port elites whose support they desperately needed to secure political authority.

The Guomindang government was an authoritarian regime led by one party. Yet compared with other contemporary one-party states, such as Nazi Germany and the Soviet Union, it was a weak government troubled by internal disunity and external threats. The formation of the international propaganda institution, however, was the outcome of power struggles among different political interest groups. It took place in a period when the survival of the Guomindang government depended on a search for foreign patrons and allies in a fast-changing international environment.[2] Yet the leftists were reluctant to depart from its anti-imperial tradition. Meanwhile, the distinction between foreign allies and threats was often unclear, due to the highly volatile political situation. Struggle for political supremacy within the regime further complicated the development of the international propaganda institution, with all major factions trying to garner propaganda resources and wield influence in the treaty-port press. Various departments that sought to influence foreign public opinion often disagreed with each other over what political stance to pursue or how to regulate the

---

1. See Mareike Svea Ohlberg's discussion on the two propaganda models in "Creating a Favorable International Public Opinion Environment: External Propaganda as a Global Concept with Chinese Characteristics" (PhD dissertation, Heidelberg University, 2013), chapter 2.
2. William C. Kirby, "The Internationalization of China: Foreign Relations at Home and Abroad in the Republican Era," in *Reappraising Republican China*, ed. Frederic Wakeman Jr. and Richard Louis Edmonds (Oxford: Oxford University Press, 2000), 188.

foreign papers. A unified international propaganda institution became possible only after Chiang Kai-shek gained absolute leadership and was able to pull together all available resources for his propaganda team led by Hollington Tong.

The international propaganda institution was not a strict modern bureaucracy where office duties and opportunities were separate from private lives. Propaganda resources were bound together by *renqing* (human feelings) cultivated in the treaty ports. The institution was built on interlocking personal networks based on native place, alumni connections, collegial experience, and chains of friendship. The Missouri mafia, the Missouri and Yenching university networks, St. John's University connections, and the *China Press* group together played a key role in forming the basic human resources for the propaganda institution. During Tong's leadership of the propaganda office, he constantly sought to make his relations with his colleagues even closer by attending to their personal needs. The living conditions in the Holly's Hotel and the International Department compound in Chongqing helped to combine office work with private domicile. The extremities of the war situation justified this design for security reasons, but it was also intended to strengthen the cohesiveness of the department and so to improve efficacy and enhance personal control. It was a network tied by common commitment, personal loyalty, and friendship that ensured the continuous flow of information despite the perilous situation for news transmission during wartime.

Although this study has dealt with the rise of the international propaganda institution, it has also narrated the tragedy of some members of the treaty-port elite who had to give up their liberal ideals during a time of national crisis. For Hollington Tong, the transition from treaty-port journalist to Guomindang official placed him in a painful dilemma of pursuing liberal journalism or submitting to conservative Guomindang culture. His experience reflected the quandary faced by many other Western-trained intellectuals at this time. Strongly influenced by liberalism during their university studies overseas, these intellectuals supported basic civil liberties and believed that a diversity of ideas constituted a necessary ingredient of a healthy society. Yet the Sino-Japanese crisis severely limited their independence. The war machine absorbed them into the militarized system, crushed their dream of creating an information oasis based on the treaty-port order within the propaganda system, and dashed their hopes of influencing the Guomindang bureaucracy from within. While the Sino-Japanese War might have provided an antidote to China's malaise and chaos, and cultivated a sense of nationalism among its mass public,[3] it also strengthened the party-state and nipped the development of liberal journalism in the bud.

Chiang's patronage of the propaganda institution derived partly from his personal friendship with Tong. Again, *renqing* was essential in the operation of the institution.

---

3. Chang-Tai Hung, *War and Popular Culture: Resistance in Modern China, 1937–1945* (Berkeley: University of California Press, 1994).

However, this very element that tied the journalists and the state together was vulnerable. Despite having been born in the same region and having been taught by Tong, Chiang's trust in Tong was limited. Chiang respected Tong's professional skills but remained cautious about his strong commitment to liberalism. Tong's views often ran contrary to the traditional Guomindang culture that emphasized ideological tutelage and personal control. Chiang would allow Tong to relax censorship as long as it did not threaten his personal prestige and ordered him to tighten it immediately when circumstances turned hostile. After moving to Chongqing, he installed Dai Li to use his intelligence apparatus to monitor the department's daily work and thus balance Tong's power in the propaganda ministry. Keenly aware of Tong's political limitations in the party, he chose Zhou Fohai, an unpredictable doyen of the party, to be minister of information, rather than promote his faithful follower. As Chen Bulei noted, Tong was much less adroit in dealing with party affairs than in organizing his propaganda office.

Throughout his professional life Tong remained fully aware of the filial nature of Chinese organizations and relationships. Because Tong taught him English in high school, Chiang always addressed Tong as "teacher." However, Tong fully understood that the title did not imply any real subservience on Chiang's part and treated Chiang as his superior both personally and professionally. While Tong's power derived from Chiang, he was mainly supported by Soong May-ling, who shared his views on liberal strategy in propaganda. Soong provided Tong with a certain degree of protection when Tong's policy contradicted Chiang's vision. Yet the close connection with Soong also led him to be regarded in the party as part of the "empress clique," which was not held in high esteem by many senior political leaders in Chiang's faction.

The suffocating political environment exhausted Tong. He resigned from the Ministry of Information immediately after the Sino-Japanese War and joined the YMCA school in New York to learn automobile mechanics. When his disciple Ye Gongchao visited him, he confided that "there is more fun repairing cars than trying to serve the government."[4] This half-joking off-the-cuff comment betrayed the deep frustrations he had felt over the past decade. However, his plan to become a mechanic was interrupted by the Civil War. He was called back to Nanjing in 1947 by Chiang to once again lead the government's international propaganda office.

Some seven decades have passed since the Sino-Japanese War. Yet a nuanced understanding of the period has seldom emerged in the public or academic debate. As Rana Mitter pointed out, without the "China Quagmire," Japan's imperial ambitions would have been much easier to fulfill. Yet China's struggle during the Sino-Japanese

---

4. Ye Gongchao, "Huainian Dong Xianguang xiansheng" [In memoriam: Mr. Hollington Tong], in Dong Xianguang xiansheng zhuisilu bianji weiyuanhui, *Dong Xianguang jiniance* [In memory of Hollington Tong] (Taipei: Dong Xianguang xiansheng zhuisilu bianji weiyuanhui, 1972), 21.

War has been largely forgotten.⁵ Official histories in mainland China exclusively attributed the victory over Japan to the leading role of the Communist Party. Scholars in Taiwan are reluctant to discuss the Nationalist government's achievements, when the Guomindang veterans had to swallow the pain and shame of the loss of the Civil War, and the increasing awareness of native identity continued to push for a Taiwan-centered perspective on history writing. In the United States and Europe, people were more attracted to the questions of "Who lost China?" or "Why did the Communists win in 1949?" instead of evaluating what the Nationalist government attempted to achieve, or could have achieved, given the context and constraints of those times.

While recovering lost stories is part of my intention, I am also interested in seeking a parallel between the past and the present. Despite the challenges, struggles, and disasters China experienced during this period—the Civil War, the Great Leap Forward, the Cultural Revolution, the reopening of its doors to the world, and the return to the international society—what we see today is a rising independent China with a strong influence on international affairs; a nation linked more and more closely with the rest of the world in economic development, political decision making and regional security; and a nation, after the Mao era, seeking to redress its isolated status in international relations, rebuild its national image, and make its political model and values more widely understood.

Since the end of the 1990s, China has put great emphasis on the development of "soft power" rather than power through coercion or warfare. At the Central Foreign Affairs Leadership Group meeting in January 2006, Party Chief and President Hu Jintao noted that the rise of China's international influence depended both on hard power and soft power. He further highlighted the significance of the latter in his political report to the Seventeenth Party Congress in October 2007, stressing the urgent need to strengthen China's soft power in response to international challenges.⁶ China's use of soft power in South Asia, Africa, and Latin America has also caught the global attention of academics and diplomats. In 2007, the then–Australian Labor Party leader Kevin Rudd (a few months before he became prime minister) handed to US president George W. Bush a copy of Joshua Kurlantzich's book *Charm Offensive: How China's Soft Power Is Transforming the World* at their meeting in Sydney.⁷ The US Congressional Research Service also conducted a lengthy report on China's soft power in South America, Asia, and Africa to assess its implications for the security and economic interests of the United States.⁸

---

5. Rana Mitter, *Forgotten Ally: China's World War II, 1937–1945* (Boston and New York: Houghton Mifflin Harcourt, 2013), 379.
6. Mingjiang Li, *Soft Power: China's Emerging Strategy in International Politics* (Plymouth: Lexington Books, 2009), 1.
7. Peter Hartcher, "Rudd Offers a Cheeky Lesson in Soft Power," *Sydney Morning Herald*, September 7, 2007.
8. US Congressional Research Service, "China's Foreign Policy and 'Soft Power' in South America, Asia, and Africa" (Washington: US Government Printing Office, 2008). https://fas.org/irp/congress/2008_rpt/crs-china.pdf.

Conclusion

The development of soft power in today's China is, of course, different from that in the 1930s. Today, China is an independent nation. Its efforts to exercise soft power are built on its growing economic, military, and political strength. The deep apprehension of the threat posed by Japan and other imperialist powers as well as the difficulties created by circumscribed sovereignty in organizing foreign propaganda in the 1930s have become history—a history that is too remote and inaccessible for those born after the war to be aware of unless they deliberately make an effort to hunt for its traces and, sometimes, be brave enough to revisit the turmoil, suffering, and pain that was exposed.

However, careful readers of history will see that many key features of those days remain present. Among the hustle and bustle of the Shanghai Bund, where Westerners today walk in and out of the historic buildings, we see a reflection of the lively and cosmopolitan Shanghai of the 1930s. When Chinese Central Television and the Xinhua News Agency began to expand their English-language services to present China's perspective to a global audience, their actions strongly echoed the attempts made by China in the 1930s to make its voice heard and its cause understood abroad. Similarly, the global development of Internet technology has transformed both the flow of information and the nature of social networks, with Microblogs (*Weibo*) and WeChat providing challenges to the Chinese government's control of information that past leaders of the Communist Party never faced. The way in which online information and social networks are transforming the public sphere today mirrors the actions of China's treaty-port papers, which embraced a wide range of divergent opinions and sought to a exert strong influence over the world media. Today, China's use of nationalism with strong Confucian overtones to fill the ideological void left by the collapse of communism,[9] again reminds us of the role nationalism played in nurturing allegiance among diverse political groups during the 1930s.

Since China reentered global society at the end of the Mao era, both China and the rest of the world have worked hard to manage its comeback. The Chinese government is eager to establish its reputation and legitimacy, while the rest of the world tentatively watches how the rise of China transforms global society. The portrayal of this economic giant but ideological heretic is a constant matter of dispute. What should China do to improve its image in the world? There are many possible answers to this question and doubtless as many critiques of whatever China does. But whatever does occur, the experience of the past, the road China has traveled, and the experiences that continue to shape its thoughts and actions will better inform us in the present.

---

9. Peter Hays Gries, *China's New Nationalism: Pride, Politics, and Diplomacy* (Berkeley: University of California Press, 2004), 8.

Glossary

A list of important personal names in pinyin, traditional form and character.

Pinyin	Traditional Form	Character
Chen Youren	Eugene Chen	陳友仁
Diao Minqian	Philip Tyau	刁敏謙
Dong Xianguang	Hollington Tong	董顯光
Gu Weijun	Wellington Koo	顧維鈞
Kong Xiangxi	H. H. Kong	孔祥熙
Li Bingrui	Edward Bing-shuey Lee	李炳瑞
Li Cai	Li Choy	李才
Lin Wenqing	Lim Boom Keng	林文慶
Peng Leshan	Mike Peng	彭樂善
Shi Zhaoji	Alfred Sze	施肇基
Song Meiling	May-ling Soong	宋美齡
Song Ziwen	T. V. Soong	宋子文
Sun Ke	Sun Fo	孫科
Tang Liangli	T'ang Leang-li	湯良禮
Wang Zhengting	C. T. Wang	王正廷
Wei Jingmeng	Jimmy Wei	魏景蒙
Wu Chaoshu	C. C. Wu	伍朝樞
Yan Huiqing	W. W. Yen	顏惠慶
Yang Guangsheng	Kwangson/Kuangson Young	楊光泩
Ye Gongchuo	Yeh Kung-cho	葉恭綽
Zhang Sixu	Samuel H. Chang	張似旭
Zhang Xinhai	H. H. Chang	張歆海
Zhao Minheng	Thomas Ming-heng Chao	趙敏恆

Other names titles and terms:

72 Hang shang bao 七十二行商報
Amō Eiji 天羽英二
Andong 安東
Ariyoshi Akira 有吉 明

Asahi shimbun 朝日新聞
Bai Chongxi 白崇禧
Bashan 巴山
Bianji ke 編輯科
Cai Tingkai 蔡廷鍇
Changchun 長春
Chen Bingzhang 陳秉章
Chen Bulei 陳布雷
Chen Gongbo 陳公博
Chen Guofu 陳果夫
Chen Lifu 陳立夫
Chen Mingshu 陳銘樞
Cheng Tiangu 程天固
Chongqing weishu silingbu jichachu 重慶衛戍總司令部稽查處
Chuanyin ke 傳音科
Chun qiu 春秋
Da wanbao 大晚報
Dagong bao 大公報
Dai Jitao 戴季陶
datong 大同
Dong Shoupeng 董壽彭
Du Xigui 杜錫珪
Du Yuesheng 杜月笙
Duiwai ke 對外科
eryu xuanchuan 耳語宣傳
Fan Changjiang 范長江
Fang Zhi 方治
Feng Yuxiang 馮玉祥
Fengtian 奉天
Fukuda Hikosuke 福田彥助
Fuxing She 復興社
Fuzhou 福州
Gan Naiguang 甘乃光
Gao Zongwu 高宗武
Geming pinglun 革命評論
Gu Mengyu 顧孟餘
Guangdong 廣東
Guangzhou/Canton 廣州
Gui Zhongshu 桂中樞

Guoji ke 國際科
Guomin/Kuomin 國民
Guomindang/Kuomintang 國民黨
Guowen 國聞
Han Deqin 韓德勤
Hankou 漢口
Hirota Kōki 広田弘毅
hou dang 后黨
hou zhi hou jue 後知後覺
Hu Hanmin 胡漢民
Hu Shi 胡適
Hu Zhengzhi 胡政之
Huang Fu 黃郛
Huang Xianzhao 黃憲照
Itagaki Seishirō 板垣征四郎
Ji Zejin 季澤晉
Jiang Guangnai 蔣光鼐
Jilin 吉林
Juntong 軍統
Kawashima Yoshiko 川島芳子
Konoe Fumimaro 近衛文麿
Kwantung 関東
Li Jishen 李濟深
Li Shizeng 李石曾
Li Zongren 李宗仁
Liang Qichao 梁啟超
Liang Shichun 梁士純
Lin Yutang 林語堂
Liu Dajun 劉大鈞
Liu Shaoqi 劉少奇
Liu Zhan'en 劉湛恩
Luo Jialun 羅家倫
Luo Wengan 羅文幹
Ma Su 馬素
Ma Xingye 馬星野
Ma Yinchu 馬寅初
Ma Zhanshan 馬占山
Mao Qingxiang 毛慶祥
Nakamura Shintaro 中村震太郎
Nichi nichi shimbun 日日新聞

Glossary

Ningbo 寧波
Pan Gongbi 潘公弼
Pei-ta-ying 北大營
pingyi jinren 平易近人
qi lian 乞憐
Quanguo baojie lianhe hui 全國報業聯合會
Quanguo baoye jujin hui 全國報業俱進會
rangwai bixian annei 攘外必先安內
Rehe/Jehol 熱河
Saitō Hiroshi 斉藤博
Shanghai nippo 上海日報
shangwei 上尉
shangxiao 上校
Shanhaiguan 山海關
Shao Lizi 邵力子
Shao Yulin 邵毓麟
shaojiang 少將
shaowei 少尉
shaoxiao 少校
Shen Jianhong 沈劍虹
Shenshi 申時
Shenyang 瀋陽
Sheying ke 攝影科
Shi Liangcai 史量才
Shidai gonglun 時代公論
Shidehara Kijūrō 幣原喜重郎
Shiozawa Kōichi 塩沢幸一
Shishi xin bao 時事新報
Si she 四社
Sun Ruiqin 孫瑞芹
Takahashi Sankichi 高橋三吉
Tan Yankai 譚延凱
Tanaka Giichi 田中義一
Tanaka Ryūkichi 田中隆吉
Tang Dechen 湯德臣
Tang Youren 唐有壬
Tang Yuanzhan 唐元湛
Tianjin/Tientsin 天津
T'ien Hsia 天下
Tōhō 東方
Uchida Yasuya 内田康哉
Wanbaoshan 萬寶山
Wang Boheng 王伯衡
Wang Chonghui 王寵惠
Wang Jiasong 王家松
Wang Shijie 王世傑
Weibo 微博
Wen Yuanning 溫源寧
Wu Tiecheng 吳鐵城
Xia Jinlin 夏晉麟
xian zhi xian jue 先知先覺
Xiao Tongzi 蕭同茲
Xikou 溪口
Xinminguo bao 新民國報
Xinwen bao 新聞報
Xiong Xiling 熊希齡
Xu Peigen 徐培根
Xu Xinliu 徐新六
Xu Zhaoyong 徐兆鏞
Yan Xishan 閻錫山
Yang Hucheng 楊虎城
Yang Yongtai 楊永泰
Yanjiuxi 研究系
Ye Chucang 葉楚傖
Yingkou 營口
Yingmei pai 英美派
Yong bao 庸報
Yoshizawa Kenkichi 芳沢謙吉
Yuan Shikai 袁世凱
Zeng Xubai 曾虛白
Zhabei 閘北
Zhang Junqi 張駿錡
Zhang Mingwei 張明煒
Zhang Pengchun 張彭春
Zhang Pingqun 張平群
Zhang Qun 張群
Zhang Xueliang 張學良
Zhang Zhuping 張竹平

Zhang Zuolin 張作霖
zhili 直隸
zhongjiang 中將
Zhongyang ribao 中央日報
Zhongyang tongxunshe 中央通訊社
Zhou Enlai 周恩來
Zhou Fohai 周佛海

Zhou Ziqi 周自齊
Zhu Jiahua 朱家驊
Zhu Qi 朱淇
Zhu Shuqing 朱書清
Zhuang Zhihuan 莊智煥
Zongwu ke 總務科

Bibliography

Archival Sources

Academia Historica, Taipei
Academia Sinica, Taipei
Chongqing Municipal Archives
Confidential US State Department Central Files, China, Internal Affairs 1930–1939
Foreign Office Files for China, 1919–1980
Guomindang Archives, Taipei
Minutes of the Standing Committee of Guomindang Central Executive Committee [Zhongguo Guomindang zhongyang zhixing weiyuanhui changwu weiyuanhui huiyi jilu]
US National Archives and Records Administration, Papers Relating to the Foreign Relations of the United States
Reuters Archives, London
The Second Historical Archives of China, Nanjing
Shanghai Municipal Council Archives
Shanghai Municipal Police Files
Special Collections of the Yale Divinity School Library
The State Historical Society of Missouri
Winston George Lewis Papers, concerning W. H. Donald, together with papers of the Donald family. Library of New South Wales, Sydney.

Newspapers and Magazines

Chicago Daily News
China at War
China Critic
China Press
China Weekly Review / Millard's Review of the Far East
Chinese Courier and Canton Gazette
Chinese Nation
Christian Science Monitor
Far Eastern Review: Engineering, Finance, Commerce
Geming pinglun 革命評論
Guowen zhoubao 國聞週報
Manchester Guardian

New York Times
North China Daily News / North China Herald
Pacific Affairs
Peiping Chronicle
Peking and Tientsin Times
Peking Leader
People's Tribune
Radio Amateur's Journal
Shanghai Evening Post and Mercury
Shanghai Times
Shen bao 申報
Time magazine
Times (London)
Xiada zhoukan 廈大周刊

Published Archival Sources

Changning weishi ziliao weiyuanhui. *Changning wenshi ziliao disiji: Xiao Tongzi he Zhongyang tongxunshe* 長寧文史資料第 4 輯：蕭同茲和中央通訊社 [Materials about Changning, vol. 4, Xiao Tongzi and the Central News Agency]. Changning: Wenshi ziliao weiyuanhui, 1988.

Chen Hongmin. *Hu Hanmin weikan wanglai handiangao* 3 胡漢民未刊往来函電稿 3 [Hu Hanmin's correspondence, vol. 3]. Guilin: Guangxi shifan daxue chubanshe, 2005.

Chongqing wenshi ziliao 重慶文史資料 [Historical materials of Chongqing], vol. 30. Chongqing: Xinan daxue chubanshe, 1988.

Documents on British Foreign Policy, 1919–1939. London: Her Majesty's Stationery Office, 1946.

Jiangsu wenshi ziliao 江蘇文史資料 [Historical materials of Jiansu], vol. 36. Nanjing: Jiangsu wenshi ziliao chubanshe, 1991.

Qin Xiaoyi, ed. *Zhongguo Minguo zhongyao shiliao chubian: Dui Ri kangzhan shiqi, xubian* 中國民國重要史料初編，對日抗戰時期，續編 [Collection of important historical materials: The anti-Japanese war; Sequel]. Taipei: Zhongguo Guomindang zhongyang weiyuanhui dangshi weiyuanhui, 1981.

Second Historical Archives. "Zeng Xubai gongzuo riji xuan 1" 曾虛白工作日記選 1 [Selection of Zeng Xubai's diary 1]. *Minguo dang'an* 民國檔案, no. 2 (2000): 27–36.

Shanghai xinwen shiye shiliao jiyao 上海新聞事業史料輯要 [Materials on the history of newspapers in Shanghai]. Taipei: Tianyi chubanshe, 1977.

Shi lüe gao ben 事略稿本 [Chiang Kai-shek's manuscripts]. Taipei: Academia Historica, 2003.

Sichuan difangzhi bianzuan weiyuanhui. *Sichuan shengzhi (waishi zhi)* 四川省志 (外事志) [Sichuan Affairs, foreign-related issues]. Chengdu: Bashu shushe, 2001.

Wang Wenbin, ed. *Zhongguo xiandai baoshi ziliao huiji* 中國現代報史資料匯輯 [Historical records on the Chinese press]. Chongqing: Chongqing chubanshe, 1996.

Xi'nan zhixing mishu chu. *Xi'nan dangwu niankan.* 西南黨務年刊 [Yearbook of the southwestern Guomindang affairs], 1932.

Zhongguo di'er lishi dang'anguan 中國第二歷史檔案館. *Minguo dang'an shiliao huibian* 民國檔案史料匯編 [Collections of historical records of the Republic of China], vol. 5, no. 1, Economy (9). Nanjing: Jiangsu guji chubanshe, 1994.

———. *Zhongguo Guomindang zhongyang zhixing weiyuanhui changwu weiyuanhui huiyilu* 中國國民黨中央執行委員會常務委員會議錄 [Minutes of the Standing Committee of the Guomindang Central Executive Committee]. Guilin: Guangxi shifan daxue chubanshe, 2000.

———. *Zhonghua Minguo shi dang'an ziliao huibian* 中華民國史檔案資料匯編 [Collections of historical records of the Republic of China], vol. 5, no. 1, Culture (1). Nanjing: Jiangsu guji chubanshe, 1994.

———. *Zhongyang dangwu yuekan* 中央黨務月刊 [Monthly of the Guomindang affairs]. Nanjing: Nanjing chubanshe, 1994.

Zhongguo renmin zhengzhi xieshang huiyi quanguo weiyuanhui wenshi ziliao yanjiu weiyuanhui 中國人民政治協商會議全國委員會文史資料研究委員會. *Wenshi ziliao xuanji* 文史資料選輯 [Selection of historical materials]. Beijing: Zhongguo wenshi chubanshe, 2000.

Zhonghua Minguo shishi jiyao bianzuan weiyuanhui. *Zhonghua Minguo shishi jiyao* 中華民國史事紀要 [Historical records of the Republican China]. Taipei: Zhongzheng shuju, 1978.

Zhongyang yinhang shiliao, 1928.11–1949.5 中央銀行史料 [Documents of the Central Bank of China, November 1928–May 1949]. Beijing: Zhongguo jinrong chubanshe, 2005.

Books and Articles

Abend, Hallett. *My Life in China, 1926–1941*. New York: Harcourt, Brace and Company, 1943.

Ahvenainen, Jorma. *The Far Eastern Telegraphs: The History of Telegraphic Communications between the Far East, Europe, and America before the First World War*. Helsinki: Suomalainen Tiedeakatemia, 1981.

Akami, Tomoko. "The Emergence of International Public Opinion and the Origins of Public Diplomacy in Japan in the Inter-war Period." *The Hague Journal of Diplomacy* 3, no. 2 (2008): 99–128.

———. *Japan's News Propaganda and Reuters' News Empire in Northeast Asia, 1870–1934*. Dordrecht: Republic of Letters, 2012.

Akio, Tsuchida. "China's 'Public Diplomacy' toward the United States before Pearl Harbor." *Journal of American-East Asian Relations* 17 (2010): 35–55.

Barrett, David P., and Larry N. Shyu, eds. *Chinese Collaboration with Japan, 1932–1945: The Limits of Accommodation*. Stanford: Stanford University Press, 2001.

Bassett, Reginald. *Democracy and Foreign Policy: A Case History, the Sino-Japanese Dispute, 1931–33*. London: Longmans, Green, 1952.

Bennett, Milly. *On Her Own: Journalistic Adventures from San Francisco to the Chinese Revolution*, edited and annotated by A. Tom Grunfeld. Armonk, NY: M. E. Sharpe, 1993.

Bernays, Edward L. *Propaganda*. New York: Liveright Publishing, 1928.

Bian, Morris L. "Building State Structure: Guomindang Institutional Rationalization during the Sino-Japanese War, 1937–1945." *Modern China* 31, no. 1 (January 2005): 35–71.

Bickers, Robert. *Britain in China: Community Culture and Colonialism, 1900–1949*. Manchester: Manchester University Press, 1999.

———. "Changing Shanghai's 'Mind': Publicity, Reform and British in Shanghai, 1928–1931." A lecture given at a meeting of the China Society on March 20, 1991.

———. "Shanghailanders: The Formation and Identity of the British Settler Community in Shanghai." *Past and Present* (1998): 161–211.

Bickers, Robert, and Christian Henriot. Introduction to *New Frontiers: Imperialism's New Communities in East Asia, 1842–1953*, edited by Robert Bickers and Christian Henriot, 1–11. Manchester: Manchester University Press, 2000.

Bix, Herbert P. *Hirohito and the Making of Modern Japan*. New York: Harper Collins Publishers, 2000.

Borg, Dorothy. *The United States and the Far Eastern Crisis of 1933–1938: From the Manchurian Incident through the Initial Stage of the Undeclared Sino-Japanese War*. Cambridge, MA: Harvard University Press, 1964.

Boylan, James R. *Pulitzer's School: Columbia University's School of Journalism, 1903–2003*. New York: Columbia University Press, 2003.

Boyle, John Hunter. *China and Japan at War, 1937–1945: The Politics of Collaboration*. Stanford: Stanford University Press, 1972.

Brune, Lester H., and Richard Dean Burns. *Chronological History of U.S. Foreign Relations: 1607–1932*. New York: Routledge, 2003.

Carr, Edward Hallett. *Propaganda in International Politics*. Oxford: Clarendon Press, 1939.

———. *The Twenty Years' Crisis, 1919–1939: An Introduction to the Study of International Relations*. London: Macmillan, 1939.

Cassel, Pär. *Grounds of Judgment: Extraterritoriality and Imperial Power in Nineteenth-Century China and Japan*. New York: Oxford University Press, 2012.

Chao, Thomas Ming-heng. *The Foreign Press in China*. Shanghai: Institute of Pacific Relations, 1931.

Chen Hongmin. *Handian lide renji guanxi yu zhengzhi: Du Hafo-Yanjing tushuguan cang "Hu Hanmin wanglai handian gao"* 函電裡的人際關係與政治：讀哈佛—燕京圖書館館藏 "胡漢民往來函電稿" [An analysis of Hu Hanmin's interpersonal relations through his correspondence]. Beijing: Sanlian shudian, 2003.

———. "Hu Hanmin nianbiao 胡漢民年表 (1931.9–1936.5)" [Chronicles of Hu Hanmin]. *Minguo dang'an*, no. 1 (1986): 119–33.

Chen, Jinxing. "Harold R. Isaacs' Trotskyist Turn in the *China Forum* Years." *Twentieth-Century China* 24, no. 1 (November 1998): 31–66.

Chen Wengan. *Kangzhan junshi yu xinwen dongyuan* 抗戰軍事與新聞動員 [Anti-Japanese war and mobilization by news]. Hankou: Zhongshan wenhua jiaoyu guan, 1938.

Ch'en, Tsung-hsi. *General Chiang Kai-shek: The Builder of New China*. Shanghai: Commercial Press, 1929.

Ch'en, Tzu-Hsiang. *The English-Language Daily Press in China*. Beijing: Collectanea Commissionis Synodalis, 1937.

Chiang Kai-shek. *Zongtong Jianggong sixiang yanlun zongji* 總統蔣公思想言論總集 [A collection of Chiang Kai-shek's thought and speeches]. Taipei: Zhongguo Guomindang zhongyang weiyuanhui dangshi weiyuanhui, 1985.

Ch'ien, Tuan-sheng. *The Government and Politics of China, 1912–1949*. Stanford: Stanford University Press, 1970.

Chihiro, Hosoya. "Britain and the United States in Japan's View of the International System, 1919–1937." In *Anglo-Japanese Alienation, 1919–1952*, edited by Ian Nish, 57–76. Cambridge: Cambridge University Press, 1982.

China's Attempt to Muzzle the Foreign Press. May 20, 1929.

"The China Lobby—Lobbying Efforts from the 1920s through World War II." *Encyclopedia of the New American Nation*. http://www.americanforeignrelations.com/A-D/The-China-Lobby-Lobbying-efforts-from-the-1920s-through-world-war-ii.html.

Clark, Katerina. *Moscow, the Fourth Rome: Stalinism, Cosmopolitanism, and the Evolution of Soviet Culture, 1931–1941*. Cambridge, MA, and London: Harvard University Press, 2011.

Clifford, Nicholas Rowland. *Spoilt Children of Empire: Westerners in Shanghai and the Chinese Revolution of the 1920s*. Hanover: Middlebury College Press, 1991.

Coble, Parks. *Facing Japan: Chinese Politics and Japanese Imperialism, 1931–1937*. Cambridge, MA: Harvard University Press, 1991.

Cohen, Warren I. *The Chinese Connection, Roger S. Greene, Thomas W. Lamont, George E. Sokolsky and American–East Asian Relations*. New York: Columbia University Press, 1978.

Creel, George. *How We Advertised America*. New York: Harper and Brothers Publishers, 1920.

Crow, Carl. *Four Hundred Million Customers*. New York: Harper Brothers, 1937.

———. "Former China Press Men Recall Paper's Early Struggles, Triumphs." *China Press*, August 29, 1931.

———. *Japan's Dream of World Empire: The Tanaka Memorial*. New York: Harner and Brothers, 1942.

———. *Newspaper Directory of China*. Shanghai: Carl Crow, 1935.

Daugherty, William E. "China's Official Publicity in the United States." *Public Opinion Quarterly* 6, no. 1 (April 1, 1942): 70–86.

Davidann, Jon Thares. *Cultural Diplomacy in US-Japanese Relations, 1919–1941*. New York: Palgrave Macmillan, 2007.

Defty, Andrew. *Britain, America, and Anti-Communist Propaganda, 1945–53: The Information Research Department*. London: Routledge, 2004.

Dong Xianguang xiansheng zhuisilu bianji weiyuanhui. *Dong Xianguang xiansheng zhuisilu* 董顯光追思錄 [In memory of Dong Xianguang]. Taipei: Dongxianguang xiansheng zhuisilu bianji weiyuanhui, 1972.

Duus, Peter, and John Whitney Hall. *The Cambridge History of Japan: The Twentieth Century*. Cambridge: Cambridge University Press, 1988.

Eastman, Lloyd E. *The Nationalist Era in China, 1927–1949*. Cambridge: Cambridge University Press, 1991.

Epstein, Israel. *My China Eye: Memoirs of a Jew and a Journalist*. San Francisco: Long River Press, 2005.

Fairbank, John K. "System in the Chinese World Order." In *The Chinese World Order: Traditional China's Foreign Relations*, edited by John K. Fairbank, 257–75. Cambridge, MA: Harvard University Press, 1968.

Fang Hanqi. *Zhongguo xinwen shiye tongshi* 中國新聞事業通史 [General history of Chinese journalism]. Beijing: Zhongguo renmin daxue chubanshe, 1992.

Feng Yue. "Jindai Jingjin diqu yingwenbao de yulun yu waijiao pingxi" 近代京津地區英文報的輿論與外交評析 [Review of the opinions and diplomatic functions of the English-language newspapers in Beijing and Tianjin in modern times]. *Beijing hangkong hangtian daxue xuebao* 23, no. 3 (2010): 90–94.

———. *Riben zai Hua guanfang bao: Huabei zhengbao, 1919–1930* 日本在華官方報：《華北正報》 [Japan's official English-language paper in China: *North China Standard*]. Beijing: Xinhua chubanshe, 2008.

———. "Zaoqi Riben zai Hua baoyeshi chutan" 早期日本在華報業史初探 [Discussion on Japan's newspaper in China in the early period]. *Riben yanjiu* 日本研究 [Japanese studies] 4 (2006): 70–74.

Feng Zhixiang. *Xiao Tongzi zhuan* 蕭同茲傳 [A biography of Xiao Tongzi]. Taipei: Zhuanji wenxue chubanshe, 1975.

Fishel, Wesley R. *The End of Extraterritoriality in China*. Berkeley: University of California Press, 1952.

Fitch, George A. *My Eighty Years in China*. Taipei: Mei Ya Publications, 1974.

Fitzgerald, John. *Awakening China: Politics, Culture, and Class in the Nationalist Revolution*. Stanford: Stanford University Press, 1996.

French, Paul. *Carl Crow: A Tough Old China Hand*. Hong Kong: Hong Kong University Press, 2006.

———. *Through the Looking Glass: China's Foreign Journalists from Opium Wars to Mao*. Hong Kong: Hong Kong University Press, 2009.

Friedman, Donald J. *The Road from Isolation: The Campaign of the American Committee for Non-participation in Japanese Aggression, 1938–1941*. Cambridge, MA: Harvard University, 1970.

Fung, Edmund S. K. *In Search of Chinese Democracy*. Cambridge: Cambridge University Press, 2000.

Gallup, George Horace. *The Gallup Poll: Public Opinion, 1935–1971*, vol. 1. New York: Random House, 1972.

Ge Gongzhen. *Zhongguo baoxueshi* 中國報學史 [A history of China's newspaper]. Hong Kong: Taiping shuju, 1964.

Goodman, Bryna. "Networks of News: Power, Language and Transnational Dimensions of the Chinese Press, 1850–1949." *China Review* 4, no. 1 (Spring 2004): 1–10.

———. "Semi-colonialism, Transnational Networks and News Flows in Early Republican Shanghai." *China Review* 4, no. 1 (Spring 2004): 55–88.

Goodman, Bryna, and David Goodman, ed. *Twentieth-Century Colonialism and China: Localities, the Everyday and the World*. London and New York: Routledge, 2012.

Goto-Shibata, Harumi. *Japan and Britain in Shanghai, 1925–31*. New York: St. Martin's Press, 1995.

Gould, Randall. *China in the Sun*. Garden City, NY: Doubleday, 1946.

Gries, Peter Hays. *China's New Nationalism: Pride, Politics, and Diplomacy*. Berkeley: University of California Press, 2004.

Guo Xuyin, ed. *Guomindang paixi douzheng shi* 國民黨派系鬥爭史 [A history of the Guomindang factional struggles]. Shanghai: Shanghai renmin chubanshe, 1992.

Hahn, Emily. *China to Me: A Partial Autobiography*. New York: Garden City Publishing, 1946.

———. *The Soong Sisters*. New York: Doran and Company, 1941.

Hamilton, John Maxwell. "The Missouri News Monopoly and American Altruism in China: Thomas F. F. Millard, J. B. Powell, and Edgar Snow." *Pacific Historical Review* 55, no. 1 (February 1986): 27–48.

Harries, Meirion, and Susie Harries. *Soldiers of the Sun: The Rise and Fall of the Imperial Japanese Army*. New York: Random House, 1991.

Harris, Lane Jeremy. "The Post Office and State Formation in Modern China, 1896–1949." PhD dissertation, University of Illinois, 2012.

Hoyt, Frederick B. "George Bronson Rea: From Old China Hand to Apologist for Japan." *Pacific Northwest Quarterly* 69 (April 1978): 61–70.

Hu Daojing. "Shanghai de ribao" 上海的日報 [Shanghai dailies]. *Shanghai xinwen shiye shiliao jiyao* 上海新聞事業史料輯要 [Materials on the history of newspapers in Shanghai]. Taipei: Tianyi chubanshe, 1977.

Hu Shi. *Hu Shi riji quanji* 胡適日記全集 *1928–1930* [Complete collection of Hu Shi's diary]. Hefei: Anhui jiaoyu chubanshe, 2001.

Huang Jianhui. "*Shenbao* jiuwen jiedu 47: Huashengdun huiyi yu chefei geguo zai Hua youju" 華盛頓會議與撤廢各國在華郵局 [News in *Shenbao*: Washington Conference and the abolition of foreign post offices in China]. *Shanghai jiyou* [Shanghai philately] 11 (2011): 41–42.

Huang Zhuoming and Yu Zhenji. "Guanyu *Shishi xin bao* de suojian suowen 關於時事新報的所見所聞 [Accounts about *Shishi xin bao*]." In *Xinwen yanjiu ziliao* 新聞研究資料 [Research materials on Chinese journalism] 19 (1983): 181–188.

Huaqiao huaren baike quanshu bianzuan weiyuanhui. *Huaqiao huaren baike quanshu, renwu juan* 華僑華人百科全書，人物卷 [An encyclopedia of overseas Chinese, personnel]. Beijing: Zhongguo huaqiao chubanshe, 2001.

Hung, Chang-tai. *War and Popular Culture: Resistance in Modern China, 1937–1945*. Berkeley: University of California Press, 1994.

Iriye, Akira. *Across the Pacific: An Inner History of American–East Asian Relations*. New York: Harcourt, Brace and World, 1967.

———. *After Imperialism: The Search for a New Order in the Far East, 1921–1931*. Cambridge, MA: Harvard University Press, 1965.

———. *The Origins of the Second World War in Asia and the Pacific*. London and New York: Longman, 1987.

Ito, Takatoshi. *Japanese Economy*. Cambridge: MIT Press, 1992.

Jansen, Marius B. *Japan and China: From War to Peace, 1894–1972*. Chicago: Rand McNally College, 1975.

Jespersen, T. Christopher. *American Images of China, 1931–1949*. Stanford: Stanford University Press, 1996.

Jia Xiutang, "Nanjing guomin zhengfu wei shouhui youzheng guanli quan suozuo de nuli" 南京國民政府為收回郵政管理權所作的努力 [The Nanjing government's efforts to restore postal control]. *Lanzhou xuekan* [Journal of Lanzhou], no. 10 (2009): 203–6.

Jordan, Donald A. *China's Trial by Fire: The Shanghai War of 1932*. Ann Arbor: University of Michigan Press, 2001.

———. *Chinese Boycotts versus Japanese Bombs: The Failure of China's "Revolutionary Diplomacy," 1931–32*. Ann Arbor: University of Michigan Press, 1991.

———. *The Northern Expedition: China's National Revolution of 1926–1928*. Honolulu: University of Hawai'i Press, 1976.

Kawakami, Kiyoshi Karl. *Japan Speaks on the Sino-Japanese Crisis*. London: Macmillan, 1932.

Kenez, Peter. *The Birth of the Propaganda State: Soviet Methods of Mass Mobilization, 1917–1929*. Cambridge: Cambridge University Press, 1985.

Kessler, Lawrence. "Reconstructing Zhou Enlai's Escape from Shanghai in 1931: A Research Note." *Twentieth-Century China* 34, no. 2 (April 2009): 112–31.

King, Frank H. H., and Prescott Clarke. *A Research Guide to China-Coast Newspapers, 1822–1911*. Cambridge, MA: Harvard University Press, 1965.

Kirby, William C. "The Internationalization of China: Foreign Relations at Home and Abroad in the Republican Era." In *Reappraising Republican China*, edited by Frederic Wakeman Jr. and Richard Louis Edmonds, 179–204. Oxford: Oxford University Press, 2000.

Koen, Ross Y. *The China Lobby in American Politics*. New York: Macmillan, 1960.

Koo, V. K. Wellington. *Gu Weijun huiyilu* 顧維鈞回憶錄 [Memoir of Wellington Koo]. Beijing: Zhonghua shuju, 1983.

Koo, V. K. Wellington. *Memoranda Presented to the Lytton Commission*. New York: Chinese Cultural Society, 1932.

Krysko, Michael A. *American Radio in China: International Encounters with Technology and Communications, 1919–1941*. Houndmills: Palgrave Macmillan, 2011.

Kuhn, Philip A. *Soulstealers: The Chinese Sorcery Scare of 1786*. Cambridge, MA: Harvard University Press, 1990.

Kushner, Barak. *The Thought War: Japanese Imperial Propaganda*. Honolulu: University of Hawai'i Press, 2006.

Lasswell, Harold Dwight. *Propaganda Technique in World War I*. Cambridge, MA: MIT Press, 1971.

League of Nations. *Report of the Commission of Enquiry of the League of Nations*. Signed at Beijing, September 4, 1932.

Lee, Chin-Chuan, ed. *Voice of China: The Interplay of Politics and Journalism*. New York: Guilford Press, 1990.

Lei, K. N., and Shanghai Bar Association. *Information and Opinion Concerning the Japanese Invasion of Manchuria and Shanghai from Sources Other Than Chinese*. Shanghai: Shanghai Bar Association, 1932.

Leong, Karen J. *The China Mystique: Pearl S. Buck, Anna May Wong, Mayling Soong, and the Transformation of American Orientalism*. Berkeley: University of California Press, 2005.

Leung, Pak-wah, ed. *Political Leaders of Modern China: A Biographical Dictionary*. Westport, CT: Greenwood Press, 2002.

Li, Mingjiang. *Soft Power: China's Emerging Strategy in International Politics*. Plymouth: Lexington Books, 2009.

Lin Yutang. *A History of the Press and Public Opinion in China*. Shanghai: Kelly and Walsh, 1937.

Liu Guoming et al., eds. *Zhongguo Guomindang bainian renwu quanshu* 中國國民黨百年人物全書 [Complete collection of biographies of key members of the Guomindang]. Beijing: Tuanjie chubanshe, 2005.

Liu Jingxiu. "Kangzhan shiqi Guomindang duiwai xuanchuan jishi" 抗戰時期國民黨對外宣傳紀事 [Chronicle of the Guomindang foreign propaganda activities during the Sino-Japanese War]. *Dang'an shiliao yu yanjiu* 檔案史料與研究 [Archives and research] 1 (1990): 82–87.

———. "Kangzhan shiqi Guomindang duiwai xuanchuan jishi (xu 1)" 抗戰時期國民黨對外宣傳紀事 (續 I) [Chronicle of the Guomindang foreign propaganda activities during the Sino-Japanese War (sequel 1)] *Dang'an shiliao yu yanjiu* 檔案史料與研究 [Archives and research] 2 (1990): 75–78.

Liu Jingxiu and Zhang Jian. "Meiguo jizhe yu Zhongguo kangzhan" 美國記者與中國抗戰 [American journalists and China's anti-Japanese war]. *Minguo dang'an* 民國檔案 [Archives of Republican China] 1 (1989): 107–16.

Liu Zhemin. *Jinxiandai chuban xinwen fagui huibian* 近現代出版新聞法規匯編 [Press regulations in modern China]. Shanghai: Xuelin chubanshe, 1992.

Loewenthal, Rudolf. "The Present Status of the Press in China." *A Reprint from the Collectanea Commissionis Synodalis* 8, no. 11 (November 1935): 929–40.

Lu, Suping. *They Were in Nanjing: The Nanjing Massacre Witnessed by American and British Nationals*. Hong Kong: Hong Kong University Press, 2004.

MacKinnon, Stephen R. "Toward a History of the Chinese Press in the Republican Period." *Modern China* 23, no.1 (January 1997): 3–32.

———. *Wuhan, 1938: War, Refugees, and the Making of Modern China*. Berkeley: University of California Press, 2008.

MacKinnon, Stephen, and Oris Friesen. *China Reporting: An Oral History of American Journalism in the 1930s and 1940s*. Berkeley: University of California Press, 1987.

MacKinnon, Stephen R., Diana Lary, and Ezra F. Vogel, eds. *China at War: Regions of China, 1937–1945*. Stanford: Stanford University Press, 2007.

Mander, Linden A. *Foundations of Modern World Society*. Revised edition. Stanford: Stanford University Press, 1947.

Manela, Erez. *The Wilsonian Moment: Self-Determination and International Origins of Anticolonial Nationalism*. Oxford: Oxford University Press, 2007.

Manning, Martin J., and Herbert Romerstein. *Historical Dictionary of American Propaganda*. Westport, CT: Greenwood Press, 2004.

Martin, Brian G. "Collaboration within Collaboration: Zhou Fohai's Relations with the Chongqing Government, 1942–1945." *Twentieth-Century China* 34, no. 2 (April 2009): 54–87.

———. *The Shanghai Green Gang: Politics and Organized Crime, 1919–1937*. Berkeley: University of California Press, 1996.

Matsusaka, Yoshihisa Tak. *The Making of Japanese Manchuria, 1904–1932*. Cambridge, MA: Harvard University Press, 2001.

Mitter, Rana. *Forgotten Ally: China's World War II, 1937–1945*. Boston and New York: Houghton Mifflin Harcourt, 2013.

———. *The Manchurian Myth: Nationalism, Resistance, and Collaboration in Modern China*. Berkeley: University of California Press, 2000.

Mittler, Barbara. "Domesticating an Alien Medium: Incorporating the Western-Style Newspaper into the Chinese Public Sphere." In *Joining the Global Public: Word, Image, and City in Early Chinese Newspapers, 1870–1910*, edited by Rudolf Wagner, 13–46. Albany: State University of New York Press, 2007.

Mizoguchi Toshiyuki. "The Changing Pattern of Sino-Japanese Trade, 1884–1937." In *The Japanese Informal Empire in China, 1895–1937*, edited by Peter Duus, Ramon H. Myers, and Mark R. Peattie, xi–xxix. Princeton, NJ: Princeton University Press, 1989.

Morris-Suzuki, Tessa. *The Past within Us: Media, Memory, History*. London: Verso, 2005.

Morrison, George Ernest. *The Correspondence of G. E. Morrison*. Cambridge: Cambridge University Press, 1976.

Morse, Hosea Ballou. *The Chronicles of the East India Company Trading to China, 1635–1834*. Cambridge, MA: Harvard University Press, 1926.

Morton, William Fitch. *Tanaka Giichi and Japan's China Policy*. Folkestone: Dawson, 1980.

Nathan, Andrew James. *Peking Politics, 1918–1923: Factionalism and the Failure of Constitutionalism*. Berkeley: University of California Press, 1976.

Nish, Ian Hill. *Alliance in Decline: A Study in Anglo-Japanese Relations, 1908–1923*. London: Athlone Press, 1972.

———. *Japanese Foreign Policy, 1869–1942: Kasumigaseki to Miyakezaka*. London: Routledge, 2002.

———. *Japanese Foreign Policy in the Interwar Period*. Westport, CT: Greenwood Publishing Group, 2002.

———. "Japan in Britain's View of the International System, 1919–1937." In *Anglo-Japanese Alienation, 1919–1952*, edited by Ian Nish, 27–56. Cambridge: Cambridge University Press, 1982.

———. *Japan's Struggle with Internationalism: Japan, China, and the League of Nations, 1931–33*. London: Kegan Paul International, 1993.

O'Brien, Neil L. *An American Editor in Early Revolutionary China, John William Powell and the "China Weekly/Monthly Review."* New York: Routledge, 2003.

O'Connor, Peter. "Endgame: The English-Language Press Networks of East Asia in the Run-up to War, 1936–41." *Japan Forum* 13, no. 1 (2001): 63–76.

———. *The English-Language Press Networks of East Asia, 1918–1945*. Folkestone and Kent: Global Oriental, 2010.

Ohlberg, Mareike Svea. "Creating a Favorable International Public Environment: External Propaganda as a Global Concept with Chinese Characteristics." PhD dissertation, Heidelberg University, 2013.

Powell, John B. *My Twenty-Five Years in China*. New York: Macmillan, 1945.

Press Union. *The Shanghai Incident Misrepresented*. Shanghai: Press Union, 1932.

Pugach, Noel H. *Paul S. Reinsch: Open Door Diplomat in Action*. Millwood: KTO Press, 1979.

Qian Suoqiao. "Gentlemen of *The Critic*: English-Speaking Liberal Intellectuals in Republican China." *China Heritage Quarterly*, nos. 30/31 (June/September 2012). http://www.chinaheritagequarterly.org/features.php?searchterm=030_league.inc&issue=030.

Ramsdell, Daniel B. "The Nakamura Incident and the Japanese Foreign Office." *Journal of Asian Studies* 25 (1965): 51–67.

Rand, Peter. *China Hands: The Adventures and Ordeals of the American Journalists Who Joined Forces with the Great Chinese Revolution*. New York: Simon and Schuster, 1995.

Ransome, Arthur. "The Shanghai Mind: An Obstacle to British Policy." *Manchester Guardian*, May 2, 1927.

Rea, George Bronson. *The Greatest Civilizing Force in Eastern Asia*. Shanghai, 1924.

———. *Japan's Place in the Sun*. Shanghai: Far Eastern Review, 1915.

———. *Japan's Right to Exist*. Shanghai, 1920.

Remer, Charles Frederick. *Foreign Investments in China*. New York: Macmillan, 1933.

Rigby, Richard W. *The May 30 Movement: Events and Themes*. Canberra: Australian National University Press, 1980.

———. "Sapajou." *East Asian History*, nos. 17/18 (June/December 1999): 131–68.

Rosenbaum, Arthur Lewis, ed. *New Perspectives on Yenching University, 1916–1952*. Chicago: Imprint Publications, 2012.

Rosholt, Malcolm Leviatt. *The Press Corps of Old Shanghai*. Rosholt, WI: Rosholt House, 1994.

Rozanski, Mordechai. "The Role of American Journalists in Chinese-American Relations, 1900–1925." PhD dissertation, University of Pennsylvania, 1974.

Salisbury, Harrison E. "China Reporting: Red Star to Long March." In *Voices of China: The Interplay of Politics and Journalism*, edited by Chin-Chuan Lee, 216–228. New York: Guilford Press, 1990.

Schmidt, Hans. "Democracy for China: American Propaganda and the May Fourth Movement." *Diplomatic History* 22, no. 1 (January 1998): 1–28.

Shen Jianhong. *Bansheng youhuan: Shen Jianhong huiyilu* 半生憂患：沈劍虹回憶錄 [Memoir of Shen Jianhong]. Taipei: Lianjing Publishing, 1989.

Shen Meijuan. *Shen Zui huiyi zuopin quanji* 沈醉回憶作品全集 [Complete collection of Shen Zui's memoir]. Beijing: Jiuzhou tushu chubanshe, 1998.

Shenshi dianxunshe. *Shinian: Shenshi dianxunshe chuangli shi zhounian jinian* 十年：申時電訊社創立十週年紀念 [Ten years: The tenth anniversary of the Shenshi agency]. Shanghai: Shenshi dianxunshe, 1934.

Shen, Shuang. *Cosmopolitan Publics: Anglophone Print Culture in Semi-colonial Shanghai*. New Brunswick, NJ: Rutgers University Press, 2009.

Shen Yiyun. *Yiyun huiyi* 亦雲回憶 [Memoir of Shen Yiyun], vol. 2. Taipei: Zhuanji wenxue chubanshe, 1968.

Shewmaker, Kenneth E. *Americans and Chinese Communists, 1927–1945: A Persuading Encounter*. Ithaca, NY: Cornell University Press, 1971.

Shi Zhaoji (Sao-ke Alfred Sze). *Shi Zhaoji zaonian huiyilu* 施肇基早年回憶錄 [Memoir of Alfred Sze about his early years]. Taipei: Zhuanji wenxue chubanshe, 1967.

Shu, Sheng-chi. "Managing International News-Agency Relations under the Guomindang: China's Central News Agency, Zhao Minheng, and Reuters, 1931–1945." *Frontier History of China* 10, no. 4 (2015): 594–644.

Simmonds, P. L. "Statistics of Newspapers in Various Countries." *Journal of the Statistical Society of London* 4, no. 2 (July 1841): 111–36.

Smedley, Agnes. *Battle Hymn of China*. London: V. Gollance, 1944.

Smythe, Lewis S. C. *War Damage in the Nanking Area: December 1937 to March 1938*. Shanghai: Shanghai Mercury Press, 1938.

Snow, Helen Foster. *My China Years*. London: Harrap, 1984.

So Wai Chor. "The Making of the Guomindang's Japan Policy, 1932–1937: The Roles of Chiang Kai-Shek and Wang Jingwei." *Modern China* 28, no. 2 (April 2002): 213–52.

Sokolsky, George Ephraim. *The Tinder Box of Asia*. New York: Doubleday, Doran and Co., 1932.

Soong, May-ling. *War Messages and Other Selections*. Hankou: China Information Committee, 1938.

Steele, Archibald Trojan. *The American People and China*. New York: McGraw-Hill, 1966.

———. *Shanghai and Manchuria, 1932: Recollections of a War Correspondent*. Tempe: Arizona State University, 1977.

Stimson, Henry Lewis. *The Far Eastern Crisis: Recollections and Observations*. New York: Harper, for the Council on Foreign Relations, 1936.

Storey, Graham. *Reuters' Century, 1851–1951*. London: Parrish, 1951.

Strauss, Julia C. *Strong Institutions in Weak Polities: State Building in Republican China, 1927–1940*. Oxford: Clarendon Press, 1998.

Sun Yat-sen. *San Min Chu-I: The Three Principles of the People*. Translated by Frank Price. Shanghai: Commercial Press, 1928.

Sun, Youli. *China and the Origins of the Pacific War, 1931–1941*. New York: St. Martin's Press, 1993.

Tang Liangli. *Wang Ching-Wei: A Political Biography*. Beijing: French Book Store, 1931.

Taylor, Philip M. *Munitions of the Mind: A History of Propaganda from the Ancient World to the Present Era*. Manchester and New York: Manchester University Press, 2003.

———. *The Projection of Britain: British Overseas Publicity and Propaganda, 1919–1939*. Cambridge: Cambridge University Press, 1981.

Teow, See Heng. *Japan's Cultural Policy toward China, 1918–1931: A Comparative Perspective*. Cambridge, MA: Harvard University Press, 1999.

Thomson, James Claude. *While China Faced West: American Reformers in Nationalist China, 1928–1937*. Cambridge, MA: Harvard University Press, 1969.

Thorne, Christopher G. *The Limits of Foreign Policy: The West, the League, and the Far Eastern Crisis of 1931–1933*. London: Hamish Hamilton, 1973.

Tien, Hung-mao. *Government and Politics in Kuomintang China*. Stanford: Stanford University Press, 1972.

Timperley, H. J. *The Japanese Terror in China*. Calcutta: Thacker, Spink and Co., 1938.

———. "Makers of Public Opinion about the Far East." *Pacific Affairs* 9, no. 2 (June 1936): 221–30.

Ting, Lee-hsia Hsu. *Government Control of the Press in Modern China, 1900–1949*. Cambridge, MA: Harvard University Press, 1974.

Tong, Hollington Kong. *Chiang Kai-shek's Teacher and Ambassador: An Inside View of the Republican China—General Stilwell and American Policy Change towards Free China*. Bloomington: Authorhouse, 2005.

———. *Dateline: China; The Beginning of China's Press Relations with the World*. New York: Rockport Press, 1950.

——— (Dong Xianguang). *Dong Xianguang zizhuan: Yi ge nongfu de zishu* 董顯光自傳：一個農夫的自述 [Hollington Tong's autobiography: A self-introduction of a farmer]. Translated by Zeng Xubai. Taipei: Taiwan xinsheng baoshe, 1973.

Totani, Yuma. *The Tokyo War Crimes Trial: The Pursuit of Justice in the Wake of World War II*. Cambridge, MA: Harvard University Asia Center, 2008.

Tsuchida, Akio. "China's 'Public Diplomacy' toward the United States before Pearl Harbor." *Journal of American-East Asian Relations* 17 (2010): 35–55.

Tsūshinshashi kankōkai, ed. *Tsūshinshashi* 通訊社史 [A history of news agency]. Tokyo: Editor, 1958.

Tyau, Min-ch'ien T. Z. *Two Years of Nationalist China*. Shanghai: Kelly and Walsh, 1930.

US Congressional Research Service Library of Congress. "China's Foreign Policy and 'Soft Power' in South America, Asia, and Africa." Washington: US Government Printing Office, 2008.

Van de Ven, Hans J. *War and Nationalism in China, 1925–1945*. London: Routledge, 2003.

Volz, Yong Z., and Chin-Chuan Lee. "American Pragmatism and Chinese Modernization: Importing the Missouri Model of Journalism Education to Modern China." *Media Culture Society* 31 (2009): 711–30.

———. "Semi-colonialism and Journalistic Sphere of Influence: British-American Press Competition in Early Twentieth-Century China." *Journalism Studies* 12, no. 5 (2011): 559–74.

Wagner, Rudolf G. "Don't Mind the Gap! The Foreign Language-Press in Late-Qing and Republican China." *China Heritage Quarterly*, nos. 30/31 (June/September 2012). http://www.chinaheritagequarterly.org/features.php?searchterm=030_wagner.inc&issue=030.

———, ed. *Joining the Global Public: Word, Image, and City in Early Chinese Newspapers, 1870–1910*. Albany: State University of New York Press, 2007.

———. "The Role of the Foreign Community in the Chinese Public Sphere." *China Quarterly* 142 (1995): 423–43.

Wakeman, Frederic E. *The Shanghai Badlands: War Terrorism and Urban Crime, 1937–1941*. Cambridge: Cambridge University Press, 1996.

———. *Spymaster: Dai Li and the Chinese Secret Service*. Berkeley: University of California Press, 2003.

Wang Boheng. "Zhongguo zhi xizibao" 中國之西字報 [Western newspapers in China]. In *Minguo congshu* 民國叢書 [A series of books on Republican China], vol. 2, no. 48, edited by Huang Tianpeng. Shanghai: Shanghai shudian, 1930.

Wang Ermin. *Wan Qing zhengzhi sixiang shi lun* 晚清政治思想史論 [The political thought of the late Qing period]. Taipei: Xuesheng shuju, 1969.

Wang Lingxiao. *Zhongguo Guomindang xinwen zhengce zhi yanjiu, 1928–1945* 中國國民黨新聞政策之研究, 1928–1945 [News policy of the Guomindang government, 1928–1945]. Taipei: Jindai Zhongguo chubanshe, 1996.

Wang Qisheng. *Dangyuan, dangquan yu dangzheng, 1924–1949 nian Zhongguo Guomindang de zuzhi xingtai* 黨員、黨權與黨爭：1924–1949 年中國國民黨的組織形態 [Party membership, power, and struggle: The organization of Guomindang, 1924–1949]. Shanghai: Shanghai shudian chubanshe, 2003.

Wen Jize. *Jiuyiba he yi'erba shiqi kang-Ri yundong shi* 九一八和一二八時期抗日運動史 [A history of the anti-Japanese movement during the Mukden and Shanghai Incidents]. Beijing: Zhongguo gongren chubanshe, 1991.

Weston, Timothy. "Mining the Newspaper Business: The Theory and Practice of Journalism in 1920s China." *Twentieth-Century China* 31, no. 2 (April 2006): 4–31.

White, Theodore Harold. *Thunder out of China*. London: Victor Gollancz, 1947.

———. *In Search of History: A Personal Adventure*. London: Cape, 1979.

Wilbur, C. Martin. "The Nationalist Revolution: From Canton to Nanking, 1923–28." In *The Cambridge History of China*, vol. 12, edited by John King Fairbank, 527–720. Cambridge: Cambridge University Press, 1983.

———. *The Nationalist Revolution in China, 1923–1928*. Cambridge: Cambridge University Press, 1983.

Willoughby, Westel Woodbury. *Foreign Rights and Interests in China*, vol. 2. Taipei: Ch'eng-Wen Publishing, 1966. First published in 1927 by the Johns Hopkins Press.

———. *The Sino-Japanese Controversy and the League of Nations*. Baltimore: Johns Hopkins Press, 1935.

Wilson, Sandra. "Containing the Crisis: Japan's Diplomatic Offensive in the West, 1931–33." *Modern Asian Studies* 29 (1955): 337–72.

———. *The Manchurian Crisis and Japanese Society, 1931–33*. London: Routledge, 2002.

Woodhead, H. G. W. (Henry George Wandesforde), and *Shanghai Evening Post and Mercury*. *Adventures in Far Eastern Journalism: A Record of Thirty-Three Years' Experience*. Tokyo: Hokuseido Press, 1935.

———. *The Sino-Japanese Crisis: Being a Reprint of a Selection of Articles Appearing in "The Shanghai Evening Post and Mercury" October 1931–June 1932*. Shanghai: Printed by the Mercury Press for the South Manchuria Railway Co., 1932.

Wu Yixiong. *Zai Hua Yingwen baokan yu jindai zaoqi de zhongxi guanxi* 在華英文報刊與近代早期的中西關係 [The English press in China and the Sino-Western relationship in the early modern times]. Beijing: Shehui kexue wenxian chubanshe, 2012.

Xia, Jinlin. *Studies in Chinese Diplomatic History*. Shanghai: Commercial Press, 1933.

———. *Wo wudu canjia waijiao gongzuo de huigu* 我五度參加外交工作的回顧 [A review of my life as a diplomat]. Taipei: Zhuanji wenxue chubanshe, 1978.

Xiao Qian (Hsiao Ch'ien). *Traveller without a Map*. Translated by Jeffrey C. Kinkley. Stanford: Stanford University Press, 1993.

———. *Xiao Qian quanji*, texie juan 蕭乾全集・特寫卷 [A complete collection of Xiao Qian, special volume]. Wuhan: Hubei renmin chubanshe, 2005.

Xiao Tongzi wenhua jijinhui choubeichu. *Zaiziji* 在兹集 [In memory of Xiao Tongzi]. Taipei: 1974.

Xiong Yuezhi, ed. *Shanghai mingren mingshi mingwu daguan* 上海名人名事名物大觀 [Shanghai: People, events and relics]. Shanghai: Shanghai renmin chubanshe, 2004. Yang, Daqing. *Technology of Empire: Telecommunications and Japanese Expansion in Asia, 1883–1945.* Cambridge, MA: Harvard University Press, 2010.

Yang Zhesheng. *Chen Bulei: Guomindang "junji dachen"* 陳布雷：國民黨"軍機大臣" [Chen Bulei: The "grand minister of state" of the Guomindang]. Shanghai: Shanghai renmin chubanshe, 1999.

Yao Fushen. "Sishe—jiu Zhongguo baoye jituanhua jingying de yici changshi" 四社—舊中國報業集團化經營的一次嘗試 [Four Agencies: A trial of press syndicate in Republican China]. *Xinwen daxue* 新聞大學 [Journalism] (Winter 1997): 57–61.

———. "Zhang Bao'an jiaoshou hua xianfu Zhang Zhuping yishi" 張報安教授話先父張竹平遺事 [Professor Zhang Bao'an's reminiscence about his father Zhang Zhuping]. *Xinwen daxue* 新聞大學 [Journalism], no. 1 (2008): 42–43.

Yeh, Wen-Hsin. *Becoming Chinese: Passages to Modernity and Beyond.* Berkeley: University of California Press, 2000.

———. *Shanghai Splendor: Economic Sentiments and the Making of Modern China, 1843–1949.* Berkeley: University of California Press, 2007.

Yen, W. W. (Yan Huiqing). *East-West Kaleidoscope, 1877–1946: An Autobiography.* New York: St. John's University Press, 1974.

———. *Yan Huiqing zizhuan* 顏惠慶自傳 [Autobiography of W. W. Yen]. Taipei: Zhuanji wenxue chubanshe, 1973.

Yenching University. *Zhongguo baojie jiaotong lu* 中國報界交通錄 [Newspapers in China] (Newspapers). Beijing: Yanjing daxue xinwen xi, 1933.

Yin Yungong. *Zhongguo xinwenjie renwu* 中國新聞界人物 [Important people in China's press]. Beijing: Zhongguo renshi chubanshe, 2002.

Young, Arthur Nichols. *China's Nation-Building Effort, 1927–1937: The Financial and Economic Record.* Stanford: Hoover Press, 1971.

Young, Louise. *Japan's Total Empire: Manchuria and the Culture of Wartime Imperialism.* Berkeley: University of California Press, 1998.

Zeng Xubai. "Kangzhan zhong de guoji xuanchuan" 抗戰中的國際宣傳 [International propaganda during the Sino-Japanese War], *Zhongguo xinwen xuehui niankan* [Yearbook of Chinese Press Institute], no. 1 (1942).

———. *Zeng Xubai zixuan ji* 曾虛白自選集 [Self-selected collection of Zeng Xubai]. Taipei: Liming wenhua shiye gufen youxian gongsi, 1981.

———. *Zeng Xubai zizhuan* 曾虛白自傳 [An autobiography of Zeng Xubai]. Taipei: Lianjing chuban shiye gongsi, 1988.

———. *Zhongguo xinwen shi* 中國新聞史 [A history of China's journalism]. Taipei: Guoli zhengzhi daxue xinwen yanjiusuo, 1966.

Zhang Kaiyuan, ed. *Eyewitnesses to Massacre: American Missionaries Bear Witness to Japanese Atrocities in Nanjing.* New York: M. E. Sharpe, 2001.

Zhang Weiying, ed. *Yanjing daxue shigao, 1919–1952* 燕京大學史稿 [A history of Yenching University, 1919–1952]. Beijing: Zhongguo renmin chubanshe, 1999.

Zhao Minheng. *Caifang wushi nian* 採訪五十年 [Fifty years of interviews]. Taipei: Longwen chubanshe, 1994.

Zhongyang tongxunshe. *Zhongyangshe liushi nian* 中央社六十年 [The Central News Agency in the past sixty years]. Taipei: Zhongyang tongxunshe, 1984.

Zhou Fohai. *Zhou Fohai riji* 周佛海日記 [Zhou Fohai's diary]. Beijing: Zhongguo shehui kexue chubanshe, 1986.

Zhou Peijing. *Zhongyangshe de gushi: 1932–1972* 中央社的故事 [The story of the Central News Agency]. Taipei: Sanmin shuju, 1991.

Zhuang Zheng. "Sun Zhongshan chuangban yingwen *Minguo xi bao*" 孫中山創辦英文"民國西報" [Establishment of the *Republican China* by Sun Yat-sen]. *Dang'an yu shixue* 檔案與史學 [Archives and history] 1 (1998): 63–64.

Index

72 Hang shang bao, 41

Abend, Hallett, 43, 60, 113, 117, 211, 243; deportation of, 81–83
Ackerman, Carl W., 92
Akira, Ariyoshi, 39, 164
Allcott, Carroll, 245
Allman, Norwood, 245
All-Union Society for Cultural Relations with Foreign Countries, 67
Amō Doctrine, 16, 160, 162–80
Amō Eiji, 162. *See also* Amō Doctrine
Anglo-Chinese Medhurst College, 191
Anglo-Japanese alliance, 55, 234
anti-Communist campaign, 125, 172
Anti-enemy Committee, Shanghai, 191, 196, 197, 207, 214, 234
antiforeignism, 2, 51, 52, 54, 57, 60, 75, 96, 101, 106; change of, 93, 115, 123, 126; dilemma of, 162. *See also* anti-imperialism
anti-imperialism, 12, 54, 61, 65, 68, 90, 101, 114, 115, 126, 253
appeasement policy, 16, 126, 130, 137, 138, 160, 162, 169, 177, 219
Armstrong, Herbert W., 105
Asahi shimbun, 98
Asia magazine, 131
Associate Press, 25, 41, 60, 228, 233
Associated Press, 25, 41, 60, 228, 233

Bai Chongxi, 211
Bates, Lilliath, 211
Bates, Miner S., 211, 214–15
Beijing government, 37, 42, 46, 50, 53, 76, 92

Belden, Jack, 247–48, 249
Bernays, Edward L., 15
Bess, C. D., 76
Bickers, Robert, 8, 22
bilingual elites, 6, 9, 12, 14, 32, 33, 42, 87, 90, 252
Birdwood, William Riddell, 100
Black Dragon Society, 170
Blue Shirts. *See* Fuxing She
Bolshevik influence, 35, 43, 54, 100. *See also* Comintern
Borodin, Mikhail, 43, 44, 60
Brady, Mary B., 216
British Foreign Office, 26, 39, 80, 235
"bureaucratic monarchy," 14
Burma Road, 219, 229, 234, 235
Burton, Basil, 215–16
Butts, J., 22
Byrna, Goodman, 9

C. C. Clique, 84, 125, 137, 225, 229, 240
cable, 5, 65, 81, 83, 84–86, 97, 102, 110, 113, 141, 142, 153, 155, 209, 210, 212, 229, 231, 248, 249
Cai Gongshi, 49
Cai Tingkai, 150
Canton Gazette, 43, 82
Canton Register, 21–22
Carr, E. H., 4–5
Cecil, Lord, 122
censorship, 10, 11, 14, 72–74, 76, 84, 109, 113, 133, 140, 141, 188, 190, 207, 208, 212, 215, 227, 242, 248, 255; on outgoing dispatches, 153–60; policy, 158–60, 204–5, 223–26, 246

Index

Censorship Office on Books and Magazines, 224
Center for Foreign Service, 67
Central Daily News, 23–24, 154
Central Executive Committee, 67, 70diagram1, 72, 77, 136, 139, 143, 240
Central Military Academy, 240
Central News Agency, 41, 70diagram1, 140–46, 159, 190, 193, 195, 202, 228, 246
Central Plains War, 88
Changchun, 96, 104
Chao, Thomas Ming-heng. *See* Zhao Minheng
Chen, Eugene. *See* Chen Youren
Chen, W. C., 42
Chen bao, 154
Chen Bingzhang, 228
Chen Bulei, 151, 255
Chen Cheng, 241
Chen Gongbo, 189, 192, 203, 241
Chen Guofu, 84, 141, 202, 225
Chen Lifu, 73, 84
Chen Mingshu, 150
Chen Youren, 43, 82, 92, 136
Cheng, Hawthorne, 149fig.10, 190
Cheng Tiangu, 138
Chiang Kai-shek, 1, 4, 12, 88, 139, 151, 208, 211, 216–17, 231, 233, 235, 243, 246, 250, 254; and *China Press*, 146, 149, 150, 152, 172; and factional struggles, 12, 69, 117, 136–37, 150, 157, 172, 189, 255; and Northern Expedition, 46, 48–49, 52, 58; and purge of Communists, 52, 137; and struggles with warlords, 72, 141, 220; challenge of, 126, 137–38, 139, 150–51, 229; foreign policy of, 12, 16, 54, 68, 125, 130–31, 140, 164, 165, 172, 185–86, 234, 236; government, 3, 16, 17, 41, 70–71, 151, 219, 233, 252; Madam Chiang Kai-shek (*see* Soong May-ling); militarizes the government, 156, 187–88, 192–93; propaganda policy of, 13, 48–49, 51, 66, 82, 116–17, 158, 186, 188, 199, 200, 227–29, 233–34, 239–42, 249; supports Central News Agency, 141–43. *See also* Tong, Hollington: and Chiang Kai-shek

Chicago Daily News, 22, 210, 211, 228
Chicago Examiner, 27
Chicago Tribune, 22
China at War, 193, 196, 224
China Campaign Committee, 197
China Critic, 7, 79, 137, 146, 172; and Amō statement, 173–74; and Shanghai Incident, 114–15; and Tanaka Memorial, 103–5; establishment of, 90–91
China Defence League, 248
China Forum, 139
China Press, 22, 91–94, 138, 140, 146, 191, 192, 193, 204, 208, 245, 254; and Amō statement, 169–73, 177, 180; and Jinan Incident, 48, 55–57, 58; and Nationalist government, 146–52; and Shanghai Incident, 114–15; establishment of, 27–30
China Republican (China Gazette), 43
China Weekly Review, 9, 22, 38, 78, 79, 82, 83, 89, 93, 102, 127, 130, 135, 136, 248; and Amō statement, 176–77; and Jinan Incident, 58–59; and Mukden Incident, 109–10; and Nanjing Incident, 212–13; and Shanghai Incident, 120–21; establishment of, 30–35
China's Industrial Commission, 37
Chinese Courier and Canton Gazette, 21
Chinese Nation, 89, 147
Chongqing Garrison Command's Guards, 227
Christian Science Monitor, 248
Christianity, 21, 144, 145, 188, 200, 204, 208, 214, 216
Chun qiu, 125
Clark, Grover, 43, 87–88
Clark, J. D., 39, 88
Clegg, Arthur, 198
Columbia University, 27, 92, 200
Comintern, 43, 79, 139
Commercial Pacific Cable Telegraph Company, 84, 85, 153, 212
Commercial Press, 113
Committee on Public Information, 5, 33, 67
Communications Clique, 92
Communist International, 105

Communist Party, 17, 99, 138–39, 185, 205–6, 219, 240–41, 245–48, 256–57; Soviet, 11. *See also* Communists; propaganda: Communist
Communists, 3, 51–52, 54, 72, 87, 125, 137, 139, 150, 158–59, 172, 206, 219, 247–49, 256
Constitutional Defence League, 79
constitutionalism, 66
consul general: of France, 43; of Japan, 33, 39; of UK, 27, 81, 133; of US, 33, 94, 127
Coolidge, Calvin, 50
Cosmopolitan Club, 191
Craddock, A. K., 39
Crane, Charles R., 27
Cripps, Stafford, 234
Croly, Herbert, 30
Crow, Carl, 28, 29, 33, 39
Cui Wanqiu, 194, 223diagram5
Cunningham, Edwin S., 33, 94, 113, 128

Da wanbao, 149, 150, 194
Dagong bao, 41, 206
Dai Jitao, 73, 240
Dai Li, 186, 195, 208, 227, 243, 255
Daily Shipping and Commercial News, 23
Daily Telegraph (London), 88, 225
Daily Telegraph, 88, 225
Daily Worker, 198
datong, 67
Daugherty, William E., 227
Deane, Hugh, 248
Diao Minqian (M. Tukzung Tyau), 42, 87
die-hardism, 26, 37, 58, 78, 79, 80, 88, 107, 108, 109
Diet, 163
Domei News Agency, 243
Donald, William H., 38, 83, 91, 93, 156–57, 203, 213–14, 235. *See also* Tong, Hollington: and William H. Donald
Dong Shoupeng (Z. B. Tong), 157, 208
Du Xigui, 147
Du Yuesheng, 116, 149, 151
Duncan, Chesney, 43
Durdin, Peggy, 205
Durdin, Tillman, 148, 149fig.10, 192, 206, 210–11, 217

East India Company, 21
Eastern Extension Telegraph Company, 84, 153
Egypt, 101, 106, 108
Eliot, Charles, 101
empress clique, 242, 255
Epstein, Israel, 225, 228
Evans, Henry, 200
Executive Yuan, 67, 77, 114, 130, 135, 156, 224
extraterritoriality, 8, 10, 12, 16, 22, 26, 32, 34, 54, 88, 93, 99, 103, 114, 204, 253; abolition of, 73–84, 99, 121, 131–36; origins of, 74–75. *See also* treaty revision
Ezra, Edward I., 30, 91

Fang Zhi, 111
Far Eastern Mirror, 196
Far Eastern Review, 37–38, 51, 83, 84, 105, 109, 127, 131, 168; and Amō statement, 168–69; and Mukden Incident, 98–101; and Shanghai Incident, 118–19
Feng Yuxiang, 43, 72, 81, 88
Fengtian Clique, 37, 42
Ferguson, J. C., 29, 93
Fessenden, Stirling, 94
Fifth Board, 186–92
Findley, William T., 91
Fitch, George A., 199, 214–15
Fitch, Geraldine, 199
Fleischer, Benjamin, 27
Foreign Agents Registration Act, 200
Four Agencies, 150–52, 157
Fox, Albert W., 77
Fox, Charles J., 76–77
French Concession, 38, 43, 112, 135, 208
Freyn, Hubert, 208
Fry, Margery, 198
Fujian rebellion, 148, 150, 164
Fukuda Hikosuke, 46
Fuxing She, 240

Gage, B. E. F., 235
Gallop poll, 1, 249
Gan Naiguang, 136
Gao Zongwu, 240

Index

Geming pinglun, 54
Georgii Avksent'ievich Sapojnikoff. *See* Sapajou
Gilbert, Rodney, 26, 80, 101
Gollancz, Victor, 198
Gould, Randall, 105–6, 120, 154, 158, 211, 233, 245
Great Northern Telegraph Company, 84, 153, 207, 212
Green, Owen Mortimer, 26–27, 78, 80–81, 101
Green Gang, 116, 149
Greene, Roger, 199
Grew, Joseph, 163, 164, 167
Gu Mengyu, 140, 239
Guangzhou (Canton), 35, 41, 43, 66, 82, 121, 138, 140, 141, 154, 229
Guangzhou Clique, 117, 177
Guangzhou government, 43, 66, 82
Gui Zhongshu, 90
Guo Moruo, 241
Guo Taiqi, 197
Guomin (Kuomin) news agency, 41, 48, 49, 136, 147
Guomindang. *See* Nationalist Party
Guomindang leftists, 33, 54, 69, 72, 125, 136, 138, 141, 149, 150, 248; Wuhan government led by, 43, 72
Guowen news agency, 41

Hahn, Emily, 227–28
Han Deqin, 247
Hankou (Hankow), 29, 54, 56, 57, 68, 121, 142, 156, 196, 198, 205, 206, 208, 215, 238
Hankow Herald, 198
Harmon Foundation, 216
Havas news agency, 25, 40
Hirota Kōki, 163, 166, 167–68, 169–70
Holcomb, Chauncey P., 91
Hong Kong, 84–85, 138, 142, 144, 152, 196, 206, 208, 220, 227, 233, 239, 240, 243, 245, 248
Hong Kong Telegraph, 43
Horiguchi Yoshinori, 243
Hornbeck, Stanley K., 168, 171, 178, 199, 216
hou dang. See empress clique

hou zhi hou jue, 66
Howard, Edwin, 27, 81, 105
Howard, Roy, 229, 234, 245
Hu Hanmin, 12, 50, 137–38, 141, 172, 177
Hu Jintao, 256
Hu Shi (Hu Shih), 33, 90, 200, 240
Hu Zhengzhi, 41
Hua min wanbao, 245
Huang Fu, 48, 50, 51, 164
Huang Xianzhao, 145
Hull, Cordell, 1, 216, 250
Hunter, E. H., 88

imperial interests, 8, 34, 55, 174; of Britain, 24, 34, 80, 106, 108; of Japan, 104, 176; of United States, 34
Imperial Maritime Customs, 88
imperialism, 9, 34, 201, 257; legacies of, 2, 6, 94; resistance of, 6, 54, 67, 88, 90, 101, 139. *See also* anti-imperialism
India, 8, 81, 100, 104, 106, 122
information order, 11, 253
intelligence, 13, 35, 38, 113, 137, 146, 151, 152, 186, 194, 195, 196, 208, 233, 234, 255
International Committee for the Nanjing Safety Zone, 211, 214
International Communications Committee, 85
International Department: against Communists, 245–49; against Wang Jingwei, 239–45; British networks of, 197–98, 235–36; changes guidelines in Chongqing; 223–26; establishment of, 192–93; settles in Chongqing, 220–23; structure of, 192–202; under air raids, 236–39; US networks of, 199–201, 233–35. *See also* Press Hotel; Radio: XGOY
International Division (Guoji ke), 69–70
International Settlement, 24, 111, 112, 115, 120, 121, 207. *See also* Shanghai Municipal Council
Investigation and Statistics Bureau, 195, 227
Iriye, Akira, 110
Isaacs, Harold, 139, 148, 149
Itagaki Seishirō, 112

Jacoby, Melville, 228, 230
Japan Advertiser, 27, 83, 167
Japanese Telegraph Administration, 84
Jehol (Rehe), 125, 126
Ji Zejin, 223diagram5, 225
Jiang Guangnai, 150
Jinan Incident, 16, 44, 46–61, 65, 88, 90, 107
Johnson, Nelson T., 83, 132–34
Journal de shanghai, 153, 212
journalistic professionalism, 10, 13, 93, 143, 145, 146, 148, 154, 156, 157, 188, 255
Judd, Walter, 199
Juntong. *See* Investigation and Statistics Bureau

Kawashima Yoshiko, 112
Keating, A. S., 21, 22
Keen, Victor, 212
Kellogg Pact, 110, 114, 116
Kerr, Clark A., 235
Kinney, Henry W., 127
Kirby, William, 11
Kirton, Walter, 42
Kong Xiangxi, 151–52, 200, 226, 228, 238
Konoe Fumimaro, 236
Koo, Wellington (Gu Weijun), 91, 92, 128–30, 138, 139
Kouichi Shiozawa, 117
Kuhn, Philip, 13–14
Kung, H. H. *See* Kong Xiangxi
Kwantung Army, 96, 97, 98, 112, 164, 185

Lampson, Miles, 27, 80, 81
Laski, Harold, 198
Lawrence, Lowell, 199
Leader, 87, 101–103, 117, 129, 136. See also *Peking Leader*; *Peiping Chronicle*
Leaf, Earl, 198–99, 215–16, 244
League of Nations, 50, 54, 99, 100, 107, 108, 109, 110, 114, 116, 125, 126–30, 138, 162, 164–66, 172–73, 175, 178, 180
Lee Yu-pu, 207
Left Book Club, 198
legal pluralism, 74
legation: American, 29, 38, 82, 87, 88, 94, 132,133, 135, 136, 139; British, 132, 133, 135, 136; French, 132, 134, 135, 136; Japanese, 117, 132
Legislative Yuan, 90, 140, 151, 164, 191
Li Bingrui (Edward Bing-shuey Lee), 87, 89, 117
Li Cai (Lee Choy), 41, 43
Li Jishen, 150
Li Shizeng, 50, 54
Li Zongren, 72, 88
Liang Shichun, 145
liberal journalism, 13, 226, 227, 245, 254
liberalism, 69, 79, 157, 204, 225, 226, 242, 253, 254, 255
Life magazine, 234, 247
Lin Wenqing (Lim Boom Keng), 89
Lin Yutang, 6n25, 90, 137
Lindley, Francis, 166
Lippman, Walter, 30
Liu, Frank, 191
Liu Dajun, 90
Liu Zhan'en, 191, 207
Lohrbas, Larry, 22
Low Key Club, 240
Luce, Henry, 234
Luo Jialun, 140
Luo Wengan, 114, 130, 134, 140
Lushan Conference (1937), 186
Lytton Commission, 126–31
Lytton Report, 130, 139

Ma Su, 43
Ma Yinchu, 90
Ma Zhanshan, 130
MacCausland, J. A., 204, 223diagram5, 228, 230
MacDonald, C. M., 234
MacMurray, John Van Antwerp, 81, 82
Magee, John, 214
Malone, Colonel L'Estrange, 80
Manchester Guardian, 26, 52, 58, 80, 191, 212, 213, 235
Manchukuo, 96, 112, 125, 127, 128, 129, 131, 163, 164, 169, 173, 175, 244
Manchuria, 3, 34, 36, 40, 58–59, 97–116, 120, 122, 125, 127–30, 163–64, 171. *See also* Manchurian crisis; Mukden; Mukden Incident

Index

Manchuria Daily News, 36, 100
Manchurian crisis, 2n3, 91, 96, 100, 105, 125, 127, 128, 165, 180. *See also* Mukden Incident; Shanghai Incident
Manila, 37, 85, 118, 152, 231
Mao Qingxiang, 233
Marco Polo Bridge, 185
Marsh, E. L., 91
Martin, Kingsley, 197–98
Matthews, Herbert L., 83
May Fourth Movement, 83, 106
May Thirtieth Movement, 53, 90, 106
McHugh, J. M., 203, 213
McKee, Frederick, 199
Meeus, Charles L., 201
Metropolitan Hotel (Nanjing), 138
metropolitan papers, 7, 8, 15, 26, 27, 36, 59–61, 107–8, 110–11, 121–23, 177–80, 211. *See also Manchester Guardian*; *New York Times*; *Times* (London)
militarism, 119, 147, 187–88, 192–93, 254
Military Affairs Commission, 156, 157, 186, 187, 192, 202, 205. *See also* Investigation and Statistics Bureau
Millard, Thomas F., 27–28, 30, 32, 82, 83, 91, 93, 144. *See also Millard's Review of the Far East*
Millard's Review of the Far East, 27n26, 30, 33, 82, 92, 93. *See also China Weekly Review*
Mills, Hal P., 245
Ministry of Communications, 67, 76, 85, 92, 131, 134, 153, 207, 227
Ministry of Finance, 42, 85, 143, 202, 242
Ministry of Foreign Affairs (China), 41, 42, 67, 77, 81, 83, 85, 87, 90, 92, 133, 134, 135, 136, 152, 172, 185, 186, 197, 242
Ministry of Foreign Affairs (Japan), 35, 36, 97, 98, 117, 127, 162, 166, 169
Ministry of Information, 41, 70, 72, 73, 77, 87, 89, 92, 141, 142, 156, 188, 255; and registration orders, 131–32; establishment of, 66–69; in Chongqing, 220–49; in Wuhan, 192–216. *See also* International Department; International Division
Ministry of Information, British, 244

Ministry of Interior, 132, 133
Misselwitz, Henry F., 60
Missouri mafia, 30, 92, 204, 254
Mitter, Rana, 103, 255
Mongolia, 40, 104, 128, 176
Moore, Frederick, 82
Morris, John, 244
Mossman, Samuel, 24
Mukai Toshiakai, 212
Mukden, 35, 96, 113, 129
Mukden Incident, 16, 33, 86, 97–111, 165, 175, 212; and Shanghai Incident, 112–30

Nagasaki, 84, 85, 86, 155
Nakamura Shintaro, 98–99
Nanjing government: and the legal control of the press, 72–73, 131–32, 153; diplomatic dilemmas of, 12, 54, 126, 130–31, 169–70, 172, 185; establishment of, 2, 16, 66, 70–71; led by Wang Jingwei, 242–43; recognition of, 50
Nanjing Incident (1927), 51, 52, 56, 60
Nanjing Incident (1937), 16, 209–16, 224
Nash, Vernon, 145
Nation, 30
National Central University, 140
National Film Censorship Board, 188
National Press Cooperating Committee (Quanguo baoye lianhe hui), 41
National Press Development Committee (Quanguo baoye jujin hui), 40
National Review, 42
National Revolutionary Army, 52, 54, 58, 59, 60
nationalism, 9, 14, 54, 55, 79, 82, 103, 106, 108, 253, 254, 257. *See also* antiforeignism; anti-imperialism
Nationalist Party: 3, 12–14, 33, 47, 49, 50, 52, 54, 139, 140, 141, 153, 192, 199, 201, 202, 206, 219, 224, 247–49, 253; and extraterritoriality, 75–78, 82, 84, 99, 131–33, 135; and treaty-port press, 43–44, 87–90, 149, 151; division of, 44, 54, 69, 136–38, 141, 150, 174, 177, 188–89, 224, 240–43, 255; ideology

of, 11, 66–68, 69, 71–73, 126, 142, 154, 156, 185, 186, 187–88, 190, 240; political culture of, 143, 156–59, 186, 189–90, 202, 226, 242, 245–46, 254–55; reorganization of, 66. *See also* Guomindang leftists; Ministry of Information; Three People's Principles

Nationalist-Communist United Front, 158, 205, 206, 219, 228, 240, 247

navy: British, 122; Chinese, 147; Japanese, 96, 111, 112, 116, 117, 118, 164, 171, 243; US, 38, 122–23, 180, 200, 203, 212

Nazi Germany, 178, 234, 253

Nazi-Soviet nonaggression pact, 234

New Culture Movement, 147

New Fourth Army Incident, 247–49

New Republic, 30, 32

New Statesman and Nation, 198

New York Herald Tribune, 212, 228

New York Times, 36, 43, 50, 82–83, 113, 117, 148, 154, 192, 200, 205, 206, 210, 211, 212, 213, 228; and Amō statement, 165, 179–80; and Jinan Incident, 52, 60–61; and Mukden Incident, 110; and Shanghai Incident, 122–23

Newsweek, 148

Nichi nichi shimbun, 53, 212

Nine Power Treaty, 114, 167, 169, 176, 180

Nineteenth Route Army, 116, 117, 148, 149, 150

Noda Iwao, 212

North China, 3, 37, 43, 88, 92, 117, 125, 126, 176, 185, 214, 246

North China Daily News, 9, 17, 29, 30, 32, 34, 39, 48, 58, 59, 83, 88, 93, 97, 98, 101, 110, 146, 178, 208, 211; and Amō statement, 174–76; and Jinan Incident, 55–57; and Mukden Incident, 105–7; and Nanjing Incident, 211; and Shanghai Incident, 119–21; establishment of, 23–27; postal ban on, 77–81. See also *North China Herald*

North China Herald, 23, 24, 120

North China Standard, 36, 37

North China Star, 76, 83, 144

Northern Expedition, 46, 49, 51, 52, 54, 76, 87, 88, 118

Nottingham, E. A., 38, 39

Ochs, Adolph S., 82

Office of Naval Intelligence of the United States, 38

Open Door policy, 32, 33, 34, 37, 38, 55, 109, 123, 144, 166, 180n92

Oriental Affairs, 131

Pan Gongbi, 151

Paris Herald, 148

Paris Peace Conference, 38, 41

patriotism, 156, 157, 207, 222

Pearl Harbor, 1, 2, 208, 249, 250, 252

Peiping Chronicle, 129, 130, 136, 143. See also *Leader; Peking Leader*

Peking and Tientsin Times, 34, 78, 88, 144

Peking Daily News, 24, 42, 92

Peking Gazette, 92

Peking Leader, 36, 42, 43, 58, 82, 87. See also *Leader; Peiping Chronicle*

Peng, Rosalind, 83

Peng Leshan, 1

Penniston, John B., 152, 208–9

People's Republic of China, 69

People's Tribune, 43, 44, 116, 119, 136–37, 174

Picard-Destelan, Henri, 76

Pittman, Key, 199

Plain Truth, 105

political tutelage, 66, 255

postal ban, 76–81, 86, 132, 133, 135, 150–51

Powell, John B., 22, 30, 32, 33, 38, 39, 83, 91, 92, 93, 144, 208, 245, 248

Pratt, F. L., 152, 157, 208

President Hoover (American Dollar Liner), 203

Press Hotel (Holly's Hotel), 226–29, 238, 254

press registration, 73

Price brothers, 198–99. *See* Price, Frank; Price, Harry

Price, Frank, 198. *See* Price brothers

Price, Harry, 198–99. *See* Price brothers

Prohme, William and Rayna, 43

Index

propaganda, 4–6, 65, 147; by Wang Jingwei regime, 243–45; channels of, 9, 41–44, 88–90, 109, 113, 136; Communist, 79, 139–40, 205–6, 245–49; dilemmas of, 54, 125–26, 130–1, 134, 160, 161, 254; division of, 12, 54–55, 136–40, 187, 189, 192, 225–26, 241–43, 254–55; efficacy of, 13, 15–16, 252, 254; guidelines, 12, 187–88, 223–24, 226, 234; in Hong Kong, 196, 206, 208, 233, 248; in Japan, 216; in Japanese-occupied Shanghai, 206–9, 243; in the United States, 198–201, 216, 234; in UK, 197–98, 215, 235; indirect, 147, 187, 190–92, 194, 196, 203–4, 209, 226–27; institution of, 11, 13, 66–67, 110–11, 140, 185–88, 192–202, 225, 252–54; Japanese, 35–9, 47–53, 58, 61, 97–101, 115, 117–19, 120, 128, 163, 165–69, 200–201, 207; on ideologies, 11, 66–71, 89, 187; Soviet influence of, 66–67,187, 253; urgency of, 42, 47, 65, 90, 110–11, 126–27, 185. *See also* "whispering propaganda"
Publication Law, 73, 131, 132, 133, 134, 135
Pulitzer School, 92

qi lian, 54
Qing dynasty, 6, 13–14, 40, 42
Qingdao, 47, 53, 121

radio, 1, 16, 70diagram1, 208, 210, 234, 237; Section, 196; station XHQC, 207; station XGOY, 229–33
Rajchman, Ludwig W. 165, 173, 175
Ramsay, Alexander, 42
Rangwai bixian annei, 125
Ransome, Arthur, 26, 80
Rea, George Bronson, 37–38, 84, 99, 127, 168
Rees, Rev. Ronald, 208
Reformed Government of the Republic of China, 207
Ren Lingxun, 143–44
Rengō news agency, 36, 102, 127, 167
renqing, 254
Republican China, 92
Research Clique (Yanjiuxi), 42

Reuters news agency, 25, 30, 35, 36, 39, 40, 41, 48, 60, 88, 93, 97, 121, 129, 142–43, 144, 211, 224, 228, 234, 244, 245
Ridge, William Sheldon, 130
Rockefeller Foundation, 199
rōnin, 120
Rosholt, Malcolm, 152, 200
Russia, 40, 84, 88, 100, 105, 163, 168, 176, 200, 212, 231. *See also* Soviet Union

Saitō Hiroshi, 166
Sapajou, 17, 45fig.4, 62fig.5, 95fig.6, 124fig.7, 161fig.12, 218fig.16, 251fig.20
Scott, Robert, 244
Shanghai Bar Association, 109
Shanghai Committee, 79
Shanghai Evening Post and Mercury, 30, 89, 106, 108–20, 127, 154, 208, 211, 233, 245
Shanghai Evening Star, 30
Shanghai Incident, 16, 96, 111–23, 125, 126, 127, 128, 148, 150, 212
Shanghai Mercury, 39, 88–89
Shanghai mind, 26, 79–80, 94
Shanghai Municipal Council, 24, 26, 77, 79, 91, 94, 112, 118, 121
Shanghai Municipal Police, 39
Shanghai nippo, 207
Shanghai Publicity Bureau, 79
Shanghai Times, 29, 38–39, 58, 109
Shanghai Truce, 125, 126, 150
Shao Lizi, 192, 239
Shao Yuanchong, 140
Shao Yulin, 195
Shaw, Bruno, 198
Shen bao, 24, 41, 93, 149, 151, 245
Shen Jianhong, 145, 146, 149fig.10, 193, 223diagram5
Shenshi News Agency, 41, 93, 149, 150
Shi Liangcai, 93, 149, 151
Shi Zhaoji (Alfred Sze), 130
Shidai gonglun, 125
Shidehara Kijūrō, 101
Shiozawa Kōichi, 111, 118
Shiratori Toshio, 167
Shishi xin bao, 41, 93, 149, 150–51
Si she. *See* Four Agencies
Simon, John, 100, 176, 178

Simpson, Lenox (Putman Weale), 88
Sino-Japanese War (first), 118
Sino-Japanese War (second), 1, 2, 12, 16, 146, 152, 185–250, 252, 254, 255
Smedley, Agnes, 245, 246, 249
Smith, Leslie C., 211
Smythe, Lewis, 215
Snow, Edgar, 144, 246, 247, 248, 249
soft power, 256
Sokolsky, George E., 34, 77, 82; deportation of, 83–84
Soong May-ling, 81, 83, 158, 188, 190, 194, 201, 202–3, 232, 235, 242, 242, 255
Soong Qing-ling, 44, 139, 206, 248
Soong, T. V. (Song Ziwen), 82, 84, 113, 114, 116, 125, 130, 135, 138, 165, 172, 173
South China Daily News, 227
South China Morning Post, 138
South Manchuria Railway, 87, 96–99, 101; Company, 36, 127
Southwest Political Council, 177
sovereignty: defence of, 4, 74; legal, 131; loss of, 5, 12, 22, 61, 75, 126, 244, 257; over Manchuria, 100, 120, 122; restoration of, 2, 7, 65, 67. *See also* extraterritoriality
Soviet Union, 4, 67, 100, 185, 219, 234, 253
St. John's University, 149, 204, 230, 254
Starr, Cornelius Vander, 89, 108, 109, 245
Steele, Archibald Trojan, 113, 120, 121, 210, 228, 247
Stefani news agency, 25
Stimson, Henry L., 2n3, 116, 121, 199
Strauss, Julia, 13, 242
Stuart, Charles, 231, 239
Sues, Ilona Ralf, 190
Sun Fo. *See* Sun Ke
Sun Ke, 37, 50, 90, 137, 164
Sun Ruiqin, 129
Sun Yat-sen, 30, 32, 37, 43, 44, 54, 66–67, 83, 90, 92, 119, 137, 198; Madam Sun Yat-sen (*see* Soong Qing-ling); thought of, 67–72, 244. *See also* Three People's Principles
Sun Yat-sen Cultural and Educational Publishing, 186
Swire, Warren, 80

Taiwan, 5, 85, 256
Takahashi Sankichi, 117
Tanaka Giichi, 53, 104; government, 52. *See also* Tanaka Memorial
Tanaka Memorial, 103–5, 116, 170
Tanaka Ryūkichi, 112
Tang Dechen, 145, 146
T'ang Leang-li. *See* Tang Liangli
Tang Liangli, 136–37, 243, 245
Tang Youren, 151
Tang Yuanzhan, 42
Tanggu Truce, 130, 137, 138, 163, 178
Tass news agency, 40
Thackrey, Theodore Olin, 108
Third National Congress, 65
Thorburn case, 99, 105
Three People's Principles, 11, 54, 67, 70, 73, 198
T'ien Hsia, 7, 191, 196
Time magazine, 131, 230, 247
Times (London), 26–27, 36, 71, 81, 156, 234; and Amō statement, 177–79; and Jinan Incident, 59–60; and Mukden Incident, 97, 107–8; and Shanghai Incident, 122
Timperley, H. J., 58, 154, 191, 197, 198, 203, 208, 211, 212, 213–16, 228, 235–36
Tōhō news agency, 35–36, 39, 40, 41, 47–48, 52, 60
Tong, Hollington K. (Dong Xianguang), 1, 14, 17, 32, 33, 43, 170, 205, 221–22, 230, 233, 234, 236, 237–38, 245, 247, 249, 254–55; and Beijing government, 92–93; and censorship, 154, 156–60, 204, 224–26; and Chiang Kai-shek, 147–48, 172, 156–57, 158, 186, 187–88, 190, 192, 200, 202–3, 225, 227, 255; and *China Press*, 91–94, 146, 148–51, 156, 157, 191, 192, 193, 222; and Fifth Board, 186–92; and intelligence, 13, 186, 194, 195, 196, 208, 227, 233, 255; and Missouri network, 91–92, 144–45, 193, 203; and Nanjing Incident, 210, 213–17; and Soong May-ling, 188, 190, 202–3, 240; and William H. Donald, 156–57, 203; factional struggles of, 159, 189,

239–43, 248, 255; in occupied Shanghai, 206–9, 243–44; propaganda principles of, 147, 158, 187, 190, 193–94, 202, 203–4, 223–24, 226. *See also* International Department
Transocean news agency, 93
Treaty of Bogue, 74
Treaty of Wanghia, 74
treaty ports, 7, 8, 11, 12, 13, 16, 22, 23, 26, 29, 30, 34, 35, 55, 58, 59, 60, 61, 73, 76, 80, 103, 129, 132, 133, 147, 148, 202, 254. *See also* extraterritoriality; treaty-port press
treaty-port press, 2, 6, 14, 15, 16, 245; and division with metropolitan papers, 23, 26–27, 60–61, 107–8, 110–11, 121–123, 179–80; as propaganda resources, 7, 10, 190–91, 202, 252–53; information order of, 11; journalists of, 12–14, 26, 76–84, 119–21, 146–52, 156–57, 190–91, 202; of British interests, 23–27, 30, 55–58, 105–7, 119–21, 174–76; of Chinese interests, 30, 42–44, 82–94, 101–5, 114–17, 146–49, 152, 169–74; of Japanese interests, 37–39, 52–53, 97–101, 117–19, 165–69; of US interests, 27–35, 58–59, 108–10, 119–21, 176–77; origins of, 21–22; transnational feature of, 7–10, 22. *See also* extraterritoriality; Shanghai mind
treaty revision, 51, 73, 79, 80, 85, 101. *See also* extraterritoriality
Trotskyism, 139
Turner, W., 35
Twenty-One Demands, 99, 169, 170, 180

Uchida Yasuya, 163
unequal treaties, 34, 68, 74
United Press, 40, 76, 93, 198, 227, 228, 244, 245
University of Missouri, 28, 30, 43, 90, 91–93, 144–45, 147, 193, 203, 243. *See also* Missouri mafia; Tong, Hollington K.: Missouri networks
USS *Panay*, 212–13
Utley, Freda, 194

Villard, Oswald Garrison, 30
Votaw, Maurice, 204, 228, 230

Wang, C. T. (Wang Zhengting), 76, 77, 81, 83, 84
Wang, H. S., 195–96
Wang Boheng, 24, 42, 43n103
Wang Chonghui, 50
Wang Jiasong, 145
Wang Jingwei, 12, 17, 44, 50, 72, 126, 130, 136–37, 177, 189, 219, 241, 242–43, 246; government, 17, 233, 243, 244, 245
Wang Shijie, 225, 241, 242, 249
Wangbaoshan Incident, 104
War Ministry of Japan, 53, 97
warlords, 3, 37, 40, 41–43, 46–47, 50–51, 54, 56, 59, 60, 61, 66, 68, 70, 71, 82, 88, 119, 141, 169, 220
Washington Conference, 76, 133
Washington Star, 166
Webb, C. Herbert, 27
Weberian bureaucracy, 13
Wei Jingmeng (Jimmy Wei), 157, 208, 216–17, 223, 225, 238
Wen Yuanning, 191, 196
Western Hills faction, 72
Whampoa Military Academy, 240
White, Theodore H., 220, 228, 236, 247
Williams, Frederick V., 200–201
Williams, Walter, 144
Wilsonianism, 5, 33
"whispering propaganda" (*eryu xuanchuan*), 216
Wolff news agency, 25
Wood, William W., 21, 22
Woodhead, Henry George Wandesforde, 34, 78, 92, 109, 127, 131
Woodman, Dorothy, 197–98
World War I, 4, 5, 30, 33, 66, 71, 85, 119, 147, 168
Wu Chaoshu (C. C. Wu), 50, 52
Wu Tiecheng, 111, 113, 118, 141, 243
Wu Tingfang, 27

Xia Jinlin, 191, 197–98, 236
Xi'an Incident, 158, 205

xian zhi xian jue, 66
Xiao Tongzi, 141–45, 190, 195, 241
Xinjiang, 25, 40, 176
Xinminguo bao, 41
Xinwen bao, 24, 93
Xu Peigen, 228
Xu Xinliu, 91
Xu Zhaoyong, 145

Yan Huiqing (W. W. Yen), 42, 114, 160
Yan Xishan, 72, 88
Yang Guangsheng (Kuangson Young), 152
Yano Makoto, 117
Yarnell, Harry E., 199
Ye Chucang, 77, 141, 151
Ye Gongchao, 222, 225
Ye Gongchuo (Yeh Kung-cho), 37, 92
Yenching University, 144–45, 193, 199, 254
Yokohama Specie Bank, 29, 38
Yong bao, 32, 93, 157, 193
Yoshizawa Kenkichi, 118
Yuan Shikai, 42, 43, 92
Yunnan, 25, 174

Zeng Xubai, 157, 193, 194, 204, 215, 222, 223, 225, 227, 230
Zhang, Pengchun, 200
Zhang Junqi, 111
Zhang Mingwei, 143
Zhang Pingqun, 228
Zhang Qun, 220, 241
Zhang Sixu (Samuel H. Chang), 41
Zhang Xinhai, 90, 159
Zhang Xueliang, 72, 81, 91, 102, 113, 117, 126, 141, 145, 158, 203
Zhang Zhuping, 30, 91, 93, 94, 149–52, 157
Zhang Zuolin, 46, 53
Zhao Minheng, 6, 24, 90, 142, 224, 228
Zhili Clique, 42
Zhongyang ribao. See *Central Daily News*
Zhou Enlai, 205, 217, 241, 247
Zhou Fohai, 239–43, 255
Zhou Ziqi, 92
Zhu Jiahua, 140, 158, 164
Zhu Qi, 42
Zhu Shuqing (S. T. Chu), 157, 208
Zhuang Zhihuan, 85